ARTICLE 8 ECHR, FAMILY REUNIFICATION AND THE UK'S SUPREME COURT

How do courts reconcile protecting family life with immigration control in human rights cases? This book addresses that question through an analysis of 11 UK Supreme Court decisions on immigration and family life, mostly focusing on Article 8 ECHR, the right to respect for family life, and starting with Huang v SSHD in 2007. The analysis is set against a national context that includes the Human Rights Act 1998 and regular controversies over immigration.

The book explains how the European Court of Human Rights jurisprudence has developed in recent years. It often still awards little weight to claims by citizens and residents to be joined by family when immigration status is in issue, particularly in the absence of children. This reflects governments' resistance to encroachment on their control over borders. The Supreme Court decisions show that, despite powers conferred by the Human Rights Act, a more nuanced position in domestic law was difficult to articulate and sustain. The book explores the way in which these problems were reflected in the changing language, argumentation, and structure of judgments, which revealed judges to be strategic actors drawing on personal and institutional values and responding to the shifting political context.

A more generous reading of Article 8 would be legally coherent but needs wider societal support to be realisable. The book ends with a discussion of how, if such support were present, the jurisprudence could give more weight to the needs of families. It is vital reading for anyone interested in families and immigration, and in the problems and potential of human rights adjudication.

Volume 29: Human Rights Law in Perspective

Human Rights Law in Perspective

General Editor: Colin Harvey
Professor of Human Rights Law
School of Law
Queen's University Belfast

The language of human rights figures prominently in legal and political debates at the national, regional and international levels. In the UK the Human Rights Act 1998 has generated considerable interest in the law of human rights. It will continue to provoke much debate in the legal community and the search for original insights and new materials will intensify.

The aim of this series is to provide a forum for scholarly reflection on all aspects of the law of human rights. The series will encourage work which engages with the theoretical, comparative and international dimensions of human rights law. The primary aim is to publish over time books which offer an insight into human rights law in its contextual setting. The objective is to promote an understanding of the nature and impact of human rights law. The series is inclusive, in the sense that all perspectives in legal scholarship are welcome. It will incorporate the work of new and established scholars.

Human Rights Law in Perspective is not confined to consideration of the UK. It will strive to reflect comparative, regional and international perspectives. Work which focuses on human rights law in other states will therefore be included in this series. The intention is to offer an inclusive intellectual home for significant scholarly contributions to human rights law.

Recent titles in this series

Specifying and Securing a Social Minimum in the Battle Against Poverty
Toomas Kotkas, Ingrid Leijten and Frans Pennings

Protecting Human Rights and Building Peace in Post-Violence Societies
Nasia Hadjigeorgiou

Collective Trauma and the Armenian Genocide: Armenian, Turkish, and Azerbaijani Relations since 1839
Pamela Steiner

The Times and Temporalities of International Human Rights Law
Edited by Kathryn McNeilly and Ben Warwick

Social Rights and the Constitutional Moment: Learning from Chile and International Experiences
Edited by Koldo Casla, Magdalena Sepúlveda, Vicente Silva, and Valentina Contreras

Article 8 ECHR, Family Reunification and the UK's Supreme Court: Family Matters?
Helena Wray

For the complete list of titles in this series, see 'Human Rights Law in Perspective' link at www.bloomsbury.com/uk/series/human-rights-law-in-perspective/

Article 8 ECHR, Family Reunification and the UK's Supreme Court

Family Matters?

Helena Wray

•HART•
OXFORD • LONDON • NEW YORK • NEW DELHI • SYDNEY

HART PUBLISHING
Bloomsbury Publishing Plc
Kemp House, Chawley Park, Cumnor Hill, Oxford, OX2 9PH, UK
1385 Broadway, New York, NY 10018, USA
29 Earlsfort Terrace, Dublin 2, Ireland

HART PUBLISHING, the Hart/Stag logo, BLOOMSBURY and the Diana logo are trademarks of Bloomsbury Publishing Plc
First published in Great Britain 2023

A catalogue record for this book is available from the British Library.

Library of Congress Cataloging-in-Publication data

Names: Wray, Helena, 1960- author.

Title: Article 8 ECHR, family reunification and the UK's Supreme Court : family matters? / Helena Wray.

Other titles: Article 8 European Court of Human Rights, family reunification and the UK's Supreme Court

Description: Oxford, UK ; New York, NY : Hart Publishing, an Imprint of Bloomsbury Publishing, 2023. | Series: Human rights law in perspective; 29 | Includes bibliographical references and index. | Summary: "This book focuses on a series of judgments by the UK's Supreme Court on the application of the right to respect for family life, contained in article 8 ECHR, to immigration decisions. These judgments have required the government to amend several aspects of its family migration policy and have become the centre of legal and political controversy, raising questions about the judicial function in a modern democracy, the influence on the legal system of European human rights law and the difficulties of controlling immigration in a globalised world. They have drawn judges into new territory and there is evidence that the senior judiciary is itself divided. Meanwhile, attempts by the government to reverse these judgments through rule changes and legislative amendment have added new layers to an already complex legal framework. In so doing, the book explains why the relationship between Article 8 and immigration is so legally and political complicated"—Provided by publisher.

Identifiers: LCCN 2022046008 | ISBN 9781509902576 (hardback) | ISBN 9781509966073 (paperback) | ISBN 9781509902590 (pdf) | ISBN 9781509902583 (Epub)

Subjects: LCSH: Family reunification—Law and legislation—Great Britain. | Emigration and immigration law—Great Britain. | Freedom of movement—Great Britain. | Great Britain. Supreme Court. | Courts of last resort—Great Britain. | Constitutional law—Great Britain. | Human rights—Great Britain. | European Court of Human Rights.

Classification: LCC KD4134 .W73 2023 | DDC 342.4108/2—dc23/eng/20221201

LC record available at https://lccn.loc.gov/2022046008

ISBN: HB: 978-1-50990-257-6
ePDF: 978-1-50990-259-0
ePub: 978-1-50990-258-3

Typeset by Compuscript Ltd, Shannon

In memory of my parents, Brenda and Tony Wray (1930–2019).
They would have celebrated this moment and I miss them.

Acknowledgements

Many people helped me to write this book. The University of Exeter gave me financial support and study leave, allowing me the necessary time to focus. I am grateful to my colleagues and friendly critics, Professor Marie-Benedicte Dembour, Professor Betty de Hart and Dr Jo Wilding, for reading the chapters and giving me such frank, supportive and useful feedback. Agnes Simic, Daniel Collins and Helena Grzywaczewska provided vital research assistance. Katie Dilger gave me invaluable insights into the world of legal practice and my sister-in-law Cate Bell gave me useful insights into Tribunal life.

I thank my husband Jem for being bloody fantastic.

Contents

Table of Cases

UK

European Court of Human Rights

Other Jurisdictions

UN Human Rights Committee (HRC)

African Commission on Human and Peoples' Rights

Table of Legislation

UK

International and Regional Instruments

Other

1

Introduction: Family Reunification, Human Rights and Judges

I. ABOUT THE BOOK

FAMILY IS CENTRAL to human existence. Most of us rely, as infants and usually throughout our lives, on a small group of others, connected by ties of biology or affinity, for material, physical and emotional support. Living in proximity to those we love most is often necessary for human happiness and security. 'Family values', however nebulous or mutable, carry strong moral weight and governments generally aim, or say they aim, to promote the well-being and stability of family life. International human rights instruments all contain commitments, sometimes spread over several clauses, that recognise the status of family and provide for its protection.

Governments do sometimes break up families, but the reasons for doing so must be weighty. A child may be removed from abusive or neglectful parents. Serious criminal offenders are separated from their family by imprisonment. Visa refusals and expulsions regularly lead to unwanted and distressing family separations. That the last of these has become so normalised reflects the assumption that immigration control is a factor of such importance that it stands alongside child abuse and serious crime as a reason to keep families apart. It is an assumption that is deeply contested, however, by thousands of binational families who cannot understand why their needs and interests carry so little weight.

This contestation is played out through politics, media and law. This book is about its playing out in human rights law, in particular, in decisions made by the UK's Supreme Court (the Court) between 2007 and 2017 on the application of Article 8 of the European Convention on Human Rights (ECHR), the right to respect for family life, under the Human Rights Act.[1] The Court's early decisions consistently centred family life. This was the first time that I had seen a court recognise the needs of binational families in an immigration context, but, as the book will show, gains were precarious and could not be sustained in the face of government opposition and a changed composition of the Court.

[1] Convention for the Protection of Human Rights and Fundamental Freedoms (European Convention on Human Rights, as amended) (Council of Europe, signed 4 November 1850, entered into force 3 September 1953) (ECHR).

The European Court of Human Rights (Strasbourg Court or Strasbourg) has also often been criticised for awarding too little weight to the claims of families separated by immigration control, and it is evident that protecting the family life of binational families through Article 8 is not straightforward. The fact that it happened at all, even for a temporary period, made me reflect on what law can and cannot do.

This led me to the underpinning thesis of this book, which is that Article 8 can and should treat family life as having the same importance as immigration control. I say it 'can' treat family life in this way because the structure of Article 8 permits that interpretation. I say 'should' as a normative and legal statement. It is normative because I believe that family life is at least as important as immigration control. It is legal because I believe that this is the best interpretation of Article 8 as it accommodates both state concerns and recognition of the right it is designed to protect. In fact, it as a modest suggestion; there are good arguments for saying that family life should prevail over immigration concerns in all but rare instances, but such a prospect is currently remote and I have confined myself to arguing that, while immigration control is important, so is family life.

However, the decisions discussed in this book show that judges can do little on their own; wider social and political acceptance of human rights values is needed for gains to be enduring.[2] The absence of this has resulted in a tortuous jurisprudence, both at Strasbourg and domestically. The tensions between immigration control and family life, and between law and politics, cannot be reconciled but only disguised. The book is therefore also a study of judges as strategic and political actors. It shows that the decisions they make are imbued with values and respond to and have consequences for other parts of the political system, while the judicial function is shown to be a contestable and negotiable part of the political constitution.[3] These are not new observations, but the book's value lies in its sustained examination of how these factors affected the development of the jurisprudence in one area. This close examination of a relatively small number of decisions has enabled new insights and understanding. It demonstrates that judges were not always transparent about what they were doing, and many features can only be understood through detailed attention and comparison across these decisions. Judges are thereby shown to be strategic political actors.

[2] The UK is not the only country that has experienced difficulties incorporating human rights into its legal and political culture; see, eg B Oomen, *Rights for Others: The Slow Home-Coming of Human Rights in the Netherlands* (Cambridge, Cambridge University Press, 2014); M Andenas and E Bjorge, 'National Implementation of ECHR Rights' in A Føllesdal, B Peters and G Ulfstein, *Constituting Europe: The European Court of Human Rights in a National, European, and Global Context* (Cambridge, Cambridge University Press, 2013) 182.

[3] L Epstein and K Weinshall, *The Strategic Analysis of Judicial Behavior: A Comparative Perspective* (Cambridge, Cambridge University Press, 2021); TT Arvind and L Stirton, 'Legal Ideology, Legal Doctrine and the UK's Top Judges' [2016] *PL* 418, 423; G Gee, R Hazell, K Malleson and P O'Brien, *The Politics of Judicial Independence in the UK's Changing Constitution* (Cambridge, Cambridge University Press, 2015).

II. CHAPTER OUTLINE

This introductory chapter presents the sociological and legal concepts used in this book. It is organised in three sections, each corresponding to an area of analysis within the book. The first concerns the family reunification question: what is family, what is family reunification and why is it so problematic? The second concerns human rights. It discusses family reunification within international human rights law, and Article 8 of the ECHR – the right to respect for family and private life. It then addresses a concept in human rights law that will be central to the legal analysis: the distinction between positive and negative obligations. The third section concerns judges: why is it argued that judges have values, what impact does this have on their judging and how is this expressed? It also discusses another key concept, 'judicial deference', and its relationship with judicial analysis of the public interest in human rights cases. The chapter ends with a discussion of the methodology used in this work, reasons for the selection of the cases discussed and the research methods.

Chapter two is designed for readers who are not already familiar with the British legal and constitutional system or with British immigration law. It is an introduction to the British constitution and court system, to the main features of the immigration control regime, including the system for appeals, and to the Human Rights Act. It outlines the system for family reunification applications and shows how the UK's history of political constitutionalism complicated the reception of human rights into the UK's legal system.

Chapter three provides a critical analysis of the European Court of Human Rights' family reunification jurisprudence under Article 8 of the ECHR. It notes that, like the Supreme Court, the Strasbourg Court has had to reconcile its commitment to family life with respect for states' sovereignty over immigration. It has done this by making state sovereignty the first consideration, which can be displaced by only a small number of applicants.

Chapter four turns to decisions made by the UK Supreme Court. It analyses the 2007 decision in *Huang*, a significant case in the history of immigration law and human rights. In contrast to preceding lower court decisions on Article 8 and family reunification, it asserted an autonomous role for the court in adjudicating on human rights and it brought family life into the centre of decision-making.[4]

Chapter five considers three decisions that continued the move begun in *Huang* towards the construction of a domestic Article 8 family reunification jurisprudence. They spoke about family migrants in a new way, placing their interests at the heart of the decision in ways that reflected the structure and spirit of Article 8, in contrast to the previous position in lower courts and, to some extent, even at Strasbourg. Even so, these judgments did not create a secure base for this new system of values, and the gains were less solid than might have been hoped; this chapter analyses why.

[4] *Huang and Kashmiri v Secretary of State for the Home Department* [2007] UKHL 11.

Chapter six continues the theme of ambiguous gains. It analyses four decisions that were regarded as hugely positive for families as they obliged the government to rethink several aspects of its policy. They continued the pattern set in chapters four and five by recognising the critical importance of family life. Yet none of them relied only or even at all on Article 8. The Court was committed to protecting family life, but was less enthusiastic about doing so at the intersections of Article 8 and immigration for reasons discussed in the chapter.

Chapter seven looks at three cases decided after the government backlash against the Court's earlier decisions, resulting in amendment to the Immigration Rules and statutory changes, although the latter did not come before the Court. By this stage, the Court was under considerable pressure and there were also internal divisions. Progressively, over three cases, the Court, now different in composition, stepped back from its previous position, explaining its decisions in part by the rule changes, but retreating further than these required. While the Court did not abandon its protective function altogether, it narrowed the field on which it asserted its authority, removed the needs and interests of families from the centre of the discussion and made government concerns more central.

Chapter eight takes inspiration from the cases discussed in chapters three to six to construct a more family-centred version of Article 8 family reunification rights while recognising that this remains an aspiration. It reflects the underpinning argument of the book that conventional articulations of Article 8 have not given family life enough weight and have underplayed the harmful and discriminatory character of controls and inequality of arms between individual and state. It shows that it is possible to design Article 8 principles that recognise the centrality of family life without disregarding the public interest in immigration control.

Chapter nine provides some brief concluding remarks. Binational family life has historically carried little weight when set against the demands of immigration control. Article 8 family reunification claims create a tension between family life and state sovereignty that courts cannot resolve. Despite some promising judgments, human rights have shifted the dial only marginally. However, the judgments analysed in chapters four to six and the discussion in chapter eight show what human rights might achieve. Law is never the whole solution, but it may be part of it; the courts can reinforce and realise norms and values, but the norms and values need a secure political and social basis.

III. FAMILY REUNIFICATION

A. Terminology: Family Reunification, Binational Families and Sponsors

Family reunification here means the process by which family members request and are granted permission to enter or remain in a state of which they are not a national. Sometimes, the aim is not, strictly speaking, 'reunification', as the family is already living together within the state, and the migrant family member is asking for status regularisation. However, the absence of status is a significant legal fact, and the law often treats such family members as if they are outside the state and are seeking 'reunification'. On other occasions, the family may not have previously lived together, or not done so for many years. However, 'reunification' rather than 'unification' is still preferred because it emphasises that the families in question have a prior existence independent of any immigration rights. Because family reunification is concerned only with compliance with immigration laws, it would be technically correct to refer to family reunification cases as 'immigration' cases. However, that would turn the focus away from the families involved and back to state interests, precisely the problem that the book discusses.

Family members who are seeking family reunification may be described as 'binational', 'cross-border' or 'transnational' families. None of these terms fits all the families under discussion, but 'binational' is used here because it emphasises the barriers that arise through the legal concept of nationality, because it includes families who may already be living in the same state and because it does not assume the particular model of family life suggested by 'transnationalism'.[5] In binational families, one party will have either citizenship or permanent residence (called 'indefinite leave to remain' or 'settlement' in British immigration law), so that families who accompany or join migrants on time-limited visas are not included in the study. The citizen or long-term resident who wants to be reunified with a family member is described as the sponsor. Strictly speaking, therefore, not all families are binational as, occasionally, the sponsor is not a British citizen and has the same nationality as the applicant. However, they have a long-term status in the UK and the immigration regime treats citizens and settled residents identically for this purpose. In the book, I make claims about the 'citizenship' rights of sponsors which I say Article 8 often fails to address and, in that context, I am using citizenship as a social rather than legal concept. There are many reasons why a long-term resident may not have naturalised, for example, prohibitions on dual nationality in the country of origin. Whether someone who has lived for decades in the UK is a citizen or a settled resident has little impact on the normative strength of their claim; the UK is their home.

In this book, legal claims may have been brought by migrants, sponsors or, occasionally, other family members. Their relationship to the proceedings will vary. Sometimes, they have brought an appeal against an unfavourable decision, when they might be described as the applicant, claimant or appellant. On other occasions, they are responding to an appeal brought by the government against a lower court ruling, so they are known as the respondent. Sometimes, they will be

[5] A transnational family lives 'some or most of the time separated from each other yet hold together and create something that can be seen as a feeling of collective welfare and unity … even across national borders': D Bryceson and U Vuorela, 'Transnational Families in the Twenty-First Century' in D Bryceson and U Vuorela (eds), *The Transnational Family: New Frontiers and Global Networks* (Oxford, Berg Publishers, 2020) 3.

appellants etc at one hearing and respondents at another. For simplicity, I have used the term 'applicant' or 'applicants' throughout to refer to the migrant and their family members. When talking about the immigration service or Home Office, I have called them 'the government'.

B. Family

'Family reunification' requires a concept of 'family'. The difficulties of defining family and its boundaries are well known and have increased in recent years as new understandings have emerged.[6] These see family as a dynamic set of practices and obligations around resource-sharing, intimacy, caring and interdependence rather than being based on biological or legal relationships.[7] Family may exist as a nuclear family unit (a couple or parent(s) with minor children) and between those with a looser biological relationship (such as aunt and niece) or none (close friends, informally adopted child). States, however, construct family narrowly in the immigration context, and this is reinforced by the ECHR jurisprudence.[8] Chapter three shows that it is almost always concerned only with 'core' family members, ie spouses and parents/minor children. While understanding has expanded to include same-sex couples, the law still excludes, in practice if not in theory, many relationships commonly thought of as family, particularly but not only in cultures originating from outside Western Europe (for example, between siblings, cousins, adult children and parents, grandchildren and grandparents, or within foster families), as well as intimate relationships which do not involve monogamous marriage or marriage-like relationships.[9] Although these relationships are occasionally recognised as constituting family life, they have not founded a successful family reunification claim.[10] As this book is concerned with family reunification in the legal context, it is equally narrow in focus, being primarily concerned with spouses, parents and minor children, and, occasionally, other close relatives such as siblings or grandparents. In so doing,

[6] For a discussion, see D Hacker, *Legalized Families in the Era of Bordered Globalizations* (Cambridge, Cambridge University Press, 2017) 46–60.

[7] C Draghici, 'Adult Children and Elderly Parents in Strasbourg Proceedings: A Misconstrued Approach to "Family Life"' (2018) 32 *International Journal of Law, Policy and the Family* 42, 53; Hacker, *Legalized Families*, 2.

[8] For a discussion, S Bonjour and L Cleton, 'Co-constructions of Family and Belonging in the Politics of Family Migration' (2021) in E Carmel, K Lenner and R Paul (eds), *Handbook on the Governance and Politics of Migration* (Cheltenham, Edward Elgar Publishing, 2021) 161–72. This narrow approach is in marked contrast with EU free movement law, where family reunification rights are more expansive, reflecting the underlying impetus to facilitate the free movement of EU citizens.

[9] See, eg T Simmons, 'Sexuality and Immigration: UK Family Reunion Policy and the Regulation of Sexual Citizens in the European Union' (2008) *Political Geography* 213. On expansion of the nuclear family, see Lady Hale, 'What Is a 21st Century Family?' (International Centre for Family Law, Policy and Practice, 1 July 2019).

[10] Bonjour and Cleton, 'Co-constructions of Family and Belonging in the Politics of Family Migration'.

it reluctantly colludes in the marginalisation of other ways of understanding family not because they do not matter, but because there are few legal rights to contest. As Mustasaari has observed, the nuclear family paradigm functions as a marker for the rights and inclusion of binational families.[11]

At the same time, immigration laws are interested in the functional as well as the legal or biological character of relationships. Article 8 ECHR protects 'family life', not family, and a successful claim depends on showing that this exists. As the next chapter will show, there are some presumptions made about family life between married couples and between parents and minor children, but perceptions about the quality of family life matter.[12] Families have always been complex, messy and changeable, and this is heightened by the immigration process, which often imposes unwanted separations or prompts strategic responses to the obstacles it creates.[13] Decision-makers, alert to the signs of a bogus relationship, may be slow to acknowledge how diverse even a nuclear family may be in terms of how it is formed (for instance, through an online community), how children may be created or cared for (for example, by step parents) or that the migration process itself creates unexpected disruptions and connections.[14] Cultural expectations shape how emotions are experienced and expressed, while perceptions about who is worthy of love are deeply embedded in colonial, racial and gender hierarchies.[15] The regulation of family reunification often relies on binary categories – genuine/bogus or forced/voluntary marriages; carer/dependant; caring/non-caring parent; economic/family migrant – that inadequately reflect the complex web of relationships and motivations of those who move across the globe to live with family members.[16] This is not incidental; gendered and racialised differentiations between worthy and unworthy family norms are central to the construction of the nation and its community.[17]

[11] S Mustasaari, 'The "Nuclear Family Paradigm" as a Marker of Rights and Belonging in Transnational Families' (2015) *Social Identities* 359.

[12] H Wray, 'Moulding the Migrant Family' (2009) *Legal Studies* 592; N Carver, 'Displaying Genuineness: Cultural Translation in the Drafting of Marriage Narratives for Immigration Applications and Appeals' (2014) *Families, Relationships and Societies* 271, 286; AM D'Aoust, 'In the Name of Love: Marriage Migration, Governmentality, and Technologies of Love' [2013] *International Political Sociology* 258.

[13] B De Hart, WM van Rossum and I Sportel, 'Law in the Everyday Lives of Transnational Families: An Introduction' (2006) 3 *Oñati Socio-Legal Series* 991.

[14] Hacker, *Legalized Families*, 288; K Charsley, B Storer-Church, M Benson and N Hear, 'Marriage-Related Migration to the UK' [2012] *International Migration Review* 861; J Leinonen and S Pellander, 'Court Decisions over Marriage Migration in Finland: A Problem with Transnational Family Ties' [2014] *Journal of Ethnic and Migration Studies* 1488.

[15] D Gebrial, 'Decolonising Desire: The Politics of Love' (*Versobooks.com*, 2017) 13; J Turner, *Bordering Intimacy: Postcolonial Governance and the Policing of Family* (Manchester, Manchester University Press, 2020).

[16] See, eg C Brettell, 'Marriage and Migration' [2017] *Annual Review of Anthropology* 81; E Beck-Gernsheim, 'The Marriage Route to Migration: Of Border Artistes, Transnational Matchmaking and Imported Spouses' [2011] *Nordic Journal of Migration Research* 60.

[17] S Bonjour and B de Hart, 'A Proper Wife, a Proper Marriage: Constructions of "Us" and "Them" in Dutch Family Migration Policy' (2013) 20 *European Journal of Women's Studies* 61.

C. The 'Problem' of Family Reunification

Family reunification has persistently been a considerable proportion, between one-third and one-half, of all immigration in many states, including the UK.[18] Effective immigration controls are broadly supported by electorates and are seen as central to the successful functioning of the modern nation state.[19] However, controlling immigration is not straightforward, and policymakers may concentrate their efforts where they have most effect.[20] In that respect, family members are an easy target as they usually actively seek permission to enter or remain and lead relatively stable and visible lives. Their admission also represents a particular challenge to governments who aim to admit only migrants deemed desirable because of skills, education or racial or cultural similarity, whereas, in family reunification, migrants are selected by families on different grounds.[21] The former French President Nicolas Sarkozy described family reunification as *immigration subie* (immigration to which the state submits) and contrasted it with *immigration choisie* (immigration desired by the state).[22] In the UK, and across northern and western Europe, there has been a growing focus on what are said to be the problematic aspects of family migration: poorly educated, culturally alien or economically unproductive applicants, the 'migrant with poor prospects' who will place a burden on welfare systems and enable the reproduction of oppressive or archaic family practices, inter-generational deprivation and ethnic segregation.[23]

At the same time, family reunification does not concern only the admission of an outsider, but also the intimate interests of a citizen or resident. Different normative questions therefore arise.[24] Refusal of a family member is a rejection on a matter that concerns a citizen's most intimate areas of life and may

[18] I Honohan, 'Reconsidering the Claim to Family Reunification in Migration' (2009) 57 *Political Studies* 769; Charsley et al, 'Marriage-Related Migration to the UK'.

[19] E Grande, T Schwarzbözl and M Fatke, 'Politicizing Immigration in Western Europe' (2009) 26 *Journal of European Public Policy* 1444.

[20] R Ford, W Jennings and W Somerville, 'Public Opinion, Responsiveness and Constraint: Britain's Three Immigration Policy Regimes' (2015) 41 *Journal of Ethnic and Migration Studies* 1391.

[21] P Regine, 'Strategic Contextualisation: Free Movement, Labour Migration Policies and the Governance of Foreign Workers in Europe' (2013) 34 *Policy Studies* 122; see also K Abrams, 'What Makes the Family Special?' (2013) 80 *Chicago Law Review* 7; S Bonjour and A Kraler, 'Family Migration as an Integration Issue? Policy Perspectives and Academic Insights' (2015) 36 *Family Issues* 1407.

[22] Assemblée Nationale, *Commission des lois constitutionnelles, de la législation et de l'administration générale de la République* (25 July 2007) Compte rendu No 7.

[23] S Bonjour and JW Duyvendak, 'The "Migrant with Poor Prospects": Racialized Intersections of Class and Culture in Dutch Civic Integration Debates' (2017) *Ethnic and Racial Studies* 882; B De Hart, 'The Odd Couple: Gender, Securitization, Europeanization and Marriages of Convenience in Dutch Family Migration Policies (1930–2020)' in AM D'Aoust (ed), *Transnational Marriage and Partner Migration: Constellations of Security, Citizenship and Rights* (Oxford, Rutgers University Press, 2022) 31.

[24] J Carens, *The Ethics of Immigration* (Oxford, Oxford University Press, 2013) 186.

have repercussions that last a lifetime. Citizens see living with their loved ones in their own country as central to their belonging, but governments do not, so that binational families experience directly the different and conflicting ways that citizenship can be understood. A citizen refused family reunification has not lost the formal attributes of citizenship; they are still, legally speaking, a member with rights of residence and political participation, yet they experience a deeper and more personal disenfranchisement.[25] Gender, class, race and ethnicity, age and sexual identity all affect the likelihood of resolution between the formal and the personal forms of belonging. Sponsors whose own membership is regarded as weak or problematic, even if they possess legal citizenship, are likely to experience greater difficulties.[26] It is not only those most immediately affected (partners, parents), but other family members, such as grandparents, who are surprised and angered to find their family lives regulated by the state. Governments cannot therefore just prevent entry, but must also explain why it is needed, reconciling their necessary support for 'family' in an abstract sense with the need to restrict family reunification in concrete cases. There is therefore a focus on the defects of the parties or of the relationship: a marriage may be designated as 'sham' or 'forced', a parent may be taken to have voluntarily abandoned a child or it is suggested that the parties need to work harder at being self-sufficient.

Many European states have accordingly implemented measures such as higher minimum age requirements, income and other financial criteria, language and knowledge tests and intrusive inquiries into family or intimate life.[27] These policies are justified in generalised terms, drawing on often racialised and gendered representations: the oppressed wife; the irresponsible or opportunistic husband; the child held back by cultural and linguistic barriers.[28] Relationships involving an irregular spouse are often conflated with sham marriages, while conventional understandings of intimacy and love become technologies for distinguishing those with sufficient emotional commitment.[29] It is not always clear what these policies actually achieve, or even whether the problem they

[25] B De Hart and F Bessels, 'Everything Went According to the Rules: Female Citizen Sponsors' Legal Consciousness, Intimate Citizenship and Family Migration Law' (2021) 28 *Identities* 37.

[26] L Block, 'Regulating Membership: Explaining Restriction and Stratification of Family Migration in Europe' (2015) 36 *Journal of Family Issues* 1433; S Bonjour and L Block, 'Ethnicizing Citizenship, Questioning Membership. Explaining the Decreasing Family Migration Rights of Citizens in Europe' (2016) 20 *Citizenship Studies* 779.

[27] S Wallace Goodman, 'Controlling Immigration through Language and Country Knowledge Requirements' (2011) 34 *Western European Politics* 235; H Wray, A Agoston and J Hutton, 'A Family Resemblance? The Regulation of Marriage Migration in Europe' (2014) 16 *European Journal of Migration and Law* 209.

[28] K Charsley, M Bolognani and S Spencer, 'Marriage Migration and Integration: Interrogating Assumptions in Academic and Policy Debates' (2017) 17 *Ethnicities* 469; Wray, 'Moulding the Migrant Family'.

[29] H Wray, 'The "Pure" Relationship, Sham Marriages and Immigration Control' in J Miles, R Probert and P Mody (eds), *Marriage Rites and Rights* (Oxford, Hart Publishing 2015) 141–65; D'Aoust, 'In the Name of Love'.

aim to remedy exists. Concerns as to, for example, forced marriage have some factual basis, but there is a tendency to overstate the problem and stretch categories to exclude a far wider range of applicants.[30] Assumed deficits in integration are another recurrent theme, but investigation often reveals a more complex picture.[31] Sometimes, measures appear pointless or even counterproductive. Preventing the genetic consequences of first-cousin marriage, for example, does not explain why Denmark prohibits admission when consanguinity is much more remote.[32] The UK's minimum income requirement was justified in large measure by the need to protect public funds, but it had the perverse consequence of forcibly pushing single parents to make welfare claims.[33] There is a sense that policy aims are often wider than or different to the specific problem under discussion.[34]

Such restrictive controls can cause acute suffering, the duration of which may be indefinite. Often, the cruelty is hiding in plain sight. The impact on a child of being separated from a loving and loved parent is shocking in almost any context but immigration, where it is perceived almost as part of the natural order.[35] This pain is not felt equally by all but is distributed according to wider patterns of racial, gender and class disadvantage, and it often reproduces older patterns of colonial domination and exclusion. Even for the most fortunate, it is a prolonged, intrusive and painful process that is not experienced by families who share a nationality.[36]

That policy causes hardship and has unclear benefits is usually a political rather than a legal question, but it can be relevant to human rights decisions, where the public interest is balanced against the adverse impact on affected individuals. This book will argue that the public interest question has received insufficient scrutiny in Article 8 family reunification decisions and that the impact on families is often minimised or glossed over.

[30] H Wray, 'The "Pure" Relationship, Sham Marriages and Immigration Control'.

[31] K Charsley, M Bolognani, E Ersanilli and S Spencer, *Marriage Migration and Integration* (London, Palgrave Macmillan, 2020); Bonjour and Kraler, 'Family Migration as an Integration Issue?'; W Schinkel, *Imagined Societies. A Critique of Immigrant Integration in Western Europe* (Cambridge, Cambridge University Press, 2017).

[32] A Liversage and M Rytter, 'A Cousin Marriage Equals a Forced Marriage: Transnational Marriages between Closely Related Spouses in Denmark' in A Shaw and A Raz (eds), *Cousin Marriages: Between Tradition, Genetic Risk and Cultural Change* (Oxford, Berghahn, 2015) 130–53.

[33] H Wray, S Grant, E Kofman and C Peel, 'Family Friendly? The Impact on Children of the Family Migration Rules: A Review of the Financial Requirements' (Children's Commissioner for England, 2015) 17.

[34] H Wray, 'What Do States Regulate When They Regulate Spousal Migration?' in D'Aoust, *Transnational Marriage and Partner Migration*, 88–105.

[35] J Bhabha, *Child Migration and Human Rights in a Global Age* (Oxford, Princeton University Press, 2014) 1–37; J Carling, C Menjívar and L Schmalzbauer, 'Central Themes in the Study of Transnational Parenthood' (2012) 38 *Journal of Ethnic and Migration Studies* 191; R Salazar Parreñas, 'Transnational Fathering: Gendered Conflicts, Distant Disciplining and Emotional Gaps' (2008) 34 *Journal of Ethnic and Migration Studies* 1057; Wray et al, 'Family Friendly? The Impact on Children of the Family Migration Rules'.

[36] J Turner and MV Espinoza, 'The Affective and Intimate Life of the Family Migration Visa: Knowing, Feeling and Encountering the Heteronormative State' (2021) 26 *Geopolitics* 357; Bonjour and Cleton, 'Co-constructions of Family and Belonging in the Politics of Family Migration'.

IV. HUMAN RIGHTS AND FAMILY LIFE

A. The Human Right to Family Life

The social, political and personal significance of family is reflected in international legal norms. Article 16(3) of the Universal Declaration of Human Rights says the family 'is the natural and fundamental group unit of society and is entitled to protection by society and the State'. There is wide acceptance in international human rights law of rights to marry and to found a family.[37] There is also a prohibition on arbitrary interference with, and a right to respect for, family life and a right for children to live with their parents.[38]

There is, however, no explicit right to family reunification across international borders. The strongest widely ratified obligation is Article 10 of the Convention on the Rights of the Child, which requires states to deal with applications for family reunification between parents and children in a positive, humane and expeditious manner.[39] In 2005, the Committee on the Rights of the Child 'reminded' states of their obligations under Article 10 when it is not in the best interests of the child to return to the country of origin.[40] Its 2017 General Comment No 22 observes that states must take the best interests of the child fully into consideration in decisions on family unity.[41] These are significant obligations, but they are general in character and cannot form the basis of enforceable rights within the UK. In practice, Article 3 of the Convention, which requires a child's interests to be treated as a primary consideration, has been more influential because of its impact on the ECHR Article 8 jurisprudence and because of its partial translation into domestic statute.[42]

Giving practical effect to family life obligations may, in principle, require family reunification. The Human Rights Committee General Comment No 19 observes that states must adopt 'appropriate measures … to ensure the unity or reunification of families, particularly when their members are separated for

[37] eg UN Universal Declaration of Human Rights (adopted 10 December, UNGA Res 217A (III) (UDHR), Art 16(1); ECHR, Art 12; International Covenant on Civil and Political Rights (adopted 19 December 1996, entered into force 23 March 1976, United Nations, Treaty Series, vol 999) (ICCPR), Art 17(2).

[38] United Nations Convention on the Rights of the Child (adopted 20 November 1989, entered into force 2 September, UNGA Res 44/25) (CRC), Arts 9, 10 and 16.

[39] ibid Art 10.

[40] Committee on the Rights of the Child, Thirty-ninth session, 17 May–3 June 2005, 'Treatment of Unaccompanied and Separated Children Outside Their Country of Origin' (2005) General Comment No 6, para 83.

[41] Joint General Comment No 3 (2017) of the Committee on the Protection of the Rights of All Migrant Workers and Members of Their Families and No 22 (2017) of the Committee on the Rights of the Child on the general principles regarding the human rights of children in the context of international migration, para 29.

[42] Borders Citizenship and Immigration Act 2009, s 55; but see *Tanda-Muzinga c France*, Requête no 2260/10, Council of Europe, European Court of Human Rights, 10 July 2014, para 76.

political, economic or similar reasons', while General Comment No 15 notes that while it

> is in principle a matter for the State to decide who it will admit to its territory … in certain circumstances an alien may enjoy the protection of the Covenant even in relation to entry or residence, for example, when considerations of non-discrimination, prohibition of inhuman treatment and respect for family life arise.[43]

However, no actual breaches have been found in respect of family reunification.[44] The regional human rights jurisprudence on family reunification has been most extensive under Article 8 of the ECHR, discussed below, although there have been some findings by the African Commission on Human Rights and the Inter-American Court of Human Rights.[45] Chapter three shows the Strasbourg jurisprudence to be limited and state centric; however, that critique must be understood not only in the regional context discussed in that chapter, but also in relation to the absence of strong global support for using family life rights to support family reunification.

B. Article 8 ECHR

Article 8 reads as follows:

> 1. Everyone has the right to respect for his private and family life, his home and his correspondence.
> 2. There shall be no interference by a public authority with the exercise of this right except such as is in accordance with the law and is necessary in a democratic society in the interests of national security, public safety or the economic well-being of the country, for the prevention of disorder or crime, for the protection of health or morals, or for the protection of the rights and freedoms of others.

This book is concerned with family life, not private life or correspondence. Determining an Article 8 family life claim requires a step-by-step analysis. This is discussed at more length in chapter three, but the key questions are:

- Is there family life?
- Has there been interference with family life?

[43] Human Rights Committee, Twenty-seventh session, 'The Position of Aliens under the Covenant' (1986) General Comment No 15, para 5.

[44] The Committee has occasionally found that expelling a well-established non-national following criminal conduct is a violation of family and private life rights. See, eg Communication No 2243/2013 *Husseini v Denmark*, views adopted on 24 October 2014; Communication No 1557/2007 *Nystrom v Australia*, views adopted on 18 July 2011; Communication No 1011/2011, *Madafferi v. Australia*, views adopted on 26 July 2004; Communication No 930/2000, *Winata v. Australia*, views adopted on 26 July 2001.

[45] 'Union Inter Africaine des Droits de l'Homme, Federation Internationale des Ligues des Droits de l'Homme, Rencontre Africaine des Droits de l'Homme, Organisation Nationale des Droits de

- Is the interference in accordance with the law?
- Is the interference proportionate?

In practice, most disputes concern proportionality, that is, the relationship between the public interest in immigration control and the harm caused to the individual. Proportionality is usually assessed by addressing the specific issues mentioned in Article 8(2), but, as chapter three will show, in family reunification cases, the Strasbourg Court uses a different method, asking whether there is a 'fair balance' between relevant factors. In so doing, it awards greater weight to the interests of the state in controlling migration, appearing to undermine the primacy of the human right, what Dembour has called the 'Strasbourg reversal'.[46] It is easy to see why the Strasbourg Court believe it needs to do that, given states' concern to control immigration, but how is it possible legally? The answer is that the Strasbourg Court has treated family reunification as a 'positive obligation' as it is asking the state to do something (to admit the family member), not as a 'negative obligation' (to refrain from refusing the family member). Appreciating the implications of this choice involves some technical legal questions that are discussed here because it is an issue that arises at many points in the book.

C. Positive and Negative Obligations and Why the Difference Matters

When I first started writing this book, I was aware of the distinction between negative and positive obligations in a general way, but I did not consider it central to this work. The Strasbourg Court has repeatedly said that, in the family reunification context, the distinction has little significance, and I took that statement at face value.[47] However, after trying and failing to find a coherent framework for the jurisprudence, I returned to the concept and things fell into place. The distinction between positive and negative obligations is the mechanism by which the priority awarded to states rather than migrant families is made legally possible, although, critically, it is not the entire explanation for the state-centric character of the jurisprudence.

The ECHR is expressed as a set of freedoms (such as freedom from interference in family life under Article 8) that create negative obligations on states (for example, not to interfere with family life). The Strasbourg Court has recognised that protecting negative rights may sometimes require that states carry

l'Homme au Sénégal and Association Malienne des Droits de l'Homme v Angola' (11 November 1997) Communication No 159/96; see also F Viljoen and L Louw, 'State Compliance with the Recommendations of the African Commission on Human and Peoples' Rights, 1994–2004' (2007) 101 *American Journal of International Law* 1, 34.

[46] M Dembour, *When Humans Become Migrants: Study of the European Court of Human Rights with an Inter-American Counterpoint* (Oxford, Oxford University Press, 2015) 118–19.

[47] eg *Jeunesse v Netherlands* (2015) 60 EHRR 17 [106].

out positive acts, so that they must take steps that enable family life to continue, leading to the concept of 'positive obligations'. As positive obligations are not the result of explicit wording within the Convention, the Strasbourg Court has been cautious about invoking them and has often applied a wider margin of appreciation.[48] Positive obligations also do not fit easily with the wording of the Convention. For example, in Article 8, when does a failure to act amount to an interference in family life? How do you apply the criterion of 'in accordance with the law' to a legal provision that does not exist?

The test for proportionality is particularly difficult. In a negative obligation case, while the Strasbourg Court's investigation is not always very rigorous, the underpinning principle is that the government must show its *action* is in the public interest and this must be linked to the interests set out in the article.[49] But how to establish that government *inaction* is 'necessary in a democratic society' in a positive case? The government may argue that it has good reasons not to act, but how should those reasons be assessed? There may be multiple possible ways to fulfil a positive obligation; must the necessity test be met for all of them? If so, the burden on states would be extensive. There are other difficulties too: taking action may involve regulating the acts of third parties (for example, through prosecution), and may require the dedication of resources that the state prefers to spend elsewhere. It can also compete with other protected rights. For these reasons, the Strasbourg Court does not usually apply Article 8(2) directly in positive obligation cases, but asks whether there is a fair balance 'between the competing interests of the individual and of the community as a whole'.[50] This is a more generalised and subjective assessment to which the Article 8(2) legitimate aims have only a 'certain relevance'.[51] The analysis may (although not necessarily) be less thorough.[52] Certainly, the structure of the proportionality assessment suggests that the Court does not attach the same priority to the protected right as in a negative obligation case.[53]

Whether a human rights claim is considered negative or positive can therefore make a considerable difference to how it is treated. The boundaries between positive and negative obligations, however, are often unclear, including in family reunification. For instance, an applicant has lived many years as an unauthorised migrant, getting married and bringing up a family. Would their removal involve a positive obligation: the government must allow them to stay despite

[48] For a discussion, see L Lavrysen, *Human Rights in a Positive State: Rethinking the Relationship between Positive and Negative Obligations under the European Convention on Human Rights* (Cambridge, Cambridge University Press, 2016) 214–21.

[49] For a summary, see V Stoyanava, 'The Disjunctive Structure of Positive Rights' (2018) 87 *Nordic Journal of International Law*, 355.

[50] *Jeunesse* (n 46) [106].

[51] *Rees v United Kingdom* App no 9532/81, (1987) 9 EHRR 56 [37]. The Court sometimes uses the term 'fair balance' as the final stage in a negative obligation Art 8(2) assessment.

[52] Lavrysen, *Human Rights in a Positive State*, 226.

[53] ibid 233; Stoyanova, 'The Disjunctive Structure of Positive Rights', 365.

the violation of national immigration laws? Or is it a negative obligation: the government is asked to refrain from expelling them? The Strasbourg Court has repeatedly said that, in family reunification cases, 'the boundaries between the state's positive and negative obligations ... do not lend themselves to precise definition', and similar principles apply in both situations.[54] However, in practice and as chapter three will show, family reunification cases are almost always treated as positive obligation cases; the question is not whether the state should refrain from acting, but whether it must act. This apparently abstract choice goes to the heart of the dilemma of family reunification and Article 8.

In a negative case, the first point of reference is the human right to family life. This is consistent with a conception of universal human rights to which states are subject. The applicant shows there is a family life with which the state has interfered, and this must be justified, placing the state on the defensive. In a positive case, the state's right to control admission and stay is treated as a pre-existing and unquestioned state of affairs; the obligation to admit arises as an exception to those controls and the default position remains exclusion, not family unity. Human rights are, in effect, an exception to state sovereignty over admission and stay. Treating family reunification as a positive obligation therefore reduces the significance of the right. This position is consistent with the often-repeated statement of the Strasbourg Court that states have the right to control the entry and stay of non-citizens, although the historical and legal origins of that claim have been questioned.[55]

The Strasbourg Court is in a difficult position. It cannot move too far ahead of states, and it is unsurprising that it has recognised states' sovereignty over their borders and treated family reunification as involving positive obligations, at least in most instances. However, family reunification is not a typical positive obligation as the usual reasons for caution in its application do not apply. The state is not asked to control the actions of third parties but of itself. There are not many ways in which the positive obligation may be implemented (the request is only for a visa or leave to remain), and implementation is straightforward, predictable and inexpensive. The government should be able to explain why restrictions in place are in the public interest as all governments have family migration policies and have decided where to draw the boundaries. There are usually no competing rights at stake beyond the 'general interest'.

All these reasons point to family reunification obligations being close to negative obligations in character and capable of being treated as such. Notably, there is no specific need for a wide margin of appreciation other than the sensitivity of the issue. It is also difficult to see how the strength of the right, once it

[54] See, eg *Jeunesse* (n 46) [106]. This evolution is relatively recent; see H Lambert, 'The European Court of Human Rights and the Right of Refugees and Other Persons in Need of Protection to Family Reunion' (1999) 11 *International Journal of Refugee Law* 427.

[55] B Schotel, *On the Right of Exclusion: Law, Ethics and Immigration Policy* (Abingdon, Routledge, 2013).

is engaged, is diminished to the point that it is a priori outweighed by another factor, the state's interest in immigration control. That is why I say that family life must bear at least the same weight as immigration control when family reunification is in issue, even within a positive obligation context. However, chapter three will show that this does not happen. The Strasbourg Court gives states a wide margin of appreciation (although it does not always describe it as such), and government claims as to the necessity of controls in that particular form are not questioned, with the result that the claims of family life are easily outweighed. This is not an inevitable consequence of treating a claim as positive, although it is easier to do it in the less structured fair balance assessment, and the overriding priority is to avoid an open challenge to states' monopoly over the terms of admission and stay.[56] The Strasbourg Court's political reluctance to confront states on immigration matters is therefore given legal expression by treating family reunification as engaging a positive obligation, and positive obligations as involving a less rigorous proportionality assessment.

This argument has been made at some length here because it does not easily emerge from reading the cases, which are rather opaque on the matter. However, once it has been understood, it explains many of the characteristics of the Strasbourg cases discussed in chapter three. It is also a submerged theme in the Supreme Court cases analysed in chapters four to seven, where it is observed that, while it was never a major theme in the jurisprudence, when the Court sought to give priority to family life, it tended to ignore or minimise the positive character of the obligation and, when it wanted to emphasise the importance of immigration control, it mentioned it more frequently.

V. JUDGES

A. Judicial Values and the Craft of Writing Judgments

The core of this book analyses how Supreme Court judges addressed the tension between family life and immigration control. The legal issues could be, and were, plausibly addressed in different ways, and judges had to draw on more than conventional legal reasoning.

Values embrace 'a wide range of concepts including belief systems, moral imperatives, political dispositions, societal expectations, social attitudes and institutional norms'.[57] They are 'abstract concepts which transcend specific situations' and their application may require little cognitive effort but will underpin

[56] It is significant that, in the rare case that family reunification is treated as involving a negative obligation, scrutiny is not necessarily more searching; see, eg *Omoregie and Others v Norway* App no 265/07 (European Court of Human Rights, 31 July 2007).

[57] R Cahill-O'Callaghan, *Values in the Supreme Court: Decisions, Division and Diversity* (Oxford, Hart Publishing, 2020) 4.

our moral and other judgments in relation to a specific dilemma.[58] It is banal in the post-Human Rights Act era to observe that decisions require value judgments, but the proposition runs counter to the ideal of the lofty, neutral, depersonalised (usually male) judge and the highly technical, precedent-based modes of reasoning that are regarded as the gold standard for advocates and judges. This tension becomes more evident when judges must adjudicate on open-textured and teleological human rights norms, presenting a challenge to the legal culture into which British lawyers and judges have been socialised. That the Human Rights Act requires judges to make some subjective decisions may be problematic, especially given limited social and other diversity among the judiciary, but it is inevitable.[59] Some Supreme Court judges have admitted that moral values and their personal philosophy plays some part in their decision-making.[60] If judges reason backwards from their preferred outcome, as it seems they often do, it is likely that the legal path that best conforms with their moral judgement will be taken if that is coherently possible.[61] The danger is not that judges use values to arrive at their decisions, but that the values are under-articulated and under-analysed.

Values are not the only influence on legal choices. Supreme Court justices are highly intelligent, but they are still human beings and may have character flaws, or make cognitive errors.[62] Extraneous factors observed in the lower courts, such as pragmatism and non-legal heuristics, are likely to be present to some degree in the higher courts also. The quality of the advocate, a factor often tied to resources, and the composition of the panel also matter. Even the presence of a single judge from a social minority appears to have an impact on how other judges formulate their position on questions that involve that minority.[63]

In practice, even a diverse judiciary will hold many values in common.[64] Judges have a strong professional identity, so that, within the constellation of values described above, institutional values, such as respect for the constitution

[58] ibid 5.

[59] Although Cahill-O'Callaghan points out that even a homogeneous judiciary will display some diversity in values, as evidenced by her research; ibid 179–80.

[60] A Paterson, *Final Judgment: The Last Law Lords and the Supreme Court* (Oxford, Hart Publishing, 2013) 259–63; R Cahill-O'Callaghan, 'The Influence of Personal Values on Legal Judgments' (2013) 40 *Journal of Law and Society* 596; A Kavanagh, *Constitutional Review under the Human Rights Act* (Cambridge, Cambridge University Press, 2009) 222–28; R Cahill-O'Callaghan, 'Reframing the Judicial Diversity Debate: Personal Values and Tacit Diversity' (2015) 35 *Legal Studies* 1.

[61] Paterson, *Final Judgment*, 196–97; L Neuberger, '"Judge Not, That Ye Be Not judged": Judging Judicial Decision-Making', FA Mann Lecture (London, 29 January 2015); Cahill-O'Callaghan, *Values in the Supreme Court*,11.

[62] JB Fischman and DS Law, 'What Is Judicial Ideology, and How Should We Measure It?' (2009) 29 *Washington University Journal of Law* 133; Neuberger, '"Judge Not, That Ye Be Not judged"'; see also L Graham, 'Lessons from Lord Hope's Diaries: Judicial Ideology and Panel Selection' (UK Constitutional Law Association, 18 June 2020).

[63] C Hanretty, *A Court of Specialists – Judicial Behavior on the UK Supreme Court* (Oxford, Oxford University Press, 2020) 239–62; Fischman and Law, 'What Is Judicial Ideology, and How Should We Measure It?', 149–50; Cahill-O'Callaghan, 'Reframing the Judicial Diversity Debate'.

[64] For an overview, see Cahill-O'Callaghan, *Values in the Supreme Court*, 9–18; NG Fielding, 'Judges and Their Work' (2011) 20 *Social & Legal Studies* 97, 115; B Barry, *How Judges Judge:*

and coherence and stability in the law, will be very significant and, particularly when intellectual skills are strong, deliberation can override emotional impulses.[65] However, where more than one coherent route is open, as will usually be the case in the Supreme Court, an individual's instinctive response, driven by their personal values, will predispose them to a particular choice.[66] As Lady Hale has said,

> the business of judging, especially in the hard cases, often involves a choice between different conclusions, any of which it may be possible to reach by respectable legal reasoning. The choice made is likely to be motivated at a far deeper level by the judge's own approach to the law, to the problem under discussion and to ideas of what makes a just result … an important project of feminist jurisprudence has been to explode the myth of the disinterested, disengaged, and distant judge.[67]

This is pertinent to family reunification. A male judge from a secure, prosperous background and a majority ethnic group (ie most senior judges) is likely to have more confidence in the capacity of a majoritarian system to identify the public interest and its relative weight than one who is not so advantaged. Judges who have emerged from the Family Court system may be more sensitised to the importance of sustaining family ties. A judge who, despite the relative privilege that goes with the judicial position, has personally experienced discrimination may be quicker to understand what that means for others even if their experience is not precisely the same: 'People who have experienced their own personal humiliations can bring that experience to the humiliations of others.'[68] Recognising these subjectivities is not to paint the judiciary as politically motivated (although some mild ideological preferences have been observed) but to recognise the inevitability of unconscious orientations and preferences.[69] The book therefore assumes that the Court's doctrinal interpretations were motivated, in part, by personal subjectivities that ran alongside and informed institutional values and doctrinal considerations. Uncovering these is an interpretive exercise; there is no reliable method for reading judicial minds, and a project of this scale, which examines only a small number of cases, cannot undertake the type of empirical work that might allow inferences to be drawn.[70] Such an interpretive exercise, however, has value provided it is carried out carefully.

Empirical Insights into Judicial Decision-Making (Abingdon, Routledge, 2020); C Guthrie, JJ Rachlinski and AJ Wistrich, 'Blinking on the Bench: How Judges Decide Cases' (2007) 93 *Cornell Law Review* 1; Arvind and Stirton, 'Legal Ideology, Legal Doctrine'.

[65] Paterson, *Final Judgment*, 123–69.

[66] ibid 259–63; Fischman and Law, 'What Is Judicial Ideology, and How Should We Measure It?'; Cahill-O'Callaghan, *Values in the Supreme Court*, 7–11.

[67] B Hale, 'Maccabaean Lecture in Jurisprudence: A Minority Opinion?' (2008) 154 *Proceedings of the British Academy* 319.

[68] ibid 321.

[69] See, eg Lord Bingham, 'Maccabaean Lecture in Jurisprudence – The Judges: Active or Passive' (2006) 139 *Proceedings of the British Academy* 55. On political leanings, see Hanretty, *A Court of Specialists*, 193–238.

[70] For a discussion, see Fischman and Law, 'What Is Judicial Ideology, and How Should We Measure It?', 133–214. For such an example, see Hanretty, *A Court of Specialists*.

One clue to judicial thinking is to consider the 'strategic nature of the judge's linguistic choices',[71] how facts and legal doctrines are presented and organised within judgments so as to direct the argument towards a particular conclusion, to 'push the existing rules a bit further in a desired direction'.[72] There has recently been increased interest in legal writing and 'legal narratives', and the Feminist Judgments Project has demonstrated the power of these choices by rewriting significant judgments from a feminist perspective without departing from the legal conventions of judicial writing.[73] Judges, particularly in the Supreme Court, are highly skilled wordsmiths as well as lawyers, and will be conscious of how their writing style – 'the specific written form in which a writer encodes an idea, a "message" that [they want] to put across'[74] – will affect reception of the judgment particularly where it concerns controversial issues.[75] Judgments are not just statements of law but communications whose aim is to persuade the reader that a particular perspective is not just plausible but inevitable.[76] To that extent, they can be consciously crafted to hide as much as they reveal.

Supreme Court judgments typically focus entirely on the legal questions and 'the parties can often … disappear from view'.[77] However, in the early cases discussed here, when the Court emphasised the needs of families, it gave more attention to the personal circumstances of migrants and their families, often humanising them as parents or spouses, or emphasising the difficulties they faced, their emotional vulnerability or their resourcefulness. It was clear that conscious decisions had been made about how their story was told (for example, whether first names or family names were used, how their relationships were described, the prominence and choice of terms to denote immigration status), as well as the placing of this narrative in the judgment. A focus on factual matters is unusual as the Court is concerned only with legal questions and the facts will have been determined at a much earlier stage. But facts are not a neutral and stable platform upon which judges construct their legal and rhetorical arguments – 'no knowledge is innocent or value free'[78] – and even Supreme Court judges can be selective as to which facts are significant and how: 'Facts are always socially constructed, no matter who presents them.'[79] Later, when

[71] E Rackley, 'The Art and Craft of Writing Judgments: Notes on the Feminist Judgments Project' in R Hunter, C McGlynn and E Rackley (eds), *Feminist Judgments: From Theory to Practice* (Oxford, Hart Publishing, 2010) 45.

[72] Rackley, 'The Art and Craft of Writing Judgements', 6.

[73] Hunter et al, *Feminist Judgments: From Theory to Practice*, 45; for a survey, see M Hanne and R Weisberg 'Introduction' in M Hanne and MR Weisberg (eds), *Narrative and Metaphor in the Law* (Cambridge, Cambridge University Press, 2018) 1.

[74] R Posner, 'Judges' Writing Styles (And Do They Matter?)' (1995) 62 *Chicago Law Review* 1421, 1421–22.

[75] DR Klinck, 'Criticising the Judges: Some Preliminary Reflections on Style' (1986) 31 *McGill Law Journal* 655.

[76] J Niemi-Kiesiläinen, P Honkatukia and M Ruuskanen, 'Legal Texts as Discourses' in G Svensson and M Davies (eds), *Exploiting the Limits of Law* (Farnham: Ashgate, 2007) 69–88.

[77] Rackley, 'The Art and Craft of Writing Judgements', 47.

[78] Niemi-Kiesiläine et al, 'Legal Texts as Discourses'.

[79] Niemi-Kiesiläine et al, 'Legal Texts as Discourses'.

the Supreme Court distanced itself from the earlier decisions, it reverted to a more conventional and impersonal style, with little detail about the applicants, and the human stories behind the cases again disappeared from view. While this marked a reversion to the norm, the contrast with the earlier decisions exposes how facts are always deployed selectively and instrumentally.

Judges also created the overall narrative, and their writing involved more than 'pure' legal writing, ie writing concerned primarily with communicating legal ideas to a legal audience through technical language.[80] Storytelling is 'determinative as well as descriptive', creating moral argument and an expectation of resolution.[81] In the early decisions, narratives undermined 'traditional forms of legal reasoning and argumentation' by conveying experiences and perspectives that had previously been excluded from legal argument and wider public discourse.[82] In later cases, the story returned to the threat posed by immigration and the duty of government to protect the public interest.

Narrative is key, but its effects can be complicated. This is clear from the early decisions, which, unusually, placed migrants and their families at the centre of decision-making. Emphasising their positive qualities and invoking compassion for them reduced the incongruity between recognising their family life claim and respecting government sovereignty over immigration control. It therefore made a moral argument for those individuals, but arguably weakened the legal impact. Migration law is founded on binaries, and public discourse also often assumes an equally strong but unrealistic dichotomy between the law-abiding, honest and productive migrant and the opportunistic, 'illegal' and self-seeking one. Compassion is easily exhausted and is a fragile basis for long-term change.[83] The judgments could be cast as applicable only to a tiny minority, and later claims could be refused because they did not meet the same exacting factual matrix. As this book argues, creating a human right to family reunification needs more than the right cases or even the right laws.

B. Judges and Deference

Proportionality – the relationship between the public interest in a policy and the harm to the individual – is central to human rights adjudication when rights are qualified. A decision on proportionality requires an understanding of the strength of the public interest: what harm is the policy designed to prevent, how effective is it and what alternatives are there? A question that came up repeatedly in the Supreme Court decisions discussed in this book was whether the

[80] Posner, 'Judges' Writing Styles', 1421–31.

[81] Rackley, 'The Art and Craft of Writing Judgments', 46; P Brooks and P Gewirtz, *Law's Stories: Narrative and Rhetoric in the Law* (New Haven, Yale University Press, 1998) 18–19.

[82] Brooks and Gewirtz, *Law's Stories*, 16.

[83] A Sirriyeh, *The Politics of Compassion – Immigration and Asylum Policy* (Bristol, Policy Press, 2018) 8.

Court should accept the government's own view on these points or reach its own conclusions and, if so, on what basis? If it went too far, it risked being seen to exceed its constitutional function (discussed in chapter two). If it was too timid, it risked under-enforcing human rights and failing to give effect to the Human Rights Act (also discussed in chapter two).

The question of judicial scrutiny of policy has been extensively analysed in the UK within the framework of 'judicial deference'. While deference concerns national constitutional arrangements, it has some relation with the margin of appreciation and the problems of the Strasbourg Court in addressing the public interest, discussed in chapter three. Deference is a controversial subject; even the term has been contested for implying a relationship of 'servility or 'gracious concession', although no viable alternative has been proposed.[84] The academic literature on deference is vast and it is not possible to do it justice here, but this section outlines the main issues and explains how they impinge on the analysis in later chapters.

Almost all judges accept that deference is sometimes appropriate; some matters cannot be determined by judges, or not by judges alone. At the same time, policy is rarely excluded from any judicial scrutiny ('spatial deference').[85] Between those poles, there is a wide range of possible approaches:

- non-doctrinal, ie deference is determined on a case by case basis. This has the advantage of flexibility, but can lead to inconsistency and unpredictability;
- formalist, where deference is based on distinctions between concepts, such as law and politics. A problem is that few matters are precisely demarcated and there is the risk of under- or over-scrutiny by the judiciary; or
- institutional, where judges assign weight as appropriate to the views of other decision-makers. The extent of deference is related to the subject matter, but there are fewer absolutes.[86]

An institutional approach is the most context sensitive. It sees deference as depending on capability and function, in contrast to a formalist approach, but is guided by principles rather than functioning ad hoc, as in the non-doctrinal approach. However, an institutional approach cannot entirely remove the uncertainty inherent in rights adjudication, as the justifications upon which it draws (such as competence, expertise or legitimacy) may be variable or contested.

Critics of deference argue that it adds an unnecessary layer to the normal judicial task of determining rights and obligations, and gives too much authority a

[84] *R (Prolife Alliance) v BBC* [2004] 1 AC 185, 240; see the discussion in L Steyn, 'Deference: A Tangled Story' [2005] *PL* 346.

[85] M Hunt, 'Sovereignty's Blight: Why Contemporary Public Law Needs the Concept of "Due Deference"' in N Bamforth and P Leyland (eds), *Public Law in a Multi-Layered Constitution* (Oxford, Hart Publishing, 2003) 339; TRS Allan, 'Human Rights and Judicial Review: A Critique of "Due Deference' [2006] *CLJ* 671; On spatial deference, see Hunt, 'Sovereignty's Blight', 347.

[86] JA King, 'Institutional Approaches to Judicial Restraint (2008) 28 *OJLS* 409.

priori to other branches of government. What is owed to them is already accommodated in the usual process of judicial determination.[87] Human rights exist to protect individuals from an over-powerful state, and interference with them, when this is permitted by qualified rights, requires substantive and adequate justification by the state. There is 'a legitimate sphere of legislative and executive autonomy', but whether legal rights have been infringed is a question for judges to decide on all the facts and circumstances.[88] There are also matters, notably the impact of policy on unpopular minorities, which courts are better placed than government to assess, particularly if assisted by good-quality evidence.[89]

The anti-deference argument, while it can be criticised for allowing unstructured and unpredictable decision-making, recognises that deference can easily shade into reluctance to give legal rights full effect. It places courts at the centre of human rights decision-making and promotes an assessment that focuses primarily on the right and its content.[90] It is also close to the position adopted by the House of Lords in the first Article 8 family reunification case discussed in chapter four, *Huang*, although its approach could also be described as non-doctrinal. This was a likely reaction to what had come before. In her critique of Allan's anti-deference position, Kavanagh observed that

> the true target of Allan's critique is not the idea of deference per se, but rather 'an illegitimate species of deference by abstention' which requires judges to submit in an absolute and routine way to … executive dictates, simply because they have a democratic stamp of approval.[91]

This, she argued, misrepresented how courts view deference. Yet, as chapter four will show, 'deference by abstention' accurately describes the lower court Article 8 family reunification cases that were overruled in *Huang*. Later chapters will show how the Court subsequently changed its view of deference, turning to an approach that hovers between institutional and formalist deference.

C. Judges and the Public Interest

In Article 8 family reunification claims, the proportionality assessment aims to find a 'fair balance' between the public interest and interference with family life.

[87] Allan, 'Human Rights and Judicial Review'.

[88] ibid 673.

[89] See, eg B Goderis and M Versteeg, 'Human Rights Violations after 9/11 and the Role of Constitutional Constraints' (2012) 41 *Journal of Legal Studies* 131, which showed fewer fundamental rights violations in countries with independent judicial review (counter-majoritarian checks) compared to those which relied on the presence of veto players in the legislative branch (majoritarian checks).

[90] For a discussion, see A Young, 'Will You, Won't You, Will You Join the Deference Dance?' (2014) 34 *OJLS* 392.

[91] A Kavanagh, 'Defending Deference in Public Law and Constitutional Theory' (2010) 126 *LQR* 222.

In *Huang*, the first Supreme Court decision discussed in this book (see chapter four), the House of Lords found that proportionality was a legal question on which courts and tribunals should reach their own conclusion. They were therefore not confined to the more limited role of reviewing the government's decision. *Huang* therefore opened the way to the judgments discussed in chapters five and six.

However, the proportionality assessment is not a single decision but a series of enquiries, including as to the strength of the public interest in immigration control, where courts had previously been previously criticised for excessive deference.[92] As family reunification decisions are made using a fair balance assessment, not the Article 8(2) factors, there is not the clear decision-making structure that there is for negative obligation cases, but a number of questions can be posed about the government's claims for immigration control measures:

1. What public or, using the language of positive obligations, general interest does the measure, for example, a minimum income requirement, language test, integration criterion or procedural obligation, serve?
2. How effective is it? What evidence is there that, for example, a minimum income requirement will reduce welfare dependency?
3. Is it necessary in this case? For example, although the sponsor does not meet an income requirement, do other factors (such as the applicant's earning capacity) mean that admission is unlikely to pose a risk to the welfare system?
4. Do the applicant's circumstances make it disproportionate? For example, although an applicant cannot meet the minimum income threshold, is the family unable to easily live elsewhere?

These questions may be addressed in more or less searching ways, and they are cumulative as well as sequential. If the policy effectively serves an important public interest under questions 1 and 2, the benefits of its application will be outweighed less often under questions 3 and 4. As chapter two shows, the European Court of Human Rights, relying on the margin of appreciation and other doctrines, assumes that the answers to the first three questions are in the government's favour. It addresses only the fourth question, and even then applies a condition of exceptionality, reflecting the weight attached to immigration control factors. The margin of appreciation is inapplicable in domestic courts, but the doctrine of deference may inhibit them in a similar manner. Subsequent chapters discuss at what point and to what extent the Supreme Court has exercised deference on the public interest.

[92] R Edwards, 'Judicial Deference under the Human Rights Act' (2002) 65 *MLR* 859; for a discussion of inconsistency in assessing proportionality, see H Samuels, 'Feminizing Human Rights Adjudication: Feminist Method and the Proportionality Principle' (2013) 21 *Feminist Legal Studies* 39, 60.

VI. METHODOLOGY

The core of this book is a study of 11 cases decided by the Supreme Court (or House of Lords, as it was formerly known). The criterion for inclusion was that the legal issue at stake was family reunification. Most of the cases concerned Article 8 ECHR, but two did not. *Mahad* was argued on Article 8 but decided on other grounds and, chapter five argues, revealed ambivalent judicial attitudes towards Article 8.[93] *Baiai* was decided under Article 12 ECHR (the right to marry and form a family) and was included because it demonstrated a developing pattern in the jurisprudence and because it concerned the core issue of the book: the rights of citizens and settled residents to family life in the UK with non-nationals.[94]

One early case was excluded: the 2009 decision in *AS (Somalia)*.[95] The applicants had asked for and been refused family reunification, and the case concerned the admissibility at appeal of facts that arose after the initial application for entry clearance was made. The substance of the decision concerned the statutory appeal provisions rather than Article 8 and did not fit within the wider jurisprudence discussed in this book, although Lady Hale suggested that the initial application, made several years earlier, might not have been refused had the other Article 8 cases already been decided at that point.[96] It was also tempting to include the 2008 decision of *EM (Lebanon)*.[97] It concerned the position under Article 8 of a Lebanese woman living in the UK with her young son, who both faced administrative removal, the likely result of which was that the son would pass into the care of his abusive father. However, while it showed the Court's willingness to make the protection of family life effective, the legal issues were different. I also considered but decided against including *Zoumbas*.[98] It concerned the expulsion of an entire family group, none of whom were British citizens or settled residents, and therefore did not engage the core interests of this book.

Also excluded are decisions that addressed extradition or deportation and Article 8, although they are mentioned when appropriate.[99] While there are some common features, particularly around the interests of children, the legal structure is different as extradition or deportation cases usually engage a negative obligation (not to extradite or deport) and the public interest is different and stronger, as both involve criminality, and extradition also involves interstate

[93] *Mahad (previously referred to as AM) (Ethiopia) v Entry Clearance Officer* [2009] UKSC 16.

[94] *R (on the Application of Baiai and Others) V Secretary of State for the Home Department* [2008] UKHL 53.

[95] *AS (Somalia) v SSHD* [2009] UKHL 32.

[96] ibid [26]–[29].

[97] *EM (Lebanon) v SSHD* [2008] UKHL 64.

[98] *Zoumbas v Secretary of State for the Home Department* [2013] UKSC 74.

[99] eg *Norris v United States* [2010] UKSC 9; *R (on the application of HH) v Westminster City Magistrates' Court* [2012] UKSC 25; *Hesham Ali v SSHD* [2016] UKSC 60; *KO (Nigeria) v Secretary of State for the Home Department* [2018] UKSC 53.

obligations. Similarly, for reasons of space, discussion of developments in the lower courts has been confined to matters that impinge on the analysis of the Supreme Court decisions. Including this added material would inevitably have resulted in a more descriptive and less analytical study, as space would have been needed to trace and explain the differences between each strand of the jurisprudence. That does not mean the issues they address are unimportant; the deportation regime, in particular, routinely involves cruel separations.[100]

The focus on a limited number of cases all centring on the theme of human rights and family reunification has allowed this book to undertake a particular type of critical exercise; it is a study not just of what the Supreme Court decided, but also how it was decided. It treats the judgments as vehicles for legal doctrine, but also as artefacts that speak to the preoccupations and problems of the society in which they were written and the perspectives of the judges who wrote them. The work pays attention to how issues are framed, how the parties are described and the prioritisation of concerns within each judgment, as well as significant inclusions and omissions. It is this analysis that enables the study to link to the wider political and social context, as well as explaining how the Court could shift its legal position throughout the period without apparently contradicting or overruling itself. The book therefore treats judges as political in the sense discussed earlier in this chapter: they are agents who are motivated by personal and institutional values, and who act consciously and often strategically in a complex constitutional and social framework.

The majority of this analysis was achieved through close study of the decisions discussed in the book and it is largely an interpretive exercise, a 'reconstruction' of the cases informed by my legal and scholarly understanding. Möller distinguishes between 'moral' and 'zeitgeist' reconstructions, ie reconstructions that have a normative or, alternatively, an explanatory purpose, although it is probably not possible to always stay true to one or the other.[101] My instincts tend towards the former and that predisposition sparked my interest in undertaking this work. However, I have largely confined explicit normative discussion to chapter eight and was conscious throughout of the need to keep a firm handle on the 'zeitgeist'; events must be understood in their context. To reinforce or challenge sometimes impressionistic findings, I undertook a content analysis that examined the occurrence of particular words, phrases or allusions within the judgments, as well as some basic characteristics such as length. This was also a qualitative analysis insofar as it relied on my interpretation of what these features meant in their context, but its methodology, which is set out in the Appendix, was designed to ensure reliable data. Some results of the content analysis are

[100] L De Noronha, *Deporting Black Britons: Portraits of Deportation to Jamaica* (Manchester, Manchester University Press, 2020).

[101] K Möller, *The Global Model of Constitutional Rights* (Oxford, Oxford University Press, 2012) 20–22.

discussed in chapters six and seven, and it has informed the analysis throughout, helping to refine and cross-check my interpretations.

In the end, however, this is a work not only about what is but what should be: 'human rights law is not agnostic on values'.[102] I believe that we need to award more value to human relationships and what they bring us: love, care, joy and, sometimes, pain. We cannot flourish as human beings without those we are closest to, and enabling binational families to live together is an entirely suitable subject matter for human rights protection, not a secondary or exceptional concern. It is with this belief that I embarked on this project, and it has infused the work that went into it.

[102] Lavrysen, *Human Rights in a Positive State*, 30.

2

Introduction to the UK's Constitutional, Court and Immigration System

I. INTRODUCTION

THIS CHAPTER IS a brief guide to the legal environment within which the Supreme Court judgments discussed in this book were decided. It is designed primarily for readers who are not already familiar with the British legal system or with the immigration law framework. It opens by outlining the basic characteristics of the British constitution and continues with a discussion of the human rights framework in the UK, particularly the Human Rights Act, before moving to an outline of how family reunification is regulated. It ends with a discussion of the court system in the UK, focusing on how immigration decisions can be challenged by appeals or judicial review. Finally, it reflects on the key points made in the chapter that are relevant to the discussion in the rest of the book.

II. THE UK'S LEGAL AND CONSTITUTIONAL FRAMEWORK

The UK consists of four countries: England, Wales, Scotland and Northern Ireland, and three legal systems: England & Wales, Scotland and Northern Ireland. Scots law has a distinctive character that was preserved following the Acts of Union in 1707, and devolution means that legislation is not always identical across the UK. For the purposes of this book, these differences have limited relevance because both human rights and immigration laws apply to the whole of the UK. The Supreme Court is the final court of appeal for all three legal systems, but cases may come to the Supreme Court via different routes, a point discussed below in the section on the court system.

The UK's constitutional arrangements are unusual. Typically, a constitution means a set of rules that legitimise government power, are a superior source of law to the legislature and are entrenched, ie capable of being changed only through a special procedure. By those standards, the UK does not have a constitution as these characteristics are not present within the UK's legal system. Rules for government exist in the form of statutes, court decisions and conventions, but there is not a single document that sets them out systematically, and they do not have a special status. Some lawyers and scholars have therefore concluded that the UK does not have a constitution in any meaningful sense. In 2014, for example, Lord Neuberger said: 'The UK famously has no constitution'.[1] There are, however, legal constraints on what governments can do, as it has found to its cost on many occasions. The courts will enforce statutory and common law rules and ensure that the executive acts within its legal powers.

Perhaps more critical than the absence of codification is the doctrine of parliamentary sovereignty and the consequent lack of entrenchment. Parliamentary sovereignty has two major components. Firstly, the legislature is the supreme body within the constitution and there is no higher authority. Secondly, there are no legal limits on how Parliament may legislate so that, subject to what is said below, no aspect of the constitution is immune from being amended or overridden by an Act of Parliament passed by a simple majority of Members of Parliament. The meaning of the British constitution is therefore not fixed. Statutes on any matter may be introduced, amended or repealed, constitutional conventions may evolve over time, or be amended or abolished by legislation, and judicial decisions can be overruled or changed via statute. Any description of constitutional arrangements in the UK is therefore provisional.

The Labour government elected in 1997 took several steps to modernise the constitution. New legislation included the Human Rights Act 1998, discussed below in section III, statutes establishing devolved legislatures with new powers in Scotland, Wales and Northern Ireland, partial reform of the House of Lords (which functions as the second legislative chamber), and the creation of a Supreme Court to replace the Judicial Committee of the House of Lords as the final court of appeal (discussed below in section VI). These were important changes that contributed to the creation of new checks within the system of government and a major devolution of power. They did not, however, alter the fundamental characteristics of the political constitution, and the risks of minority rights being overridden and of executive dominance remain. The separation of powers between legislature and executive is quite weak, with considerable legislative power delegated to ministers. A minister is accountable to Parliament but, if they retain the support of the governing party, they may face limited sanction.

The tendency towards a majoritarian and executive-led political system has been reinforced by recent events. The Brexit referendum and its aftermath took the UK closer towards a 'populist democracy'.[2] The tortuous process of leaving

[1] Lord Neuberger, 'The Role of Judges in Human Rights Jurisprudence: A Comparison of the Australian and UK Experience', speech at the Supreme Court of Victoria (Melbourne, 8 August 2014) [8].

[2] S White, 'Brexit and the Future of the UK Constitution' (2022) 43 *International Political Science Review* 359, 364.

the EU led to unprecedented attacks on judges who required the government to exercise its constitutional powers lawfully, with one national newspaper memorably describing them in a front-page headline as 'Enemies of the People'.[3] There has been an increase in broadly drafted statutes that give the executive wide power to make or amend law, with Brexit legislation raising particular concerns.[4] The election of Boris Johnson's Conservative government in 2019 led to intensified hostility to checks on government, with plans to reform the Human Rights Act and to introduce legislation that reduces the scope for judicial review and restricts public protest.[5]

It is too early to say whether we are seeing a long-term shift towards a more centralised, authoritarian and populist politics or whether the pendulum will swing back. In either event, the attachment to parliamentary sovereignty is deep rooted and likely to endure. Within this political constitution, legal constraints come principally from common law principles developed by the courts. Judges see their function as to give effect to parliamentary intention and it is doubtful that judges would refuse to enforce an explicitly worded but oppressive statute.[6] Some constraints, however, inhibit unlawful executive action and demand more of the legislature in certain situations. These include the concept of the rule of law, common law rights and interpretive principles.

Of these, the most fundamental is the rule of law, although it is not a concept with a single accepted meaning. At its most basic, it requires only that governments act lawfully, a minimal but still critical standard. While it can also refer to standards for making and implementing law, or norms of substantive justice, its function within the UK has primarily been to ensure compliance with the law.[7] The rule of law is protected through supervision by the courts in the form of judicial review of acts by public authorities. As immigration appeal rights have contracted, judicial review has become a more important remedy for those subject to immigration control, so its limitations must be understood. Judicial review happens when a court is asked to consider whether a public body,

[3] R Breeze, '"Enemies of the People": Populist Performances in the Daily Mail Reporting of the Article 50 Case' (2018) 25(October) *Discourse, Context & Media* 60.

[4] N Barber and A Young, 'The Rise of Prospective Henry VIII Clauses and Their Implications for Sovereignty' [2016] *PL* 113; A Kouroutakis, 'The Henry VIII Powers in the Brexit Process: Justification Subject to Political and Legal Safeguards' (2021) 9 *The Theory and Practice of Legislation* 97.

[5] Ministry of Justice, *Human Rights Act Reform: A Modern Bill Of Rights – A Consultation to Reform the Human Rights Act 1998* (CP 588, December 2021); Ministry of Justice, *Judicial Review Reform The Government Response to the Independent Review of Administrative Law* (CPP 408, March 2021); Ministry of Justice, *Judicial Review Reform Consultation: The Government Response* (CP 477, July 2021); Police, Crime, Sentencing and Courts Act 2022; Bill of Rights Bill, HC Bill (2022–23) [117].

[6] This possibility has occasionally been canvassed judicially; see, eg *Jackson v HM Attorney General* [2005] UKHL 56 [102] (Lord Steyn), [107] (Lord Hope), [159] (Lady Hale). For a discussion, see T Mullen, 'Reflections on Jackson v Attorney General: Questioning sovereignty' (2007) 27 *Legal Studies* 1.

[7] Useful introductions to the rule of law in the British legal system include T Bingham, 'The Rule of Law' (2007) 66 *CLJ* 67; House of Lords Select Committee on the Constitution, *Relations between the Executive, the Judiciary and Parliament* (HL 2006–7, 151), Appendix 5.

including the immigration authorities, has acted unlawfully. This may mean that it has acted outside its powers, has engaged in procedural impropriety, has made an error of law or has acted improperly by, for example, failing to consider all relevant matters. These are questions of process that do not consider the substance of the decision but how it was made.

A decision may also be unlawful because it is 'irrational' in the sense that it is so unreasonable that it could not have been reached by any reasonable person. The threshold for intervention on these grounds is high and the intensity of scrutiny is variable. Where matters concern political or economic judgment, scrutiny is less intensive. Where fundamental rights are engaged, courts engage in 'anxious scrutiny', a more demanding standard but one that is still concerned with reviewing government action rather than the inherent merits of the decision. It is less exigent than proportionality, the standard for assessing qualified human rights. The question of whether courts should apply anxious scrutiny to the government's view of proportionality in human rights cases or reach their own decision was central to the decision in *Huang*, discussed in chapter four.

The courts have also developed a 'fledgling' conception of common law rights protection.[8] The concept of rights does not fit easily into the common law tradition, where individuals are free to act unless constrained by law, and the emphasis has been on enhanced procedural rather than substantive rights; hence the anxious scrutiny standard of review where fundamental rights are in issue, and explicit wording is needed if a statute is to interfere with such rights. Judges have acted to protect the integrity of the legal process, ensuring, for example, access to the courts, the finality of court judgments and the inadmissibility of evidence obtained by torture.[9] Interpretive principles also inhibit casual constitutional change, as a 'constitutional statute' may only be repealed or amended by explicit words. Defining a 'constitutional statute' is not straightforward, but paradigm examples include the Human Rights Act, devolution statutes and legislation providing for elections. Such legislation is still an ordinary statute that may be repealed in whole or part by subsequent legislation without any special process, but, unlike other statutes, it cannot be amended or repealed by implicit language.[10]

In summary, therefore, the British constitution is distinctive for being neither codified nor entrenched. Constitutional rules and fundamental rights can be overridden by the legislature, although explicit words are required. This is a consequence of the doctrine of parliamentary sovereignty.

[8] T Hickman, *Public Law after the Human Rights Act* (Oxford, Hart Publishing, 2010) 101–08. For a useful comparison between common law rights protection and rights under the Human Rights Act, see M Elliot, 'Beyond the European Convention: Human Rights and the Common Law' (2015) 65 *Current Legal Problems* 85.

[9] *R (on the application of UNISON) v Lord Chancellor* [2017] UKSC 51; *R (Evans) v Attorney-General* [2015] UKSC 21; *A and others v. Secretary of State for the Home Department* [2005] UKHL 71; see also Lady Hale, 'UK Constitutionalism on the March?', keynote address to the Constitutional and Administrative Law Bar Association Conference, 12 July 2014.

[10] For a discussion, see F Ahmed and A Perry, 'Constitutional Statutes' (2016) 37 *OJLS* 461.

III. THE HUMAN RIGHTS ACT 1998

It was in this context that the Human Rights Act was enacted in 1998 and implemented in 2000. As primary legislation, it has the highest force of law under the UK's constitution, but, as just discussed, it can be amended or repealed by express language in a later Act of Parliament (as the government plans to do at the time of writing).[11] Its purpose is to give 'further effect to rights and freedoms guaranteed under the European Convention on Human Rights'.[12] Section 1 identifies the 'Convention Rights' covered by the Act, and includes Article 8, the subject of this book. Although Convention Rights are not entrenched constitutional rights, the provisions of the Act mean that they have played a significant role in developing the UK's public law.

Section 2 of the Act obliges courts and tribunals to take European Court of Human Rights (Strasbourg Court or Strasbourg) jurisprudence 'into account'. To 'take into account' is not the same as to 'follow' and the domestic courts have some freedom of action, although how much has been the subject of debate. It is a plausible interpretation of the Human Rights Act to say that it permits courts to move beyond the Strasbourg cases. Lord Bingham said in 2004 that the courts should 'keep pace with the Strasbourg jurisprudence as it evolves over time: no more but certainly no less'.[13] This was taken as saying that domestic courts could not go 'beyond' the Strasbourg cases, but what this means is a complex question. Going directly against the Strasbourg jurisprudence might be unwise, although it is not expressly prohibited. However, the Strasbourg cases are guides not precedents in the common law tradition. Sometimes, there is no clear principle to apply, either because the jurisprudence is not clear or it is absent. The Human Rights Act requires domestic courts to adjudicate on human rights claims so they cannot refrain from addressing questions only because there is no authority from Strasbourg. In such cases, courts must take the Strasbourg jurisprudence a step further, drawing on principles established in cognate decisions. Courts may also go further and depart from the Strasbourg jurisprudence when it is believed that the Strasbourg Court has not fully appreciated the UK position or the jurisprudence is out of date.[14]

[11] Ministry of Justice, *Human Rights Act Reform: A Modern Bill Of Rights – A consultation to reform the Human Rights Act 1998* (CP 588, December 2021); Queen's Speech 2022, www.gov.uk/government/speeches/queens-speech-2022; Bill of Rights Bill.

[12] Human Rights Act 1998, Preamble.

[13] *R (Ullah) v Special Adjudicator* [2004] UKHL 26 [20].

[14] The literature discussing these points includes R Masterman, 'Aspiration or Foundation? The Status of the Strasbourg Jurisprudence and the "Convention Rights" in Domestic Law' in H Fenwick, G Philipson and R Masterman (eds), *Judicial Reasoning under Human Rights* (Cambridge, Cambridge University Press, 2017) 57; F Klug and H Wildbore, 'Follow or Lead? The Human Rights Act and the European Court of Human Rights (2010) 6 *European Human Rights Law Review* 621; T Bingham, 'The Human Rights Act' (2010) 6 *European Human Rights Law Review* 568; E Bjorge, 'National Supreme Courts and the Development of ECHR Rights' (2011) 91 *International Journal of Constitutional Law* 5; C Knight and T Cross, 'Public Law in the Supreme Court 2011–2012'

It may also be appropriate when that Court has applied a wide margin of appreciation.[15] Human rights implementation is a shared responsibility between the Strasbourg and national courts.[16] The margin of appreciation recognises that some issues are best determined at a national level, particularly if the issue is balancing the interests at stake, where national courts have a particular understanding. While a Council of Europe Member State cannot drop below the 'floor' of protection provided by Strasbourg, enhanced 'domestic' protection by the courts may be permitted under national constitutional arrangements. It is legitimate to see section 2 as permitting a court to find that Article 8 in the domestic context requires something different than at Strasbourg.[17] As will be seen, the question of whether the UK Supreme Court has gone further than Strasbourg became a live political question, but, to the extent that the Court did surpass the Strasbourg jurisprudence, it acted within its legislative mandate.

Section 3 creates an interpretative obligation: 'So far as it is possible to do so, primary legislation and subordinate legislation must be read and given effect in a way which is compatible with the Convention rights.' This permits the reinterpretation of all Acts of Parliament, and of subordinate legislation made under powers granted by Acts of Parliament irrespective of the original intention. In the words of Lord Neuberger, this gives courts 'something of a blank cheque', leading to 'a subtle but significant adjustment to the balance of power between the legislature and the judiciary'.[18] The interpretative obligation, however, does not extend to the Immigration Rules, which determine the entry of family members to the UK, as they are not legislation but, as discussed below, 'rules of practice'.

Where a Convention Rights-compliant interpretation of primary legislation (or of subordinate legislation where primary legislation dictates the outcome) is not possible, the Court must make a declaration of incompatibility under section 4. The incompatible legislation remains in place, but can be amended by a government minister through an expedited procedure under section 10 of the Act. A declaration of incompatibility carries moral and political weight and draws attention to the need to remedy the human rights violation, but it cannot do more. The Court has used its powers to declare primary legislation incompatible sparingly.[19] This is not only due to judicial reticence; many human rights

(2012) 17 *Judicial Review* 330; H Fenwick, 'The Human Rights Act or a British Bill of Rights: Creating a Down-Grading Recalibration of Rights against the Counter-Terror Backdrop?' [2012] *PL* 468; L Graham, 'Going Beyond, and Going Against, the Strasbourg Court' (UK Constitutional Law Association, 11 January 2022).

[15] The Rt Hon Lord Reed, President of the Supreme Court of the United Kingdom, 'Response to a Call for Evidence produced by the Independent Human Rights Act Review', para 9; Lord Neuberger, 'The Role of Judges in Human Rights Jurisprudence', para 40; Graham, 'Going Beyond, and Going Against, the Strasbourg Court'.

[16] Bjorge, 'National Supreme Courts and the Development of ECHR Rights'.

[17] Masterman, 'Aspiration or Foundation?'.

[18] Lord Neuberger, 'The Role of Judges in Human Rights Jurisprudence', [14].

[19] B Dickson, *Human Rights and the United Kingdom Supreme Court* (Oxford, Oxford University Press, 2013) 72–78; Equality and Human Rights Commission, 'Independent Human Rights Act

claims, including those discussed in this book, have involved executive policies, including those contained in the Immigration Rules, and these are not covered by the section 4 provisions.

Instead, policies, as well as most subordinate legislation and individual decision-making, are examined under section 6 of the Act, which requires public authorities to act compatibly with Convention Rights. Public authorities include courts and tribunals, as well as 'any person certain of whose functions are functions of a public nature' (but not Parliament, which can still therefore legislate in ways that do not comply with Convention Rights).[20] Section 6 brings the Human Rights Act into the heart of immigration control. Government ministers, policymakers and immigration officials are all bound by section 6 in respect of their policies and their individual decisions. Appeals and judicial reviews are adjudicated by specialist tribunals and courts, supervised by the higher courts, all of whom must also act compatibly with Convention Rights under section 6.

After implementation of the Human Rights Act, those representing migrants and their families began to use Article 8 arguments in appeals and judicial reviews of immigration decisions. These arguments led to prolonged judicial proceedings that eventually made their way to the top of the court system and the cases discussed in this book. However, in these claims, the focus was often the individual decision, although there were some judicial reviews of the Immigration Rules themselves. The question of when the Immigration Rules would be unlawful under section 6 became a live issue discussed in the decisions analysed in this book.

Implementation of the Human Rights Act was a pivotal moment for the UK's constitution. As the discussion earlier showed, the concept of substantive rights, as opposed to procedural guarantees, was not well embedded in the UK's constitutional and legal system.[21] The Act changed the constitutional dynamic by introducing a new conception of rights, by giving them a democratic imprimatur through legislation and by giving courts a critical role in determining their content. Yet it purposefully did not undermine the principle of parliamentary supremacy and the UK remains a country with a largely political constitution. Those promoting the Act hoped that the legislature would be an active partner with the courts in the promotion of human rights.[22] Many of the mechanisms for rights protection introduced by or associated with the Act, such as ministerial statements of compatibility under section 19 or the Joint Committee for Human Rights, involve the legislature. Parliament can still legislate in contravention of Convention Rights if it so chooses, but must do so consciously. The Act

Review Call for Evidence (March 2021): Response of the Equality and Human Rights Commission' (3 March 2021) 23.

[20] Although, if they do so knowingly, they must declare their intention; see Human Rights Act 1998, s 19.

[21] Hickman, *Public Law after the Human Rights Act*, 101–08.

[22] S Chakrabarti, 'Rights and Rhetoric: The Politics of Asylum and Human Rights Culture in the United Kingdom' (2005) 32 *Journal of Law and Society* 131.

therefore represented only a modest shift from a political to a legal constitution and, it was said, struck an 'elegant balance between respect for Parliament's legislative supremacy and the legal security of the Convention rights'.[23]

In so doing, however, it left unresolved the underlying tension between human rights and majoritarian democracy. Human rights must sometimes prevent the majority from overbearing the minority, and the principle of parliamentary sovereignty does not provide a final fail-safe, whatever its other virtues. The tension may be resolved by treating human rights as acting in tension with democracy (consistent with a majoritarian conception of democracy) or as constitutive of it (consistent with deliberative models).[24] The Human Rights Act does not point definitively in either direction: it is 'structured so as to neither wholly accept nor wholly reject faith in Parliament nor fear of what it might do'.[25] Its ambiguity derives from the political compromise upon which it is based whereby rights are interpreted judicially but their application ultimately depends on political will.[26] It is unsurprising that Parliament did not resolve that tension through the Act. It is difficult to imagine the legislature acting to change the constitutional settlement by stripping itself of authority in favour of the judiciary and there was no popular support for such a step. The White Paper that preceded the Bill emphasised the importance of upholding parliamentary sovereignty.[27] Lord Irvine, the Lord Chancellor who sponsored the Bill in Parliament, saw the Act as representing a new balance, but one in which parliamentary supremacy would not be dislodged.[28]

In summary, an unambiguous statutory provision that gives rise to a human rights violation must be resolved by Parliament, but instances of outright incompatibility are relatively uncommon. Usually, other responses are possible, and the judiciary has gained substantial new powers in that regard. If legislation can be reinterpreted to meet human rights standards, then that route must be taken. Secondary legislation, policies and executive practice, including immigration decisions, can be found to be incompatible and thus unlawful under section 6 of the Act. Judges also determine the meaning of human rights, subject to section 2 of the Act. Human rights norms are expansive and open textured; they cannot

[23] *International Transport Roth GmbH v Secretary of State for the Home Department* [2002] EWCA Civ 158, [2003] QB 728 [71] (Lord Justice Laws).

[24] E Anderson, 'Democracy: Instrumental vs. Non instrumental Value' in T Christiano and J Christman (eds), *Contemporary Debates in Political Philosophy* (Oxford, Blackwell, 2009) 213–27; see also M Gordon, *Parliamentary Sovereignty in the UK Constitution: Process, Politics and Democracy* (Oxford, Hart Publishing, 2015) 1–10.

[25] D Dixon, *Democracy and the Human Rights Act: Republican Analysis of Citizen Power* (Abingdon, Routledge, 2017) 4.

[26] J Hiebert, 'The Human Rights Act: Ambiguity about Parliamentary Sovereignty' [2013] *German Law Journal* 2253.

[27] Home Office, *Rights Brought Home: The Human Rights Bill* (Cm 3782, 1997); J Wright, 'Interpreting Section 2 of the Human Rights Act 1998: Towards an Indigenous Jurisprudence of Human Rights' [2009] *PL* 595, 597–98; Labour Party Manifesto (1997), www.labour-party.org.uk/manifestos/1997/.

[28] Dixon, *Democracy and the Human Rights Act*, 18–19.

be parsed for legislative intent or a literal meaning. The Act has thus created a new dynamic in which the judiciary plays a critical role in determining what human rights require and how they should be applied.

This has taken the judiciary into new areas of activity, requiring them to adjudicate on matters that touch more closely on policy than before; they have been 'pitchforked into ruling on the most contentious issues of the day – asylum seekers' rights, balancing press freedom and privacy, prisoners' rights, the rights of soldiers on active service, prisoners' votes, the right to be assisted to die'.[29] This was a difficult step for judges socialised into the British system of parliamentary sovereignty and common law freedoms. This book will show that deciding human rights questions does not mean deciding policy but deciding whether policy is human rights compatible. The difference, however, may mean little to many critics. The Act was criticised from inception for giving too much authority to an unelected judiciary and it became associated in public and media discourse with assisting 'foreign criminals' and other unworthy subjects.[30] Its 'elegant balance' opened a new era in the constitutional history of the UK, but it did not resolve the tension between the foundational principle of parliamentary sovereignty and the function of human rights in protecting individuals and minorities. Instead, it turned the spotlight onto the judiciary in ways that many have found uncomfortable, and which are discussed in later chapters.

IV. REGULATING FAMILY REUNIFICATION IN THE UK

Family reunification has been the subject of extensive and intrusive regulation since it emerged as a controversial issue in the 1960s, when immigration controls were first imposed on some Commonwealth subjects.[31] It was severely restricted from the early 1970s until 1997 and most affected were Commonwealth migrants, particularly from South Asia, and their British born children. There was some liberalisation after 1997 under the Labour government, but this was reversed under the Conservative/Liberal Democrat coalition government, which came to power in 2010 and was committed to reducing 'net migration' to the 'tens of thousands'. In 2012, it amended the Immigration Rules for family members, removing almost all rights to sponsor elderly and dependent relatives, and imposing tough financial and other conditions for the sponsors of spouses and partners. Both changes have caused great anguish to affected families.

The sponsorship of elderly parents and other adult dependent relatives was already difficult, and it now became almost impossible, with the reformed regime

[29] Lord Neuberger, 'The Role of Judges in Human Rights Jurisprudence', [5].

[30] KD Ewing, 'The Human Rights Act and parliamentary democracy' (1999) 62 *MLR* 79; R Hamlin, '"Foreign Criminals," the Human Rights Act, and the New Constitutional Politics of the United Kingdom' (2016) 4 *Journal of Law and Courts* 437.

[31] On the regulation of family migration in general and spousal migration before 2010, see H Wray, *Regulating Marriage Migration into the UK: A Stranger in the Home* (Farnham, Routledge, 2011).

described by one MP as a 'ban masquerading as a rule'.[32] The changes have predominantly affected sponsors who are migrants to the UK and have subsequently settled or naturalised. While only a very few claims can now succeed, those who come from poor countries are doubly disadvantaged as the Rules now require that paid-for care must be unaffordable in the country of origin, a condition that is easier to meet in respect of, for example, Canada than Bangladesh. The introduction of these criteria was justified almost entirely in economic terms, with a focus on the likely burden of the elderly and vulnerable on health and other services. This ignored the contribution of these family members to the quality of family life, and the impact upon citizens and residents who could not care for their loved ones as other families might, whatever the ties and obligations. The result has been an impoverished family life, guilt, distress and immense practical problems, as care must be organised at long distance.[33]

The new conditions for spouses and partners, introduced in 2012, included a minimum income requirement (MIR) for the sponsor of at least £18,600 per year, available without the support of the incoming spouse, parents or other benefactors. Shortfalls in income could be made up only through substantial amounts of capital. The MIR is discussed in more depth in chapter seven; it is sufficient to note here that, on implementation, it exceeded the earnings of a significant proportion of the adult population and its effects on families were devastating. A report by the Children's Commissioner for England showed serious social, psychological and other harms to children and parents due to the prolonged separation, the stress of trying to achieve the minimum income for the requisite period, leading to excessive working hours and constant anxiety about losing work, and the uncertainty of knowing when the situation will be resolved.[34] The impact has been sharply differentiated, with women, the young, some ethnic groups and those living outside London and the South East more severely affected. While the rule is therefore discriminatory, its target is arguably more diffuse than the earlier controls; analysis has highlighted its impact amongst the majority as well as the minority ethnic population.[35] It is arguable that family reunification has become a more mainstream concern, a process that is likely to be intensified now that Brexit has turned EU citizens into migrants.

Family reunification through the admission of minor children (under 18) to join parents living here has been less controversial than other aspects of the family migration system. Applications when both parents are present in the UK are relatively straightforward, although accommodation and basic maintenance requirements must be met. However, where one parent is elsewhere, children

[32] HC Deb 19 Jun 2013, vol 564, col 261WH.

[33] Joint Council for the Welfare of Immigrants, 'Harsh, Unjust, Unnecessary: Report on the Impact of the Adult Dependent Relative Rules on Families & Children' (July 2014).

[34] H Wray, S Grant, E Kofman and C Peel, 'Family Friendly? The Impact on Children of the Family Migration Rules: A Review of the Financial Requirements' (Children's Commissioner for England, 2015) 37–58.

[35] ibid 37–58.

are admitted only if the UK parent has had sole responsibility for the child's upbringing, or there are serious and compelling family or other considerations which make exclusion undesirable. Both are difficult conditions to establish, the latter particularly so. However, it can also, at least in principle, be used to allow children to join a relative who is not a parent, although such applications rarely succeed.[36] It is also possible for a parent to apply to join a child in the UK if they are not in a relationship with the other parent.

V. THE IMMIGRATION CONTROL FRAMEWORK IN THE UK

The power to control the admission and stay of non-national family members is governed by the Immigration Act 1971.[37] The Act is now more than 50 years old and has been amended and supplemented by a substantial number of later statutes. Section 3(1) requires those without a 'right of abode', as defined in section 2 of the Act, to have leave to enter the UK. For reasons connected to the UK's colonial history, the 'right of abode' applies to British citizens but not to other types of UK citizenship (mainly British Overseas Citizens and British Overseas Territories Citizens). A few Commonwealth citizens also have the right of abode, but these exceptions are now rare; for most practical purposes, non-nationals need leave to enter. The Act also allows conditions to be placed on admission, and provides powers of investigation, detention and enforcement against those who do not have leave.

The detailed framework for implementation is the Immigration Rules, a voluminous and confusing set of rules that often change several times a year. Section 1(4) of the Immigration Act requires that the Rules and amendments to them are laid before Parliament and take effect unless disapproved by Parliament, a very rare event. This limited scrutiny means that they have only a weak democratic mandate, an issue that arose in some decisions discussed in this book. The precise legal status of the Immigration Rules was previously much contested, but it is now clear that they are rules of practice, not subordinate or secondary legislation.[38] The consequence is that they are not interpreted as legislation but 'according to the natural and ordinary meaning of the words used'.[39]

The Immigration Rules are binding on the government, and it is unlawful for it to impose conditions that are not contained in the Rules.[40] However, the government may act more generously than the Rules require through granting leave to enter or remain in the UK outside the Immigration Rules (Leave outside the Rules or LOTR). Where the government has a policy for granting LOTR

[36] For examples of unsuccessful applications, see *PO (Democratic Republic of Congo) v ECO* [2013] EWCA Civ 1571; *Mundeba* (s 55 and [297(i)(f)]) [2013] UKUT 88 (IAC).

[37] *R (on the application of Munir) v SSHD* [2012] UKSC 32; *R (on the application of Alvi) v SSHD* [2012] UKSC 33.

[38] *Hesham Ali v SSHD* [2016] UKSC 60 [17] (Lord Reed).

[39] *Mahad v SSHD* [2009] UKSC 16 [10] (Lord Brown).

[40] *Alvi* (n 37) [87].

in specific circumstances, it must be consistently followed.[41] LOTR provides an outlet for compelling cases that do not fit within the Rules and has often been used when a refusal would breach the government's obligations under the Human Rights Act. The possibility of LOTR has been an important consideration when the Supreme Court has had to decide if the Rules are compatible with Convention Rights, a question that arises repeatedly in this book. LOTR is not an entirely satisfactory solution however, as it is a long route to a permanent status and can leave applicants in a prolonged limbo. The government is also reluctant to see widespread grants of LOTR as this undermines the consistency and predictability of their policy.

While overall responsibility for immigration policy lies with the Home Office, the immigration service is administered by a discrete body. The identity of this body and its precise relationship with the Home Office have varied over time, but the responsible body at the time of writing is UK Visas and Immigration, which sits inside the Home Office. The Home Office itself has been widely criticised for its poor performance on immigration, having overseen the Windrush and numerous other less well-publicised scandals.[42]

A non-national who wants to come to the UK to live as a family member must obtain both a visa (also called entry clearance) and leave to enter. These are usually issued simultaneously at a visa post. A family member present in the UK can apply in-country for leave to remain as a family member only in limited circumstances, a question that arose in *Chikwamba*, discussed in chapter five. Spouse and partner visas are granted for two and half years initially and must then be renewed for the same period, with indefinite leave to remain (sometimes called settlement) now granted only after five years (compared to two years before 2012). Other family members (mainly children, as adult dependent relatives now enter only rarely) joining citizens or settled residents are given indefinite leave to enter as soon as the application succeeds. Grants of leave based on human rights result in indefinite leave only after 10 years and meanwhile are usually subject to restrictions on access to public funds, including most welfare support.

The period before spouses and partners are eligible for indefinite leave to remain is commonly called the 'probationary period' and can be a stressful time. The migrant spouse or partner can work and receive healthcare during this period (having paid a 'health surcharge' on application), but they are not eligible for public funds, and leave is dependent on continuing compliance with conditions as to income, accommodation etc. Applications are complex and expensive. The costs of even a straightforward spouse application are close to £10,000 from first application to settlement.[43] Those on a 10-year route face even more prolonged insecurity and expense.

[41] *Mandalia v SSHD* [2015] UKSC 59 [29].

[42] See, eg Home Affairs Committee, *The Windrush Generation* (HC 2017–19, 990); A Qureshi, M Morris and L Mort, 'Beyond the Hostile Environment' (London, Institute for Public Policy Research, 2021).

[43] K Charsley, E Agusita, H Wray, R Mohabir, C Coombs and P Ballmi, 'Kept Apart: Couples and Families Separated by the UK Immigration System' (Bristol, University of Bristol, 2020), 12.

VI. APPEALS AND THE COURT SYSTEM

Grounds for appeal against refusal of leave to enter or remain are now confined to human rights or asylum claims, meaning, in the family context, a claim based on Article 8 of the European Convention on Human Rights (ECHR).[44] Until 2014, appeals could be brought on wider grounds, including that a decision was not in accordance with the Immigration Rules or that discretion should have been exercised differently.[45] Since then, if there are errors in the decision-making process, there are opportunities for administrative review or reconsideration by the immigration service. Otherwise, an unsuccessful applicant can bring a judicial review on the basis that the decision shows illegality, irrationality or procedural impropriety. A substantial proportion of human rights appeals and judicial reviews succeed.[46]

Bringing an appeal or judicial review is a stressful, prolonged and expensive process. Legal aid for most immigration matters was withdrawn in 2012 and parties must either fund themselves, find a voluntary service to assist them (rare in an age of austerity) or hope to be funded by legal aid on an 'exceptional' basis. Immigration lawyers are unevenly distributed across the UK and finding a good, affordable adviser can be difficult.[47] Civil legal proceedings in the UK are adversarial in character, meaning that the preparatory work of gathering evidence, undertaking background research and so on is carried out by the parties and their lawyers, making the quality of legal support particularly important; legal representation makes a significant difference to the chances of success.[48] Recourse against defective immigration decisions is thus available only to those with sufficient resources and resilience.

Immigration appeals are heard by a specialised tribunal. Initial appeals are heard in the Immigration and Asylum Chamber of the First Tier Tribunal. An appeal based on an error of law is possible, with permission, from the First Tier Tribunal to the Asylum and Immigration Chamber of the Upper Tribunal. The two-tier Tribunal has been part of the UK Tribunal Service since 2010, a change that reinforced its institutional independence and its status as a legal adjudicatory body. Tribunal judges are experienced legal professionals appointed by an independent commission. From the Upper Tribunal, a further appeal on a point of law may be made, with permission, to the Court of Appeal of England and Wales, the Court of Session (Inner House) in Scotland or the Court of Appeal in Northern Ireland. Occasionally, a further appeal lies to the Supreme Court. Judicial reviews are usually heard in the High Court in England and Wales or

[44] Nationality Immigration and Asylum Act 2002 (NIAA 2002), s 84 after amendment; amended on 20 October, 2014.

[45] NIAA 2002, s 84 before amendment.

[46] On judicial review, see Ministry of Justice, *Judicial Review Reform Consultation: The Government Response* (CP 447, July 2021) para 35; Free Movement, 'Half of All Immigration Appeals Now Succeed' (*freemovement*, 13 June 2019).

[47] J Wilding, 'Droughts and Deserts. A Report on the Immigration Legal Aid Market' (Brighton, University of Brighton and Joseph Rowntree Charitable Trust, 2019) 39.

[48] C Bevan, 'Self-Represented Litigants: The Overlooked and Unintended Consequence of Legal Aid Reform' (2013) 35 *Journal of Social Welfare and Family Law* 54.

Northern Ireland, or the Court of Session (Outer House) in Scotland, although some are heard by the Upper Tier Tribunal. Appeals lie through the various Courts of Appeal and then the Supreme Court.

The Supreme Court is the highest appeal court in the UK and hears appeals on points of law of the greatest public importance. It was formed in 2009, taking over from the Judicial Committee of the House of Lords, which had previously performed this function and was now abolished. While the Supreme Court did not have any increased powers, the change of name and of physical and institutional context, alongside the constitutional changes of the 1990s, arguably encouraged a more constitutional approach to the law.[49] The Supreme Court hears only about 60 cases per year. That so many Article 8 migration-related cases have been heard by the Court reflects the difficulties connected to this issue.[50] With rare exceptions, hearings are in open court, and are live streamed.[51] Twelve justices are usually appointed at any one time, including a President and Vice-President, with five hearing each case unless particular circumstances apply, for example, that the Court is asked to depart from its own previous decision, or the case is of high constitutional or great public importance. A panel of seven sat in *MM (Lebanon)* and *Agyarko*, both discussed in chapter seven, indicating the significance of those decisions.[52] While there have been efforts to make the judiciary more representative in recent years, the Supreme Court is still overwhelmingly white, privately educated and male.[53] Lady Hale, appointed in 2017, was the first female Supreme Court justice and brought a distinctive perspective and presence.[54] Since then, three female justices have been appointed although, at the time of writing, only one was still on the panel (retirement is required at the age of 75, having risen in 2022 from 70).[55] There is yet to be a Supreme Court justice from a non-white ethnic community.

The common law system works through a system of judicial precedent, which means that the legal principle of a case (ratio decidendi) decided by a 'superior court of record' is binding on all courts below it in the hierarchy, and usually on other courts at the same level. The Upper Tribunal, High Court, Courts of Session, Courts of Appeal and Supreme Court are all courts of record,

[49] L Neudorf, 'The Supreme Court and the New Judicial Independence' (2012) 1 *Cambridge Journal of International and Comparative Law* 25; K Malleson, 'The Evolving Role of the Supreme Court' [2011] *PL* 754; J Murkens, 'Judicious Review: The Constitutional Practice of the UK Supreme Court' (2018) 77 *CLJ* 349.

[50] As well as the family reunification cases discussed in this book, the Supreme Court has heard a significant number of cases on article 8 and criminal deportation or extradition.

[51] Supreme Court Rules 2009 (2009 No 1603 (L 17)) para 27.

[52] www.supremecourt.uk/procedures/panel-numbers-criteria.html.

[53] See www.supremecourt.uk/about/biographies-of-the-justices.html; see also The Sutton Trust/Social Mobility Commission, 'Elitist Britain 2019: The Educational Backgrounds of Britain's Leading People', 55.

[54] See, eg R Hunter and E Rackley, 'Lady Hale: A Feminist Towering Judge' in R Abeyratne, and I Porat (eds), *Towering Judges: A Comparative Study of Constitutional Judges* (Cambridge, Cambridge University Press, 2021) 78–95.

[55] Judicial Pensions and Retirement Act 1993, s 4.

and their decisions are binding on the First Tier Tribunal, which hears most appeals. Strictly speaking, only those legal principles needed to reach a decision are binding, but other statements of law (sometimes called obiter dicta) are authoritative, particularly when they come from the higher courts. For instance, in *Huang*, the first domestic decision discussed in this book in chapter four, the legal issue was the decision-making function of the Tribunal. However, the judgment also set out the criteria for success in an Article 8 claim, and these were (or should have been; see chapters four and five) adopted, given that they came from the House of Lords.[56]

The character of these binding legal principles is not always clear-cut. Judgments can be long, with many legal points explored. In appellate courts, each judge on a panel may deliver an independent judgment, arriving at the same conclusion via a different route. Justices are also not always explicit about which of the legal arguments they use within each judgment is determinative. While there is often now more signposting than before, it can be hard to say exactly what legal point forms the ratio and there can still therefore be room for disagreement about the exact meaning of a judgment. A Supreme Court judgment can easily be interpreted in different ways. Variations in interpretation may reflect the different sense that judges have of their function, depending on where they sit in the judicial system. The Tribunal, while institutionally separate, is much closer to the immigration system than higher courts; it is, in effect, 'part of the broader process for implementing government policy'.[57] That does not mean that Tribunal judges lack independence, but it does mean that the fulfilment of policy objectives is likely to weigh more heavily. At several points in this book, it will be observed that the Tribunal was sometimes slow to appreciate the significance of Supreme Court decisions that required adjustment to policy and some (not all) Tribunal judges seemed to identify closely with government concerns. Higher court judges, meanwhile, are more likely to engage in detailed textual analysis, comparing different authorities in a highly technical way, while still often seeking to avoid conflict with government.[58]

VII. CONCLUSION

This chapter has been a necessarily brief account of the UK's constitutional arrangements, human rights protection, family reunification provision, immigration control and court system. For any reader who would like to know more, there is a vast literature on all these subjects, including some that has been referenced here. The focus in this chapter has been on those elements that may

[56] *Huang v Secretary of State for the Home Department* [2007] UKHL 11.

[57] R Thomas, *Administrative Justice and Asylum* (Oxford, Hart Publishing, 2011) 281.

[58] See, eg J Campbell, 'The Role of Lawyers, Judges, Country Experts and Officials in British Asylum and Immigration Law' (2020) 16 *International Journal of Law in Context* 1.

be unfamiliar to a non-legal or non-British reader, and which are necessary to understand the analysis in later chapters. The essential points are, firstly, that the UK has a political constitution which is governed by the doctrine of parliamentary sovereignty. Acts of Parliament are the highest form of law and there are no entrenched constitutional rights. Common law rights offer mainly procedural guarantees, and interference with these, with fundamental rights and with 'constitutional statutes' requires explicit statutory words.

The Human Rights Act brought most of the ECHR into the UK's legal system in the form of 'Convention Rights', but it does not prevent statutes from being enacted that conflict with those rights, and it may be repealed or amended through ordinary legislation, a step that is in prospect at the time of writing. The introduction of human rights into a legal culture based on parliamentary sovereignty and judicial restraint was not straightforward. The Act ensures that Parliament retains the last word on legislation that might violate human rights, but, otherwise, judges were granted considerable new powers. Consequently, judges have been more politically exposed. They have powers which, under the Act, they are legally obliged to exercise, and these have taken them into areas of adjudication which they had previously avoided.

Family reunification has always been tightly regulated, with much tighter controls over the admission of spouses and dependent relatives since 2012. These are mainly implemented through administrative rules, and the application system is complex, expensive and prolonged. Appeals against decisions may now only be brought on human rights grounds, and access to legal remedies requires substantial resources and resilience.

The UK's court system is precedent based, with the legal decisions of higher courts all binding on courts beneath them or, often, in the same place on the hierarchy. Appeals against refusal of applications for family reunification are heard in a specialised tribunal. Legal and procedural errors may be challenged through judicial review heard in the High Court (or Court of Session in Scotland). In both cases, affordable and appropriate legal advice can be difficult to access. Further appeals can proceed, on the basis of legal error and with permission, through various appellate courts, and a few cases that engage points of law of the greatest public importance are heard by the Supreme Court. The Court's intensive engagement with Article 8 shows the problems involved in reconciling immigration control and the protection of family life.

3

The European Court of Human Rights: Strait is the Gate

I. INTRODUCTION

THIS CHAPTER ANALYSES the Article 8 family reunification jurisprudence of the European Court of Human Rights (ECtHR, Strasbourg Court or, in this chapter only, just the Court) and shows that the Court has developed doctrines that enable some, but not many, claims to succeed. That Article 8 protects some families is a positive development, but the jurisprudence remains state-centric, reflecting the Court's difficult position as a supervisory supranational body dependent on the support of many diverse states. The aim of this chapter is to unpick the Court's methods to show where it has advanced, and where and how it has kept the brakes on the Article 8 family reunification jurisprudence.

The next section of the chapter asks why family reunification is such a difficult issue for the Court. It reflects on the historical context and the reasons for treating family reunification as a positive obligation, first discussed in chapter one. After that, the chapter discusses each component of Article 8. It begins by analysing the Court's approach to family life under Article 8(1), observing that it usually recognises family life between spouses, and between parents and minor children, but imposes conditions that make it difficult to establish family life between other family members. The chapter then turns to Article 8(2) and looks first at how the Court has treated the public interest in immigration control, showing that the need for immigration policies, however draconian, is assumed, reflecting a wide margin of appreciation. The chapter than examines the fair balance proportionality assessment. It observes that while there is now welcome clarity as to the relevant factors, the way these are balanced in practice means that two predominate: children's interests and state sovereignty over immigration policy. The latter is, in effect, double counted as it is considered both in its own right and because it underpins the doctrine of 'precarious residence', under which claims made when there is not a stable immigration status can succeed only 'exceptionally'. The result is that success is possible only in a narrow set of circumstances, and the chapter analyses what these seem to be. The conclusion to the chapter looks at the problems of this jurisprudence for domestic courts.

II. WHY IS FAMILY REUNIFICATION AND ARTICLE 8 SO PROBLEMATIC?

There has been wide criticism of the Strasbourg Court's Article 8 family reunification jurisprudence. This has often been inconsistent in character, arguing variously that the Court has failed to protect either migrants' or states' interests, or is either insufficiently or excessively ambitious. Most academic commentators and some judges believe that the Court has veered too far towards protecting states' interests, but the opposite view has also been put forward, particularly by dissenting judges in violation decisions.[1]

This inconsistency reflects polarised perspectives on the role that the Court should play in family reunification. On one view, any engagement with migration-related questions is a bold step on an issue seen as critical to state sovereignty and not directly covered by the European Convention on Human Rights. There is no interstate consensus that would support the Court using Article 8 to enhance protection, and the Court will be particularly cautious about extending protection in its absence: 'It is not … the Court's role to engineer changes in society or to impose moral choices.'[2] Quite the contrary, the pressure from states has been explicitly for the Court to withdraw from asylum and immigration matters.[3] Overstepping the boundaries in this area could be destructive in terms of the court's legitimacy and authority. From another perspective, however, the protection of family life is a fundamental right that receives widespread support in human rights law, applies to all within the jurisdiction, including non-nationals, and engages the rights of citizens and residents in intimate areas of their lives where they would normally expect strong protection.[4] The content of human rights evolves as society changes and, although inter-state consensus

[1] The critical literature includes H Lambert, 'The European Court of Human Rights and the Right of Refugees and Other Persons in Need of Protection to Family Reunion' (1999) 11 *International Journal of Refugee Law* 427; S Lagoutte, 'Surrounding and Extending Family Life: The Notion of Family Life in the Case-Law of the European Court of Human Rights' (2003) 21 *Mennesker og Rettigheter* 292; D Thym, 'Respect for Private and Family Life under Article 8 ECHR in Immigration Cases: A Human Right to Regularize Illegal Stay?' (2008) 57 *ICLQ* 87; T Spijkerboer, 'Structural Instability: Strasbourg Case Law on Children's Family Reunion' (2009) 11 *European Journal of Migration and Law* 271; A Farahat, 'The Exclusiveness of Inclusion: On the Boundaries of Human Rights in Protecting Transnational and Second Generation Migrants' (2009) 11 *European Journal of Migration and Law* 253; M Dembour, *When Humans Become Migrants: Study of the European Court of Human Rights with an Inter-American Counterpoint* (Oxford, Oxford University Press, 2015) 19–20; A Farahat, 'Enhancing Constitutional Justice by Using External References: The European Court of Human Rights' Reasoning on the Protection against Expulsion' (2015) 28 *Leiden Journal of International Law* 303; M Klaassen, 'Between Facts and Norms: Testing Compliance with Article 8 ECHR in Immigration Cases' (2019) 37 *Netherlands Quarterly of Human Rights* 157.

[2] L Wildhaber, 'The European Court of Human Rights in Action' (2004) 21 *Ritsumeikan Law Review* 83, 86.

[3] C Bosch March, 'Backsliding on the Protection of Migrants' Rights? The Evolutive Interpretation of the Prohibition of Collective Expulsion by the European Court of Human Rights' (2021) 35 *Journal of Immigration Asylum and Nationality Law* 315.

[4] R Cholewinski, 'Family Reunification and Conditions Placed on Family Members: Dismantling a Fundamental Human Right' (2002) 4 *European Journal of Migration and Law* 271, 274.

is an important element in that evolution, it is not an absolute or mechanical concept.[5] While there is a 'family resemblance' between European states' family migration controls, not all of them have adopted the restrictive policies that have brought certain governments repeatedly before the Court.[6] It is arguable that too much authority has been ceded in this domain.

The question in issue – immigration control as an inherent feature and emblematic issue of state sovereignty pitched against the right of citizens and residents to live with family in their own home – is a microcosm of a wider debate about the Court's function. As Benhabib has said: 'From a philosophical point of view, transnational migrations bring to the fore the constitutive dilemma at the heart of liberal democracies: between sovereign self-determination claims on the one hand and adherence to universal human rights principles on the other.'[7]

This chapter shows that the Strasbourg Court has attempted to resolve this tension through doctrines that ensure that all but a small class of applications must fail. It can thereby claim to protect the family life of binational families, while not impinging in any significant way on state sovereignty. This argument must recognise that almost all applications fail anyway; only about 2 per cent of all applications result in a violation finding.[8] The point is not that Article 8 family reunification applications fail more than others but that violation findings are framed narrowly, making family reunification adjudication a search for exceptional personal circumstances rather than a critical scrutiny of state practice. To the extent that rights have been constitutionalised, that general principles have been developed to guide states, these are not expansive.[9]

Yet the fact that they have developed at all shows the Court's ability to gradually raise standards. Family reunification rights were not in contemplation when the Convention came into being. Its creators' primary concern was to protect citizens from autocratic states, and the *travaux préparatoires* did not consider the position of migrants under Article 8.[10] Unlike the American

[5] See L Wildhaber, A Hjartarson and S Donnelly, 'No Consensus on Consensus? The Practice of the European Court of Human Rights' (2013) 33 *Human Rights Law Journal* 241; K Dzehtsiarou, *European Consensus and the Legitimacy of the European Court of Human Rights* (Cambridge, Cambridge University Press, 2015) 206.

[6] See H Wray, A Agoston and J Hutton, 'A Family Resemblance? The Regulation of Marriage Migration in Europe' (2014) 16 *European Journal of Migration and Law* 209; see also variations in the scores of Council of Europe states on the MIPEX website, www.mipex.eu/family-reunion.

[7] S Benhabib, *The Rights of Others: Aliens, Residents and Citizens* (Cambridge, Cambridge University Press, 2004) 2; see also G Letsas, *A Theory of Interpretation of the European Convention on Human Rights* (Oxford, Oxford University Press, 2007).

[8] In 2020, only 5% of applications involved a judgment, with over 80% found inadmissible and the rest struck out. Of 1901 judgments, 762 (41%) found at least one violation. European Court of Human Rights, *Analysis of Statistics 2020* (January 2021); European Court of Human Rights, *Violations by Article and by State 2020*, www.echr.coe.int/Documents/Stats_violation_2020_ENG.pdf.

[9] For a discussion of constitutionalisation, see S Greer and L Wildhaber, 'Revisiting the Debate about "Constitutionalising" the European Court of Human Rights' (2012) 12 *Human Rights Law Review* 655.

[10] E Bates, 'The Birth of the European Convention on Human Rights – and the European Court of Human Rights' in J Christoffersen and M Madsen (eds), *The European Court of Human Rights*

or Universal Declarations of Human Rights, the Convention does not include rights to asylum or nationality.[11] Rights relating to nationality, free movement and expulsion appear only in later optional protocols.[12] Migrants are mentioned in the main Convention only in Article 16, which permits restrictions on aliens' political activity, a response to extension of the Convention to all 'within the jurisdiction' of a contracting state.[13]

The Court started to develop its jurisprudence on Article 8 and migration only in the 1980s, and there has been hesitancy ever since.[14] One problem has been that of recognising and valorising the interests at stake. Family reunification concerns both sponsors, who are citizens or residents, and migrants.[15] In principle, the Court considers the rights of the entire family, but it has, in practice, been difficult to make sponsors' interests central to decision-making. The state's act or omission is directed at the migrant, who usually brings the complaint, and this is reflected in the reasoning. Even when other family members join the proceedings, the migrant is almost always listed in the judgment as the first applicant.[16] While this may reflect the ordering of the parties in the application, that, in turn, reflects lawyers' perceptions of the Court's focus.

Abdulaziz holds one clue as to why sponsors have found it hard to be heard.[17] The legal question in this claim was the interference with the three female sponsors' human rights. They were subject to a near prohibition on the admission of husbands that did not apply to men sponsoring wives. All had lived many years in the UK and one was a British citizen, who was also treated differently to female citizen sponsors born or having a parent born in the UK and whose husbands could enter. The rules were thus shot through with discrimination.

between Law and Politics (Oxford, Oxford University Press, 2013) 17–42; European Commission of Human Rights, 'Preparatory Work on Article 8 of the European Convention on Human Rights', information document prepared by the Secretariat of the Commission, 9 August 1956; see also D Thym, 'Residence as Defacto Citizenship? Protection of Long Term Residence under Article 8 ECHR' in R Rubio-Marin (ed), *Human Rights and Immigration* (Oxford, Oxford University Press, 2014) 109.

[11] Convention for the Protection of Human Rights and Fundamental Freedoms (European Convention on Human Rights, as amended) (Council of Europe, signed 4 November 1850, entered into force 3 September 1953) (ECHR), Art 13 (right to leave and enter own country), Art 14 (right to seek asylum) and Art 15 (nationality rights); UN Universal Declaration of Human Rights (adopted 10 December, UNGA Res 217A (III)), Art XVIII (right of residence and freedom of movement), Art XIX (nationality rights), Art XXVII (right to seek and receive asylum); American Declaration of the Rights and Duties of Man (Inter-American Commission on Human Rights (IACHR), adopted 2 May 1948), Art XXVII (right of asylum).

[12] ECHR, protocol nos 4 and 7.

[13] Dembour, *When Humans Become Migrants*, 44–51.

[14] J Christoffersen and MR Madsen, 'Introduction: The European Court of Human Rights between Law and Politics' in Christoffersen and Madsen, *The European Court of Human Rights between Law and Politics*, 2–3. For discussion of earlier decisions, see C Draghici, *The Legitimacy of Family Rights in Strasbourg Case Law: Living Instrument or Extinguished Sovereignty* (Hart Publishing, 2017) 341–42.

[15] *Guliyev and Sheina v Russia* App no 29790/14, [2018] ECHR 330 [43].

[16] eg *Omoregie v Norway* App no 265/07 (ECtHR, 31 July 2008).

[17] *Abdulaziz Cabales and Balkandali v United Kingdom* (1985) 7 EHRR 471.

The Strasbourg Court paid considerable attention to the sponsors' immigration history, although the issue was their husbands' status.[18] It found the gender discrimination unlawful under Articles 8 and 14 (prohibition of discrimination in Convention rights) but that the UK could lawfully distinguish between naturalised and birth citizens 'to avoid the hardship which women having close ties to the UK would encounter if, on marriage, they were obliged to move abroad in order to remain with their husbands'.[19] This, it found, was 'an objective and reasonable justification'.[20]

From inception, therefore, the UK-based sponsors' claims as citizens and residents were treated as contingent. In finding no violation of Article 8 alone, the Court observed that family life had been created after settlement in the UK and states were under no general obligation to respect a couple's choice of joint residence. The applicants had not shown that there were obstacles to residing 'in their own or their husbands' home countries', or special reasons why that could not be expected of them. Further, the women had always known that their husbands were not eligible to enter or stay in the UK.[21] The impression is of applicants who were not legal or social citizens but guests. The judgment set the tone for decades to come, creating a template under which sponsors are responsible both for their dilemma and for resolving it by moving elsewhere.

Article 8 family reunification claims emerged in a very specific context. Those that culminated in *Abdulaziz* came largely from former colonial subjects subject to policies designed to keep them outside the metropole.[22] Others came from guest workers to European states.[23] Sponsors were of migrant origin and their belonging was seen as provisional. When sponsors with no migrant background started to appear, governments and the Court did not treat them differently, although discrimination between different types of citizen had been endorsed by *Abdulaziz* (and was later rejected in *Biao*).[24] In a theme that has persisted to the present day, sponsors with no migrant background are assimilated to those that have such a background, not vice versa. They are all expected to accept the consequences of their decision to form a binational family. The result is that the

[18] ibid [60].

[19] ibid [87].

[20] ibid [88]; it is doubtful that such a finding would be made today after the Grand Chamber judgment in *Biao v Denmark* discussed later in this chapter.

[21] *Abdulaziz* (n 17) [60].

[22] Dembour, *When Humans Become Migrants*, 96–109; on the connections between postcolonialism and family migration controls, see also J Turner, 'The Family Migration Visa in the History of Marriage Restrictions: Postcolonial Relations and the UK Border' (2015) 17 *British Journal of Politics & International Relations* 623,643; H Wray, *Regulating Marriage Migration into the UK: A Stranger in the Home* (first published Farnham, Ashgate, 2011, Abingdon, Routledge, 2016); SK van Walsum, GR Jones and S Legene, 'Belonging and Membership. Postcolonial Legacies of Colonial Family Law in Dutch Immigration Policies' in M Schrover and DM Molony (eds), *Gender, Migration and Categorisation. Making Distinctions between Migrants in Western Countries, 1945–2010* (Amsterdam, Amsterdam University Press, 2013) 149–73.

[23] eg *Sen v Netherlands* App no 31465/96, (2001) 36 EHRR 81, [2001] ECHR 888.

[24] *Biao v Denmark* App no 38590/10 (GC, 24 May 2016), [2016] ECHR 455, (2017) 64 EHRR 1.

interests of citizens and residents have never been at the centre of the Court's jurisprudence and the Court has continued to see family reunification as primarily a question of migration rather than of family.

This reflected the priorities of states and led, as chapter one showed, to family reunification being treated as involving a positive obligation, in that refusal of admission is the norm to which family life may require an occasional exception, although, as the discussion in this chapter will show, the Court may take a different position if the migrant family member has already held an immigration status. Treating family reunification primarily as a positive obligation is not just a formal question, but has had a major impact on how applications have been treated by the Court. This is evident to some degree in how family life is approached, discussed in the next section, and has been very significant in shaping the proportionality assessment, discussed in the following two sections.

III. ARTICLE 8(1): FAMILY LIFE

This section will demonstrate that the Court has defined 'family life' narrowly, primarily by imposing a test for interference with certain types of family life that can rarely be met by binational families. In relationships between parents and their minor children and between married couples, the Strasbourg Court often accepts there is interference in family life even if they are currently separated. In other relationships, the Court needs more to find that there is family life and more still to find that there is interference. One explanatory factor is the assumption that family reunification involves a positive obligation. In *Marckx*, some years before *Abdulaziz*, violation of a positive obligation was found to exist as soon as interference was established under Article 8(1) without considering proportionality under Article 8(2).[25] If this approach had prevailed, the only way to confine the number of successful claims would be to ensure that interference was found only in a restricted number of cases, and this may partially explain the Court's reluctance to interpret Article 8(1) family life expansively. However, since at least 1994, it has been clear that a proportionality assessment can be carried out in a positive obligation claim, and the desire to keep family life narrowly defined must have additional wellsprings.[26]

In the early years of Article 8 family reunification claims, governments wanted to limit the admission of the family members of colonial subjects and guest workers to avoid what was called 'chain migration', the idea that admitting family members would lead to new claims by these arrivals, and an unending stream of family migrants.[27] The connection between this concern

[25] *Marckx v Belgium* App no 6833/74 (13 June 1979).

[26] *Keegan v Ireland* (1994) 18 EHRR 342.

[27] For a discussion, see H Wray, 'Moulding the Migrant Family' (2009) *Legal Studies* 592; N Carver, 'Displaying Genuineness: Cultural Translation in the Drafting of Marriage Narratives for Immigration Applications and Appeals' [2014] *Families, Relationships and Societies* 271.

and the Court's narrow treatment of family was exemplified by the Court's response to the UK's discriminatory immigration policies. In the 1970s and 1980s, the UK government refused thousands of children and wives of workers from former colonies, principally South Asia, because applications were considered fraudulent as the parties were not 'related as claimed'; men were accused of sponsoring women to whom they were not married and children of whom they were not the father. The procedures involved were unreliable, widely criticised at the time and led to decades of heart-breaking separation.[28] Once DNA testing was possible, it showed that almost all the parties were 'related as claimed', and wives now had to be admitted. However, the children were, by then, adults. In a cluster of applications, the Commission accepted that the original decision had been incorrect but, as bad faith could not be shown, applications would be considered without reference to the historic injustice and were consequently refused.[29]

Refusing to admit these adult children limited the numbers arriving and ensured that they could not sponsor further entrants. It was legally possible because Article 8 prohibits interference with family life, and family life must therefore already exist. This was interpreted as meaning there was no obligation to permit a family who are currently separated to live together. This argument, however, has not been consistently deployed. In relationships between parents and their minor children and between married couples, the Strasbourg Court usually accepts that family life requires them to cohabit even if they are currently separated, that, in the recent words of the Court, there is a 'potential relationship'.[30] The Court has, however, been unwilling to assume that family life exists in other relationships. The distinction is not based on Article 8 itself, but on cultural assumptions about which types of family life require cohabitation, although, as will be seen, the problem is less the fact of a distinction and more how the distinction is drawn.

A. Married and Unmarried Couples

In *Abdulaziz*, the Strasbourg Court agreed that immigration control potentially engages Article 8 and rejected the government's submission that family life was confined to couples already living together 'with the legitimate expectation of

[28] For cases brought before the Commission, see, eg *Kamal v UK* App no 8378/78 (14 May 1980) or *Alam and Khan* App no 2991/66 (17 December 1968). For a discussion of these procedures and their consequences, see Wray, *Regulating Marriage Migration into the UK*, 105–36.

[29] *Ullah v UK* App no 17712/91 (Commission Decision 14 October 1992; *M v UK* App no 19153/91 (1 July 1992); *TA and HN v UK* App no 19577/92 (Commission Decision 8 January 1993); *Miah and Islam v UK* App no 19546/92 (31 March 1993); *KM v UK* App no 20516/92 (31 March 1993); *Afzal v UK* App no 28853/95 (9 April 1997).

[30] *Valdís Fjölnisdóttir and others v Iceland* A No 71552/17 (18 May 2021) [57].

the enjoyment of it in that country'.[31] This was a significant step; it had not previously been clear that Article 8 applied to couples separated by immigration controls.[32] *Abdulaziz* therefore established a presumption of family life for married couples and that this normally requires cohabitation (although the presumption may be displaced if the parties have voluntarily spent substantial periods apart or a marriage is believed to be one of convenience).[33]

This presumption does not extend to other forms of intimate relationship, such as unmarried heterosexual couples, engaged couples or polygamous relationships where family life must be demonstrated.[34] To treat a same-sex couple differently to an opposite-sex couple would be discrimination. Where same-sex couples cannot access marriage or other official recognition, refusing family reunification to a committed same-sex couple when it would be granted to married opposite-sex couples is discriminatory, even if unmarried opposite-sex couples are also excluded.[35] More complex sexual identities and intimate relationships have not been part of the discussion in this context.

That couples who cannot show a legal tie such as marriage must establish the existence of their relationship seems common sense, but it risks a circular argument. Immigration controls mean that these couples cannot cohabit in the state and, because they do not cohabit, they do not have a family life that requires cohabitation. However, in *Pajić*, an Article 14 and Article 8 discrimination case, the Court found interference in family life when the parties had been able to live together only sporadically, suggesting openness to a more expansive approach.[36]

B. Minor Children and Parents

Claims can arise when either the child or the parent is outside the state or when a parent faces expulsion due to lack of status. Claims sometimes succeed but, if

[31] *Abdulaziz* (n 17) [61], [62].

[32] Dembour, *When Humans Become Migrants*, 99–102.

[33] *Valmont v UK* App no 36385/97 (23 March 1999); *Schembri v Malta* A No 66297/13 (19 September 2017). On the problematic aspects of designating a marriage of convenience, see H Wray, 'The "Pure" Relationship, Sham Marriages and Immigration Control' in J Miles, R Probert and P Mody (eds), *Marriage Rites and Rights* (Oxford, Hart Publishing, 2015) 141–65. Some judges have argued that family life does not exist where the couple has a 'precarious' status despite cohabitation and even the birth of children; see *Omoregie* (n 16), Concurring Opinion of Judge Jebens; see also the discussion below on precarious family life.

[34] eg on polygamous relationships, see *EA and AA v Netherlands* (1992) 72 DR 118 [121]–[123] where the father maintained contact and thus his family life. Unmarried heterosexual relationships may also found a claim: *Johnston v Ireland* (1986) EHRR 203; *Keegan* (n 26) [44]; *Marckx* (n 25) [31]; *Alim v Russia* App no 39417/07 (27 September 2011); For affianced couples, see *Wakefield v UK* App no 15817/89 (1 October 1990).

[35] *Vallianatos v Greece* (2014) 59 EHRR12; *Pajić v Croatia* App no 68453/13 (23 February 2016); *Tadeucci and McCall v Italy* App no 51362/09 (30 June 2016); see also N Koffemann, '*Taddeucci and McCall v. Italy*: Welcome Novelty in the ECtHR's Case-Law on Equal Treatment of Same-Sex Couples' (*Strasbourg Observers*, 27 July 2016).

[36] *Pajić v Croatia* (n 35).

they fail, it may be because there is no family life, there is no interference or the interference is proportionate under Article 8(2). Judgments are not always very specific as to which, and the position of children is also considered in the discussion of proportionality in section V below. Even so, the Strasbourg Court has made some specific findings about Article 8(1) family life and children.

In both its general and immigration jurisprudence, the ECtHR assumes that family life exists between minor children and their parents from birth even if the parents stop being married or living together.[37] Where there has never been marriage or cohabitation, the Court looks for evidence that family ties exist.[38] Relevant factors include the nature of the parents' relationship, whether the child was planned, whether the father recognised the child and parental involvement in the child's upbringing.[39] Relationships between an adoptive parent and child are, in principle, protected even in the absence of cohabitation and close de facto ties, but more is needed to recognise the intra-family adoptions that are customary in some cultures.[40] Some biological parents must also do more; although he ultimately succeeded, a Nigerian father struggled to overcome both the mother's unilateral decision to exclude him from his children's lives and the explicit suspicion that he was using the relationship to remain in Germany.[41]

If family life exists, there must still be interference. Expulsion of the entire family unit is not interference if they can relocate together.[42] There may also be no interference if the family does not already live together. In a cluster of cases involving the Netherlands, the Court supported the government's position that parents who had voluntarily left their children could not expect their later admission.[43] Given the family's circumstances, the Court's conclusion in *Gül* that refusal to admit the child was not interference suggested that any prior separation between parents and child would prevent a successful future claim.[44] Similarly, in *Adnane*, the Court said that Article 8 'does not guarantee a right as such to choose the most suitable place to develop family life'.[45] However, *Sen* in 2001 found that the eldest child's entry was required as 'the most adequate means for the applicants to develop family life', given the problems of reintegrating the

[37] *Keegan* (n 26); *L v Netherlands* App no 45582/99 (1 June 2004) [36]; *Berrehab v Netherlands* (1989) 11 EHRR 322.

[38] *L v Netherlands* (n 37) [36]; *Kroon and Others v Netherlands* (1994) Series A No 297-C, [30].

[39] *Kroon and Others* (n 38) [30]; *Joseph Grant v UK* App no 10606/07 (8 January 2009); *Onur v UK* App no 27319/07 (17 February 2009).

[40] *Pini and others v Romania* (2005) 40 EHRR 13, [143]–[146]. For recognition of a well-established relationship amounting to 'family life', see *Singh v ECO New Delhi* [2004] EWCA Civ 1075, while for refusal to find the same, see *X and Y v UK* (1978) 12 D&R 32.

[41] *Anayo v Germany* (2012) 55 EHRR 5. See B De Hart, 'Superdads: Migrant Fathers' Right to Family Life before the European Court of Human Rights' (2015) 18 *Men and Masculinities* 448 for a discussion of the gendered and racialised aspects of the *Anayo* case.

[42] See *Slivenko v Latvia* (2004) 39 EHRR 24 [97].

[43] F Staiano, 'Good Mothers, Bad Mothers: Transnational Mothering in the European Court of Human Rights' Case Law' (2013) 15 *European Journal of Migration and Law* 155.

[44] *Gül v Switzerland* (1996) 22 EHRR 93 [43].

[45] *Adnane v Netherlands* App no 50568/99 (6 November 2001).

younger children in the state of origin of the parents.[46] A similar approach was taken in *Tuquabo-Tekle* in 2005. Even so, claims by children for admission have not always succeeded.[47] Single mothers, in particular, have faced difficulties, and older children have been found to no longer need the day-to-day care of their parents.[48]

If a parent facing expulsion lives apart from their child, the child cannot follow the parent abroad, but whether expulsion is interference depends on the intensity of the ties and the status of the parent. In *Berrehab*, the divorced applicant was assisted by his regular contact with his daughter, his financial contribution and the support of his former wife. In addition, his residence permit had been withdrawn.[49] A less committed father also succeeded in *Ciliz*.[50] In other similar cases, there was interference even if claims failed on proportionality grounds.[51] All these cases were treated as negative obligation claims as they involved fathers whose residence permits had been withdrawn or not renewed. On the other hand, two claims involving mothers who lived apart from their children succeeded even though they had never held a regular status and a positive obligation was engaged; maternal ties seemed to outweigh these disadvantages more easily.[52]

While family life usually exists between parents and minor children and interference often does, that is rarely the case for relationships between children and other relatives. Outside the immigration context, children may have family life with wider relatives despite the absence of cohabitation and close de facto ties.[53] In the immigration context, family life has been found when children already lived with the relatives.[54] However, an orphaned child, for example, cannot rely on Article 8 to join relatives who want to care for them. In these cases, the argument again has a circular quality. Family life cannot develop because border controls prevent the family living together, but without living together, family life is insufficient and border controls will prevail. Few claims asking for the admission of children to join wider relatives have even been made, reflecting the limitations of Article 8 in this respect.[55]

[46] *Sen* (n 23).

[47] *Tuquabo-Tekle v Netherlands* App no 60665/00 (1 December 2005), [47], [48]; see Spijkerboer, 'Structural Instability'; Draghici, *The Legitimacy of Family Rights in Strasbourg Case Law*, 348–49.

[48] Staiano, 'Good Mothers, Bad Mothers'; S Van Walsum, 'Against All Odds: How Single and Divorced Migrant Mothers Were Eventually Able to Claim Their Right to Respect for Family Life' (2009) *European Journal of Migration and Law* 295; *Berisha v Switzerland* App no 948/12 (30 July 2013).

[49] *Berrehab* (n 37).

[50] *Ciliz v Netherlands* App no 29192/95 (11 July 2000).

[51] *Dilek v Netherlands* (1999) 27 EHRR CD244; *Eshak v Sweden* App no 33758/96 (10 September 1997).

[52] *Nunez v Norway* (2011) 58 EHRR 17; *Rodrigues da Silva and Hoogkamer v Netherlands* (2007) 44 EHRR 34.

[53] *X, Y and Z v UK* (1997) 24 EHRR 143; *Kroon and Others* (n 38).

[54] *Butt v Norway* App no 47017/09 (4 December 2012).

[55] In *Nsona*, the Court was concerned primarily with adult deception of the authorities rather than with assessing the relationship between child and aunt: *Nsona v Netherlands* App no 23366/94 (28 November 1996).

C. Adult Relatives

In *Slivenko*, the Grand Chamber said that, in expulsion and extradition cases, family life is 'normally limited to the core family'.[56] It found there was no family life with the first applicant's elderly parents, as they 'did not belong to the core family and … have not been shown to have been dependent members of the applicants' family', a position criticised from within the Court.[57] In support of its position, the majority cited *Marckx* in 1973, and the 1968 admissibility decision of *X v Germany*.[58] *Marckx* concerned the legal position of an illegitimate child, and focused on the maternal relationship, but did not suggest that only parental relationships are protected. *X v Germany* involved a refugee's relationship with his nephew and niece living in a children's home. The Court found there was no family life, and the claim was inadmissible; he had little relationship with them and had even been prohibited from contact. It is difficult to see how these fact-specific cases could justify such a conclusion.

Notwithstanding, dependency was thereby established as the test for family life. Unless it involves young adults still living with their parents, it is interpreted as requiring something beyond the 'normal ties of affection' between family members.[59] In practice, this means both financial dependency and extreme vulnerability must be present. The emphasis on financial dependency particularly disadvantages those whose relatives are in low-income countries where care is relatively inexpensive and can be funded by the sponsor, as, even if dependency and therefore family life is found, this can continue without admitting the applicant. Care is thereby treated as fungible, as if there is no difference between institutional or paid for services and care by relatives in a home setting. The requirement of vulnerability is equally troubling. Physical, psychological and material support flow in different directions over time or even simultaneously; a physically disabled relative may be an important source of emotional support, for example.[60] It is ironic that grandparents' potential contribution to family life is irrelevant to their own claims, but its availability has been cited as a reason to refuse the admission of children.[61]

Even co-residence in the same state does not meet the Article 8(1) test if there is no explicit authorisation by the state. In *Slivenko*, the Grand Chamber said that, in its case law on expulsion and extradition, 'family life' means 'the effective "family life" established in the territory of a Contracting State by aliens lawfully

[56] *Slivenko* (n 42) [94].

[57] ibid [97], Partially Concurring Opinion of Judge Spielmann [4].

[58] *Marckx* (n 25); *X v Germany* App no 3110/67 (19 July 1968).

[59] *Aliyev v Ukraine* App no 78228/14 (10 June 2021) [40]; *Senchishak v Finland* App no 5049/12 (18 November 2014) [57]; *Ayoola v UK* App no 33185/96 (23 October 1997); *SS v UK* App no 10375/83 (10 December 1984). For a general discussion, see S Pellander, 'Traces of Dependency: Manifestations of Elderly Family Migration across Policy Arenas' ('The Problematisation of Family Migration' workshop, University of Amsterdam, 4–5 June 2015).

[60] For a discussion, see Pellander, 'Traces of Dependency'.

[61] *Berisha* (n 48).

resident there'.[62] This is exemplified by *Senchishak*, where an elderly, sick Russian woman lived with her daughter in Finland for several years while her claim for a residence permit was determined.[63] Because residence had not been authorised (although it was not unlawful), it was treated as precarious (see section VB below) and discounted, a formalistic approach that was criticised in the dissenting opinion.[64] The Court's approach invokes the circular argument mentioned earlier in relation to other non-nuclear family members: if the family does not already live together, there is no interference if admission is refused, but the claim arises precisely because co-residence is not authorised. Government immigration policies are put in an unassailable position, family life is treated as frozen at the moment of migration, and its changeable and multifaceted character is ignored.[65]

The Court seems to treat family reunification claims as a category apart. In the non-immigration case of *Emonet*, for example, the Court found in favour of an adult child who left home, married and divorced. As a result of severe illness, she needed care from her mother and her mother's partner. Adoption by the partner, desired by all the parties, would sever the legal bond between mother and daughter. The Court found that there was dependency and thus family life, even though they had not lived together for many years and did not intend to. There was no mention of financial dependency, and the 'additional factors of dependence, other than normal emotional ties', were established through the unspecified 'care and support' shown to the daughter.[66] As family life existed, 'the national authorities were under an obligation to allow those family ties to develop', resulting in a violation finding.[67] The applicant in *Ayoola*, in contrast, had serious physical and mental health problems but was to be expelled after living in the UK for 14 years. She saw her mother, brothers, nephews and nieces very often and her claim of dependency due to her poor mental health was supported by unchallenged psychiatric evidence. However, the government's argument that there was no family life as dependency was not financial and the parties did not cohabit was endorsed by the Commission, which concluded that removal would not interfere with family life.[68]

The real difference, it is submitted, between *Emonet* and *Ayoola* was not the degree of need or the character of family life, but the consequences of finding a violation.[69] The admission of adult relatives has been tightly controlled

[62] *Slivenko v Latvia* App no 48321/99 (9 October 2003).

[63] *Senchishak* (n 59); see also *AS v Switzerland* App no 39350/13 (30 June 2015).

[64] *Senchishak* (n 59), Dissenting Opinion of Judges Bianku and Kalaydjieva, 13.

[65] See C Draghici, 'Adult Children and Elderly Parents in Strasbourg Proceedings: A Misconstrued Approach to "Family Life"' (2018) 32 *International Journal of Law, Policy and the Family* 42.

[66] *Emonet and others v Switzerland* (2009) 49 EHRR 11 [35], [37]; see also *Pla and Puncerneau v Andorra* App no 69498/01 (13 July 2004); *Mustafa and Armagan Akin v Turkey* App no 4694/03 (6 April 2010); *Boyle v UK* App no 16580/90 (9 February 1993).

[67] *Emonet* (n 66) [82].

[68] *Ayoola* (n 59); on financial dependency, see also *SS v UK* (n 59).

[69] At the time *Ayoola* was decided in 1997, the Court had already started to apply proportionality in Art 8 positive obligation cases, so the Commission should not have been motivated by fear that finding interference would lead straight to a violation.

for many years in European states, particularly those with expensive welfare and health systems.[70] Yet, whether those controls are necessary, given the cost to family life, is an Article 8(2) proportionality question, not an Article 8(1) family life question. This is occasionally recognised. In *FN v UK*, the applicant was a traumatised asylum seeker whose claim of brutal gang rape was disbelieved.[71] She lived for eight years in the UK with her aunt before being returned to Uganda. The Court accepted there was family life with her aunt but still found that removal was proportionate under Article 8(2). The decision endorsed awful suffering, but at least the Court focused on the appropriate issue: whether the applicant's family ties outweighed the state's interest in immigration control.

D. Family Life: Discussion

In 1967, almost 20 years before *Abdulaziz*, the application in *Alam and Khan* was found admissible, leading to a friendly settlement.[72] The sponsor's minor son had twice been refused admission because the authorities did not accept that they were related, as the sponsor, an illiterate mill worker from Pakistan, could not produce documents showing paternity. Dembour reports that a similar case, lodged on the same day but concerning the admission of an elderly father, was inadmissible.[73] Thus, from the outset, two interrelated features were visible. The first was the association between resistance to recognising family ties, particularly by wider family members, and post-colonial anxiety; sponsors were overwhelmingly from former colonies or were otherwise of migrant descent. They were treated not as citizens asking to live in their own home with those they love, but as having made instrumental choices with consequences they must accept.[74] The second was the Strasbourg Court's narrow view of family life that could, in practice, found a claim (spouses, parents and minor children) and family life that could not (adult children and parents, other relatives). By restricting the meaning of family life in this way, the Court could reject more claims at the Article 8(1) stage and spare states from scrutiny, however slight, under Article 8(2). However, it has led to a narrow and impoverished understanding of family, an argument explored further in chapter eight.

[70] See H Askola, '(No) Migrating for Family Care in Later Life: *Senchishak v Finland*, Older Parents and Family Reunification' (2016) 18 *European Journal of Migration and Law* 351; *Britcits v SSHD* [2017] EWCA Civ 368.

[71] *FN v UK* App no 3202/09 (17 September 2009).

[72] *Alam and Khan* (n 28).

[73] Dembour, *When Humans Become Migrants*, 99–102.

[74] For more on this, see B De Hart, 'Love Thy Neighbour: Family Reunification and the Rights of Insiders' (2009) 11 *European Journal of Migration and Law* 235, 252; Staiano, 'Good Mothers, Bad Mothers'; Van Walsum, 'Against All Odds'.

IV. ARTICLE 8(2) PROPORTIONALITY 1: IMMIGRATION CONTROLS, POSITIVE OBLIGATIONS AND THE MARGIN OF APPRECIATION

Once Article 8(1) is engaged, a violation finding may be avoided only by showing that interference is proportionate under Article 8(2). The Court has been criticised for its failure to assess state justifications for refusing family reunification, handing states a significant advantage; in effect, they can decide where to set the bar on admission in all but rare cases. This is achieved through two interrelated mechanisms: the Court's treatment of proportionality in positive obligation claims and the margin of appreciation, discussed here; and the character of the fair balance assessment, discussed below.

The proportionality assessment is different in negative and positive obligation cases. A negative obligation assessment follows the structure of Article 8(2) and examines the lawfulness of interference, whether it serves an aim set out in Article 8(2) or is 'necessary in a democratic society'. Sometimes, the Court describes the final stage of its assessment as finding a 'fair balance' between these factors. This is not the same exercise, however, as a 'positive obligation' fair balance assessment. Proportionality in positive obligation cases is not expressly regulated by the Convention. Article 8(2) is sometimes applied by analogy, but there are practical difficulties.[75] How far must a government justify failure to act? Is the burden even on the government? Must the positive obligation be fulfilled to its maximum possible extent and how many alternative courses of action should be considered? To what extent must it be shown that the positive act requested will not have other harmful consequences?[76] To avoid these difficulties, the Court usually applies a 'fair balance' test, where the 'general interest of the community' is weighed against the individual interest, and the Article 8(2) factors have a 'certain relevance'.[77] This is a pragmatic response to the difficulties, although some critics have argued that it is casuistic, and accords insufficient weight to the human rights norm.[78]

The Court has consistently said that family reunification may engage both positive and negative obligations. In practice, it usually treats claims as positive, unless the state has issued and withdrawn a residence permit.[79] It has also said that similar principles apply to both, which is usually but not always true.[80] The Court is consistent, however, in finding that, in both negative and positive obligation cases, the government does not have to justify its immigration policy. Thus, in *Berrehab*, a negative case, the Court said that its function 'is not to

[75] M Klatt and M Meister, *The Constitutional Structure of Proportionality* (Oxford, Oxford University Press, 2012) 108.

[76] For a discussion of these, see ibid 108.

[77] *Rees v United Kingdom* App no 9532/81 (17 October 1986) [37]; see also [107].

[78] eg S Tsakyrakis, 'Proportionality: An Assault on Human Rights' (2009) 7 *International Journal of Constitutional Law* 468.

[79] eg *Berrehab* (n 37).

[80] ibid; eg *Ciliz* (n 50); *Omoregie* (n 16).

pass judgment on the Netherlands' immigration and residence policy as such' but to consider whether the interference was excessive in the particular case.[81] The 'necessity' of, ie the public interest in, controls was not analysed, and the violation finding was based entirely on Mr Berrehab's circumstances. In positive obligation cases, the Court arrives at the same destination by positing states' right 'as a matter of well-established international law ... to control the entry of aliens into its territory and their residence there'.[82] Scholars have questioned the legal origins of the doctrine, but it functions to remove immigration policy from the Court's purview, so that there is no evaluation of its benefits.[83] Immigration controls thus become an unquestionable and pre-existing legal fact, to which human rights are an occasional exception, Dembour's 'Strasbourg reversal'.[84]

The Court also justifies its approach by reference to the 'margin of appreciation', under which the Court allows states discretion in the implementation of rights. The margin of appreciation recognises the Court's supervisory status and limited capacity, and the need for state support.[85] As the margin widens, the level of scrutiny of state conduct decreases, and a wide margin of appreciation risks turning the Court into the guardian of process alone, particularly where it has not set minimum substantive standards.[86] The Court commonly says in family reunification cases that states have only a 'certain' margin of appreciation, but the margin is, in reality, wide at least so far as the public or general interest is concerned, a point sometimes made by dissenting judges.[87]

The difference this distinction makes can be understood by comparing the two *Biao* judgments. They concerned a naturalised Danish citizen whose wife was refused admission due to the 'combined attachment' requirement in Danish

[81] *Berrehab* (n 37) [29]; see also *Alim* (n 34) [93].

[82] *Jeunesse v Netherlands* (2015) 60 EHRR 17 [100].

[83] See Dembour, *When Humans Become Migrants*, 117–18; SS Juss, 'Free Movement and the World Order' (2004) 16 *International Journal of Refugee Law* 289; B Schotel, *On the Right of Exclusion: Law, Ethics and Immigration Policy* (Abingdon, Routledge, 2013).

[84] Dembour, *When Humans Become Migrants*, 118–19.

[85] L Lavrytsen, *Human Rights in a Positive State: Rethinking the Relationship between Positive and Negative Obligations under the European Convention on Human Rights* (Cambridge, Intersentia, 2017) 168–70. See, eg *Goodwin v UK* App no 28957/95 (11 July 2002); *Hämäläinen v Finland* App no 37359/09 (GC) 16 July 2014; *Gaskin v UK* App no 10454/83 (7 July 1989); *B v France* App no 13343/87 (25 March 1992); see also V Stoyanova, 'The Disjunctive Structure of Positive Rights under the European Convention on Human Rights' (2018) 87 *Nordic Journal of International Law* 344; A Mowbray, *The Development of Positive Obligations under the European Convention on Human Rights by the European Court of Human Rights* (Oxford, Hart Publishing, 2004) 127–88.

[86] *Von Hannover v Germany* (2012) 55 EHRR 15 [107]; *MA v Denmark* App no 6697/18 (GC, 9 July 2021) [148]. On the risks of process rights, see D Spielmann, 'Allowing the Right Margin: The European Court of Human Rights and the National Margin of Appreciation Doctrine: Waiver or Subsidiarity of European Review?' (2012) 14 *Cambridge Yearbook of European Legal Studies* 381; J Kratochvíl, 'The Inflation of the Margin of Appreciation by the European Court of Human Rights' (2011) 29 *Netherlands Quarterly of Human Rights* 324, 330.

[87] See, eg Joint Dissenting Opinion of Judges Villiger, Mahoney and Kjølbro in *Biao* App no 38590/10 (25 March 2014) [OIII-30]; Joint Dissenting Opinion of Judges Villiger, Mahoney and Silvis in *Jeunesse* (n 82) [8]; Dissenting Opinion of Judge Thór Vilhjálmsson in *Berrehab* (n 37).

law, under which a couple had to show that their combined attachment to Denmark was greater than their combined attachment to any other state.[88] The rule particularly disadvantaged Danes with a migrant background, as an exemption applied after 28 years of citizenship so that those born Danish were exempt from age 28. Naturalisation in Denmark required many years' residence, and Mr Biao, who entered Denmark aged 22, would have been 59 before being exempt. Meanwhile, the enforced separation from his wife made compliance with the combined attachment requirement itself almost impossible.

Where Article 14 is invoked, particularly on grounds of ethnicity, the margin of appreciation is narrowed.[89] Mr Biao argued that the attachment requirement exemption discriminated by ethnicity as naturalised citizens were more likely to come from minority ethnic groups. The Chamber disagreed and determined the claim on Article 8 grounds alone, finding there was no violation.[90] The Grand Chamber found discrimination by ethnicity and looked more closely at the government's justification.[91] The difference this made can be understood by returning to the list of questions, set out in chapter one, that a court might ask itself when addressing the general interest in immigration control in a positive obligation case:

1. What public or general interest does the measure serve?
2. How effective is it?
3. Is it necessary in this case?
4. Do the applicants' circumstances make its application disproportionate?

In its assessment under Article 8 alone, the Chamber addressed only the fourth question, considering matters relating to the couple's personal situation: if they could live elsewhere or whether they knew about the combined attachment criterion before they applied. It found that the national authorities had not 'acted arbitrarily or otherwise transgressed the margin of appreciation'.[92] The Court did not evaluate the benefits of the combined attachment requirement.

In contrast, the Grand Chamber applied a narrow margin of appreciation, resulting in much deeper analysis. It observed that Mr Biao had lived in Denmark for over 10 years and had strong ties, was proficient in Danish language and social knowledge, and was self-sufficient. It therefore considered question 3 – whether such a draconian integration measure was needed in this instance. It also addressed question 2 by asking if the policy itself was effective. The

[88] *Biao* v *Denmark* App no 38590/10 (25 March 2014); *Biao v Denmark* (2017) 64 EHRR 1.

[89] eg in *Hode v UK* (2013) 56 EHRR 27, differences between family reunification rights for refugees and for migrant workers and students could not be justified. In *Ponomaryovi v Bulgaria* App no 5335/05 (21 June 2011), it was a breach of Art 14 in conjunction with Art 2 of Protocol 1 to charge lawfully present non-nationals for their secondary education. A series of cases on access to welfare payments by non-nationals also found that discrimination was not justified; see, eg *Dhahbi v Italy* App no 17120/09 (8 April 2014).

[90] *Biao v Denmark* App no 38590/10 (25 March 2014) [59].

[91] *Biao v Denmark* (2017) 64 EHRR 1 [138].

[92] *Biao v Denmark* App no 38590/10 (25 March 2014) [59].

government's case was found to be 'based on rather speculative arguments' and the policy excluded consideration of those factors that could have reassured the authorities on integration.[93] The Court also observed that some of the government's arguments reflected 'negatively on the lifestyle of Danish nationals of non-Danish ethnic extraction' and did not 'provide sufficient justification for a difference in treatment'.[94] However, the majority did not find that the policy had a discriminatory intent and did not expressly address question 1.[95] Even so, it was a searching examination.

Such in-depth scrutiny occurred only because Article 14 was engaged.[96] Under Article 8 alone, the existence of immigration control is its own sufficient justification, and the individual must show that their personal circumstances merit an exception. It is unusual for bright line rules to be accepted as being in the public interest without further examination, even in positive obligation cases, particularly when, as here, the usual reasons for a wide margin in positive cases are absent.[97] The margin of appreciation has become not a calibrated means of addressing the problems of supranational supervision, but is a blunt instrument that weights the proportionality assessment in favour of the state. The Court clearly does not want to force states to regularise irregular residence or admit unwanted migrants, given the need for continuing state support. However, from a rights perspective, that a group's interests are excluded from national understanding of the 'public interest' is normally a reason to narrow the margin of appreciation.[98] The tension between these two pressures is rarely admitted openly: the Court often says it applies a 'certain', not a 'wide', margin of appreciation and that similar principles apply to positive and negative claims, although the principles that it usually applies, discussed in the next section, make sense only in the context of a positive obligation and a wide margin of appreciation.[99] The tension sometimes becomes visible in dissenting opinions to violation findings. In *Jeunesse*, for example, the minority criticised the grant of residence to an irregular migrant, saying that the 'margin of appreciation, which was wide in such circumstances, has undergone a hot wash in this case'.[100]

While the margin of appreciation usually makes immigration policies unassailable unless Article 14 discrimination is present, there are occasional hints of a more expansive approach. The Grand Chamber in *MA* said that inability to show sufficient resources to provide for basic family subsistence could be a reason

[93] *Biao v Denmark* (2017) 64 EHRR 1 [125].

[94] ibid [126].

[95] ibid [121]; see also the Concurring Opinion of Judge Pinto de Albuquerque [19].

[96] Problems with Art 14 discrimination are discussed further in ch 8, s VI.

[97] See ch 1, s IVC; Lavrytsen, *Human Rights in a Positive State*, 68; see also Stoyanova, 'The Disjunctive Structure of Positive Rights'; Mowbray, *The Development of Positive Obligations*, 127–88.

[98] Farahat, 'The Exclusiveness of Inclusion'.

[99] See, eg *Jeunesse* (n 82) [106]. This evolution is relatively recent; see Lambert, 'The European Court of Human Rights and the Right of Refugees', 429.

[100] *Jeunesse* (n 82), Joint Dissenting Opinion of Judges Villiger, Mahoney and Silvis, [4].

for refusal.[101] All the cases cited by the Chamber involved applicants where basic self-sufficiency was an issue, although, in *Hasanbasic*, this did not prevent a violation finding.[102] The implicit corollary of their words was that a standard higher than subsistence might not be sufficient. In other words, the Court would not necessarily accept any income criterion without question. This was an interesting if veiled hint and too much should not be read into it. In general, the Court has avoided the challenges presented by Article 8 family reunification cases by refusing to examine the public interest in immigration policies. Some cases still succeed, however, and the next section looks at how these arise by examining the fair balance assessment.

V. ARTICLE 8(2) PROPORTIONALITY 2: FAIR BALANCE

The most up-to-date guidance on a family reunification fair balance assessment was provided in 2021 by the Grand Chamber in *MA v Denmark*.[103] It observed that the presence of one or several of the following factors made a violation finding less likely:

- family life was created when those involved knew that the immigration status of one party meant that family life within the state would be precarious from the outset;
- the sponsor or applicant has limited ties to the host country;
- there are no insurmountable obstacles to the family living in the other state;
- the sponsor cannot show sufficient resources to provide for basic family subsistence.

On the other hand, an accumulation of the following factors might result in an obligation to grant family reunification:

- the sponsor or the applicant has a settled status in or strong ties to the host country;
- family life was created when there was already a residence status;
- children are involved;
- there are insurmountable or major obstacles to living in country of origin.

This elaborated on the guidance in *Jeunesse* in 2016 and, together, these decisions make it easier to understand when a claim might succeed – a positive development. However, in practice, some factors are particularly important, and this can only be understood from looking more closely at how they have functioned in decisions. The following sections do this by dividing the criteria into

[101] *MA* (n 86) [134].
[102] *Hasanbasiç v Switzerland* App no 52166/09 (11 June 2013).
[103] *MA* (n 86) [134]–[135].

three categories: those relating to obstacles to relocating and ties to the state; immigration control factors; and the best interests of children.

A. Insurmountable Obstacles to Relocation and Ties to the Contracting State

From a UK perspective, 'insurmountable obstacles' are significant because of their role in the domestic jurisprudence (discussed in later chapters), but they have only a limited function in the Strasbourg cases. It is not even clear that the criterion is that obstacles must be 'insurmountable'. In both *Abdulaziz* and *Gül*, for example, the Court merely said that the applicants had not shown 'obstacles' to establishing family life elsewhere.[104] The Court in *Berisha* referred to 'major obstacles'.[105] The Commission has also used words such as 'significant', 'objective' or 'practical' obstacles.[106] This suggests that 'insurmountable' should not be interpreted too literally, although it remains the most common term.

'Insurmountable obstacles' first appeared in unsuccessful admissibility decisions.[107] If an application was admissible, the phrase did not feature in the reasoning, although it sometimes appeared in an indicative checklist.[108] It then found its way into Chamber and Grand Chamber judgments, but again mainly in non-violation findings. In *Kaplan*, for example, the Court used it when discussing the children where there was no violation but not the child where there was a violation.[109] It did not appear in the successful admissibility decision

[104] *Abdulaziz* (n 17) [68]; *Gül* (n 44) [42].

[105] *Berisha* (n 48) [57]–[58].

[106] *Jaramillo v UK* App no 24865/94 (23 October 1995); *PP v UK* App no 25297/94 (16 January 1996); *Tella v UK* App no 31612/96 (21 May 1997); *Esen v Netherlands* App no 37312/97 (21 October 1997); *Bajsultanov v Russia* App no 54131/10 (12 June 2012).

[107] *X v UK* App no 9088/80 (6 March 1982); *X, Y and Z v UK* App no 9285/81 (6 July 1982); *Dilawar v UK* App no 12408/86 (12 March 1987); *MA v UK* App no 12392/86 (13 July 1987). *Jaramillo* (n 106); *Ebibomi v UK* 29622/95 (29 November 1995); *Bibi v UK* App no 26290/95 (16 January 1996); *PP* (n 106); *Larbie v UK* App no 25073/94 (28 February 1996); *Choudry v UK* App no 27949/95 (13 May 1996); *Altuntas v Austria* App no 25918/94 (15 May 1996); *Poku v UK* App no 26895/95 (15 May 1996); *Gorman v UK* App no 32339/96 (9 April 1997); *ER v UK* App no 32214/96 (21 May 1997); *Schneider v UK* App no 37003/97 (15 January 1998); *Mitchell v UK* App no 40447/98 (24 November 1998); *Ajayi v UK* App no 27663/95 (22 June 1999); *Solomon v Netherlands* App no 44328/98 (5 September 2000); *Useinov v Netherlands* App no 21292/00 (11 April 2006); *Priya v Denmark* App no 13594/03 (6 July 2006); *Angelov v Finland* App no 26832/02 (5 September 2006); *Konstatinov v Netherlands* App no 16351/03 (26 April 2007); *M v UK* App no 25087/06 (24 June 2008); *Narenji Haghighi v Netherlands* App no 38165/07 (14 April 2009); *Biraga v Sweden* App no 1722/10 (3 April 2012); *KM v Russia* App no 46086/07 (29 April 2010); *Olgun v Netherlands* App no 1859/03 (10 May 2012); *I v Netherlands* App no 24147/11 (10 July 2012); *K v Netherlands* App no 33403/11 (25 September 2012); *Imamovic v Sweden* App no 57633/10 (13 November 2012); *Naibzay v Netherlands* App no 68564/12 (4 June 2013); *Bolek v Sweden* App no 48205/13 (28 January 2014); *JM v Sweden* App no 47509/13 (8 April 2014); *Smith v Ireland* App no 52223/13 (24 June 2014). *Tella* (n 106); *Esen* (n 106).

[108] eg *Tuquabo-Tekle v Netherlands* App no 60665/00 (19 October 2004); *Omoregie v Norway* App no 265/07 (22 November 2007).

[109] *Kaplan v Norway* App no 32504/11 (24 July 2014).

in *Omoregie*, but it did in the Chamber's non-violation finding.[110] In *Sezen*, the majority found a violation of Article 8 without using the term, but it appeared in the dissenting opinion.[111] In successful claims, such as *Rodrigues da Silva and Hoogkamer*, *Alim* and *Nunez*, it was mentioned in the checklist of factors, but the Court did not go on to consider whether obstacles were insurmountable.[112] In *Butt* and *Jeunesse*, the Court found that there were no insurmountable obstacles but there was still a violation.[113] In no instance did a claim succeed only because there were insurmountable obstacles, but equally none failed only because they did not exist. The 'insurmountable obstacles' criterion seems to function mainly as a long stop to ensure that the Court does not destroy the possibility of family life by refusing a claim.[114] For that reason, it is more significant in the forced migration context, where it has informed the more favourable treatment of refugee sponsors, and that may explain the greater emphasis placed on it in *MA*.[115] The existence of insurmountable obstacles is not, however, a precondition for success.

While claims do not fail therefore only because there are no insurmountable obstacles, the Court has also said repeatedly that states have no obligation to respect the choice by married couples of their country of residence, an observation made in *Abdulaziz* and many times since.[116] In practice, ties to the host state play only a limited role, particularly where the migrant party has not held a regular status.[117] Even citizen sponsors' ties have not been considered in depth, with the emphasis on the possibility of relocation. In *Omoregie*, for example, the Court acknowledged that the applicant's Norwegian wife 'would probably experience some difficulties and inconveniences' settling in Nigeria.[118] It also mentioned that she had lived in South Africa, reducing residence in two different African countries to a single experience. These observations disposed of her entire life in her country of birth and nationality: her other family, social contacts, professional life and cultural attachments, as well as her concerns about living conditions in Nigeria.[119] The consequence of finding that family life can continue if the parties relocate is that the consequences of separation are irrelevant as that is a choice made by the parties. If Mrs Omoregie and the

[110] *Omoregie* (nn 108 and 16) [66]; see also *Arvelo Aponte v Netherlands* App no 28770/05 (3 November 2011); *Biao v Denmark* App no 38590/10 (Decision 25 March 2014); *Muradeli v Russia* App no 72780/12 (9 April 2015); *Akbulut v UK* (2012) 55 EHRR SE10; *Antwi v Norway* App no 26940/10 (14 February 2012).

[111] *Sezen v Netherlands* (2006) 43 EHRR 30.

[112] *Rodrigues da Silva and Hoogkamer* (n 52) [39]; *Alim* (n 34); *Nunez v Norway* (2014) 58 EHRR 17.

[113] *Butt* (n 54) [88]; *Jeunesse* (n 82) [117].

[114] eg see *EP and AR v Netherlands* App nos 43538/11 and 63104/11 (11 July 2017) [96].

[115] *Mugenzi v France* App no 52071/09 (10 July 2014); *Tanda-Muzinga v France* App no 2260/10 (10 July 2014); *MA* (n 86) [134], [138], [145].

[116] *Abdulaziz* (n 17) [68].

[117] eg *Jeunesse* (n 82) [116].

[118] *Omoregie* (n 16) [66].

[119] ibid [48].

couple's daughter remained in Norway, 'nothing should prevent [them] from coming to visit the first applicant for periods in Nigeria'.[120]

The marginalisation of the sponsor occurs even when, as in *Omoregie*, their interests have been raised specifically by the parties. Elsewhere, for instance in *Arvelo Aponte*, where the husband and son were Dutch citizens expected to move to Venezuela despite 'a certain degree of social and economic hardship', they were not even parties to the claim.[121] There is a feedback loop here: if the Court is uninterested in these questions, applicants and their lawyers are less likely to raise them, ensuring that they are not addressed. Whatever the causal dynamics, the net effect is that, even where claims succeed, the situation of the sponsor has often not carried much weight.

That said, there has been some development in the cases. In *Jeunesse* in 2016, the Grand Chamber said that 'the extent of the ties in the Contracting State' was a relevant factor, without specifying whose ties.[122] However, in its application of those principles, it noted that all the other members of the applicant's family were Dutch nationals and had a right to enjoy family life with each other in the Netherlands.[123] In *MA* in 2021, the Court said that factors in favour of family reunification included when 'The person requesting family reunification had achieved a settled status in the host country or had strong ties with that country'.[124] The wording was not very clear but, from the context, it seems that they meant the sponsor. This could suggest a possible shift towards more focus on the painful dilemmas of sponsors. If so, this would be a positive step, as discussed further in chapter eight.

B. Immigration Control and Precariousness

This chapter has already observed that the Strasbourg Court assumes that an immigration control measure always serves the general or public interest. The consequence is that the obligation to admit a non-national is an exceptional case for which a strong argument must be made. From this flows the doctrine of 'precariousness', expressed typically as follows:

> Another important consideration will also be whether family life was created at a time when the persons involved were aware that the immigration status of one of them was such that the persistence of that family life within the host State would be precarious from the outset. The Court has previously held that where this is the case it is likely only to be in the most exceptional circumstances that the removal of the non-national family member will constitute a violation of Article 8.[125]

[120] ibid [66].
[121] *Arvelo Aponte* (n 110) [60].
[122] *Jeunesse* (n 82) [107].
[123] *Jeunesse* (n 82) [115].
[124] *MA* (n 86) [135].
[125] *Konstatinov* (n 107).

Family life may be described as precarious when an applicant is an irregular migrant,[126] has a short-term residence permit,[127] is subject to an expulsion order even if not yet in force,[128] is an asylum seeker or rejected asylum seeker,[129] or when residence or citizenship has been obtained through fraud or suspected fraud.[130] While the term is usually invoked when family life started after entry, it has been used when it predates entry, including in admission claims when the parties cannot comply with ordinary immigration laws.[131] In short, family life will always be precarious unless created under a status that has expired or been withdrawn.[132] Although an exception has been made when there was no knowledge of the irregularity, family life formed when there is not already a regular immigration status is generally at the risk of the parties and the state does not have to assist them.[133]

To treat family life as precarious when immigration status is absent has some normative logic; it inhibits applicants from presenting a fait accompli through cynical disregard for immigration laws.[134] It can even be seen as progressive as it recognises that a claim arising from irregular residence will not automatically fail.[135] The problem, however, is that immigration status is often unstable and uncertain, and its absence involves different degrees of personal responsibility.[136] In *Omoregie*, for instance, the relationship began before Mr Omoregie's asylum claim was determined, ie while toleration of his presence was mandated by international law. There followed several years of appeals and applications under asylum and family reunification laws, interspersed with periods of irregularity.[137] He did not deceive or evade the authorities and tried persistently to obtain a regular status. Yet his residence was treated as precarious in the same way as that of, for example, Mr Antwi or Ms Nunez, who both used forged documentation.[138] On this analysis, precariousness is not a way to protect states from deception and manipulation, but ensures their ability to control immigration is never compromised.

The doctrine creates a circular argument in favour of the state: applicants are ineligible for family reunification because immigration laws apply to them, but

[126] *Rodrigues da Silva and Hoogkamer* (n 52); *Guliyev and Sheina v Russia* App no 24650/02 (19 June 2008); *Jeunesse* (n 82); *Nunez* (2014) (n 112).

[127] *Ejimson v Germany* App no 58681/12 (1 March 2018); *Arvelo Aponte* (n 110).

[128] *MA v Denmark* App no 58363/10 (8 July 2014).

[129] *Omoregie* (n 16); *Nnyanzi v UK* App no 21878/06 (8 April 2008); *SJ v Belgium* App no 70055/10 (GC, 19 May 2015).

[130] *Antwi* (n 110).

[131] *Konstatinov* (n 107); *Biao v Denmark* (2017) 64 EHRR 1.

[132] *Useinov* (n 107).

[133] *Butt* (n 54).

[134] eg *Omoregie* (n 16) [64].

[135] Thym, 'Respect for Private and Family Life under Article 8 ECHR'.

[136] A Kubal, 'Conceptualizing Semi-legality in Migration Research' (2013) 47 *Law and Society Review* 555.

[137] *Omoregie* (n 16).

[138] *Antwi* (n 110); *Nunez* (2014) (n 112).

they cannot challenge their application because the same laws have made family life precarious. In *Biao*, the applicants' complaint concerned the 'combined attachment' requirement in Danish law. The Chamber observed that the parties knew that their family life was precarious – because they knew about the attachment requirement.[139] In *Senchisak*, the applicant applied for a residence permit on the day of her arrival in Finland as permitted by Finnish law, but, because it was eventually refused, the majority found that the family life created during five years spent together in Finland was precarious and carried no weight.[140] In this form, precariousness represents a form of double counting; states already have a wide margin of appreciation as regards immigration controls, and precariousness discounts the countervailing value of family life. Certainly, its absolute character normalises onerous immigration controls, passing both moral responsibility and risk to the family and devaluing relationships because of when they began. It also empties Article 8 of much of its effective content. Article 8 concerns family life, not immigration, and there is little coherence in finding that family life, a social fact, does not exist or count because of a legal construct. The 'precariousness' doctrine is therefore problematic, and this is explored further in chapter eight.

Although precariousness means that almost all family reunification claims fail, some 'exceptional' cases succeed. A common feature in violations is that the Court finds the state's claim to sovereignty over immigration has been weakened by a procedural problem or defect.[141] Sometimes, this accords with the Court's supervisory role, for example when it finds that the domestic authorities failed to carry out a proper balancing exercise or the process was defective in another way.[142] However, in other instances, the focus is on reasons to mitigate the pre-eminence of immigration controls. There may be a prior unexercised right of residence, individuals could not easily access immigration procedures or the state was dilatory in pursuing an irregular resident.[143] In *Sen*, it was noted that, unlike *Gül*, the sponsors had always resided lawfully under a work permit and, in *Osman*, that the daughter had a previous lengthy lawful residence.[144] In *Tuquabo-Tekle*, the Court observed that the daughter's admission had been delayed because her mother had misunderstood the relevant law.[145]

In these cases, the Court acknowledges a problem with application of the law but not with the law itself and thereby avoids impinging on state sovereignty over

[139] *Biao v Denmark* App no 38590/10 (5 March 2014) [57].

[140] *Senchishak v Finland* [2014] ECHR 1295.

[141] I owe this insight to the perceptive PhD thesis of Eva Hilbrink: E Hilbrink, 'Adjudicating the Public Interest in Immigration Law: A Systematic Content Analysis of Strasbourg and Luxembourg Case Law on Legal Restrictions to Immigration and Free Movement' (PhD Thesis, Vrije Universiteit Amsterdam, 2017).

[142] *Guliyev and Sheina* (n 15); *El Ghatet v Switzerland* App no 56971/10 (8 November 2016); *Alim* (n 34); *Sezen* (n 111); *Tanda-Muzinga* (n 115).

[143] *Rodrigues da Silva and Hoogkamer* (n 52) [43]; *Nunez* (2011) (n 52); *Alim* (n 34) [88]. *Butt* (n 54).

[144] *Osman v UK* (2000) 29 EHRR 245.

[145] *Tuquabo-Tekle* (n 47).

substantive rules. However, these mitigations seem to arise only when the Court also finds a violation in a positive obligation claim. In numerous non-violation findings, the Court has found that official delays or tolerated presence do not affect precariousness.[146] Yet, in *Nunez*, the Court observed that the expulsion order was not made until nearly four years after the applicant's unlawful residence was brought to the attention of the authorities.[147] In *Rodrigues da Silva and Hoogkamer*, the Court concluded that lawful residence might have been possible, distinguishing this claim from one where this was never possible.[148] In *Jeunesse*, the Grand Chamber noted that lengthy toleration of the applicant's unlawful presence 'enabled the applicant to establish and develop strong family, social and cultural ties in the Netherlands'.[149] What these three cases had in common was a new focus by the Court on the best interests of children, the other key factor in the fair balance assessment, which is discussed in the next section.

C. Best Interests of Children

The family reunification jurisprudence has begun to reflect wider international commitments to protecting children's best interests. Article 3 of the Convention of the Rights of the Child (1989), on which the Court has drawn in its Article 8 jurisprudence, says that, in all actions concerning children, their best interests must be a primary consideration.[150] While this is a relative obligation (children's interests are not paramount), it is a welcome development as children's interests were previously routinely subordinated to the interests of immigration control.[151] The best interests principle may apply within two broad factual matrices: the admission or expulsion of a parent and an application by a child to join the family unit. The best interests of the child as a free-standing factor were first mentioned in an expulsion case: *Rodrigues da Silva and Hoogkamer*.[152] Unlike previous violation findings such as *Berrehab*, which involved fathers who had held a regular status, the mother never had leave so that family life was precarious, and a powerful counterbalancing factor may have been thought necessary.[153] In *Nunez* and *Jeunesse*, the Court also found in favour of mothers who lacked immigration status, and referred explicitly to Article 3.[154]

[146] *Omoregie* (n 16); *Arvelo Aponte* (n 110); *Useinov* (n 107); *Konstatinov* (n 107).
[147] *Nunez* (2014) (n 112) [82].
[148] *Rodrigues da Silva and Hoogkamer* (n 52) [43].
[149] *Jeunesse* (n 82) [116].
[150] United Nations Convention on the Rights of the Child (adopted 20 November 1989, entered into force 2 September, UNGA Res 44/25), Treaty No 27531, United Nations Treaty Series, 1577, Art 3; see also *Neulinger v Switzerland* (2012) 54 EHRR 31.
[151] See, eg *Sorabjee v UK* App no 23938/94 (Decision of the Commission (Plenary) 23 October 1995); *Poku* (n 107); *Omoregie* (n 16); *Solomon* (n 107).
[152] *Rodrigues da Silva and Hoogkamer* (n 52) 34.
[153] *Berrehab* (n 37); *Ciliz* (n 50).
[154] *Nunez* (2011) (n 52) [84]; *Jeunesse* (n 82) [109].

On the admission of children, *Sen* in 2001 found major obstacles to the family's return: the parents' long legal residence, and the birth and education of two children in the Netherlands. In this context, and given the younger children's interests, admission of the eldest child was 'the most adequate way to continue family life'.[155] It is not clear that the circumstances in *Sen* were more compelling than in the earlier non-violation decision of *Gül*, nor that it represented a significant doctrinal advance as it has not been consistently applied since.[156] In *Berisha* and *IAA*, older children were refused admission because, it was assumed, they needed less close care and attention, an argument contested by the minority in *Berisha*.[157] Older children did succeed in *Tuquabo-Tekle* and *Osman*, but there were particular factors: the mother's enforced flight as a refugee in *Tuquabo-Tekle*, and the daughter's involuntary departure from and previous residence in Denmark in *Osman*.[158] Claims also succeeded where there were procedural defects, particularly in a forced migration context.[159]

While there have been some positive developments, childhood is still not consistently awarded the same value in family reunification as in other areas of the Court's jurisprudence.[160] The Grand Chamber in *Jeunesse* in 2014 found that national bodies must 'give effective protection and sufficient weight to the best interests of the children',[161] articulating what previous decisions implied, but it is still not clear what is required. The child's age and the strength of the child–parent bond seem to be relevant, and the Court has been more attentive when parents are separated so that family relocation is not possible, but decisions cannot easily be categorised.[162] The danger is inconsistency or decisions that rely on unsubstantiated assumptions and gender norms.[163] Yet articulating a principled position is not straightforward, given the lack of consensus within the Court. For instance, in 2012, some years after *Rodrigues da Silva and Hoogkamer*, the Court in *Kaplan* still felt able to say that:

> Weighty immigration policy considerations … militate in favour of identifying children with the conduct of their parents, failing which there would be a great risk that the parents exploit the situation of their children in order to secure a residence permit for themselves and for the children.[164]

[155] *Sen v Netherlands* (2001) 36 EHRR 81 [40].

[156] For a discussion, see Spijkerboer, 'Structural Instability'; Draghici, *The Legitimacy of Family Rights in Strasbourg Case Law*, 348–49.

[157] *Berisha* (n 48); *IAA v UK (*2016) 62 EHRR SE19, Dissenting Opinion of Judges Jočienė and Karaka, [5].

[158] *Tuquabo-Tekle* (n 145); *Tanda-Muzinga* (n 115); *Osman v UK* (2015) 61 EHRR 10. For a discussion, see Spijkerboer, 'Structural Instability'; Draghici, *The Legitimacy of Family Rights in Strasbourg Case Law*.

[159] *Tanda-Muzinga* (n 115).

[160] For a discussion, see S Trotter, 'The Child in European Human Rights Law' (2018) 81 *MLR* 452.

[161] *Jeunesse v Netherlands* App no 12738/10 (GC, 3 October 2014) [120].

[162] C Smyth, 'The Best Interests of the Child in the Expulsion and First-Entry Jurisprudence of the European Court of Human Rights: How Principled Is the Court's Use of the Principle?' (2015) 17 *European Journal of Migration and Law* 70.

[163] De Hart, 'Love Thy Neighbour'; De Hart, 'Superdads', 448–67; Staiano, 'Good Mothers, Bad Mothers', 180.

[164] *Kaplan* (n 109) [86].

While a different view later prevailed in *Nunez* and *Jeunesse*, the dissenting opinions in those cases show the depth of anxiety. In *Nunez*, for example, the minority feared that 'this case will send the wrong signal, namely that persons who are illegally in a country can somehow contrive to have their residence "legitimised" through the expedient of marriage and of having children'.[165] It is perhaps understandable, given this lack of consensus in the Court, that judges supporting a more child-oriented jurisprudence are reluctant to draw fire by articulating clear principles. The result, however, is that while the significance of children's interests is detectable in the cases, their weight is imprecisely defined.

D. Fair Balance: Discussion

While immigration considerations remain both weighty and incontestable, some factors predispose the Court towards finding a violation, and national authorities must carry out a proper assessment of them. Yet the odds remain stacked in favour of the state. In *MA*, the Grand Chamber said that 'one or several' negative factors would make the Court 'reluctant' to find a violation, while 'several' positive factors must be 'cumulatively' present for there to be a violation.[166] *MA* also confirmed that 'precarious' family life, ie most positive obligation cases, will only 'exceptionally' result in an obligation to accept the applicant.[167]

Leaving aside Article 14 discrimination cases, I have identified only two Article 8 family reunification claims that have succeeded without a minor child as part of the family unit. One was *Hasanbasiç*, where a residence permit was not renewed after a brief departure.[168] This was treated as a negative obligation case and the state's reasons for refusal were considered insufficient, given the applicant's many years of lawful residence. The other was *MA v Denmark* in 2021, which concerned a three-year waiting period for family reunification without an individualised assessment for a beneficiary of subsidiary protection.[169] Otherwise, successful claims have all involved minor children either as parties or as members of the family. In all these cases, the Court found a reason why immigration control factors have been weakened. This, it is submitted, is not coincidental. The presence of children and the demands of immigration control are distilled representations of the tension to which the jurisprudence has been subject since the Court first acknowledged that family reunification comes within Article 8: humanity's need for intimacy and care against state sovereignty over immigration. That does not mean that other factors are immaterial, but they are secondary.

[165] *Nunez* (2014) (n 112), Joint Dissenting Opinion of Judges Mijoviç and De Gaetano [1].
[166] *MA* (n 86) [134], [135].
[167] ibid [134].
[168] *Hasanbasiç* (n 102).
[169] *MA* (n 86).

Immigration control and children's interests may be at the core of the fair balance assessment, but the role each plays in relation to the other is unclear. The mitigation of immigration control factors has barely been articulated. It is possible that the Court looks for defects only when it is already sympathetically disposed because children are present. Expediency is suggested, for example, by *Omoregie*, where the majority, who did not find a violation, mentioned only the applicant's lack of status, while the dissenting judge noted that he was permitted to marry in contravention of Norwegian law.[170] In *Rodrigues da Silva and Hoogkamer*, the Court said of the applicant's irregular residence: 'by attaching such paramount importance to [the applicant's irregular status], the authorities may be considered to have indulged in excessive formalism'.[171]

This uniquely strong wording was arguably designed to distract from the new direction taken by the Court in respect of the child's interests. Some judges have criticised the absence of a clear position. In his concurring opinion in *Nunez*, Judge Jubens supported the majority, but wished 'the reasoning of the judgment to be clearer with regard to the impact of the interest of the children and those of the applicant herself'.[172] In *Jeunesse*, the dissenting opinion also criticised the majority for having, in effect, established new principles on the relative weight of children's interests without saying so:

> [I]t must be observed that most of these seemingly fundamental jurisprudential developments are not reflected in the applicable general principles as hitherto formulated by the Court in its case-law and reiterated in the current judgment. They appear only under the surface in the application of these principles to the facts of the case.[173]

If reliance on apparent state failure in implementing controls is used to covertly support an expansion in Article 8 protection for claims involving children, it is likely to interact dynamically with the perceived strength of children's claims. Taken overall, the cases suggest that fathers must make a more compelling case than mothers and that age is a factor. The Berisha children were teenagers, and their expulsion was proportionate despite their parents' efforts to regularise their situation.[174] Mr Antwi had day-to-day care of his child, whereas Ms Nunez had lost parental responsibility due to her imminent expulsion. Both had deceived the authorities for many years, yet the Court found a violation only in respect of Ms Nunez.[175] Ms da Silva had never been lawfully resident and was not the full-time carer of her child, but she succeeded.[176] Mr Omoregie made

[170] *Omoregie* (n 16), Dissenting Opinion of Judge Malinverni joined by Judge Kovler. It is questionable whether the blanket prohibition suggested in the Opinion would comply with Article 12 ECHR; see *O'Donoghue v UK* (2011) 53 EHRR 1.

[171] *Rodrigues da Silva and Hoogkamer* (n 52) [44].

[172] *Nunez* (2011) (n 52), Concurring Opinion of Judge Jubens.

[173] *Jeunesse* (n 161), Dissenting Opinion by Judges Villiger, Mahoney and Silvis [8].

[174] *Berisha* (n 48).

[175] *Antwi* (n 110); *Nunez* (2011) (n 52).

[176] *Rodrigues da Silva and Hoogkamer* (n 52).

his first application for residence while still an asylum seeker, had lived with his daughter and never misled the authorities, but his claim failed.[177]

It is hard to find a totally consistent pattern. Some claims by fathers without immigration status succeed and some by mothers fail.[178] Beliefs both about what children need and what role those needs should play will vary between judges. De Hart has argued that the Court is concerned with particular characteristics of fatherhood and Staiano that single mothers are particularly stigmatised.[179] Each case has numerous variables, making firm conclusions difficult. Did Ms Nunez succeed because of the government's delays and the distress of her children, or did Mr Antwi fail because he and his wife were both of Ghanaian origin and could relocate? How significant was Ms Jeunesse's lost Dutch nationality?

Despite the difficulties of interpretation, however, it does appear that violation findings have predominantly involved young children (*Nunez*, *Zakayev and Safanova*) or older children where particular circumstances obtained (*Turquabo-Tekle*, *Osman*), and fathers where precariousness was absent (*Berrehab*, *Ciliz*) or mothers with some claim to mitigate precariousness (*Rodrigues da Silva and Hoogkamer*, *Nunez*, *Jeunesse*). In this way, the Court has reduced the tension between states' authority over immigration and children's claims. It is a pragmatic approach, but it lacks transparency and full justification.

VI. CONCLUSION

The apparent 'universality' of human rights hides a multitude of exclusions and limitations.[180] The family reunification jurisprudence accepts states' claims to sovereignty over admission and stay as a pre-existing norm. Most claims are filtered out through jurisprudential tests that apply at three points in the decision process: existence of or interference in family life; the margin of appreciation; and the fair balance assessment. Successful cases have two common factors: the family unit contains a minor child; and the state's authority over immigration control has been weakened in some respect. Exceptions have involved claims based on discrimination or, more rarely, forced migration.

The outcome is that family life rights amount to an imprecisely defined right to parent or be parented, with some recognition of the moral and practical significance of childhood, enabling a few children or parents to construct a viable claim. While their interests do not always prevail, the child is still the

[177] *Omoregie* (n 16).

[178] *Zakayev and Safanova v Russia* App no 11870/03 (11 February 2010); *Arvelo Aponte* (n 110); *Alleleh v Norway* App no 569/20 Court (23 June 2022).

[179] De Hart, 'Superdads', 448–67; Staiano, 'Good Mothers, Bad Mothers'.

[180] B Ibhawoh, 'Human Rights for Some: Universal Human Rights, Sexual Minorities, and the Exclusionary Impulse' (2014) 69 *International Journal* 612, 614; see also O Onazi, 'Towards a Subaltern Theory of Human Rights' (2009) 9 *Global Jurist* No 8.

principal beneficiary of rights that are, in theory, universal. By recognising a limited category of 'ideal migrant victims', the Court can legitimise the routine exclusion of other applicants who are taken to have freely accepted the risks of migration.[181] Other problematic issues, such as the narrow meaning of family life or the extensive reach of 'precariousness', therefore receive little attention. Sponsors, whether citizens or residents, are almost invisible; their needs are subordinated to the claims of national immigration laws, and they are, in effect, assimilated to the position of their non-citizen family member.

That states must sometimes ensure that children are not separated from a parent undoubtedly represents progress, but it is still a modest ambition for a universal human right that has, in other contexts, evolved to increase protection from state interference in the intimate and private sphere.[182] The Article 8 right that emerges in this context is not only exiguous, but also does not have a reliable and predictable content. There is no clear state obligation on which applicants can rely. Rather, there are factors which occasionally predispose the Court to a favourable position. The sense that more should be done with Article 8 has been expressed through dissenting and minority opinions, although other opinions advocate a more conservative position; the majority in these cases may, with some reason, say they represent a compromise position. However, those opinions which advocate a more pro-migrant position effectively highlight the extent to which merely the existence of a national boundary limits the effectiveness of Article 8. For instance, on the narrow meaning of family life, Judge Spielmann commented in *Shevanova* that the restrictive case law, which 'appears to be confined to the sphere of expulsions, greatly impoverishes the notion of "family life"'.[183] In *Senchishak*, the dissenting opinion not only regarded the decision as morally mistaken, but observed the factual parallels between, and different outcomes in, that case and the non-immigration decision in *Emonet*.[184]

Dissenting and minority opinions have also challenged the overwhelming weight awarded to government priorities. In *Omoregie*, the joint dissenting opinion found that the applicant's administrative offences were insufficient grounds to break up a family.[185] In *Gül*, Judge Martens observed that:

> [T]he European Court of Human Rights has to ensure, in particular, that State interests do not crush those of an individual, especially in situations where political

[181] CY Furusho, 'The "Ideal Migrant Victim" in Human Rights Courts: Between Vulnerability and Otherness' in M Duggan (ed), *Revisiting the 'Ideal Victim': Developments in Critical Victimology* (Bristol, Bristol University Press, 2009) 123.

[182] Even in the family reunification context, it is arguable that the Court has understated the strength of obligation in international law; see, eg *Biao v Denmark* (2017) 64 EHRR 1, Concurring Opinion of Judge Pinto de Albuquerque [23]–[24].

[183] *Shevanova v Latvia* App no 58822/00 (GC, 15 June 2006), Dissenting Opinion of Judge Spielmann [8].

[184] *Senchishak* (n 59), Dissenting Opinion of Judges Bianku and Kalaydjieva; *Emonet* (n 66).

[185] *Omoregie* (n 16), Dissenting Opinion of Judge Malinverni joined by Judge Kovler [12].

> pressure – such as the growing dislike of immigrants in most member States – may inspire State authorities to harsh decisions.[186]

Perhaps the boldest call yet is in the concurring opinion of Judge Pinto de Albuquerque in the Grand Chamber decision in *Biao*:

> Instead of addressing the issue of family protection within the framework of immigration policy from a principled, standard-setting perspective, the Court has preferred until now to hide behind the pure casuistic treatment of the 'exceptional circumstances' of each case, occasionally resolving the human problem of the applicant, and thus giving the appearance of leaving the general picture of State discretion in this field of law untouched ... The day will come, hopefully sooner rather than later, when the Court will take the simple but courageous step of concluding, in an unequivocal manner, that the right to family life does warrant family reunification.[187]

His was a lone voice, however; the other minority opinions believed the majority in *Biao* had already gone too far in its cautious violation finding. There is no judicial consensus for even the incremental advances in the jurisprudence which have taken place. Even if, as Judge Pinto de Albuquerque suggests, the Court recognises a right to family reunification, it will still be necessary to determine the conditions for its exercise, although such a debate would at least address the correct human rights question: the rights of those who seek the Court's protection. At present, the margin of appreciation means that the state's reasons for refusal are not evaluated, and violation findings are contingent on a narrow range of exceptional personal circumstances. This is so whether family reunification is treated as involving a positive or negative obligation, although the doctrines adopted by the Court reflect not just the margin of appreciation, but the assumption that any obligation on the state is positive in character; the state's right to control immigration is treated as a prior legal fact. The consequence, particularly in the absence of children, is that family life, the concept that Article 8 is designed to protect, becomes an abstract, decontextualised entity that can exist anywhere, and the interests of individuals, whether migrants, citizens or residents, have little independent weight.

It would be wrong, however, to see this as the entire story. Slowly, through the cases, the Court has begun to develop a set of principles that, while they do not yet amount to a right to family reunification, outline the possible contours of such a right – an argument that is developed in chapter eight. For present purposes, the question is the implications of this chapter for an analysis of the UK Supreme Court's Article 8 family reunification jurisprudence. Specific doctrinal issues are relevant; how should family life, 'precariousness', the interests of children, 'insurmountable obstacles' or failure to comply with procedural

[186] *Gül* (n 44); Dissenting Opinion of Judge Martens [15].

[187] *Biao v Denmark* (2017) 64 EHRR 1, Concurring Opinion of Judge Pinto de Albuquerque [29]–[30].

requirements be interpreted? Human rights concepts such as proportionality must be translated into a different legal tradition. But the overarching question is functional. A supranational Court performs a different role to a domestic Court and the extent of the potential difference is magnified by the margin of appreciation that applies only in the supranational context. A domestic court, while subject to its own constraints, would not necessarily exceed its powers by exercising closer scrutiny, with implications for how all these issues may be treated. The issue is whether and how that should happen under the Human Rights Act. As subsequent chapters show, this question was to trouble the Supreme Court for more than a decade.

4

Huang: *Breathing Life into Article 8*

I. INTRODUCTION

THE 2007 JUDGMENT of *Huang* was a defining moment in the UK's history of family reunification and human rights. It was also significant for the overall development of UK human rights law, taking its place with other pivotal human rights cases.[1] This chapter puts it in a different context, seeing it as the start of a remarkable series of cases, discussed over this and the next three chapters, in which the House of Lords/Supreme Court (the Court) first established and then largely retreated from a new approach to human rights family reunification claims. This enabled courts to look more closely at government claims and give more weight to family life under Article 8. While it concerned a technical legal issue – the role of appellate courts and tribunals in assessing the human rights compatibility of immigration decisions – *Huang* also talked about binational families in a new way, including in one of the most humane passages to have appeared in any immigration judgment, and which brought to the fore the nature of the interests at stake:

> Human beings are social animals. They depend on others. Their family, or extended family, is the group on which many people most heavily depend, socially, emotionally and often financially. There comes a time at which, for some, prolonged and unavoidable separation from this group seriously inhibits their ability to live full and fulfilling lives.[2]

Rereading this passage in mid-2022 gives a jolt. It is difficult to imagine it being written now and it invokes a different, more optimistic age when human rights seemed to offer new ways of doing law. It was a decision that came at a particular time and out of a particular context, and must be understood in that light. The next two sections of the chapter explain that context, the battles on human rights and immigration that preceded *Huang*, and why the Court may have been ready to intervene in this way at this point. Section IV identifies the legal problems that *Huang* addressed, and section V sets out the legal findings. Section VI looks more closely at how the judgment was constructed, how the Court brought the human need for family life into the legal assessment and established a new

[1] See, eg M Amos, 'Separating Human Rights Adjudication from Judicial Review – *Huang v Secretary of State for the Home Department and Kashmiri v Secretary of State for the Home Department*' (2007) 6 *European Human Rights Law Review* 679; T Hickman, *Public Law after the Human Rights Act* (Oxford, Hart Publishing, 2010) 128–72.

[2] *Huang and Kashmiri v Secretary of State for the Home Department* [2007] UKHL 11[18].

relationship between the claims of family and of immigration control, as well as how it talked about families subject to immigration control. Section VII looks at the aftermath of *Huang*, particularly at how the lower courts responded. It shows that its reception was not straightforward, reflecting both the difficulties of changing a deep-seated institutional culture and some ambiguities in the judgment itself. Section VIII brings these threads together, summarising both what was remarkable and what was problematic in the decision.

II. THE IMMIGRATION BATTLEGROUND

By the time of the *Huang* judgment, there had already been several tussles between the courts and the government, reflecting tension between human rights values and government priorities in immigration control. There were two aggravating factors: the human rights commitments had been explicitly made by the self-same government through statute, the highest form of UK law, and the government had reacted to previous human rights decisions that went against them by attempting to remove judicial oversight. Underpinning all this were government problems in managing migratory pressures.

In 1997, the Labour Party, led by Tony Blair, won the general election by a decisive majority, ending 18 consecutive years of Conservative government. The new government unofficially designated itself 'New Labour' and presented itself as a modernising force in politics, a contrast to both the previous government's right wing Thatcherite ideology, and the trade union militancy and state interventions associated with 'Old Labour'. Its election manifesto included a commitment to giving citizens 'statutory rights to enforce their human rights in the UK courts', and to 'lead' in Europe and internationally, including through advocacy for human rights. On immigration, it promised 'firm control over immigration', with applications decided 'speedily and fairly'. It also promised some liberalisation, notably changes to the notorious 'primary purpose' rule, which had enabled the refusal of thousands of spouses from former Commonwealth countries.[3] The primary purpose rule was removed shortly after the 1997 election, and there followed passage of the Human Rights Act in 1998 and the extension of race discrimination laws to public authorities in 2000, including the immigration service unless specifically exempted.[4]

In contrast to previous Conservative administrations, the Labour government embraced the benefits of immigration, at least in its early years, adopting a positive tone and admitting increased numbers of migrants for work, study and family life.[5] From 2000, it became easier to obtain a work permit, and the first

[3] Labour Party Manifesto, 1997, 'New Labour Because Britain Deserves Better', www.labourparty.org.uk/manifestos/1997/; for a detailed analysis of the primary purpose rule, see H Wray, *Regulating Marriage Migration into the UK* (Abingdon, Routledge, 2011) 56–68, 88–102, 122–31.

[4] Race Relations (Amendment) Act 2000.

[5] For a discussion of the non-family migration policies, see W Somerville, *Immigration under New Labour* (Bristol, Policy Press, 2010).

points-based schemes were implemented. When 10 states joined the EU in 2004, the UK was one of only three Member States (alongside Sweden and Italy) that allowed immediate labour market access without transitional controls. There were further liberalising changes to the family route, including better provision for domestic abuse survivors, unmarried and same-sex partners, and couples who had lived together abroad, reflecting 'modern' practices and mores.[6] The immigration regime was 'one of the most expansive in Europe'.[7]

However, ambivalence was soon evident. The government was willing to acknowledge the benefits of migration, but it also had little choice as migratory pressures were already increasing; the first increases in work permits had been in 1995 under the previous regime.[8] Not all this immigration was of the desired kind. The number of irregular migrants increased, possibly to more than half a million.[9] Asylum applications grew from 32,500 in 1997 to 84,130 in 2002.[10] In the meantime, public support for immigration was cautious and later became hostile. Even in 1995, approximately two-thirds of the population believed immigration should be reduced, and this increased to nearly three-quarters by 2003.[11] The salience of immigration as a political issue increased dramatically from the late 1990s, peaking around 2007.[12] Delays became endemic; resolving asylum claims routinely took months or years, and those who did not meet Refugee Convention criteria might have a human rights remedy now available via the domestic courts.[13] Conscious that public concern risked undermining wider trust in political institutions, the government aimed to show that it was in control, its aim becoming '*the comprehensive management of all forms of migration*, whether forced or voluntary' (emphasis in original).[14]

In the early 2000s, therefore, the government introduced the concept of 'managed migration', including a 'five-year plan' and 'new asylum model'. The result was constant organisational, legal and regulatory change. Six immigration statutes were passed between 1999 and 2009, and there were continuous changes to the Immigration Rules. There were, for example, more than 25

[6] H Wray, *A Stranger in the Home* (Abingdon, Routledge, 2011) 158–59.

[7] E Consterdine, 'Managed Migration under Labour: Organised Public, Party Ideology and Policy Change' (2015) 41 *Journal of Ethnic and Migration Studies* 1433.

[8] J Salt, 'International Migration and the UK. Annual Report of the UK SOPEMI Correspondent to the OECD' (London, UCL Migration Research Unit, 2009) 92.

[9] IR Gordon, K Scanlon, T Travers, and CME Whitehead, 'Economic Impact on the London and UK Economy of an Earned Regularisation of Irregular Migrants to the UK' (London, Greater London Authority, 2009).

[10] Somerville, *Immigration under New Labour*, 65.

[11] Somerville, *Immigration under New Labour*, 132–33.

[12] R Ford, W Jennings and W Somerville, 'Public Opinion, Responsiveness and Constraint: Britain's Three Immigration Policy Regimes' (2015) 41 *Journal of Ethnic and Migration Studies* 1391.

[13] Convention relating to the Status of Refugees (adopted 28 July 1951, entered into force 22 April 1954) 189 UNTS 137.

[14] D Flynn, 'New Borders, New Management: The Dilemmas of Modern Immigration Policy' (2005) 28 *Ethnic and Racial Studies* 463; L McLaren, *Immigration and Perceptions of National Political Systems in Europe* (Oxford, Oxford University Press, 2015).

just between the start of 2004 and the end of 2006. The government wanted to welcome economic migrants, combat irregular migration, reduce asylum claims, offer reassurance on security and promote the integration of the UK's ethnic minorities, objectives that often collided. The titles of White Papers published in this period reflect the ambivalence: *Secure Borders, Safe Haven: Integration with Diversity in Modern Britain* (2002) or *Controlling our Borders: Making Migration Work for Britain* (2005).[15] The ordering is significant; the safety of the resident population and control over admission were preconditions for refuge, integration and 'making migration work'. Security concerns now prevailed over the presumed benefits of migration and international legal obligations, and, during this period, the government maintained, strengthened and introduced new security-oriented controls.[16]

The government also suffered some significant judicial defeats under the Human Rights Act. In *A v SSHD* in 2004, the House of Lords found that the indefinite detention of foreign terror suspects discriminated by nationality or immigration status and breached Articles 5 and 14 of the European Convention on Human Rights (ECHR).[17] Legislation passed in 2002 required that financial support be refused to an asylum seeker who had not made a claim 'as soon as reasonably practicable' after arrival.[18] It was applied to those who delayed only a few days or even hours before making their asylum claim, leaving them without resources or accommodation.[19] In 2005, in *Limbuela*, the House of Lords found that where this caused enforced destitution, it would breach Article 3 ECHR.[20] This judicial brake was a source of frustration for the government. Although he refrained from commenting adversely on higher court decisions, David Blunkett, then the Home Secretary, said in 2003 of lower court judgments on the asylum provisions:

> Frankly, I'm personally fed up with having to deal with a situation where Parliament debates issues and the judges then overturn them. We were aware of the circumstances, we did mean what we said and, on behalf of the British people, we are going to implement it.[21]

Blunkett expressed his frustration again on other occasions, while media outlets echoed and amplified his sentiments.[22] Concern went beyond the Human Rights

[15] Home Office, *Secure Borders, Safe Haven: Integration with Diversity in Modern Britain* (White Paper, Cm 5387, 2002); HM Government/Home Office, *Controlling Our Borders: Making Migration Work for Britain – Five Year Strategy for Asylum and Immigration* (White Paper, Cm 6472, 2005).

[16] Somerville, *Immigration under New Labour*, 39–50; J Hampshire, 'Disembedding Liberalism? Immigration Politics and Security since 9/11' in TE Givens, GP Freeman and D Leal (eds), *Immigration Policy and Security: US, European and Commonwealth Perspectives* (Abingdon, Routledge, 2009) 109–29; N Yuval-Davis, F Anthias, and E Kofman, 'Secure Borders, Safe Haven and the Gendered Politics of Belonging: Beyond Social Cohesion' (2005) 28 *Ethnic and Racial Studies* 513.

[17] *A and others v SSHD* [2004] UKHL 56.

[18] Nationality, Immigration and Asylum Act 2002, s 55.

[19] S Chakrabarti, 'Rights and Rhetoric: The Politics of Asylum and Human Rights Culture in the United Kingdom' (2005) 32 *Journal of Law and Society* 131.

[20] *R (on the application of Limbuela) v SSHD* [2005] UKHL 66.

[21] A Travis, 'Blunkett to Fight Asylum Ruling' *The Guardian* (London, 20 February 2003).

[22] R Rawlings, 'Review, Revenge and Retreat' (2005) 68 *MLR* 378, 393–94.

Act to incorporate long-standing resistance to 'common law constitutionalism'.[23] It was not human rights, per se, that were the problem, but the assertion of authority by the judiciary. Rawlings summarised the overall sentiment through his juxtaposition of representative quotations: 'If public policy can always be overridden by individual challenge through the courts, then democracy itself is under threat.' It is 'time for judges to learn their place'. They do not 'have the right to override the will of the House, our democracy or the role of Members of Parliament in deciding the rules'.[24]

In late 2003, a new Immigration Bill included a clause that ousted the supervisory powers of the courts in asylum and immigration decisions, whether on human rights or other grounds, citing a steep increase in asylum judicial reviews and appeals.[25] While there was some judicial sympathy for the litigation burden, there was a forceful reaction to the ouster clause on rule-of-law grounds from lawyers, ex-judges and parliamentarians, including the former Lord Chancellor Lord Mackay. As Rawlings observed, a Labour government committed both to human rights and protection of the vulnerable could not justify its position, and the clause was abandoned.[26]

By the time of *Huang*, therefore, there had already been skirmishes between the judiciary and the government over asylum, immigration and human rights, and perhaps a sense also that the government could not have it all ways. It could not take credit for human rights legislation and expect that legislation to be applied without inconvenience to them. The price for legitimising painful executive decisions by reference to human rights norms was shared authority with judges and, while the judiciary might cooperate with such outsourcing, it would do so on its own terms. The ouster clause episode raised the stakes, showing the government was ready both to limit judicial autonomy and to back down. It is against that background that the right to family life became the next judicial flashpoint. This was not a surprise; family reunification had become a fraught question.

During the early years of the New Labour government, British citizens and residents continued to choose overseas spouses in significant numbers, while others married irregular migrants and asylum seekers who were already present. Concern crystallised around two factors: fears of abuse of the family route by opportunistic and manipulative migrants, and the presumed integration deficits and problematic marriage practices of some, principally South Asian, minority communities.[27] Already in 1998, a government White Paper mentioned 'ample evidence to show that large numbers of bogus marriages are being contracted

[23] ibid 368, 380.
[24] ibid 397.
[25] ibid 384–96.
[26] ibid 403–08.
[27] For a more detailed discussion, see H Wray, *Regulating Marriage Migration into the UK: A Stranger in the Home* (first published Farnham, Ashgate, 2011, Abingdon, Routledge, 2016) 139–54.

in the UK every year'.[28] The government began to assimilate sham marriages to wider national security; the 2002 *Secure Borders, Safe Haven* White Paper even had a chapter headed 'Marriage/family visits and war criminals'.[29] In that White Paper, the epithet 'bogus' appeared nine times and 'sham' appeared twice, always in relation to marriage and with an explicit connection to organised crime and corruption.[30] The problem was presented as widespread despite the absence of reliable evidence. While some sham marriages may have taken place, it is likely that the actual number was smaller than suggested and the sham marriage itself remained an ambiguous and elusive concept.[31]

The other factor was the perception that some practices, particularly involving young or arranged marriages in families of South Asian descent, inhibited social cohesion and successful incorporation. To avoid overt stigmatisation, governments often adopted an apparently paternalistic stance, expressing concern, for example, for women without access to English language or work opportunities, or who were victims of forced marriage.[32] The 'immigrant woman' was a 'troubled figure', suffering from the oppressive and archaic cultural practices of her family and passing on these values and other disadvantages, educational, social and cultural, to her children.[33] Some of these issues, forced marriage in particular, were of real social and political concern, but there was a tendency to generalise, suggesting a wider hostility to arranged marriage. Ann Cryer MP, for example, connected forged documents, forced marriage, sham marriage, chain migration, first-cousin marriage, lack of integration and educational underachievement with binational marriages in her constituency.[34] A less scattergun but still assertive tone was evident in the 2002 White Paper:

> While embracing the diverse nature of our society, there are certain norms in relation to marriage in this country which we recognise as acceptable. For example … we do not recognise polygamous households. Neither will we tolerate forced marriages. A man or woman must be free to decide whether to enter into marriage.[35]

[28] Home Office, *Fairer, Faster, Firmer: A Modern Approach to Immigration and Asylum*, (Cmnd 4018, 1998) para 11.4.

[29] Home Office, *Secure Borders, Safe Haven: Integration with Diversity in Modern Britain*, (Cm 5387, 2002) ch 7.

[30] ibid 18, 100.

[31] There is a reference to 700 reports of suspicious marriages in a one-year period, but it is not clear how many were eventually established as bogus: ibid 100; H Wray, 'An Ideal Husband? Marriages of Convenience, Moral Gatekeeping and Immigration to the UK' (2006) 8 *European Journal of Migration and Law* 303; H Wray, 'The "Pure" Relationship, Sham Marriages and Immigration Control' in J Miles, R Probert and P Mody (eds), *Marriage Rites and Rights* (Oxford, Hart Publishing, 2015) 141–65.

[32] I Gedalof, 'Unhomely Homes: Women, Family and Belonging in UK Discourses of Migration and Asylum' (2007) 33 *Journal of Ethnic and Migration Studies* 77; H Wray, 'Moulding the Migrant Family' (2009) 29 *Legal Studies* 592.

[33] I Gedalof, 'Unhomely Homes: Women, Family and Belonging in UK Discourses of Migration and Asylum' (2007) 89–90; Wray, 'Moulding the Migrant Family', 592.

[34] Wray, 'Moulding the Migrant Family', 602.

[35] Home Office, *Secure Borders, Safe Haven*, 19.

In a controversial passage of the Executive Summary, David Blunkett, then Home Secretary, said: 'We also believe there is a discussion to be had within those communities that continue the practice of arranged marriages as to whether more of these could be undertaken within the settled community here.'[36]

The government thus saw both a need and a right to intervene in marriages with an overseas partner, and there were numerous legislative and rule changes. New notice requirements for marriage and a duty on marriage registrars to report suspected sham marriages were enacted in 1999.[37] In 2002–03, the 'probationary period' before settlement increased from one to two years, and the minimum age of entry and sponsorship was increased to 18, followed by a further rise to 21 in 2008.[38] From 2003, partners in the UK without long-term leave could no longer 'switch' status in-country, but had to leave and apply for re-entry.[39] In 2004, a 'certificates of approval' scheme placed drastic restrictions on the rights of non-nationals to marry, making it effectively impossible for those without long-term immigration status.[40] As the next two chapters show, many of these measures were challenged for human rights compatibility and ended up before the Supreme Court.

III. A SENSE OF JUDICIAL PURPOSE

The decision in *Huang* and those discussed in the next two chapters gave the impression of a Court committed to ensuring that family life received due recognition in the immigration context. This reflected wider changes in the Court's role. In 2007, at the time of *Huang*, the Court was still officially the Appellate Committee of the House of Lords and was institutionally attached to the legislature.[41] However, legislation creating the Supreme Court had been passed in 2005 and, while it would not be inaugurated until 2009, observers anticipated a different kind of court emerging, one that would 'take on some, though by no means all, of the characteristics of a constitutional court'.[42] But the House of Lords was already more 'constitutional' in character, not only due to the

[36] ibid 18.

[37] Immigration and Asylum Act 1999, s 24.

[38] Wray, 'Moulding the Migrant Family', 605–6.

[39] ibid 605–06.

[40] Asylum and Immigration (Treatment of Claimants, etc) Act 2004, ss 19–25. The scheme was later found to be a breach of Art 12 (right to marry and found a family) and Art 14 ECHR (non-discrimination), and was eventually abolished; *Baiai v SSHD* [2008] UKHL 53; *O'Donoghue v United Kingdom* App no 34848/07, (2011) 53 EHRR 1; see Wray, 'The "Pure" Relationship, Sham Marriages and Immigration Control', 141–66.

[41] Darbyshire describes a Law Lord dictating his judgment from his rooms within Parliament against the background of a TV screen relaying parliamentary proceedings: P Darbyshire, *Sitting in Judgment* (Oxford, Hart Publishing, 2011), 396.

[42] Vernon Bogdanor speaking in 2006 and quoted in K Malleson, 'The Evolving Role of the UK Supreme Court' [2011] *PL* 754, 755.

Human Rights Act, but also because of increased constitutional legislation and public law litigation. The change to a Supreme Court did not cause but reflected the evolving judicial role; a Supreme Court was 'a more accurate reflection of the Court's true position and independence within the British constitutional system'.[43] By 2007 and *Huang*, the Court would already have been conscious of an increased constitutional focus to its work.

If the judiciary was already more central to resolving issues of social as well as private significance, then to what purpose? The Court chose its own workload. It heard *Huang* and the other Article 8 cases because it considered them important, and this would have reflected, at least in part, some personal priorities. Lord Bingham, who led the *Huang* panel, saw the protection of fundamental rights as inherent to the rule of law.[44] He noted 'a heightened sense of the judges' duty to respect and defend fundamental principles' and said it was 'desirable that judges should on occasion give decisions that are deeply unwelcome to the powers that be'.[45] He also said:

> [I]t is not the ordinary, financially secure majority for whom human rights protection really matters. It is the vulnerable and outcast members of society who stand to gain – children, mental patients, immigrants, asylum seekers, despised racial minorities, prisoners and criminals.[46]

This sense of law's potential to hold government to account sat alongside a keen sense of the limits to judicial authority; not every injustice could be remedied judicially, and Lord Bingham distinguished between executive and legislative acts, but where there was the power to act, including under the Human Rights Act, judges should not shirk that responsibility. *Huang* and the other cases discussed in this book are consistent with the constitutional principle of parliamentary sovereignty but, within those limits, there is a vision of law that speaks to a deeper moral purpose to which judges may contribute.

Lord Bingham was not alone. Lady Hale strongly supported a human rights culture, as did Lord Hoffmann, albeit more cautiously.[47] Lady Hale's family law background would have sharpened her appreciation of why family life matters. She had already noted that Article 8 cases involved not only a foreign national, but also 'other members of his core family group', and that interference was

[43] ibid 755.

[44] T Bingham, *The Rule of Law* (London, Penguin Books, 2010).

[45] T Bingham, *Lives of the Law: Selected Essays and Speeches* (Oxford, Oxford University Press, 2011) 146.

[46] T Bingham, 'The Human Rights Act' (2010) 6 *European Human Rights Law Review* 568, 575; see also T Bingham, 'The European Convention on Human Rights: Time to Incorporate' in T Bingham (ed), *The Business of Judging: Selected Essays and Speeches: 1985–1999* (Oxford, Oxford University Press, 2000) 131–40.

[47] Bingham, 'The European Convention on Human Rights',131–40; Bingham, *The Rule of Law*, 67–68; J Rozenberg, 'Judges Would Regret Human Rights Act Repeal, Warns Lady Hale' *The Guardian* (London, 14 March 2013); E Metcalfe, 'The Strange Jurisprudence of Lord Hoffmann: Human Rights and the International Judge' (2009) 2 *UCL Human Rights Review* 35; J Jowell, 'Judicial Deference: Servility, Civility or Institutional Capacity' [2000] 592.

directly caused by the UK's government's acts and omissions.[48] Each member of the *Huang* panel had sat on the panels in either *A v UK* on indefinite detention or in *Limbuela* on asylum seeker support, while Lord Bingham and Baroness Hale had been present in both. Finding against the government on immigration matters using human rights was not new to them.

IV. THE LEGAL PROBLEM ADDRESSED BY *HUANG*

Huang altered an approach towards human rights in immigration set early in the evolution of domestic human rights. *Mahmood*, decided by the Court of Appeal in 2000 shortly after the Human Rights Act came into effect, concerned a failed asylum seeker from Pakistan married to a British citizen and the father of British citizen children but who did not qualify for in-country regularisation.[49] He claimed that his anticipated removal would breach Article 8.[50] The issue for the Court of Appeal was the standard of scrutiny by the courts of the removal decision. Laws LJ acknowledged that the conventional judicial review standard, which required a decision to be irrational or procedurally defective before it could be overturned, was too 'exiguous'.[51] Instead, he followed other pre-Human Rights Act jurisprudence which held that, where fundamental rights were in issue, the appropriate standard was 'anxious scrutiny'.[52] Using that approach, he found against the applicant.

Anxious scrutiny was a relatively demanding standard, a requirement that there be a 'reasoned justification' for any decision, but it was concerned with the decision-making process, not its substance.[53] When applied to human rights proportionality, it required decision-makers to have undertaken the fair balance assessment with sufficient care, and to have considered all facts and competing considerations. Provided that was the case, the actual decision remained one for the decision-maker to make. A perverse decision would suggest that insufficient care has been exercised and courts might consider the weight accorded to a particular factor to be unreasonable, but the decision-maker retained a 'margin of discretion' and the court would not undo the decision only because they would have struck the balance differently.[54]

Although anxious scrutiny was more demanding than traditional judicial review, it still required decision-makers to act unreasonably before decisions could be overturned. It applied both to judicial review applications, which

[48] *R (Razgar) v SSHD* [2003] EWCA Civ 840 [43]–[44].
[49] *R (on the application of Mahmood) v SSHD* [2001] 1 WLR 840.
[50] ibid [28]–[30].
[51] ibid [18].
[52] ibid [18]–[19]. The standard of 'anxious scrutiny' had previously been invoked by the House of Lords in complex asylum cases: *Bugdaycay v SSHD* [1987] AC 514.
[53] For a discussion of anxious scrutiny, see P Craig, 'Judicial Review and Anxious Scrutiny: Foundations, Evolution and Application' [2015] *PL* 60.
[54] See *Samaroo v SSHD* [2001] EWCA Civ 1139.

ensured the legality of government action, and appeals, which were concerned with the decision itself, curtailing the latter's effectiveness.[55] It did not permit enquiry into the public interest, as immigration policy was considered an 'area of discretion' where the government could operate without intervention by the court, a form of 'spatial deference'.[56] It followed that the government's view of whether refusal was proportionate, as expressed in the Immigration Rules, would almost always prevail and only 'exceptional' cases could succeed. Alongside this restrictive finding, *Mahmood* also suggested that refusal would only be disproportionate if there were insurmountable obstacles to return, basing this on the criterion of the European Court of Human Rights (ECtHR, Strasbourg Court or Strasbourg), even though it functioned at Strasbourg as just one factor, not a precondition.[57]

In consequence, it was almost impossible to win an Article 8 claim; insurmountable obstacles were almost never found and very few cases were sufficiently 'exceptional'. Refusals made painful reading. The migrant, usually male and resident without authorisation, may have been a father caring for a disabled child, a husband working long hours to support his family or a stepfather said by a psychiatrist to have given stepchildren their first experience of familial stability.[58] Yet, provided the relevant factors had been considered, removal, even if it would destabilise the family or lead to years of separation, was proportionate. It was only the government's own egregious failings that might allow an occasional case to succeed.[59]

Outside the immigration arena, the House of Lords had begun to find anxious scrutiny insufficiently rigorous in human rights cases, saying in 2001:

> Assessing proportionality requires more than determining whether a decision is within the range of rational or reasonable decisions but an assessment of whether the decision-maker has struck the correct balance and therefore, if necessary, of the relative weight to be accorded to relevant interests and considerations.[60]

In 2006, it said: 'The domestic court must now make a value judgment, an evaluation, by reference to the circumstances prevailing at the relevant time … Proportionality must be judged objectively, by the court.'[61]

It was still not clear if the House was moving to a full assessment of human rights or just an even more intense anxious scrutiny review, but it was clear that

[55] *Blessing Edore v SSHD* [2003] EWCA Civ 736.

[56] *Mahmood* (n 49) [38] per Lord Phillips; *Samaroo* (n 54); For a discussion, see G Clayton, 'Prediction or Precondition? The House of Lords judgment in *Huang and Kashmiri*' (2007) 21 *Journal of Immigration Asylum and Nationality Law* 311.

[57] *Mahmood* (n 49) [55]; see also ch 3, s VA.

[58] Wray, *Regulating Marriage Migration into the UK: A Stranger in the Home*, 181, 189; H Wray, '"A Thing Apart": Controlling Male Family Migration to the United Kingdom' (2015) 18 *Men and Masculinities* 424.

[59] For example, *Shala v SSHD* [2003] EWCA Civ 233; *Abbas v SSHD* [2005] EWCA Civ 992.

[60] *R (on the application of Daly) v Secretary of State for the Home Department* [2001] UKHL 26 [27] (the passage was obiter and therefore not binding, but would be influential).

[61] *R (Begum) v Governors of Denbigh High School* [2006] UKHL 15 [30] (Lord Bingham).

the *Mahmood* version of anxious scrutiny was considered unsuitable for these non-immigration human rights applications. Even so, there was little impact on immigration, where the conditions of exceptionality and insurmountable obstacles were an almost complete block to success.

Meanwhile, other problems were emerging with the *Mahmood* anxious scrutiny test. When facts were undisputed and all relevant considerations had been addressed, the only issue was the fair balance assessment, and the original decision was upheld even if the judge might personally have decided it differently. When, however, there was disagreement as to factual findings or the decision-maker had failed to address all relevant issues, the judge had to undertake their own fair balance assessment and could substitute their own view of where the balance fell, resulting in more intense judicial scrutiny.[62]

By the time *Huang* came to the House of Lords, therefore, there were two legal approaches to judicial human rights assessments, one in immigration and one elsewhere. There was lack of clarity as to what the approach outside immigration was and an inconsistent approach within immigration. The dominant version of anxious scrutiny in immigration cases excluded entire areas of government activity from scrutiny and made it almost impossible for an Article 8 claim to succeed. It is easy to see why the House of Lords saw a need for clarification.

V. THE LEGAL FINDINGS IN *HUANG*

The specific legal issue in *Huang* was whether, in deciding appeals, courts were confined to anxious scrutiny, following *Mahmood*, or whether they should make their own assessment of human rights compatibility. The case therefore concerned interpretation of the relevant appeals legislation, a technical issue, but the outcome would be momentous for ensuring independent judicial scrutiny of the human rights compatibility of government decisions.

The *Huang* judgment established three legal principles:

1 Appellate courts should reach their own decision on human rights compatibility in an appeal. They were not confined to reviewing the decision under appeal.
2 In assessing proportionality, courts must allocate 'appropriate weight' to legislative and executive views, but this was part of the normal judicial function and there was no additional process under the doctrine of 'deference'.
3 The provisions of the Immigration Rules were only the starting point for assessing human rights compliance, so cases did not have to be 'exceptional' to succeed on human rights grounds.

[62] I Macdonald, 'ECHR Article 8: Bringing the UK Courts Back in Step with Strasbourg' (2008) 22 *Journal of Immigration Asylum and Nationality Law* 293, 298; A Vaughan, 'The Tribunal's New Role in Article 8 Statutory Appeals' (2007) 21 *Journal of Immigration Asylum and Nationality Law* 129.

The findings were interconnected. As courts would now reach their own decision on human rights compatibility (1), they needed a method for assessing the original decision, and the Court gave guidance in (2). (3) is the natural consequence of (2). As the government's view on Article 8 compliance did not automatically merit greater respect from courts, the Article 8 assessment should be approached with an open mind. While the Immigration Rules were relevant, a decision under the Rules was 'the point at which to begin, not end, consideration of the claim under Article 8'.[63] Hence, the Article 8 assessment should be an open evaluation, and that precluded any test of exceptionality.[64]

In rejecting a specific doctrine of deference, the Court risked being accused of moving into the policy arena and of contradicting its previous position.[65] It addressed this by distinguishing between decisions on policy, made by government, and decisions on human rights compatibility, made by judges. An appellate court would not decide the merits of a policy, or even of a decision made under the policy, but only whether that decision was human rights compliant.[66] Doing that required some assessment of the policy, however, in order to assess the strength of the public interest and whether interference in family life was justified.[67] The question was whether the Court would accept the government's assessment of the strength of the public interest or make its own, and it was here that the question of deference became relevant. The Court rejected the tortuous debates that had evidently been aired in the hearing, as well as in the lower courts and academic literature, in favour of a more straightforward approach:

> We think, with respect, that there has been a tendency, both in the arguments addressed to the courts and in the judgments of the courts, to complicate and mystify what is not, in principle, a hard task to define, however difficult the task is, in practice, to perform.[68]

In making a proportionality assessment, an appellate body must establish the facts with care, and consider and weigh the points in favour of refusal, with particular reference to Article 8(2) factors. According to the Court, this was

> performance of the ordinary judicial task of weighing up the competing considerations on each side and according appropriate weight to the judgment of a person with responsibility for a given subject matter and access to special sources of knowledge and advice.[69]

[63] *Huang* (n 2) [6].
[64] ibid [6]; Clayton, 'Prediction or Precondition? The House of Lords judgment in *Huang and Kashmiri*'.
[65] *Daly* (n 60) [32].
[66] *Huang* (n 2) [13]; see also A Brady, *Proportionality and Deference Under the UK Human Rights Act: An Institutionally Sensitive Approach* (Cambridge, Cambridge University Press, 2012).
[67] *Huang* (n 2) [13].
[68] ibid [14].
[69] ibid [16].

'Weighing' and 'weight' both appear in this passage, but they are used in different ways; the decision-maker's judgment as to the public interest must be given 'appropriate' weight, but deciding how the public interest should be weighed against other considerations, notably the interference in family life, was a judicial task.

The Court saw the public interest as a matter of ordinary judgment rather than one requiring specialist knowledge:

> There will, in almost any case, be certain general considerations to bear in mind: the general administrative desirability of applying known rules if a system of immigration control is to be workable, predictable, consistent and fair as between one applicant and another; the damage to good administration and effective control if a system is perceived by applicants internationally to be unduly porous, unpredictable or perfunctory; the need to discourage non-nationals admitted to the country temporarily from believing that they can commit serious crimes and yet be allowed to remain; the need to discourage fraud, deception and deliberate breaches of the law; and so on.[70]

These immigration control factors would only form part of the assessment. The parties' personal circumstances should also be assessed: it was 'important that the facts are explored, and summarised in the decision, with care, since they will always be important and often decisive'.[71] The Court also said: 'Much will depend on the individual circumstances: the age, health and vulnerability of the applicant, the character of family relations, cultural factors and conditions in the country of origin.'[72]

This suggested an enquiry that was concerned with the impact on the individual and went beyond the state-oriented perspective emerging from the Strasbourg Court at that time, which mentioned only 'insurmountable obstacles' and the extent to which family was 'ruptured' on the side of the migrant.[73] The result was that the fair balance assessment was more evenly weighted than in the Strasbourg context:

> The ultimate question [is whether refusal] in circumstances where the life of the family cannot reasonably be expected to be enjoyed elsewhere, taking full account of all considerations weighing in favour of the refusal, prejudices the family life of the applicant in a manner sufficiently serious to amount to a breach of the fundamental right protected by article 8. If the answer to this question is affirmative, the refusal is unlawful and the authority must so decide.[74]

It followed that the exceptionality test was incorrect. The Court said:

> It is not necessary that the appellate immigration authority … need ask in addition whether the case meets a test of exceptionality. The suggestion that it should is

[70] ibid [16].
[71] ibid [15].
[72] ibid [18].
[73] In eg *Rodrigues da Silva and Hoogkamer v Netherlands* (2007) 44 EHRR 34, which had been issued in January 2006.
[74] *Huang* (n 2) [20].

> based on an observation of Lord Bingham in *Razgar* above, para 20. He was there expressing an expectation … that the number of claimants not covered by the Rules and supplementary directions but entitled to succeed under article 8 would be a very small minority. That is still his expectation. But he was not purporting to lay down a legal test.

While the sense of the Court's words is reasonably straightforward, these two passages proved difficult to apply in practice. The second, in particular, caused problems: there was no longer a test of exceptionality, but only a very few cases would succeed. This was, in the words of Gina Clayton, a 'prediction not a pre-condition', but it meant that lower court judges now had to decide which of the 'very small minority' of cases should now succeed without applying a criterion of exceptionality, a problem discussed further in the next section of this chapter. Even so, the passages marked a major departure in Article 8 family reunification cases, and they were unique at that point for their recognition that family life should carry significant weight in Article 8 family reunification decisions. It was clearly an intentional reorientation, and the next section of this chapter shows that the Court's commitment to the human right to family life was expressed not only as a legal argument, but through the language and structure of the judgment.

VI. 'HUMAN BEINGS ARE SOCIAL ANIMALS'

The *Huang* judgment was a single composite judgment, a relatively uncommon occurrence and one that Lord Bingham, who led the Court, did not usually support unless there was a particular need for legal certainty.[75] It was also quite short, at 22 paragraphs, and written in a direct, unequivocal style. The aim was to assert judicial autonomy and expertise in human rights matters, reject automatic deference to government and establish a consistent but flexible approach to proportionality that could apply across the entire human rights spectrum. To this extent, *Huang* can be understood as part of a broader argument about how courts should exercise their powers under the Human Rights Act. That does not, however, explain the way in which the House of Lords framed this particular decision. This section considers these aspects further, looking first at how the Court articulated its role as a domestic human rights court and secondly at how it prioritised and expressed the value of family life.

The Court in *Huang* barely discussed the Strasbourg jurisprudence and did not seek to justify the principles it set out in terms of alignment with Strasbourg; this was about domestic law and domestic human rights. The only Strasbourg case cited was the foundational decision in *Abdulaziz*, already two decades old at that point, while 12 domestic cases were mentioned. There were

[75] A Paterson, *Final Judgment: The Last Law Lords and the Supreme Court* (Oxford, Hart Publishing, 2013) 101–02.

later suggestions that *Huang* went beyond Strasbourg principles, which were narrower at that time than now (this was prior to decisions such as *Jeunesse* or *Nunez*), and it is true that the fair balance assessment was more generously cast than the Strasbourg equivalent.[76] However, it is arguably more accurate to say not that the Court departed from Strasbourg principles, but that it approached them from a different direction.

The test of whether the family can 'reasonably be expected' to live abroad suggested a test that was more generous than 'insurmountable obstacles', but 'insurmountable obstacles' were never a criterion in the Strasbourg cases and the Strasbourg Court had found that an obligation might arise to allow admission as 'the most adequate means for the applicants to develop family life', a condition that was closer to a reasonableness test.[77] Precariousness was also not explicitly mentioned by the Court in *Huang*, although it had already appeared in the Strasbourg cases, but it was implicit in the references to considerations in favour of refusal and to the damage caused by unduly porous controls. Strasbourg principles were therefore present, but they were expressed less absolutely. Consistent with this, the Court rejected a test of exceptionality, and the judgment suggested a more fine-grained and closer analysis than was usual in Strasbourg. This was congruent with the Court's function. The Strasbourg Court's supervisory function assumed that signatory states had their own mechanisms for ensuring human rights were fully assessed and that domestic actors were better placed to understand the detailed factors involved. Judicial engagement in that process had been authorised by parliament through the Human Rights Act and the Court therefore applied Strasbourg principles in a domestic context.

This domestic perspective was evident also in the discussion of states' right to control admission. At paragraph 5, the Court recognised the power of sovereign states to control migration but departed from the conventional Strasbourg formula by saying:

> [T]he power to admit, exclude and expel aliens was among the earliest and most widely recognised powers of the sovereign state. But it seems unlikely that any developed state has ever enforced, or sought to enforce, a blanket rule to exclude the entry of all foreign nationals. Some exceptions were always made ...[78]

This had a different emphasis to the wording used by the Strasbourg Court in *Abdulaziz* and elsewhere: 'as a matter of well-established international law and subject to its treaty obligations, a State has the right to control the entry of non-nationals into its territory'.[79]

The Strasbourg formulation enabled state immigration controls to be presented as deriving from a pre-existing and superior legal source upon which

[76] For more, see ch 3, s V.

[77] *Tuquabo Tekle and Others v The Netherlands* [2005] ECHR 803, [47]; also: *Sen v Netherlands* (2001) 36 EHRR 81.

[78] *Huang* (n 2) [5].

[79] *Abdulaziz Cabales and Balkandali v United Kingdom* (1985) 7 EHRR 471 [67].

applicants sought to encroach, although state sovereignty over admission was a political rather than a legal principle.[80] In its formulation, the Court in *Huang* ensured that the opposite order prevailed. It did not mention international law, as it was irrelevant; within the UK's dualist legal system, statute law is the supreme source of law. Instead, it acknowledged the state's power to control admission, but saw it as a concrete exercise of power whose boundaries were subject to the rule of law. The competing legal constraints were to be found in the Human Rights Act, a statute based on obligations in international law, and the Immigration Rules, administrative rules with weak democratic credentials. The superior democratic status of the Human Rights Act was further emphasised when the Court said that, through the Human Rights Act, 'Parliament not only enabled but required the Convention Rights … to be given effect as a matter of domestic law in this country'.[81] In other words, the Court had an obligation to use the statutory powers endowed by the Act to apply human rights values domestically.

While the *Huang* judgment may therefore be justified as having paid due account to the Strasbourg cases and as acting in accordance with the powers granted by parliament, it also displayed an energetic commitment to human rights values and to the role of the courts in ensuring these were observed. Marie Dembour has written about the 'Strasbourg reversal', where, in contrast to the usual ordering of priorities, the Strasbourg Court made human rights an exception to state sovereignty over immigration control in its Article 8 jurisprudence.[82] After the Human Rights Act, domestic courts had enthusiastically adopted the Strasbourg reversal, with the result that Article 8 had almost no impact on immigration. *Huang* reversed, or at least neutralised, the Strasbourg reversal. It acknowledged that family reunification involved a positive obligation and that a fair balance assessment was required, but saw family life as central to that assessment.[83] It instigated what Lord Bingham elsewhere called 'a subtle but significant re-calibration of the relationship between the individual and the state'.[84]

The judgment started conventionally by identifying the legal question at issue. It did this not by heading into the dangerous territory of immigration, human rights and Article 8, but by referring to the relevant statutory appeal provisions, a low-key opening that suggested the judgment was a routine exercise in judicial interpretation. There followed a brief factual account of the lives of the applicants, establishing them as individuals as well as immigrants. Mrs Huang was in her 60s, with close family living in the UK. Mr Kashmiri was a young man who, alone out of his parents and siblings, had been refused

[80] See ch 3, s IV.
[81] *Huang* (n 2) [8].
[82] M Dembour, *When Humans Become Migrants: Study of the European Court of Human Rights with an Inter-American Counterpoint* (Oxford, Oxford University Press, 2015) 118–19.
[83] *Huang* (n 2) [18], [20]; on the significance of this, see ch 1, s IVC.
[84] Bingham, *Lives of the Law: Selected Essays and Speeches*, 178.

indefinite leave as a refugee. When their immigration status was mentioned, it was in neutral terms: 'Neither of the applicants qualifies for the grant of leave to remain in this country under the Immigration Rules and administrative directions currently promulgated.'[85]

As well as the word 'currently', the paragraph talked elsewhere of rules and directions 'in force from time to time'.[86] There was an implicit contrast between changeable, provisional Immigration Rules and the underlying and permanent values represented by human rights. In the words elsewhere of Lady Hale, 'While the Rules and policies come and go, Article 8 is there forever'.[87]

This opening may be contrasted with the first sentence in the Court of Appeal decision of *Mahmood*, implicitly overruled by *Huang*, which said: 'This appeal is brought against the judgment of Owen J … when he dismissed the appellant's application for judicial review of the Secretary of State's decision to remove him from this country as an illegal entrant.'[88]

The words 'illegal entrant' coloured the entire tone of the judgment. Biographical details were narrated sceptically and structured around Mr Mahmood's immigration status: doubt was cast, with no explanation, on the date and mode of his 'clandestine' arrival in the UK. It said that Mr Mahmood, '[h]owever', married a British citizen shortly before his asylum application was refused, implying that one purpose of the marriage was to frustrate removal. It was noted that Mr Mahmood's wife had come with her family from Pakistan aged 13, suggesting that she could easily return. The asylum appeal was said to have been pursued without 'any great vigour' and the only basis for legal challenge was his marriage and the birth of two children.[89] In brief, he appeared to epitomise the opportunistic migrant exploiting the UK's receptivity to human rights to undermine immigration controls.

The protagonists in the *Mahmood* and *Huang* judgments were framed in opposing ways within their respective judgments, but the gulf between them was perhaps less than may be imagined. Potentially negative facts about the protagonists mentioned by the Court of Appeal in *Huang* did not appear in the House of Lords judgment.[90] Mrs Huang was a doctor with no noted health problems who divided her time between China and the UK. She was separated from her UK-resident husband and her claim relied on the relationship with her adult daughter and her grandchildren. Another child lived outside the UK, and she had siblings and a mother in China. Her situation would have drawn little sympathy from the Strasbourg Court. Mr Kashmiri chose to remain in Iran as an

[85] *Huang* (n 2) [4].
[86] ibid [4].
[87] B Hale, 'Families and the Law: The Forgotten International Dimension' (2009) 21 *Child and Family Law Quarterly* 413, 414.
[88] *Mahmood* [1].
[89] ibid [4]–[15].
[90] *Huang v Home Secretary* [2005] EWCA Civ 105.

adult following the departure of the rest of his family, joining them only later. As he made an unsuccessful claim for asylum after arrival, he would have entered the UK either 'clandestinely' (as Mr Mahmood had done) or under a visa obtained through misrepresentation. He was described by an adjudicator as having 'low credibility'.[91]

Meanwhile, a critical reading of the *Mahmood* judgment revealed some potentially sympathetic features: there was no indication that Mr Mahmood had evaded the authorities and no suggestion of a sham marriage. The couple had two children and he appeared to be a committed husband and father who worked to support the family. It was not explained why the asylum claim failed. His wife's family, while of Pakistani origin, were all settled in the UK, so relocation would have been difficult and perhaps impossible for her. These facts could have been used to contextualise and humanise the application but, in common with most other courts at this time, this was not attempted.

As the Court observed in *Huang*, the underlying facts were not material to the legal principles, but it was expedient that the courts' respective narratives reduced the cognitive dissonance between facts and outcome.[92] In itself, this was not unusual; judges commonly construct their judgments as persuasively as possible. The novelty in *Huang*, and the judgments that followed, was that the narrative should allow the humanity of the migrant protagonist to emerge. Similarly, as remarked above and unlike previous courts (including *Mahmood*), the Court did not embark on a tour of the mainly negative Strasbourg cases.[93] Instead, it described them as examples of where the line had been drawn in a variety of factual situations and said that 'the main importance of the case law is in illuminating the core value which article 8 exists to protect', positing Article 8 as an underlying principle and a source of rights. It continued with the passage quoted at the start of the chapter, which bears repeating:

> Human beings are social animals. They depend on others. Their family, or extended family, is the group on which many people most heavily depend, socially, emotionally and often financially. There comes a time at which, for some, prolonged and unavoidable separation from this group seriously inhibits their ability to live full and fulfilling lives.[94]

This remarkable passage evoked the human interests in family reunification that had previously been almost entirely absent. In contrast to the usual perspective, where the migrant was presented as a disruptive outsider who may be using family ties for self-seeking reasons, the Court here asserted the value and primacy of

[91] ibid [12].
[92] ibid [3].
[93] *Mahmood* [38] per Lord Phillips.
[94] *Huang* (n 2) [18].

human relationships and interdependence, an 'ethics of care', that is 'a form of moral reasoning based on an understanding of individuals as embedded within webs of relationships rather than as disconnected, free-floating entities'.[95]

It was only at this point that the Court observed that Article 8 does not confer on individuals and families the right to choose where to live, going on to identify the key question as being that of proportionality, which required a 'fair balance' between competing considerations. However, the Court approved a conventional Article 8(2) proportionality analysis, reinforcing the impression that it saw family reunification as close to being a negative right. It was unique in a further respect. The Court contrasted statutory policy that had been the subject of wide discussion in Parliament where all interests were represented with the Immigration Rules, 'which are not the product of active debate in Parliament'.[96] These words, taken on their own, suggested a familiar demarcation between executive rules and legislation. However, the Court continued: 'where non-nationals seeking leave to enter or remain are not in any event represented'.[97] These brief words indicated a willingness to contemplate the contra-majoritarian character of human rights. This should not be overstated; these were a handful of words that were not repeated in later decisions and all the jurisprudence discussed in this book was consistent with the constitutional principle of parliamentary sovereignty but, within those limits, there was a vision of law that spoke to a deeper moral purpose, and this first found expression in *Huang*.

VII. THE AFTERMATH OF *HUANG*

In *Huang*, the Court mandated a more family-oriented approach to Article 8, in which judges played a more central role. It rejected the 'exceptionality test' but predicted that only a small number of cases would succeed. As usual, the Court of Appeal had to interpret the decision.[98] After a series of cases addressing different aspects of the judgment, the Court of Appeal gave the following general guidance to the Tribunal:

- The threshold to engage article 8(1) was not particularly high;
- The key issue would usually be article 8(2) proportionality, where a fact-specific and structured decision was required;

[95] R Hunter, C McGlynn and E Rackley, 'Feminist Judgments: An Introduction' In R Hunter, C McGlynn and E Rackley (ed), *Feminist Judgments: From Theory to Practice* (Oxford, Hart Publishing, 2010), 21.

[96] *Huang* (n 2) [17].

[97] ibid [17].

[98] See *AH (Philippines) v Secretary of State for the Home Department* [2007] EWCA Civ 376; *MT (Zimbabwe) v Secretary of State for the Home Department* [2007] EWCA Civ 455; *KR (Iraq) v SSHD* [2007] EWCA Civ 514; *KD (Sri Lanka) v SSHD* [2007] EWCA Civ 1384.

- That cases would succeed only rarely was a prediction that arose from the strong public interest in immigration control.[99]

The rejection of the exceptionality test was expressed by the Court of Appeal in a way that emphasised its limited impact:

> The effect of their Lordships' decision (and, if we may say so, the intended effect of this court's decision) in *Huang* has thus not been to introduce a new interpretation of art.8 but to clarify and reiterate a well understood one. While its practical effect is likely to be that removal is only exceptionally found to be disproportionate, it sets no formal test of exceptionality and raises no hurdles beyond those contained in the article itself.[100]

The passage was subtly written, but the words 'no formal test of exceptionality' and 'only exceptionally found' ensured that the idea of exceptionality was still very much present in the minds of decision-makers. The pre-eminence of government concerns was further in evidence some months later when, discussing the fair balance assessment post-*Huang*, Moses LJ said, again in the Court of Appeal:

> I would therefore reject the suggestion … that the scales start at a point of even balance. The starting point is the need to maintain fair and consistent immigration control. It will therefore be difficult to outweigh the impact of that starting point for an appellant such as this, who has no claim to remain under the rules, to establish, nevertheless, that he and his family should be entitled to do so, by virtue of the rights enshrined in article 8.[101]

This did not reflect the passage in *Huang* cited earlier which posited the fair balance assessment in a more balanced way.[102] Even if family reunification continued to be treated as a positive right, such a position failed to award sufficient weight to the claims of family life under Article 8.

The response of the Court of Appeal suggested unease at the potential breadth of the new mandate, and this was amplified within the Tribunal. Decisions straight after *Huang* treated the expectation that only a small minority of cases would succeed as indicating that there would be no increase, although that was not stated in the *Huang* judgment.[103] In June 2007, less than three months after the *Huang* judgment, a panel of the Tribunal that included the President of the Tribunal, Henry Hodge, said:

> although 'exceptionality' is not in itself a legal test, the evaluation of the evidence in order to answer the ultimate question … [is] the same as [it was] before the Appellate Committee of the House of Lords delivered its opinion in *Huang* … It is not the case,

[99] *AG (Eritrea) v SSHD* [2007] EWCA Civ 801.
[100] ibid [25] per Sedley LJ.
[101] *LK (Serbia)* [8] per Moses LJ.
[102] *Huang* (n 2) [20].
[103] For example, *MM v SSHD* [2007] UKAIT 00040; *Kl v SSHD* [2007] UKAIT 00044; *VS v SSHD* [2007] UKAIT 00069.

> in our judgement, that applicants will find it easier to succeed under Article 8 than was previously the case.[101]

If the same outcome applied irrespective of *Huang*, nothing of substance had changed and the exceptionality test remained an invisible criterion. While it is understandable that lower courts, in clarifying decisions, wanted to avoid raising unrealisable expectations, this suggested a deeper reluctance. Some immigration judges certainly did not relish their extended mandate. Mark Ockelton, a former Vice President of the Tribunal, wrote in 2015 that 'The decision in *Huang*, desirable as it might be in principle, is the route to decisions that are, and were always bound to be, less than fully informed, irrational, inconsistent, and uncontrollable'.[105]

Ockelton's argument was that *Huang* had given judges wide discretionary powers over an issue that they were unqualified to assess. He wanted to see courts and tribunals return to a review function.[106] His account of the practical difficulties had some force, as *Huang* demanded a new, more labour-intensive approach. There was also an element of self-protection: if the law set out unambiguous criteria, judges could not be criticised for applying them, but if admission or refusal was a matter of judicial discretion, judges risked political or public criticism. Yet, it can also be argued that Ockleton identified too closely with the government: all his arguments showed that he feared too many applicants succeeding. For example, he did not consider the problems of separated families, but he did cite the risk that undeserving applicants might mislead courts as to the strength of their family ties, and pointed out that Article 8 did not prevent family separation when a parent goes to prison, a telling analogy.[107] Equally, while re-emphasising the 'exceptional' character of successful applications, the Court of Appeal did not explore the likelihood that too many people had been refused under the former regime, or reflect on the sorts of cases that might now succeed, suggesting a sense of responsibility towards government that did not extend to migrants and their families.

In consequence, the actual impact of *Huang* in securing recognition of family life was limited as lower courts absorbed the decision into their pre-existing executive-oriented framework. Shortly after *Huang*, the Tribunal, again headed by the President, heard an appeal (*AM (Third party support)*) by an elderly appellant in poor health who had been displaced from Somalia to Ethiopia, from where he applied to join his wife in the UK.[108] She was also

[104] *AM v ECO, Addis Ababa* [2007] UKAIT 00058 [46]–[47]; for a discussion, see Macdonald, 'ECHR Article 8: Bringing the UK Courts Back in Step with Strasbourg', 300.

[105] M Ockelton, 'Article 8 ECHR, the UK and Strasbourg: Compliance, Cooperation or Clash? A Judicial Perspective' in KS Ziegler, E Wicks and L Hodson (eds), *The UK and European Human Rights: A Strained Relationship?* (Oxford, Hart Publishing, 2015) 215, 218.

[106] ibid 222.

[107] ibid 220.

[108] *AM (Third party support) v Entry Clearance Officer (Addis Addaba, Ethiopia)* [2007] UKAIT 00058.

disabled, and it was accepted that both parties had 'suffered, both physically and psychologically' as a result of war and separation, and that they could live together only in the UK so that refusal would mean indefinite separation for this long-married couple.[109] They would be supported financially in the UK by close family members in well-paid employment. The Tribunal set these factors against the interests of maintaining immigration controls, the limited family life they could enjoy by phone and the company in Ethiopia of an adult son, and decided this was not 'one of the very small minority of cases which, although it is not covered by the Rules and supplementary directions, is entitled to succeed under Article 8'.[110] The decision minimised several key findings in *Huang*. The shadow of exceptionality continued to loom, and the standard applied appeared higher than the reasonableness test established in *Huang*. The public interest in immigration control was considered in only a general way, not in relation to the parties' circumstances, and incorrectly took the Immigration Rules as the reference point. While the Tribunal was correct (at that time) to find that reliable support from family members was not permitted under the Immigration Rules, its availability should have been considered separately under Article 8. It is usual for lower courts to refine and interpret higher court judgments, but here the direction of travel was towards the most government-friendly of possible interpretations.

VIII. THE SIGNIFICANCE OF *HUANG* AND ITS LIMITS

This book has devoted an entire chapter to *Huang* because it was a remarkable decision and critical to the story of Article 8 in British immigration law. Without *Huang*, the cases discussed in the next two chapters could not have happened. It made courts central to protection of human rights and, by creating a common approach to proportionality, it ended the treatment of immigration as a special case of almost absolute executive discretion. The public interest in effective immigration control remained a powerful factor, but the judgment opened a space in which the value of family life could also receive proper consideration and used new judicial language in talking about family and immigration. The Court did this in a context where immigration, including family reunification, was as contentious as ever and where the courts had previously declined to use Article 8 to protect family life despite policies that fractured binational families on a regular basis. It was one of the boldest and most imaginative of all House of Lords/Supreme Court judgments.

It also contained gaps and ambiguities, notably the prediction that only a small minority of appeals would still succeed. The previous section showed

[109] ibid [55].
[110] ibid [56].

that some lower courts relied on this prediction to conclude that the number of successful appeals would be no greater than before, minimising the impact of the ruling. While it was true that most refusals under the Immigration Rules would still not breach Article 8 read as a whole, the *Huang* judgment suggested that, in previous appeals, the Court had been insufficiently active in protecting family life. The logical consequence was that some appeals that had previously been refused would now be accepted. It is improbable that the Court really intended that appellants would not find it easier to succeed than before, even if the proportion of successful appeals remained small. Yet the Court avoided saying so explicitly. It perhaps did not believe it needed to, and it would have wanted to avoid unnecessarily antagonising the government and raising expectations.

In so doing, however, it provided a life raft for judges reluctant to give full effect to the spirit of the *Huang* judgment. Applying *Huang* meant, as Ockelton complained, judges now had to reason in unfamiliar ways.[111] Insofar as that required an individual evaluation, it was a reasonable expectation. Such evaluations are routine in, for example, asylum. However, individual circumstances were only one part of the assessment; decision-makers had to weigh them against the public interest in immigration control. The *Huang* judgment gave some general guidance, but did not comprehensively address its complexities. As a result, subsequent courts failed to engage with the public interest in a meaningful way. In *AM (Third party support)*, for example, discussed in the previous section, the Tribunal, headed by the President of the Tribunal, did not take the availability of third party financial support into account in its Article 8 assessment. Instead, just as it did pre-*Huang*, it considered only whether there were any reasons connected to the applicants' own circumstances that made refusal disproportionate, applying a threshold so high that a blameless, elderly couple in poor health could not live out their last years together.

There was thus a disjuncture between the overall meaning of the *Huang* judgment and its reception by the lower courts. This, it is suggested, reflected differences in how the judicial function was conceptualised. The House of Lords set out a single approach to human rights that would apply across the whole justice system. It implicitly treated the Tribunal as part of that system and as subject to the same norms and constraints. Making individualised decisions that duly acknowledged human rights might be difficult, but it was the task in hand. Administrative justice scholars, however, see the Tribunal as having an ambiguous position within the justice system: 'tribunal adjudication is an institutional process by which public policy can be administered'.[112] Normal judicial values and processes apply, but priorities such as efficiency,

[111] M Arden, 'Proportionality: The Way Ahead' [2013] *PL* 54.

[112] R Thomas, *Administrative Justice and Asylum Appeals* (Oxford, Hart Publishing, 2011) 9.

consistency and the implementation of policy weigh more heavily.[113] It is not surprising that some Tribunal judges, and the Court of Appeal hearing appeals from the Tribunal, were unenthusiastic about interpreting *Huang* in ways that would increase tension with these institutional priorities and expose judges to increased political fire.

A further potential problem lay in the treatment – or, rather, the non-treatment – of the Strasbourg cases. It was noted earlier that *Huang* cited only one Strasbourg case: *Abdulaziz*. The Court's overall treatment of Article 8 was not inconsistent with other Strasbourg cases, given that the margin of appreciation had been removed, but it did lean towards a generous interpretation of that jurisprudence, and the Court did not undertake a more precise mapping exercise: 'the main importance of the case law is in illuminating the core value which article 8 exists to protect'.[114] More detail was not required as the legal issue at stake was the role of the courts, not the application of human rights in any particular instance. However, given their new responsibilities, courts needed guidance, and the absence of more detail at this juncture therefore suggested some reluctance to be explicit about the precise relationship between domestic and ECtHR jurisprudence, a highly sensitive issue and one where there may have been internal disagreement. This relative silence on the Strasbourg cases was reproduced in later cases and it left the Court vulnerable to political criticism for having 'gone beyond' or 'misapplied' Strasbourg.

A final challenge of *Huang* was that it contained the seeds of future tension within the Court itself. There were two distinct conceptual threads in *Huang*. One concerned the authority of the courts, reflected in the finding that judges should reach their own decision on proportionality. The other concerned the recognition of family life rights in the immigration sphere even where this may conflict with government priorities. In *Huang*, these two threads were closely intertwined. Promoting the human rights of migrants was congruent with affirming judicial authority, and this may be one reason why the Court was willing to act so assertively. Subsequent chapters will explore whether that continued to be the case or if the threads started to pull in different directions.

IX. CONCLUSION

Huang was a remarkable case that talked about family and migration in a new way and brought family life into the heart of Article 8 decision-making on immigration, from where it had been almost entirely absent. It aligned immigration with other policy areas so that it was no longer almost immune from judicial

[113] For a general discussion of administrative justice, see M Adler, *Administrative Justice in Context* (Oxford, Hart Publishing, 2010).

[114] *Huang* (n 2) [18].

human rights scrutiny. However, it was unclear about the implications of removing the exceptionality condition, and it did not explain the relationship between its findings and the Strasbourg jurisprudence. While *Huang* resolved some urgent issues and breathed life into Article 8 family reunification claims, there were questions left unresolved and it set the scene for new tensions to emerge. These are explored in subsequent chapters.

5

*'Good News from on High': The First Post-*Huang *Phase*

I. INTRODUCTION

THIS CHAPTER IS the first of three that discuss the House of Lords/Supreme Court (the Court) family reunification decisions after *Huang* in 2007. It analyses the first three post-*Huang* House of Lords judgments, called here the first post-*Huang* phase as they shared some common characteristics. This was not surprising, as they were delivered on the same day, 25 June 2008, by the same panel, which included three members who had also sat in *Huang*: Lords Bingham and Brown and Lady Hale. The decisions reinforced the new approach in *Huang* and resulted in improved protection for binational families. The legal findings in each judgment were quite modest but were collectively significant, countering the executive-oriented interpretations of lower courts even after *Huang*. They showed how the application of human rights in a national context without the constraint of the margin of appreciation can result in small but significant shifts in favour of binational families. They also demonstrated a new language and new ways of structuring judgments that suggested an invigorated approach to the judicial function, borne from the possibilities created by the Human Rights Act. To have three such positive cases coming out together was an exciting moment for immigration lawyers. A blog post reporting them was headlined 'Good news from on high' and a prominent set of barristers' chambers threw a party to celebrate.[1] However, the decisions were not without problems. This chapter will show that, despite the Court's energy and commitment, it was not straightforward for it to use Article 8 to protect binational family life in the absence of wider political consensus. The Court's reasoning was subtle, and the meaning of these decisions was not always well understood by lower courts, which operated in a different institutional culture.

The chapter first considers each case in turn. It starts with *Beoku-Betts*, where the Court found that a statutory appeal must consider the Article 8 rights of the entire family, ending a practice whereby only the migrant's rights would be considered, while those of a spouse or child had to be represented in

[1] 'Good News from on High' (*Free Movement*, 25 June 2008); the party was reported to the author by a member of the Chambers involved.

a separate and expensive judicial review. The second decision was *Chikwamba*, which considered whether an application to live in the UK could be made from inside the UK, a procedural issue that had wide practical ramifications. The Court found it would often be disproportionate to require the claimant to go abroad to make an application. The final case, *EB (Kosovo)*, determined that excessive delay by the government could affect the proportionality of removal. It also confirmed that disapproval of the exceptionality condition in *Huang* meant that the standard for deciding if the family could relocate abroad was 'reasonableness', not 'insurmountable obstacles'.

There follows an analysis of what these cases achieved. They showed the potential value of Article 8 in protecting the family life of binational families. They helped to ensure that all relevant rights were considered and that proportionality assessments were based on a fact-sensitive assessment. They introduced a new language and style of judgment that made family life and the individuals involved central to the decision. In the two proportionality decisions, they paid attention to the government's reasons for interfering in family life, acknowledging government concerns but declining to show automatic deference. This section also discusses whether the Court exceeded the European Court of Human Rights (Strasbourg Court or Strasbourg) jurisprudence. It observes that this was not a binary question and argues that, while the decisions sat at or just beyond the generous end of the Strasbourg spectrum, the Court undertook a closer examination of the relevant factors identified by Strasbourg, rather than creating new ones. This was congruent with the Strasbourg Court's own doctrines of subsidiarity and the margin of appreciation. The question was whether the Court was acting within its constitutional powers under domestic law, and this was the case.

There were, however, areas of uncertainty. The Court said little about the relationship between its decisions, the Strasbourg cases and the Human Rights Act. Some key passages were expressed ambiguously, making them hard to interpret. While the focus on the human story in each case was refreshing, these had to carry a lot of weight in the judgments, particularly in *Chikwamba* and *EB (Kosovo)*, and it is not clear that they always did so successfully. It is suggested that the Court was anxious not to be perceived as undermining immigration controls. Emphasising the individual humanity of protagonists enabled it to avoid being explicit about the tension between family life and immigration control, but it sometimes seemed to suggest a binary between 'deserving' and 'undeserving' migrants.[2] While the analysis suggests this was not the intention, lower courts, faced with new and uncomfortable principles for decision-making, tended to fall back on this divide, setting high factual thresholds for success.

[2] See, eg B Anderson, *Us and Them? The Dangerous Politics of Immigration Control* (Oxford, Oxford University Press, 2013); H Jones, Y Gunaratnam, G Bhattacharyya, W Davies, S Dhaliwal, E Jackson and R Saltus, 'Un/deserving Migrants and Resisting Dehumanisation' in HJ Gunaratnam, Y Bhattacharyya, G Davies, W Dhaliwal, E Jackson and R Saltus (eds), *Go Home?: The Politics of Immigration Controversies* (Manchester, Manchester University Press, 2017) 120–40.

II. *BEOKU-BETTS*: INCLUDING ALL THE FAMILY

The first of the three decisions analysed here, *Beoku-Betts*, did not address Article 8 proportionality and fair balance.[3] While it is therefore discussed more briefly, it made a key contribution to protecting the family life of binational families. The issue was whether, in an Article 8 appeal, the rights of all family members should be considered or just those of the appellant. If only the appellant's interests were in contemplation, a tribunal or court could take account of the impact of separation on other family members only so far as it affected the appellant. This led to artificially constructed arguments and decreased protection, as the impact on a child, for example, could be considered only through the prism of how their distress affected the parent. Yet, a situation that is devastating for a child might be less critical to the parent's well-being, while the parent's wrongdoing would more easily outweigh interference in their own family life than in their child's. There were practical problems also; if the relative's rights were not considered at the appeal, they had to be asserted through a separate judicial review application, an expensive additional process for which few families had the resources.

Like *Huang*, the case centred on interpretation of ambiguous wording in the appeals legislation.[4] The applicant, a failed asylum seeker who lived with his mother and siblings in the UK, argued that the family life protected by Article 8 was a 'single family life', incorporating the ties and needs of all family members.[5] The Court, led by Lord Brown, ruled unanimously in his favour, finding that there is 'one family life' for Article 8 purposes and therefore the human rights of the entire family should be considered in the appeal, reversing the findings of the Immigration Appeal Tribunal and the Court of Appeal.[6]

While questions of public interest and fair balance were therefore not relevant, the judgment was consistent with the others discussed here in its focus on family life, which was foregrounded through explicit language. For example, Baroness Hale observed that to adopt a narrow approach would miss the 'central point of family life', where 'the whole is greater than the sum of its individual parts'.[7] More indirectly, the family who brought the appeal was portrayed sympathetically. Their circumstances were discussed early in the judgment, and they were described as having 'understandably sought refuge' in the UK even though their asylum claims were rejected.[8] The reader is told the first names of the appellant's siblings and their circumstances, including how well one sister

[3] *Beoku-Betts v SSHD* [2008] UKHL 39.

[4] Nationality, Immigration and Asylum Act 2002, s 84 provided for a right of appeal on the grounds that the decision was incompatible with appellant's Convention rights or was otherwise not in accordance with the law.

[5] *Beoku-Betts* (n 3) [20].

[6] For a discussion, see D Seddon, 'Case Comment: Beoku-Betts v Secretary of State for the Home Department' (2008) 22 *Journal of Immigration Asylum and Nationality Law* 358.

[7] *Beoku-Betts* (n 3) [4].

[8] ibid [8].

was doing at school and another's employment at a law firm. The appellant's six-month irregular residence after his visa expired and before he made his asylum claim was noted only in passing and attributed to an error. None of this was necessary for the legal argument, but it evoked the human issues at stake as a preliminary to the legal analysis.

The Strasbourg jurisprudence was used sparingly. In his lead judgment, Lord Brown cited two cases: *Sezen*, where the Strasbourg Court had criticised domestic authorities for failing to consider the impact of criminal deportation on the applicant's 'functioning family unit', and *Mokrani*, where additional elements of dependence existed between adult family members.[9] The factual scenario in neither case was particularly relevant, but their citation enabled Lord Brown to say that: 'Time and again, the Strasbourg case law emphasises the crucial importance of family life.'[10] As with *Huang*, the Strasbourg jurisprudence was posited as a source of rights, rather than a series of limitations, and Lord Brown quoted the passage in *Huang* cited in the previous chapter, which affirmed the 'core value which article 8 exists to protect'.[11]

While there was therefore a commitment to family life, it was also a pragmatic judgment concerned with the efficacy of human rights decision-making. The government had a legal duty under the Human Rights Act to consider the position of all family members while, if a claim reached Strasbourg, the family's interests would also be considered together. It was illogical to require separate proceedings in respect of the same immigration decision only at this stage. Lord Brown asked what 'could be less convenient' than the narrow approach?[12] Lady Hale described it as 'artificial and impracticable'.[13]

In finding that the interests of all family members must be considered, the judgment had a significant practical effect on the conduct of appeals. However, it could have been more explicit about what was now required.[14] Was family life a single entity, was it a series of relationships, each of which must be evaluated from the perspective of each party, or was it both? Lord Brown said:

> Once it is recognised that … 'there is only one family life', and that, assuming the appellant's proposed removal would be disproportionate looking at the family unit as a whole, then each affected family member is to be regarded as a victim …

Lady Hale said in her concurring judgment:

> [The narrow approach] also risks missing the central point about family life, which is that the whole is greater than the sum of its individual parts. The right to respect

[9] *Sezen v Netherlands* (2006) 43 EHRR 30 [49]; *Mokrani v France* (20030 40 EHRR 123 [33].
[10] *Beoku-Betts* (n 3) [37].
[11] ibid [40].
[12] ibid [43].
[13] ibid [4].
[14] See, eg *R (Mansoor) v SSHD* [2011] EWHC 832; *AF (Jamaica) v SSHD* [2009] EWCA Civ 240; *R (on the application of Rainford) v SSHD* [2008] EWHC 2474; *Stephenson v SSHD* [2010] EWHC 704; *Card v SSHD* [2009] EWHC 2128.

> for the family life of one necessarily encompasses the right to respect for the family life of others, normally a spouse or minor children, with whom that family life is enjoyed.[15]

Both statements pointed towards considering both the family as a single unit and the interests of each individual separately, but they were not explicit that this was the case. Both approaches could be important. Looking at family life as a whole avoided an over-concentration on the strength of each individual tie, with the risk, for example, that a vulnerable adult relative, all of whose family live in the UK, might be found to have an insufficient tie with any of them.[16] More commonly, however, the danger was that an emphasis on family life as a whole failed to specifically consider the rights of each family member. There is a difference between observing, for example, that a parent's expulsion will have an impact on a child and a structured examination that puts the child's Article 8 rights at the centre of the assessment. The Court did not say specifically that the latter was needed, although this was implied when Lord Brown asked 'What could be less convenient than to have the appellant's article 8 rights taken into account in one proceeding ... [and] other family members' rights in another'.[17]

However, subsequent courts did not always undertake a full Article 8 assessment in respect of other family members. It was, for example, considered that the requirements of *Beoku-Betts* were satisfied if the decision-maker had considered the family member's situation without a discrete human rights assessment.[18] Even the Court of Appeal was occasionally rather casual about ensuring that the Article 8 rights of each individual were fully considered.[19] The issue often arose in respect of children, and it took the *ZH (Tanzania)* decision, discussed in the next chapter, for their interests to be further recognised.

III. *CHIKWAMBA*: APPLYING IN-COUNTRY OR ABROAD

The second decision handed down that day was *Chikwamba*.[20] Ms Chikwamba was an asylum seeker allowed to remain in the UK after her claim was rejected due to conditions in Zimbabwe. By the time removals were reinstated, she had married a Zimbabwean refugee and the couple had a daughter. She made an application under the Immigration Rules to remain as a spouse, which was refused as the Rules required her application to be made from abroad. The legal question was the proportionality of forcing her to return to Zimbabwe to apply for readmission. It therefore concerned the preliminary procedural issue of where the substantive application, whether under the Immigration Rules or

[15] *Beoku-Betts* (n 3) [4].
[16] *ZB (Pakistan) v SSHD* [2009] EWCA Civ 834.
[17] *Beoku-Betts* (n 3) [43].
[18] *R (on the application of Myckoo) v SSHD* [2008] EWHC 2778.
[19] *DS (India) v SSHD* [2009] EWCA Civ 544; *MA (Turkey) v SSHD* [2009] EWCA Civ 1018.
[20] *Chikwamba v SSHD* [2008] UKHL 40.

under Article 8, should be made. The Court found unanimously that it would be disproportionate to require Ms Chikwamba to leave the UK to make her application.

Ms Chikwamba's was a test case; the policy of requiring applications to be made from outside the UK had caused extensive hardship as spouses and partners were forced back to troubled regions.[21] While, in principle, decisions to require return were subject to an Article 8 assessment, they were almost invariably found to be proportionate. Problems for families arose due to the expense and other difficulties of returning to troubled regions, travelling to the visa post, and funding accommodation and living costs for the duration of the application process. Meanwhile, the UK-based family would be without a carer or provider, creating practical and financial problems, and making a successful application under the Immigration Rules more difficult if employment or housing were lost in consequence. In principle, visa officers should apply Article 8 as well as the Immigration Rules when deciding the substantive application from abroad, but it seems that this almost never happened.[22] Any appeal would be heard in the UK without the applicant, putting the parties at a disadvantage.

Instances where it was considered proportionate to require return included a father deeply engaged in caring for his disabled daughter and other children while working to support the family. His wife could not cope financially and practically without his support. Another involved a father who had to return to chaotic post-war Iraq, obtain travel documents, undertake an expensive and dangerous journey to Jordan, negotiate border controls and stay in a hotel while awaiting a decision that could have as easily been made in the UK.[23] Applications made from abroad could take months to process, or longer if an appeal was necessary. If the application was refused and the appeal failed, the appellant was already abroad, the government was saved the trouble of expelling them and separation would be permanent.

Chapter four showed how, in *Huang*, the Court treated proportionality as a legal question to be judicially determined and rejected a specific doctrine of deference, saying that government claims as to the public interest would be given 'appropriate weight'. *Chikwamba* showed what that can mean in practice. The government claimed the policy of requiring return was in the public interest as it prevented 'queue-jumping', which was unfair to those waiting abroad. This argument was rejected by the Court as those waiting abroad were not delayed by in-country applications; if anything, the reverse was true as they reduced the

[21] For more background on the case, see C Walsh, 'Unhappy Families and Use of Article 8 for Failed Asylum Seekers' (2009) *Denning Law Journal* 153, 157; see also H Wray, *Regulating Marriage Migration into the UK. A Stranger in the Home* (Abingdon, Routledge, 2011) 159–62.

[22] This has long been widely believed, but there is little hard data supporting or disproving the thesis. Some evidence supporting the thesis was submitted to the Supreme Court in the case of *MM (Lebanon) v SSHD* discussed in ch 7 (witness statement is available from the author).

[23] H Wray, '"A Thing Apart": Controlling Male Family Migration to the United Kingdom' (2015) 18 *Men and Masculinities* 424.

queue. The real rationale was to deter unauthorised entry through imposing the 'very substantial disruption' of being forced abroad to regularise. This was not an objectionable aim, but whether removal for this reason was proportionate would be context-dependent; the expulsion must fulfil the purpose of the policy and its benefits must outweigh disruption to family life.[24]

Thus, after *Chikwamba*, the question was not whether there were exceptional factors relating to individual hardship that made return disproportionate but whether, in all the circumstances, the interference caused by return was justified. Relevant factors included the duration and extent of family disruption, if refusal abroad would lead to a further human rights appeal and whether the visa officer was best placed to assess the claim.[25] On the public interest front, the Court distinguished between a claimant who entered irregularly to pursue an asylum claim and one who deliberately and cynically flouted immigration controls. As a result, the entire framing of the argument changed; in his lead judgment, Lord Brown described a previous case, *Ekinci*, as, 'on any view, an exceptional case'.[26] Mr Ekinci was a failed asylum seeker who had engaged in substantial deception and faced only short-term exile to Germany. Lord Brown suggested that such cases would now be the exception: 'only comparatively rarely, certainly in family cases involving children, should an article 8 appeal be dismissed on the basis that it would be proportionate and more appropriate for the appellant to apply for leave from abroad'.[27]

The Court did not refer to any Strasbourg cases, although Article 8 proportionality was at the heart of the decision. At that point, there had been no specific rulings in Strasbourg on this issue.[28] In the period after *Chikwamba*, the Strasbourg Court found it proportionate to require migrants to leave to comply with procedural requirements,[29] and in 2014 it said in *Jeunesse*:

> [I]n principle, Contracting States have the right to require aliens seeking residence on their territory to make the appropriate request from abroad. They are thus under no obligation to allow foreign nationals to await the outcome of immigration proceedings on their territory.[30]

It might seem, therefore, that the Court was out of step with the direction of travel at Strasbourg. However, the position was more complex. Both Lord Brown's words cited above and Baroness Hale's short concurring judgment suggested that the presence of a child was significant.[31] Making the impact

[24] *Chikwamba* (n 20) [40]–[41].
[25] ibid [42].
[26] ibid [29]; *Ekinci v SSHD* [2003] EWCA Civ 765.
[27] *Chikwamba* (n 20) [44].
[28] Although the doctrine of 'precariousness' had already emerged: *Rodrigues da Silva and Hoogkamer v Netherlands* (2007) 44 EHRR 34 [39].
[29] *Biraga v Sweden* App no 1722/10 (3 April 2012); *Mbuisa v UK* App nos 22897/09 and 37369/12 (10 September 2013); *Bolek v Sweden* App no 48205/13 (28 January 2014).
[30] *Jeunesse v Netherlands* (2014) 60 EHRR 17 [101].
[31] *Chikwamba* (n 20) [8].

on children critical was consistent with the increasing emphasis at Strasbourg on children's interests in family reunification, which had started to be explicit in 2007.[32]

However, while the presence of a child clearly strengthened a claim, it was not a precondition. Also relevant, according to Lord Brown, was the reason for entry. A person who entered with a 'genuine' asylum claim was in a different position to one who entered with the intention of residing without authorisation. A person with a 'genuine' asylum claim would be a refugee and the point in *Chikwamba* would not be in issue, so Lord Brown could not have meant to refer only those in that position. His counterexample of irregular migrants coming to pursue studies was equally unrepresentative of typical *Chikwamba*-type applicants and his words seemed to be examples cited only to emphasise the broad range of possible circumstances. Taken as a whole, therefore, the judgment did not suggest that the Court intended only a few deserving applicants or those with children to succeed, even if the most undeserving could still be excluded, and, in that light, it could be read as going further than Strasbourg. However, any advance was modest; it was still possible to refuse claims when required by the public interest and the decision did not concern matters of substance but the process for making an application. It was less that the House of Lords was out of step with Strasbourg than that it was a different court fulfilling different functions, a point discussed further in section V.

However, the Court was not very specific about what it had done, and the Human Rights Act and the Strasbourg cases were not referenced. Instead, the Court found other ways to convey the message that the policy was objectionable. Lord Brown presented Ms Chikwamba in a favourable light, aided by some unusual facts. For example, she was a woman, whereas most appellants in her situation were male.[33] While gender was not formally a factor, it has been found to affect how the ties of parenthood are considered.[34] She married and conceived a child while she had temporary leave so was not irregular at that point and, as her husband was a refugee, he could not travel to Zimbabwe. These features were highlighted early in the judgment and there was also an emphasis on the 'genuine' character of the marriage. The parties were further humanised: the reader was told that Ms Chikwamba's husband was a childhood friend, and that their daughter was called Bianca.[35] The question thus became the impact of an over-rigid policy on a sympathetic couple who could be contrasted with undeserving migrants such as Mr Ekinci, the 'exceptional' case mentioned earlier.

[32] In January 2008, the government announced plans to review its reservation on immigration and nationality matters to the Convention on the Rights of the Child – HC Deb 14 January 2008, vol 470, col 649.

[33] Wray, '"A Thing Apart"', 431.

[34] ibid 439–40; B de Hart, 'Superdads: Migrant Fathers' Right to Family Life before the European Court of Human Rights' (2015) 18 *Men and Masculinities* 448.

[35] *Chikwamba* (n 20) [5], [12], [13].

The problem was that the binary between deserving and undeserving migrants was largely a construct. Almost all claimants fell somewhere between these two poles and could be presented in different and competing ways. This was true also for Ms Chikwamba. The judgment mentioned some facts that could have been given more weight by an unsympathetic observer: her asylum claim was dismissed for lack of credibility, and she had married and conceived a child knowing her status was precarious. She had two children in Zimbabwe by a previous relationship and family in Harare, who presumably could support her during her return.[36] There was also some uncertainty over whether an application made under the Immigration Rules would succeed.[37] All this information was in the judgment, but it was not emphasised. The latter point, in particular, was glossed over, with the Court saying 'No one apparently doubts that, in the longer term, this family will have to be allowed to live together here'.[38] Ms Chikwamba had not absconded, used a false identity or committed criminal offences, so did not fall into the most unmeritorious categories, but her claim was no stronger than that made by many others.

Chikwamba allowed some claims to succeed that would otherwise have failed, but decision-makers and judges had to decide which these were.[39] As with *Huang*, they seemed anxious not to interpret the decision overgenerously. For example, one issue was whether success under *Chikwamba* required an unequivocal claim to live in the UK. The Court had noted that Ms Chikwamba might not succeed under the Immigration Rules, but said that the family would eventually be reunited in the UK, presumably through a successful substantive Article 8 claim.[40] The judgment did not say that inevitable success under Article 8 or under the Immigration Rules was a precondition for in-country determination, but this was how it was sometimes interpreted. Subsequent courts said, for example, that Ms Chikwamba's claim for long-term admission had been 'invincible', and that the principle in *Chikwamba* applied only when there was an 'unassailable case for entry clearance', or where 'an application for entry clearance from abroad would be granted'.[41] This reduced the scope of the judgment. The outcome of a long-term application often cannot be predicted. A decision under the Immigration Rules would address different issues, such as the couple's financial position or housing, to those in an Article 8 application. In a substantive Article 8 application, both interference and the public interest would be greater and require more consideration. While a strong *Chikwamba* claim was

[36] ibid [10].
[37] ibid [18].
[38] ibid [46].
[39] For a further discussion, see Walsh, 'Unhappy Families and Use of Article 8 for Failed Asylum Seekers',170–71.
[40] *Chikwamba* (n 20) [46].
[41] *SZ (Zimbabwe) v SSHD* [2009] EWCA Civ 590 [18]; *GA (Iraq) v SSHD* [2009] EWHC 2403 (Admin) [18]; *Goran Kadr Ahmed v SSHD* [2009] EWHC 2403 (Admin) [18]; *Hiahong Chen v SSHD* [2015] UKUT 189 (IAC) [39].

likely to mean a strong substantive Article 8 claim (and vice versa), the Court did not make that a precondition, and proportionality in each claim must be assessed on its own merits. However, some lower courts, by demanding certainty as to the ultimate outcome, blunted the potential impact of *Chikwamba*.

Later courts also seemed uncertain as to the extent to which the factual scenario in *Chikwamba* or its equivalent had to be replicated. Less than a month after the judgment, the Court of Appeal heard a *Chikwamba*-related appeal.[42] The case turned on procedural issues and there was evident irritation at an apparently misconceived application, leading to some tart observations about the differences between the two cases. It was noted that when Ms Chikwamba married, she had permission to be in the UK, whereas the appellant here had disappeared from view for around two years. It was assumed that Ms Chikwamba would have taken her daughter to Zimbabwe while this male applicant would leave his son with his mother.[43] The weakness of the case moved Buxton LJ to describe the facts in *Chikwamba* as 'extreme'.[44] While this was said in a particular context, it aided the impression that parties must meet a high factual threshold to benefit from the *Chikwamba* decision. For example, the High Court said in respect of a subsequent judicial review:

> This [application] is, it must be recognised, a very different factual situation from that in *Chikwamba* where requiring the applicant to return to 'very harsh' conditions in Zimbabwe meant a separation both from her infant daughter for whose care she was responsible and from her spouse.[45]

Government representatives predictably advocated for this narrow interpretation.[46]

Not all decisions took such a minimal approach and some parties benefited from the decision. However, by 2012, the Court of Appeal in *Hayat* had to restate the legal principles involved: insisting on an application from abroad may be Article 8 interference, particularly where children were adversely affected, and there must be a good reason why it was needed.[47] A fact-sensitive assessment was required, and the government must do more to justify interference than in a substantive Article 8 assessment. Following a successful application, any substantive Article 8 claim will be decided in the usual way and the outcome may be different; the parties in *Hayat*, for example, succeeded on *Chikwamba* but failed on the substantive application. The clarity provided in *Hayat* was welcome, but reflected the extent to which the judgment had previously been poorly applied.

Although it was not straightforward, when applied correctly, *Chikwamba* enabled more nuanced decision-making, as demonstrated by the decision in

[42] *TG (Central African Republic) v SSHD* [2008] EWCA Civ 997.
[43] ibid [3], [5].
[44] ibid [6].
[45] *Wray v SSHD* [2010] EWHC 3301 [79]–[80].
[46] 'Should I Stay or Should I Go?' (*Free Movement*, 25 November 2011).
[47] *Hayat and others v SSHD* [2012] EWCA Civ 1054.

Kotecha and Das.[48] Mr Kotecha was a Tanzanian national who overstayed his student visa for three years without contacting the authorities. When he married a British citizen, he applied for leave to remain, but was expected to return to Tanzania to make the application. The couple had no children and applications in Tanzania were decided within 30 days, often less. The High Court found it was proportionate for Mr Kotecha to make his application from abroad. Ms Das came with her child to the UK from Bangladesh on a spouse visa. Her husband died, she remarried and gave birth to a further child, but failed to apply for new leave. She was the children's primary carer and her husband worked. If she could not apply in-country, she would either return to Bangladesh alone, depriving her children of their usual carer for an uncertain period, or take them with her, disrupting her elder child's education and separating father and child. It could take up to three months to reach a decision on the application. The government argued that *Chikwamba* did not apply because Mr Das and the children might travel with Ms Das to Bangladesh, where life was not subject to the 'harsh and unpalatable' conditions of Zimbabwe and the period of separation would be shorter than in *Chikwamba*. The Court, however, found that it would be disproportionate, correctly finding that such a high threshold was not required. There was a gulf between Mr Kotecha and Ms Das in their circumstances and their relationship with immigration control. Pre-*Chikwamba*, they would almost certainly have been treated identically. After *Chikwamba*, their differences could be recognised, although, it must be acknowledged, only after application to the High Court.

IV. *EB (KOSOVO)*: DELAY, PROPORTIONALITY AND REINFORCING *HUANG*

The third decision handed down that day was *EB (Kosovo)*.[49] It concerned the impact of government delay on proportionality, a major issue at that time due to inefficiencies in decision-making. Many asylum applicants had to wait years for a decision and, in the meantime, began relationships and formed families, leading to Article 8 claims when the asylum claim was eventually refused. This instance concerned a young man from Kosovo who had come to the UK aged 13 and claimed asylum. His application was subject to a delay of more than four and a half years, by which time changed circumstances in Kosovo led to its rejection. He was also no longer eligible under a policy that, had his case been dealt with earlier, would have led to a permanent status. Instead, he was due to be removed despite having a family life in the UK. The legal question for the

[48] *R (on the application of Anand Narencha Kotecha and Ruma Rani Das) v SSHD* [2011] EWHC 2070.

[49] *EB (Kosovo) v SSHD* [2008] UKHL 41.

Court was 'what bearing (if any) does delay by the decision-making authorities have on a non-national's rights under article 8?'[50]

The Court of Appeal had already found that excessive delay would occasionally make it disproportionate to apply the procedural requirement to apply from abroad (the issue in *Chikwamba*).[51] In *EB (Kosovo)*, the question was whether delay could be relevant to the substantive claim; earlier decisions had been limited by the requirement pre-*Huang* of exceptionality, so a new approach was needed.[52] Lord Bingham in his lead judgment said that delay may be relevant in three ways:

- The applicant's personal and social ties and roots in the community would be correspondingly deeper;[53]
- The failure of the authorities to act over a prolonged period was likely to reduce the parties' sense of precarity so that relationships would deepen;[54]
- Delay due to 'a dysfunctional system which yields unpredictable, inconsistent and unfair outcomes' might reduce the weight otherwise accorded to the requirements of immigration control.[55]

The first way recognised what was likely to be factually true, that family or private life would be stronger. The second was said to 'depend on no legal doctrine but on an understanding of how, in some cases, minds may work'.[56] It suggested mitigation of the precariousness factor, the principle that little weight be attached to relationships knowingly formed 'under the shadow of severance by administrative order'.[57] The third envisaged a reduction in the weight attached to the public interest in immigration control if delay was due to a 'dysfunctional system which yields unpredictable, inconsistent and unfair outcomes'.[58] That did not mean that governments could not amend their policies over time, and not all delay resulted from a 'dysfunctional' system, but the loss of a right to remain due to government failings could be relevant to proportionality.[59]

In a dissenting judgment, Lord Brown accepted the first two of Lord Bingham's points, although he thought that the second point should not be taken too far, but he did not accept the third. He reasoned that the public interest in immigration control had not diminished and that courts should therefore treat it in the normal way.[60] Delay might therefore lead to a strengthening of the

[50] ibid [1].
[51] *Shala v SSHD* [2003] EWCA Civ 233; *Akaeke v SSHD* [2005] EWCA Civ 947.
[52] *HB (Ethiopia) v SSHD* [2006] EWCA Civ 1713 [24]; *Strbac v SSHD* [2005] EWCA Civ 848 [25].
[53] *EB (Kosovo)* (n 49) [14].
[54] ibid [15].
[55] ibid [16].
[56] ibid [15].
[57] ibid [15].
[58] ibid [16].
[59] See D Seddon, 'Case Comment: EB (Kosovo) v Secretary of State for the Home Department' (2008) 22 *Journal of Immigration Asylum and Nationality Law* 360, 362.
[60] *EB (Kosovo)* (n 49) [39]–[42].

appellant's claim but not to a weakening of the government's. Lord Bingham's point, however, was that the weight attached to the public interest, not the public interest itself, would be diminished. In immigration cases, unlike deportation, the public interest is the generalised need for an enforceable policy rather than the risk presented by any individual. Extreme government delay had deprived EB of a right to long-term residence from which his cousin, with whom he arrived, had benefited and this was only because of government inefficiency. It was hard to see how the public interest now required his expulsion. Lord Brown's dissent anticipated more profound future disagreement. It suggested that he was willing to see Article 8 provide remedies in individual cases but not for it to challenge government assessment of the public interest.

Lord Brown also suggested that Lord Bingham had paid insufficient attention to Strasbourg, and it is true that Lord Bingham barely mentioned the Strasbourg cases, focusing principally on the previous domestic cases.[61] Lord Brown referred to the non-violation findings in *Konstatinov* and *Nnyanzi*, although neither was precisely on point. In *Konstatinov*, the authorities failed to make a decision on a residence permit for seven years, during which time the applicant gained several criminal convictions, making her eligible for deportation on those grounds.[62] In *Nnyanzi*, the applicant waited four years for her human rights appeal to be heard, but an earlier hearing would not have changed the outcome.[63] As Lord Brown himself observed, these cases suggested limits to the *EB (Kosovo)* principles, not that they were incorrect. Later developments at Strasbourg suggested that, by treating delay as relevant to proportionality, the Court was in tune with Strasbourg. In 2014, some six years after *EB (Kosovo)*, the Strasbourg Court found that a state's toleration of lengthy irregular residence was relevant to proportionality.[64]

In addition to the specific findings on delay, Lord Bingham said that:

> [I]t will rarely be proportionate to uphold an order for removal of a spouse if there is a close and genuine bond with the other spouse and that spouse cannot reasonably be expected to follow the removed spouse to the country of removal, or if the effect of the order is to sever a genuine and subsisting relationship between parent and child.[65]

This reiterated the principles in *Huang*, which, as the previous chapter showed, were not always clearly understood. It was later cited as an example of the Court going further than Strasbourg (see chapter seven) through displacing the tests of insurmountable obstacles and exceptionality. This critique, however, oversimplified the Strasbourg position. 'Insurmountable obstacles' has never been a criterion and the Strasbourg Court has treated government failings as mitigating

[61] ibid [7], [15].

[62] *Konstatinov v Netherlands* App no 16351/03 (24 September 2007).

[63] *Nnyanzi v UK* (2008) 47 EHRR 18.

[64] *Jeunesse* (n 30) [116]; in relation to a refugee, see *Tanda-Muzinga v France* App no 2260/10 (10 July 2014).

[65] *EB (Kosovo)* (n 49) [12].

the exceptionality test.[66] Even so, the passage was certainly at the generous end of the jurisprudence, a point pursued below.

More even than in *Beoku-Betts* and *Chikwamba*, the judgment in *EB (Kosovo)* humanised the appellant, placing him at the centre of the narrative. Lord Bingham opened by summarising his immigration history. Instead of then commencing an analysis of the legal issues, he went further into the appellant's personal story. His family was forced from its home in 1999, when the applicant and his cousin, both children, became separated from their family and joined a convoy to Macedonia. After living in refugee camps, the boys came together to the UK and applied for asylum. They stayed with foster parents before joining the family of an uncle in the UK. The appellant went to school and entered sixth form, where, aged 18, he formed a relationship with a young Somali national, Latifa Quresh (while EB himself remained anonymised, Latifa was called throughout by her first name), who had indefinite leave to remain. Latifa was pregnant and abandoned by another man and, after her birth, the appellant treated Latifa's daughter as his 'own', 'informally adopted' child.[67] The couple lived together at the uncle's house, and they planned to marry. Latifa conceived another child, but miscarried. Lord Bingham then proceeded to detail the government's delays and errors in dealing with the appellant's asylum claim and lawyers' efforts to resolve them. By the end of these paragraphs, he had evoked a young, traumatised couple trying to build a secure family unit after tragic beginnings and crossed not by the stars but by an incompetent and heartless bureaucracy.

By the time Lord Bingham moved onto the legal issues, therefore, removal of EB appeared more an act of state-sponsored cruelty than a necessary protection of the nation state. The narrative reversed the Strasbourg reversal not through legal argument, but by invoking 'the core value which article 8 exists to protect', the care and love that human beings show to each other.[68] Discussion of the same facts by the Court of Appeal and the first instance adjudicator revealed how prioritising immigration control over family life required a reverse process of dehumanisation. In the Court of Appeal, EB was only one of four parties. Discussion of his circumstances was thus inevitably more cursory, but it also appeared only mid-way through the judgment, after a discussion of the limited relevance of Article 8 (based on the pre-*Huang* requirement of exceptionality). The focus was almost entirely on the immigration history. EB's partner was described as 'LQ, a Somali lady', and EB is said to 'have accepted' her child, a more distanced presentation than that of Lord Bingham.[69] The first instance decision was quoted in the Supreme Court judgment, and revealed an even more

[66] See ch 3, s VA.
[67] *EB (Kosovo)* (n 49) [4], [18].
[68] *Huang v Home Secretary* [2007] UKHL 11 [18].
[69] *HB (Ethiopia* (n 52) [31]–[32].

brusque and unsympathetic attitude, as well as some dismissive and objectifying language:

> [His girlfriend] is Somali. She looks at least Asian he says by relatively light skin tone. She could return with him. He says she would receive racist treatment. I am not referred to any cogent evidence of that. It may be that she may receive such racist treatment here if it amounted to verbal abuse. It may not. All of this is to be frank speculation on the part of the appellant. It does not establish that she cannot return with him ... Even were she not able to return with him she has family in the UK including mother and brother ... He would be able to telephone. He would be able to write. He is not married. He can apply to come in to the country in the normal way. The child ... is young and cannot have yet bonded with him at one year old. There are no exceptional grounds for allowing the applicant to remain although he has been here nearly 5 years and has a family life of sorts.[70]

Like *Chikwamba*, the decision in *EB (Kosovo)* made life more complex for the lower courts, but, as the specific issue of delay was only one part of a broader proportionality assessment, it could be absorbed relatively easily into the reasoning, although there was sometimes a tendency, including in government guidance, to treat the case as turning on its facts rather than expressing an underlying principle.[71] More significant was the clarification that, after *Huang*, the test for removal was 'reasonableness', not 'insurmountable obstacles'. This made a concrete difference to how decisions were made, although the number of Court of Appeal and High Court decisions on these questions, even some years later, suggest that some decision-makers and first instance judges found these principles difficult to apply.[72]

V. REFLECTIONS ON THE FIRST PHASE DECISIONS

EB (Kosovo), *Beoku-Betts* and *Chikwamba* were, like *Huang*, remarkable decisions. The legal changes were not, in themselves, dramatic and concerned statutory interpretation or executive policy, and substantive Article 8 issues were relevant only in *EB (Kosovo)*. However, they collectively demonstrated how Article 8 could function to protect family life and represented a dramatic departure in approach and tone. *Beoku-Betts* recognised that an appeal that did not consider the rights of all family members led to inadequate rights protection

[70] *EB (Kosovo)* (n 49) [17].

[71] *RQK [Assisted Person]* [2011] CSOH 199 [39]; *Secretary of State for the Home Department v SU (Pakistan)* [2017] EWCA Civ 1069 [57]; 'New Home Office Article 8 policy' (*Free Movement*, 18 September 2008).

[72] eg *R (on the application of Omoruyi) v SSHD* [2008] EWHC 3120 (Admin); *VW (Uganda) v SSHD* [2009] EWCA Civ 5; *WB (Pakistan) v SSHD* [2009] EWCA Civ 215; *MA (Pakistan) v SSHD* [2009] EWCA Civ 953; *AO (Iraq) v SSHD* [2009] CSOH 168; *SL (Vietnam) v SSHD* [2010] EWCA Civ 225; *RM (Iran) v SSHD* [2012] CSOH 53; *Milan Gurung v The Entry Clearance Officer, New Delhi* [2016] EWCA Civ 358.

for other family members, who might often be more vulnerable than the main claimant. Requiring applicants to return abroad, the issue in *Chikwamba*, was, on the surface, an administrative requirement but, in practice, a substantial obstacle that often led to serious disruption or permanent separation that was mitigated in *Chikwamba*. The principal impact in *EB (Kosovo)* came from its express repudiation of the 'insurmountable obstacles' test, which previously acted as an almost complete bar to a successful claim. It also recognised that the strength of a family life claim in relation to the public interest in immigration control could be weakened by excessive delay. In brief, through these decisions the Court required a more flexible, fact-sensitive approach. The public interest in immigration control remained strong, but family life factors had to be properly considered and put into the balance. They demonstrated how the assertion in *Huang* of an autonomous role for the judiciary under the Human Rights Act could result in subtle but important adjustments.

The belief that family life mattered was reflected in the language of the judgments. The individuals were discussed sympathetically. All of them used first names at least some of the time and, although each of the applicants in these cases was a failed asylum seeker who had entered or remained without leave, their immigration status was discussed briefly and neutrally; terms such as 'illegal entry' were absent. Their personal circumstances appeared early in each judgment and received considerable attention (taking up more than 20 per cent of Lord Bingham's judgment in *EB (Kosovo)*). When discussing the relationships in issue, their depth and significance were emphasised: EB did not just 'accept' his partner's child, but 'treated her as his own'; Ms Chikwamba's marriage was 'a genuine consequence of the attachment that had grown between these two young people'.[73] Sponsors also moved out of the shadows: Latifa, EB's partner, was not patronised as 'a young lady', but respected as an individual with her own story; Mr Magaya, Ms Chikwamba's husband, was described as a childhood friend of his wife, a refugee and a father who faced separation from his wife and child. Coming from the UK's highest court, whose function is to decide points of law of 'the greatest public or constitutional importance', the space given to the human stories was a statement of their legal, not just their human, significance. The public interest in immigration control was still important, but the Court also brought family life to the fore.

The Court was later criticised for going beyond the Strasbourg jurisprudence.[74] At first glance, this critique has some force, given the Strasbourg Court's narrow vision of Article 8 discussed in chapter three and the absence in these three judgments of substantial engagement with the Strasbourg cases. This chapter has already suggested that, on close examination, the Court's conclusions were at the generous end of the Strasbourg spectrum but did not exceed it, or did so only

[73] *Chikwamba* (n 20) [5].

[74] See the discussion in ch 7, s II.

marginally. However, the idea of going 'beyond Strasbourg' is too simplistic a framework. While the House of Lords' language in all the judgments was more sympathetic than at Strasbourg, the legal consequence of these three cases was to require a closer examination of Strasbourg-generated factors, not to make them irrelevant. This closer examination was consistent with the doctrines of subsidiarity and the margin of appreciation, doctrines that reflected the difficulties for the Strasbourg Court in ruling on a huge number of claims across a diverse range of signatory states, so that states act as the main protector of rights, with the Strasbourg Court in a supervisory role. The active engagement of the domestic authorities was thus inherent in the protection of human rights and the form of that engagement was a matter for national constitutional arrangements. The relevant question was whether the Court was acting within its constitutional powers under domestic law, and this was clearly the case. The Human Rights Act required domestic courts to make human rights-compliant decisions that took account of, but were not completely confined by, the Strasbourg cases. There was, in Lord Bingham's words, no 'licence to freewheel', but there was also no obligation to adhere unreflectively to doctrine.[75] In *Chikwamba* and *EB (Kosovo)*, the Court applied the underlying principles in ways that recognised the different context and the absence of the margin of appreciation and required courts to undertake a deeper, fact-sensitive investigation.

One consequence of the Court's approach was that there was more evaluation of the public interest than was usual at Strasbourg. Here it is useful to return to the list in chapter one of questions that a court might ask in relation to the public or general interest:

1. What public (or general) interest does the measure serve?
2. How effective is it?
3. Is it necessary in this case?
4. Do the applicants' circumstances make it disproportionate?

The Strasbourg Court usually considers only question 4, and even then applies an exceptionality condition if residence is 'precarious'. *Huang* authorised a more searching approach, and this took place in both *Chikwamba* and *EB (Kosovo)*. *Chikwamba* saw the Court address all four questions. It answered questions 1 and 2 by finding that the policy aim of deterring opportunistic irregular migration was in the public interest but that the policy itself was over-inclusive as it failed to differentiate between motives for entry and overstay. The Court also addressed question 3 by finding that, while a procedural requirement might be lawful, it was not needed for someone in Ms Chikwamba's situation. Finally, it addressed question 4 because it considered the impact on Ms Chikwamba, her husband and their daughter of separation and found that the public interest did not outweigh the interference in their family life.

[75] Lord Bingham, 'The Human Rights Act' (2010) 6 *European Human Rights Law Review* 568, 572.

EB (Kosovo) recognised that a policy of enforcing immigration control through the removal of irregular migrants was generally in the public interest so that questions 1 and 2 were answered for the government. It addressed question 3 by finding that the weight of the public interest could be reduced in some circumstances. Finally, it emphasised the importance of question 4 by recognising the problems of relocation for the spouse or partner and the importance of maintaining a parent–child relationship.

These decisions therefore enabled courts to take a more enquiring approach to family reunification claims. This should not be overstated; some cases would now succeed but many others would not, despite some hard choices for the families involved.[76] Further, as the discussion here has shown, lower courts tended to interpret them narrowly and their impact was sometimes less than hoped for. One factor that has already been mentioned in relation to *Huang* was possible identification by some Tribunal judges with the concerns of the government.[77] The switch from almost automatic refusal to a considered, fact-sensitive assessment required a new, time-consuming approach and culture, and the decisions were not always easy to apply. If near-automatic refusals were now unlawful, so were near-automatic acceptances, but where the line should be drawn depended on the answers to some difficult questions: to what extent should the needs of a child outweigh a poor or deceptive immigration history? What sacrifices should a sponsor reasonably be asked to make to move abroad? It is not surprising that these questions had to be worked out through subsequent appeals and judicial reviews.

In doing so, lower court judges had to apply new legal principles contained in judgments that sometimes appeared to face both ways. This began with *Huang*, discussed in the previous chapter, where the Court rejected the test of exceptionality and predicted that only 'a very small minority' would still succeed, but did not specifically say that the numbers accepted were likely to increase. This led some lower courts to conclude that nothing of substance needed to change, with the result that the 'reasonableness' test and the rejection of 'insurmountable obstacles' had to be restated in *EB (Kosovo)*. But *EB (Kosovo)* did not entirely resolve the tension. They key passage in the judgment said:

> It will, for example, recognise that it will rarely be proportionate to uphold an order for removal of a spouse if there is a close and genuine bond with the other spouse and that spouse cannot reasonably be expected to follow the removed spouse to the country of removal, or if the effect of the order is to sever a genuine and subsisting relationship between parent and child. But cases will not ordinarily raise such stark choices, and there is in general no alternative to making a careful and informed evaluation of the facts of the particular case.[78]

[76] For an example, see *VW (Uganda)* (n 72).
[77] See ch 4, s VIII.
[78] *EB (Kosovo)* (n 49) [12].

The first sentence suggested an accommodating test; immigration lawyers would probably say that a substantial number, if not the majority, of their clients could meet it, particularly given the troubled and impoverished regions from where many applicants came. However, the next sentence suggested that these cases were, in fact, the exception: 'cases will not ordinarily raise such stark choices', implying that these factors would often not apply. The test was more generous than before but, taken as a whole, the passage was ambiguous and later courts could take different meanings from it.

A similar ambiguity was present in *Chikwamba*, where Lord Brown said:

> I am far from suggesting that the Secretary of State *should* routinely apply this policy [of allowing in-country applications] in all but exceptional cases. Rather it seems to me that only comparatively rarely, certainly in family cases involving children, should an article 8 appeal be dismissed on the basis that it would be proportionate and more appropriate for the appellant to apply for leave from abroad. (emphasis in original)[79]

It would have been easy for subsequent decision-makers to understand how to apply such a test in practice.[80] The Court was trying to do something new with human rights, but would have been anxious about going too far or raising unrealisable expectations. The result seems to have been uncertainty and thus imprecision about where the new boundaries should be sited. There was a space in which applicants could now succeed, but its dimensions were difficult to measure, leaving lower courts to work this out. While lower courts commonly have to interpret higher level decisions, here there was particular uncertainty and an absence of detailed legal guidance.

This was not surprising; Article 8 requires fact-sensitive decisions, and guidance was therefore difficult to deliver. In this context, factual narratives had to do a lot of work. This chapter has already mentioned the sympathetic treatment of the claimants, but this was subtly done. The Court wove favourable factors into the narrative, while countervailing factors were presented neutrally and briefly. In *Chikwamba*, for example, the applicant's other two children, her relatives in Harare and the failure of her asylum claim for lack of credibility were mentioned in passing, the emphasis being on her new relationship and younger child. In *Beoku-Betts*, the applicant's overstaying was also mentioned only very briefly and explained as a misunderstanding. In *EB (Kosovo)*, there were two competing narratives, but the unfavourable assessments of the lower courts were presented as quotations and only after a lengthy and sympathetic account at the start of the judgment. The Court seemed to be doing something quite complex here, saying that these applicants had important interests that demanded respect and attention even if they were not model migrants in all respects. Given the unsympathetic accounts that had predominated earlier, they sought to redress the balance by putting more emphasis on their humanity. The aim was to ensure more balanced and finely grained human rights assessments.

[79] *Chikwamba* (n 20) [44].

[80] The paragraph was later said not to lay down a 'legal test': *Kotecha and Das v SSHD* [48].

This message, however, was not necessarily received as such by lower courts. Instead, the sympathetic factors became the only ones that counted, leading to the tendency discussed earlier to set very high criteria for subsequent success. *Chikwamba*, for example, was said to need an 'unassailable' case for entry clearance even though that is not what the judgment said.[81] It is perhaps not surprising that lower court judges, struggling to differentiate the small number of meritorious applicants, treated the emphasis by the Court on the parties' sympathetic qualities as setting a standard that few could meet. There were not a few deserving cases which a more discerning examination would identify but thousands of families who needed to live together in the UK despite the absence of immigration rights. The pressures on the Tribunal would have created a preference for bright-line rules and, in some instances at least, sympathy for executive concerns that would push them to more restrictive interpretations.[82] There was perhaps a gap in mutual understanding. Senior justices rarely had direct experience of immigration advocacy or adjudication, particularly at Tribunal level. None of the House of Lords panel in these cases had prior expertise in immigration law and they may not have appreciated the difficulties of executing such a nuanced test in the Tribunal environment and the need therefore for more explicit guidance. They may also have been anxious about drawing political attention to what they were doing.

In summary, these cases saw the Court acting to protect family life, while pulling back from addressing all issues directly, leading to some lack of clarity. The decisions were entirely proper constitutionally and the judgments were concerned with policy, not legislation or even the Immigration Rules, but the Court's reticence suggested awareness that even such modest advances could be controversial, and it was less explicit than it might otherwise have been about what it was doing. The rather subtle character of the judgments meant that the Tribunal, situated at the sharp end of immigration adjudication, sometimes found it difficult to give enough weight to family life or to carry out the nuanced assessments that were needed. These problems did not detract from the significance or boldness of these decisions, or the difference that they made, but they were not easy to execute.

VI. CONCLUSION

The three decisions discussed in this chapter were, like *Huang*, remarkable. Uniquely in the history of British immigration control, they centred the predicaments of binational families and used human rights to create a space in which their claims could be acknowledged. In so doing, they reversed the 'Strasbourg reversal' by treating Article 8 as a guiding principle, putting family life at the

[81] *SZ (Zimbabwe)* (n 41) [18].
[82] See ch 4, s VIII.

heart of the evaluation and critically evaluating government claims as to the public interest. This reordering was reflected in the argument but also in the structure and language of the judgments and the focus on the human dilemmas and difficulties faced by applicants.

The decisions were made using judicial powers under the Human Rights Act and the Court acted within the scope of its authority. It 'took account' of the Strasbourg jurisprudence and did not depart from its underlying principles but applied them in a domestic context, without the deference of the wide margin of appreciation that had previously been adopted by the domestic courts. The result was a fact-sensitive approach that took the claims of family life seriously and was willing to interrogate the public interest justification for interference. This was a new and unusual approach to immigration, although it may have been more familiar in family law.

The Court therefore acted boldly in an area where courts had previously shown extensive executive deference. This may be why the Court did not always show how it arrived at its conclusions, omitting to address all the steps along the way. The consequence was that lower courts did not always know what to make of these judgments and were sometime overcautious in applying them, reflecting also some wider institutional anxiety and the inherent problems of creating guidelines for inherently fact-sensitive decisions in such a charged area. The next chapter shows how, in a series of later cases, the Court addressed the protection of family life in claims that drew on statute and the Immigration Rules and, in so doing, modified its approach, notably by avoiding sole reliance on Article 8 in the immigration context.

6

*Still Family First: The Second Post-*Huang *Phase*

I. INTRODUCTION

THIS CHAPTER CONTINUES the analysis of the post-*Huang* cases in the House of Lords/Supreme Court (the Court). It discusses four decisions made in the three-year period from 2008 to 2011. It shows that the Court continued to use its authority, post-*Huang*, to determine human rights compatibility in ways that protected family life, and the decisions had a significant impact on government policies. However, the Court ended the period seriously divided for the first time and exposed to overt government criticism.

I describe these decisions as the second post-*Huang* phase, distinguishing them from the first phase, discussed in the previous chapter. This requires some justification as the distinctive, unified character of the decisions is not immediately obvious. They did not all even address Article 8, they were decided over a period of two years and the judicial panel was not the same throughout. At the same time, there were some continuities with the first phase, including a shared acknowledgement of the importance of family life and considerable overlap in the judges involved.[1] Yet, my argument is that they can be considered as a distinct phase. Collectively, they moved beyond the assessment of policy and looked at the compatibility with human rights of the Immigration Rules and statutory law. None of them relied solely on Article 8 but drew on a wider range of legal resources. They also reverted to a more conventional style of decision-making. They suggested that the Court remained willing to use its human rights jurisdiction to protect family life but was cautious about relying too heavily on Article 8 and the more personal style of judgment of the first phase.

The chapter opens with two decisions that did not involve Article 8. Their treatment is therefore quite brief, but they are included because they speak to the concern of this book with the reunification of binational families in the

[1] Although Lord Bingham retired in 2008, shortly after the first phase, Lord Brown sat on all the cases in both phases, Lady Hale on all except *Mahad*, and Lord Hope on all except *Baiai* and *Quila*. Lead judgments were given in both phases by Lord Brown (*Beoku-Betts*, *Chikwamba* and *Mahad*) and Lord Bingham (*EB (Kosovo)* and *Baiai*).

UK, while the absence of Article 8 was, in one of them at least, significant. The first is *Baiai*, which concerned a statutory scheme that interfered with the right to marry under Article 12. The decision was congruent with the wider picture of a Court committed to protecting family life, it deployed comparable forms of reasoning and the clear character of the Article 12 right underlined the uncertainty of Article 8. The second case is *Mahad*, where the Court was asked if Article 8 required interpretation of the maintenance requirements in the Immigration Rules to permit financial support by third parties. The Court found that the Rules already permitted third party support and made no substantive comment on Article 8.

The third decision, *ZH (Tanzania)*, was one of the most important Article 8 cases decided by the Court. The issue was the impact of children's best interests – in this instance, British citizen children – on decisions concerning the expulsion of their parents. In applying Article 8, the Court drew on Article 3 of the Convention on the Rights of the Child and its incorporation into British law through statute. The final decision, *Quila*, challenged an amendment to the Immigration Rules that raised the minimum age of sponsorship and admission for marriage from 18 to 21. It was decided under Article 8 alone, but the Court stressed the non-immigration aim of the policy and pointed also to the relevance of Article 12.

The chapter then discusses what these decisions tell us about the themes and arguments of this book. It observes that, perhaps encouraged by their success in the first phase, applicants now asked the Court to address the compatibility of the Immigration Rules and statute. The Court continued to give weight to the claims of family life and was prepared to engage with these questions, but it no longer relied on the intersection of Article 8 with family reunification alone. The judgments were also pragmatic about what they could achieve even if this was not as wide-ranging or secure as might be hoped.

The chapter concludes by observing that the decisions in this and the two previous chapters were unprecedented in terms of judicial protection for binational families, but they pushed against the limitations of Article 8. Article 8 could not become a robust tool without wider understanding and support for the values it embodied. This became more evident as claimants asked the Court to move beyond the evaluation of administrative practice. While the decisions discussed in this chapter showed the Court responding positively, there were the first signs of judicial unease and of wider political dissent, anticipating the hostile political climate and the Court's later decisions, which are analysed in the following chapter.

II. *BAIAI*: THE RIGHT TO MARRY

Baiai was an application for judicial review of a statutory scheme (the certificates of approval scheme) implemented in 2005, which restricted the right to marry of non-nationals in the UK.[2] The challenge was under Article 12 of the European Convention on Human Rights, which reads: 'Men and women of marriageable age have the right to marry and to found a family, according to the national laws governing the exercise of this right.'

Article 12 does not contain a public interest exception, but limits on the right may be imposed by national law. The European Court of Human Rights (ECtHR, Strasbourg Court or Strasbourg) has upheld restrictions based on, for example, consent, capacity, age, place of marriage, consanguinity and monogamy, but government measures must not 'impair the essence of the right' or be arbitrary or disproportionate.[3]

Under the certificates of approval scheme, non-EEA nationals who did not have indefinite leave to remain or a visa granted for the specific purpose of marriage had to apply and pay for a 'certificate of approval' to marry. This was granted only to those who had long-term leave to be in the UK, such as students or workers, and only then if that leave was not about to expire. Visitors, irregular migrants, almost all asylum seekers and migrants nearing the end of their leave were refused, with no investigation of the marriage. The stated aim of the certificates of approval scheme was the detection and prevention of sham marriages, but its impact was much wider, preventing the marriages of thousands of non-nationals regardless of their relationship. In so doing, the government could pre-empt post-marriage claims based on Article 8 or EU law.[4]

The judgment was delivered in July 2009, led by Lord Bingham with no dissent. It found that the scheme violated Article 12. Lord Bingham observed that Article 12 was a strong right, widely recognised in international law, and that national restrictions may relate only to issues connected to the marriage itself, such as capacity or consent. A marriage of convenience was not protected by Article 12 and measures which detected and prevented only such marriages would not violate Article 12. While states might make inquiries to establish that a marriage was not sham, they 'must never injure or impair the substance of the right' through rules which prevented an entire category of individuals from marrying because some might not be genuine.[5] The certificates of approval scheme was a blanket prohibition and therefore an unlawful infringement of the right to marry.[6] The fee of £295 (or £590 if both partners were subject to the scheme) was excessive.[7] In consequence, the regulations and guidance that

[2] *Baiai and others v SSHD* [2008] UKHL 53.

[3] For a recent discussion of the Strasbourg cases, see European Court of Human Rights, *Guide on Article 12 of the European Convention on Human Rights* (31 August 2021); for a summary of the cases at the time of the *Baiai* judgment, see paras [13]–[21] of that judgment.

[4] *Baiai* (n 2) [6]; for a further discussion, see H Wray, 'An Ideal Husband? Marriages of Convenience, Moral Gate-Keeping and Immigration to the UK' (2006) 8 *European Journal of Migration and Law* 303.

[5] *Baiai* (n 2) [14].

[6] ibid [31].

[7] ibid [30].

contained the policy were unlawful. The governing statute, which created powers of investigation but did not set out the details of the scheme, was mostly compatible with Article 12, but a provision that exempted those marrying in the Church of England breached Articles 12 and 14 as it discriminated by religion.[8] A declaration of incompatibility with Convention Rights under section 4 of the Human Rights Act was upheld as regards this exemption, although by the time of the judgment the government had agreed to remove it.

As with Article 8, one question was how far the Court should assess the government's justification of its policy. The government argued that the scheme concerned 'an area of broad social policy where the judgment of the legislature and executive should be given considerable weight'.[9] This, Lord Bingham said, was 'too sweeping'. While some political judgements were involved, for example, as to the prevalence of marriages of convenience,

> the court cannot abdicate its function of deciding whether as a matter of law the section 19 scheme ... violated the respondents' right to marry guaranteed by article 12. The answer to that question does not turn on considerations of broad social policy but on an accurate analysis of the scheme and the law.[10]

Article 12 did not involve a proportionality assessment, but it did require an evaluation of the effect and purpose of national laws and, as the passage just cited shows, the Court saw itself as having an autonomous function in that regard, reflecting the position in *Huang* on Article 8 proportionality. Using this approach, the Court determined that the scheme went further than necessary to detect sham marriages. This was not surprising; the applicants had also succeeded in all lower court proceedings, and the Court's findings were later approved in a separate case brought in Strasbourg.[11] The right to marry was confirmed as fundamental and only narrowly qualified. In her concurring judgment, Lady Hale referred to historical bans on mixed marriages in Nazi Germany and the USA, and constitutional guarantees in South Africa, where apartheid laws had previously restricted marriage.[12] Restrictions on the marriage rights of migrants therefore transcended purely migration-related considerations.

In its analysis, the Court referred to Article 8, but principally to note its weakness compared to the right to marry.[13] Article 8 rights are less directly protected ('respect for') and explicitly qualified by specific public interests, in contrast to the much narrower exception in Article 12. However, there was a common question: what did the right protect? Kesby said of *Baiai* that the issue was 'not the legitimacy of the immigration policy but the scope of the right

[8] Asylum and Immigration (Treatment of Claimants, etc) Act 2004 (as originally enacted), s 19(1).
[9] *Baiai* (n 2) [25].
[10] ibid [25].
[11] *O'Donoghue and Others v the United Kingdom* App no 34848/07 (14 November 2010).
[12] *Baiai* (n 2) [44].
[13] ibid [15].

to marry'.[14] Despite the differences between Article 12 and Article 8, the same question arose under Article 8: what does the right protect? In *Huang*, the Court referred to 'the fundamental right protected by article 8'.[15] *Chikwamba* and *EB (Kosovo)* recognised a government duty to protect family life and considered when and how interference would be lawful. There was thus some similarity in the underlying structural issue, but whether interference was permitted under Article 12 depended only on the reason for the interference, whereas Article 8 required a fair balance assessment of all the facts. It followed that individual circumstances were less significant and the judgment contained little about the parties' personal situation, and did not use the empathetic language and style of the first phase judgments. There was, however, an extensive exegesis of the Strasbourg jurisprudence. Lord Bingham did not mention any domestic precedents, although there was a brief discussion by Lady Hale. The argument was thus framed confidently around the Strasbourg jurisprudence.

III. *MAHAD*: THIRD PARTY SUPPORT

Mahad, decided in December 2009, was the first judgment by the newly formed Supreme Court discussed in this book.[16] It concerned the rules for ensuring the financial self-sufficiency of family migrants after their arrival. At that time (the position is now significantly more restrictive), the Immigration Rules required applicants for admission to show that the family unit would be 'adequately maintained', a relatively modest test, linked to welfare support levels. The issue was whether funds provided by parties other than the sponsor ('third party support') could be used to show that maintenance was adequate. The question before the Court was whether Article 8 required the Immigration Rules to be construed to permit third party support. The Rules addressed the position of children, spouses and dependent adult relatives all in slightly different ways, and lower courts had reached sometimes conflicting positions as to whether third party support was permitted in each case.[17]

A fundamental problem for the applicants was that, as the government pointed out, *Huang* had already decided that the Immigration Rules do not have to comply with Article 8, as leave under Article 8 can be granted outside the Rules. If the case had ended there, the claim would have achieved little. While confirmation that Article 8 might require third party support to be permitted outside the Immigration Rules, without detailed argument and a concrete,

[14] A Kesby, 'Internal Borders and Immigration Control: New Prospects and Challenges' (2010) 2 *European Human Rights Law Review* 176, 187.

[15] *Huang v Secretary of State for the Home Department* [2007] UKHL 11 [20].

[16] *Mahad and others v SSHD* [2009] UKSC 16.

[17] *MW (Liberia) v SSHD* [2007] EWCA Civ 1376; *AM (Ethiopia) v Entry Clearance Officer* [2008] EWCA Civ 1082; *AA (Bangladesh) v SSHD* [2005] UKAIT 105; *Mahad (Ethiopia) v ECO* [2008] EWCA Civ 1082.

fact-based claim, it would have been of little value. Instead, Lord Brown, in a judgment endorsed by the entire panel, sidestepped the issue by focusing on the meaning of the Immigration Rules. Administrative rules were not to be 'construed with all the strictness applicable to the construction of a statute or a statutory instrument but, instead, sensibly according to the natural and ordinary meaning of the words used'.[18]

He therefore compared the wording of the relevant paragraphs within the context of the Rules as a whole and concluded that they already permitted third party support, given the policy aim implicit in the Rules, which was to ensure new entrants did not need to access public funds. He found government objections unconvincing. The credibility of support could be verified in the usual way, and commitments, if necessary, made legally binding. He observed that evidence of financial security was always precarious to some degree and third party support was no different in that regard.[19] He saw the issue as one of common sense: 'Are rich and devoted uncles (or, indeed, large supportive immigrant communities such as often assist those seeking entry) really to be ignored in this way?'[20]

Lord Kerr, in his concurring judgment, expanded on the theme:

> The vaunted precariousness of support from a third party source is, in my opinion, no greater than that which might arise in the course of the ordinary vagaries and vicissitudes of life. Promised employment may not materialise or may last for only a short time. Dependence on benefits received by the family member who is settled in the United Kingdom may cease. As Lord Brown has pointed out, there is no warrant for (and much to be said against) the view that third party support occupies a particular category of uncertainty.[21]

Lord Collins reflected on the narrow view of family taken by the government:

> The overall point in these appeals is that the arguments for the Secretary of State were founded on the model of a nuclear self-supporting family, which is far removed from the reality of the situation in the typical immigration case. This is not a new phenomenon. Members of immigrant communities have always supported each other.[22]

Although the Court based its decision on the wording of the Rules and did not consider Article 8, it therefore considered the policy arguments for the Rules and found the government's justification unimpressive. It also suggested that government concerns could be overcome through undertakings or joint sponsorship.[23] In this respect, the judgment recalled the critical analysis of policy aims in *Chikwamba*, but without reliance on Article 8.

[18] *Mahad* (n 16) [10].
[19] ibid [19], [20].
[20] ibid [19].
[21] ibid [54].
[22] ibid [45].
[23] ibid [20], [32]–[33].

Legal commentators had not expected this pragmatic approach.[24] It enabled migrants to rely on third party support but avoided finding the Rules incompatible and the consequent uncertainty of separate Article 8 decisions made outside the Rules. The judgment was instantly effective, but its efficacy would last only so long as the Rules were unchanged. In fact, they were amended in 2012, changing the maintenance requirements in ways discussed in the next chapter. In the interim, however, a few Tribunal decisions showed how the *Mahad* decision enabled a more flexible approach to maintenance for the benefit of families.[25]

The judgment suggested little enthusiasm for engaging with Article 8. Lord Brown said of the Article 8 argument:

> Obviously, were the Secretary of State now to amend the rules to exclude third party support – and Parliament not then disapprove them – it might well become necessary to [engage with Article 8]. The argument could possibly be affected by the precise form of amendments.[26]

Had the case been decided under Article 8, the Court would have had to address the difficult question of whether and when the Immigration Rules will be unlawful if leave outside the Rules can be granted. There was likely some relief that a solution was available without addressing that question.

IV. *ZH (TANZANIA)*: THE BEST INTERESTS OF CHILDREN

ZH (Tanzania), handed down on 1 February 2011, remains one of the Supreme Court's most influential decisions, affecting the treatment of children under immigration control well beyond family reunification.[27] The appeal concerned two British citizen children born in the UK to an irregular Tanzanian woman and her British husband, from whom she had separated without, it seems, having applied for regularisation. She had, however, made three unsuccessful asylum applications, two using a false identity. Without the children's claim, there would have been no defence to her expulsion. The father had significant health problems, but saw the children regularly. It was unlikely that he could either care for them alone in the UK or visit them in Tanzania. The children would almost certainly leave the UK with their mother, removing them from their place of nationality, residence and education and ending the relationship with their father.

[24] '3rd Party Support Judgement' (*Free Movement*, 20 December 2009).

[25] *Yarce (Adequate Maintenance: Benefits: Spain) Re* [2012] UKUT 425 (IAC); *Jahangara Begum and others (maintenance – savings) Bangladesh* [2011] UKUT 00246 (IAC).

[26] *Mahad* (n 16) [31].

[27] *ZH (Tanzania) v SSHD* [2011] UKSC 4. See also R Taylor, 'Putting Children First: Children's Interests as a Primary Consideration in Public Law' (2016) 28 *Child & Family Law Quarterly* 45,65; J Pobjoy, 'The Best Interests of the Child Principle as an Independent Source of International Protection' (2015) 64 *ICLQ* 327, 338; A Christie, 'The Best Interests of the Child in UK Immigration Law' (2013) 16 *Nottingham Law Journal* 16.

The 'over-arching issue' was the weight of the children's best interests in the decision to remove or deport one or both of their parents and when a parent might be expelled if the consequence was the enforced departure of a citizen child.[28]

The starting point in Lady Hale's lead judgment was Article 8 and, for the first time in the judgments analysed so far, there was an extended discussion of the Article 8 Strasbourg cases. Lady Hale pointed to the priority awarded to children's interests in the then recent judgment of *Rodrigues da Silva and Hoogkamer*, which concerned the planned expulsion of a mother without status who had a young, Dutch citizen daughter.[29] She observed that there was a disjuncture between the severity of the precariousness principle, expressed in that judgment, and the violation finding that followed. Lady Hale thereby went straight to the heart of the issue: chapter three demonstrated that Strasbourg's severity towards migrants without status was softened only when a child was affected. Lady Hale also anticipated the express incorporation into the Article 8 proportionality assessment of the obligation in Article 3 of the Convention on the Rights of the Child, which requires that in all actions concerning children, their best interests should be 'a primary consideration'.[30] At that time, it had been mentioned only in *Neulinger*, which concerned parental abduction of a child.[31] Lady Hale referred to *Neulinger* and the obligation under Article 3 to explain that 'It is not difficult to understand why the Strasbourg Court has become more sensitive to the welfare of the children who are innocent victims of their parents' choices'.[32] This anticipated the express mention of Article 3 in the subsequent family reunification decisions of *Nunez* and *Jeunesse*.

Lady Hale also noted that Article 3 was now a binding obligation on the UK government in immigration and nationality matters, following removal of the UK's reservation to the Convention in 2008. The 'spirit, if not the precise language', had been incorporated into section 55 of the Borders, Citizenship and Immigration Act 2009, which provided that immigration functions must be fulfilled 'having due regard to the need to safeguard and promote the welfare of children who are in the United Kingdom'.[33] The remainder of the judgment analysed how the Article 3 duty affected the Article 8 proportionality assessment, and the legal analysis is rich in references to decisions from other jurisdictions, materials from international conventions and monitoring bodies, and academic commentary. The findings were, in effect, 'Article 8 plus', and did not depend only on the fragile thread of the Strasbourg decisions. The statutory duty was particularly important as it created a direct obligation on government.

[28] *ZH (Tanzania)* (n 27) [1].
[29] *Rodrigues da Silva and Hoogkamer v Netherlands* (2007) 44 EHRR 729.
[30] United Nations Convention on the Rights of the Child (adopted 20 November 1989, entered into force 2 September, UNGA Res 44/25), Art 3.
[31] *Neulinger v Switzerland* (2010) 28 BHRC 706.
[32] *ZH (Tanzania)* (n 27) [21].
[33] ibid [23].

While children's interests were not paramount but primary, they had to be 'considered first' and not diluted by the shortcomings of their parents, although their interests might, on balance, be outweighed by the cumulative effect of other considerations, including those of immigration control.[34] In his concurring judgment, Lord Kerr seemed to go even further: 'Where the best interests of the child clearly favour a certain course, that course should be followed unless countervailing reasons of considerable force displace them.'[35] Nationality was particularly important. Lady Hale observed that, while it was not a 'trump card', nationality was of particular importance in assessing a child's best interests.[36] The significance of citizenship was emphasised even more strongly by Lord Hope in his assenting judgment: 'The fact of British citizenship does not trump everything else. But it will hardly ever be less than a very significant and weighty factor against moving children who have that status to another country …'[37]

While children's interests now carried more weight, they could still be outweighed by the public interest. The overall test was whether it was 'reasonable' to expect the child to live in the other country, a child-centred test but not the same as saying that it must be in the child's best interests to do so. Even so, it was clear that more was required than before to justify a decision against their interests. Decision-makers must identify a child's best interests, treat them as the single most important consideration and show why they should be overridden. It is arguable that these obligations were not new, but the authority of the Supreme Court in this and the subsequent case of *Zoumbas* ensured that the necessity of a serious, structured consideration was impressed on lower courts and decision-makers.[38] Children ceased to be 'parcels', appendages of their parents; they were now the holders of rights that must be respected, even at some cost to the presumed necessities of immigration control.[39] Sketchy and uninformed assessments that did not address the issues properly were liable to be overturned.[40] Some critics suggested that, in consequence, children's interests

[34] ibid [25]–[33]; see also Taylor, 'Putting Children First: Children's Interests as a Primary Consideration in Public Law'; J Eekelaar, 'The Role of the Best Interests Principle in Decisions Affecting Children and Decisions about Children' (2015) 23 *International Journal of Children's Rights* 3.

[35] *ZH (Tanzania)* (n 27) [45]; see also Eekelaar, 'The Role of the Best Interests Principle in Decisions Affecting Children and Decisions about Children'.

[36] *ZH (Tanzania)* (n 27) [30].

[37] ibid [41].

[38] J Fortin, 'Are Children's Best Interests Really Best? *ZH (Tanzania) (FC) v Secretary of State for the Home Department*' (2011) 74 *MLR* 932; *Zoumbas v Secretary of State for the Home Department* [2013] UKSC 74; for an example, see *LD (Zimbabwe) v SSHD* [2010] UKUT 278 (IAC).

[39] *ZH (Tanzania)* (n 27) [32]; see also J Bhabha, *Child Migration and Human Rights in a Global Age* (Princeton, Princeton University Press, 2014) 12.

[40] For example, *JO, CU, AU, BU v SSHD* [2014] UKUT 00517 (IAC); *R (on the application of Project for the Registration of Children of British Citizens) v SSHD* [2021] EWCA Civ 193; *ST (a child) v SSHD* [2021] EWHC 1085; *R (on the application of MG (Iran)) v SSHD* [2015] EWHC 3142; see also Pobjoy, 'The Best Interests of the Child Principle as an Independent Source of International Protection', 338–39.

were now effectively paramount.[41] This was clearly not the case in extradition and criminal deportations, where the public interest was both stronger and more specific.[42] Nor did the judgment say that children's interests could be displaced only by other rights-based considerations or that there was a public interest in promoting the best interests of children.[43] However, it was certainly more difficult to expel the parents of citizen children if there was no criminality. There might, though, still be times when the child could reasonably travel with the parent or where the parent–child relationship was insufficiently strong to outweigh the public interest in immigration control.

This book has observed that the Article 8 Strasbourg jurisprudence gave little regard to the interests of sponsors and other family members in remaining in their own homes. *ZH (Tanzania)* made citizenship significant, at least for children. In this, Lady Hale again anticipated developments. While the Strasbourg cases had not, at that point, given weight to a child's nationality in the migration context, one month after *ZH (Tanzania)*, the *Zambrano* judgment in the European Court of Justice found that a non-EU citizen parent could not be expelled if this would force an EU citizen child to leave the EU.[44] In *Genovese*, in October 2011, the Strasbourg Court found that citizenship formed part of a person's social identity and fell within Article 8 private life so that the discriminatory attribution of a child's nationality breached Article 14 with Article 8.[45] The children's Dutch nationality was a factor cited by the Strasbourg Court when finding a violation in *Jeunesse* in 2014.[46] These developments, of which *ZH (Tanzania)* was part, were welcome; for decades, children's nationality had been treated as an incidental, formal matter. States were not required to ensure that its child citizens were practically enabled to exercise their legal right to live within its boundaries and the separation of families or the 'constructive' deportation of children when their parents were expelled had been regarded as normal, barely meriting regretful comment.[47]

If *ZH (Tanzania)* improved the position of citizen children in family reunification, there were fewer direct benefits for children outside the UK and non-citizen

[41] P Glen, 'The Removability of Non-citizen Parents and the Best Interests of Citizen Children: How to Balance Competing Imperatives in the Context of Removal Proceedings' (2012) 30 *Berkeley Journal of International Law* 1,34; R English, 'Analysis: Children's "Best Interests" and the Problem of Balance' (*UK Human Rights Blog*, 2 February 2011).

[42] On extradition, see, eg the troubled judgment in *HH v Deputy Prosecutor of the Italian Republic, Genoa* [2012] UKSC 25. On deportation, see *SS (Nigeria) v SSHD* [2013] EWCA Civ 550.

[43] *ZH (Tanzania)* (n 27) [28].

[44] Case C-34/09 *Ruiz Zambrano v ONEm* [2011] EUECJ; see also Fortin, 'Are Children's Best Interests Really Best?'.

[45] *Genovese v Malta* App no 53124/09 (2014) 58 EHRR 25.

[46] *Jeunesse v Netherlands* [2014] ECHR 1309. For a discussion of children's nationality and human rights, see D Prabhat and J Hambly, 'Bettering the Best Interests of the Child Determination: Of Checklists and Balancing Exercises' (2017) 25 *International Journal of Children's Rights* 754.

[47] See Lady Hale in *ZH (Tanzania)* (n 27) [20]; Fortin, 'Are Children's Best Interests Really Best?'; C Sawyer, 'Not Every Child Matters: the UK's Expulsion of British Citizens' (2006) 14 *International Journal of Children's Rights* 157.

children. The section 55 duty applied only to children in the UK, so children living abroad with a non-citizen parent were reliant entirely on Article 8 if that parent could not meet the Immigration Rules.[48] Where their lives in the other country were settled and care was adequate, the parent's admission was often not considered necessary.[49] However, the largest group of children who derived limited benefit from *ZH (Tanzania)* were non-citizen children in the UK. The admission of the family members of child refugees was barely affected, although there was the occasional exception.[50] Families in the UK where parents faced expulsion and the children did not have citizenship also derived less benefit. They obtained no advantage from the added weight that citizenship conferred, but there was another factor. Under British nationality law, a non-citizen child will usually have two non-citizen parents and removal involves the whole family unit. Family reunification questions would arise only if the child had an independent claim to remain, and the *ZH (Tanzania)* judgment did not provide new grounds for such a claim. Lady Hale's list of factors that applied to the best interests assessment of non-citizen children was mainly confined to those relevant to an Article 8 private life claim: the child's integration in this country, length of absence from the other country, living and care arrangements.[51] She also included the loss of relationships with parents or other family members, but these would rarely come into play if the whole family was to be removed. Meanwhile, the social or health benefits and educational opportunities that flowed from living in the UK attached only to claims concerning citizen children, even though they were important also for non-citizen children.

As Article 8 private life rights were already available to these children, the judgment did not provide substantive change, although they gained from the procedural requirement to have their interests specifically and properly considered.[52] This was made clear in the Supreme Court's 2013 judgment in *Zoumbas*, which concerned such a family who originated from the Congo.[53] The Court said that the children's best interests assessment should proceed on the basis that the parents will be removed if they have no right to live in the UK. In almost all cases, it would be in the children's best interests to go with their parents, particularly as factors such as superior health care or education would

[48] *T (s.55 BCIA 2009: Entry Clearance: Jamaica)* [2011] UKUT 483 (IAC).

[49] *SG (Child of Polygamous Marriage: Nepal)* [2012] UKUT 265(IAC); *SD v Entry Clearance Officer Colombo* [2020] UKUT 00043(IAC) [105].

[50] *R (on the application of FWF) v SSHD* [2021] EWCA Civ 88; *SSHD v ZAT* [2016] EWCA Civ 810; *R (on the application of FTH) v SSHD* [2020] EWCA Civ 494; *AT and another (Article 8 ECHR – Child Refugee – Family Reunification) Eritrea* [2016] UKUT 227 (IAC).

[51] *ZH (Tanzania)* (n 27) [29].

[52] See, eg *Tinizaray v SSHD* [[2011] EWHC 1850; *R (on the application of SQ (Pakistan)) v Upper Tribunal Immigration and Asylum Chamber* [2013] EWCA Civ 1251; *HH (AP) v SSHD* [2012] CSOH 83.
EV (Philippines) v SSHD [2014] EWCA Civ 874; *JW (China), MW (China) v SSHD* [2013] EWCA Civ 1526; *ZS (Jamaica) & Anr v SSHD* [2012] EWCA Civ 1639; *Jogee and Manderson v SSHD* [2017] EWCA Civ 2715.

[53] *Zoumbas* (n 38).

not form part of the assessment: '[The children] were not British citizens. They had no right to future education and health care in this country.'[54]

It is correct that there are no rights to future education or healthcare independent of presence in the state, but, where rights do exist, they are not dependent on citizenship. Universal rights to healthcare and education, for example, appear in the Convention on the Rights of the Child.[55] There has always been some provision in British law and policy for children to remain after some (usually seven) years' residence because the disruption of moving would be disproportionate.[56] The Court's statement was therefore arguably an oversimplification, but it reflected concern that allowing social rights, such as educational opportunities, to found the basis of an Article 8 family life, as opposed to private life, claim would overextend the scope of the Article 8 right. It would certainly have attracted controversy. *ZH (Tanzania)* was therefore a bold decision, but it was also a pragmatic one. While the application of the section 55 duty would be important across a range of immigration and asylum claims, the immediate impact on Article 8 and family reunification was confined to citizen children at least one of whose parents was an irregular migrant in the UK. For that group, however, it was significant.

Lady Hale's judgment was carefully crafted to achieve that effect. Its scholarly character was different to the style and structure of the decisions discussed in the previous chapter. It referred to many Strasbourg cases, alongside other sources, and there were few efforts to personalise the claim. The children's names were, for obvious reasons, initialised, and no further identifying details were provided. There was also no need to ensure a sympathetic understanding of their parents. Quite the reverse; the point to establish was that children's claims would transcend parental wrongdoing in a significant number of cases.[57]

V. *QUILA*: FORCED MARRIAGE AND THE MINIMUM AGE FOR SPONSORSHIP OR ENTRY

The final decision discussed in this chapter is *Quila*.[58] It concerned a change to the Immigration Rules implemented in 2008 that raised the minimum age for sponsorship or admission as a spouse from 18 to 21, a policy that had been

[54] ibid [24].

[55] The United Nations Convention on the Rights of the Child, Arts 24 and 28; see also Committee on the Rights of the Child General Comment No 14; on the best interests principle, see J Fortin, 'Children's Rights – Flattering to Deceive' (2014) 26 *Child and Family Law Quarterly* 51; J Eekelaar, 'Beyond the Welfare Principle' (2002) 14 *Child and Family Law Quarterly* 237; Prabhat and Hambly, 'Bettering the Best Interests of the Child Determination: Of Checklists and Balancing Exercises'.

[56] Christie, 'The Best Interests of the Child in UK Immigration Law'. On the recent position, see 'Can Children and Parents Apply to Remain after Seven Years' Residence?' (*Free Movement*, 18 October 2021).

[57] *ZH (Tanzania)* (n 27) [5].

[58] *Quila v SSHD* [2011] UKSC 45.

implemented in several European states and was permitted under EU law.[59] The stated aim of the change was to reduce the incidence of forced marriage. The limited data available suggested that some forced marriages involved overseas marriages, about one-third involved young people aged between 18 and 21, and most (although not all) had South Asian, principally Pakistani or Bangladeshi, backgrounds.[60]

Using immigration controls to prevent forced marriages was controversial despite the human rights violations and criminal offences involved in forced marriage. The minimum age for marriage in the UK was, and remains, 18 (or 16 with parental consent), and those marrying spouses from overseas would now be treated differently, leading to charges of discrimination against communities who tend to marry at a younger age.[61] There was scepticism as to the effectiveness of measures based on age and the wisdom of intervening through immigration controls. Overseas arranged marriages had been subject to restrictive immigration measures for decades, and some perceived the change to be one more form of stigmatisation and exclusion. Critics pointed to the extensive interference in the married lives of couples in unforced marriages, and suspected that the measures were partly driven by adverse perceptions of these marriages.[62] In 2002, the government had suggested that ethnic minority communities should look for partners within the UK, and overseas arranged marriages within these populations were often seen as tainted by such problems as perpetuation of oppressive family norms, sham marriage and first-cousin marriage.[63] The blanket character of the prohibition suggested that, at the least, enabling couples in unforced young arranged marriages to live together was a low priority.[64]

Two overseas spouses applied for judicial review of the rule. Amber Quila, a British citizen, met and married her Chilean husband when she was 17; as his visa was about to expire, marriage was the only route for them to stay together in the UK. His application to remain was refused and she had to choose between moving to Chile or pursuing her plans for study in the UK. Bibi was a Pakistani citizen who married her British husband when she was 18. Her application for admission was also refused on age grounds. Lord Wilson, a former Family Court judge, gave the lead judgment in October 2011, with assent from Lords Phillips and Clarke and a concurring judgment by Lady Hale. The Court found that the policy breached Article 8 in these individual cases and found it hard to imagine

[59] Council Directive (EC) 2003/86 of 22 September 2003 on the right to family reunification.

[60] *Quila* (n 58) [11].

[61] Foreign and Commonwealth Office/Home Office, *Forced Marriage Statutory Guidance: Consultation Paper* (London, TSO, 2008) 9.

[62] See, eg M Dustin and A Phillips, 'Whose Agenda Is It? Abuses of Women and Abuses of "Culture" in Britain' (2008) 8 *Ethnicities* 405.

[63] See ch 4, s II.

[64] Home Office, *Secure Borders, Safe Haven: Integration with Diversity in Modern Britain* (Cm 5387, 2002), 18. For a discussion, see H Wray, 'Moulding the Migrant Family' (2009) 29 *Legal Studies* 592, 600; H Wray, *Regulating Marriage Migration into the UK: A Stranger in the Home* (Farnham: Ashgate, 2011) 167–73.

circumstances where refusal of an applicant in an unforced marriage would not be a violation. Lord Brown, however, dissented.

There were two main legal issues: interference with family life under Article 8(1) and proportionality under Article 8(2). On interference, as both couples had barely cohabited, the government argued that family life 'had scarcely been established' or was 'relatively undeveloped', making interference insignificant. It cited *Abdulaziz*, where interference was not found, to argue a higher threshold was needed in admission cases.[65] Lord Wilson dismissed this argument; *Abdulaziz* was 'an old decision' and would not be followed.[66] Lady Hale agreed, saying that any distinction between admission and expulsion cases should be based on the 'facts and circumstances', analysed under Article 8(2).

Lord Wilson's proportionality assessment in *Quila* followed the structure of Article 8(2), treating the Article 8 obligation as if it were negative.[67] The Court recognised that reducing the incidence of forced marriage was a legitimate aim and accepted a connection between the policy and the aim, despite the absence of a direct relationship in the cases before them.[68] The key question was proportionality. It was observed that the government must justify interference, although the burden could not be represented by a legal standard such as the 'balance of probabilities'.[69] It was, rather, that the Court must be persuaded overall that the policy was necessary and proportionate, and that a different, less intrusive measure would not be equally effective. He referred to the finding in *Huang* that there was no specific doctrine of deference. Rather, the judgments of the Secretary of State would carry 'appropriate weight … to the extent, in particular, that she was likely to have had access to special sources of knowledge and advice'. He also recalled that the Court in *Huang* had not found the Immigration Rules to have 'the imprimatur of democratic approval'.[70]

Using this approach, Lord Wilson found that the government had failed to discharge the burden on it. The case for the policy was confined to a government report, which 'believed' there would be benefits to raising the spouse visa age, and equivocal support in a public consultation.[71] Against the proposal was a commissioned academic report which recommended against lifting the age, but it was rejected by the government on quality grounds and disregarded by the Court.[72]

[65] *Abdulaziz and Balkandali v UK* App no 9473/81, [1985] ECHR 7.
[66] *Quila* (n 58) [30]–[43].
[67] ibid [71].
[68] ibid [8]; see also R Williams, 'Structuring Substantive Review' [2017] *PL* 99, 104–07.
[69] *Quila* (n 58) [44].
[70] ibid [46].
[71] Home Office/UK Border Agency, *Marriage Visas: The Way Forward* (2008); Home Office/Border and Immigration Agency (2007) 'Marriage to Partners from Overseas: A Consultation Paper' (December 2007).
[72] M Hester, K Chantler, G Gangoli, J Devgon, S Sharma and Ann Singleton, *Forced Marriage: The Risk Factors and the Effect of Raising the Minimum Age for a Sponsor, and of Leave to Enter the UK as a Spouse or Fiancé(e)* (Bristol, University of Bristol, 2007).

A Home Affairs Select Committee report also urged caution.[73] A later report found some benefit to the victims of forced marriage but did not assess the interference in unforced marriages.[74] As a whole, the government had failed to consider all the relevant factors or to show any relative sense of the harm caused by action or inaction.[75] Lord Wilson outlined 10 questions that had not been addressed and concluded that the government had not established that the policy would effectively deter forced marriages, that it had explored other, less intrusive measures and that the policy benefits outweighed the interference in unforced marriages: 'On any view it is a sledge-hammer but [the Secretary of State] has not attempted to identify the size of the nut.'[76]

This was a searching examination. This becomes clear if one returns to the list of questions in chapter one setting out what a court might ask itself about the public interest:

1. What public or general interest does the measure serve?
2. How effective is it?
3. Is it necessary in this case?
4. Do the applicants' circumstances make it disproportionate?

Lord Wilson addressed question 1, finding that preventing forced marriage was in the public interest. He also addressed question 2, finding the government's approach was overinclusive, as it targeted all marriages within the age group and it was not known how many of these were forced. The policy of allowing admission in 'exceptional, compassionate circumstances' was insufficient to satisfy question 3, as entry was not permitted when the marriage was unforced. The policy was also too inflexible to satisfy the requirements of question 4.

The conclusion, however, was not that the Immigration Rule containing the minimum age requirement was invalid, but that individuals' Article 8 rights would often be violated. In this way, the Court avoided ruling on the human rights compatibility of the Immigration Rules and passed the problem back to the government:

> [W]hile decisions founded on human rights are essentially individual, it is hard to conceive that the Secretary of State could ever avoid infringement of article 8 when applying the amendment to an unforced marriage. So in relation to its future operation she faces an unenviable decision.[77]

Lord Brown's strong dissent, despite the Court's finessing of the point, treated the majority judgment as one that held the relevant Immigration Rule itself to

[73] Home Affairs Select Committee, '*Domestic Violence, Forced Marriage and 'Honour'-Based Violence* (HC 2007–08, 263-I).

[74] *Quila* (n 58) [55].

[75] ibid [58]; Y Tew, 'And They Call It Puppy Love: Young Love, Forced Marriage and Immigration Rules' (2012) 71 *CLJ 18*,21; C Knight and T Cross, 'Public Law in the Supreme Court 2011–2012' (2012) 17 *Judicial Review* 330.

[76] *Quila* (n 58) [58].

[77] ibid [59].

be incompatible, not the individual decision.[78] He found the evidence presented by the government more persuasive than had Lord Wilson and Lady Hale, and noted the acceptance of a similar minimum age criterion elsewhere in Europe. He was critical of Lady Hale's finding that 'the right to marry is just as important as the right not to marry',[79] saying that she

> cannot possibly mean by this that the postponement by up to three years of a couple's wish to live together as man and wife in this country involves just as great a violation of human rights as a forced marriage.[80]

Lady Hale's words were taken a little out of context by Lord Brown.[81] For her, it was not a question of equivalence between the human rights violations in each case but that all rights must be taken seriously. However, his underpinning argument is important. In most immigration cases, the public interest is the generalised benefit of a functioning immigration system, whereas here the issue was a direct and serious violation of another's human rights, and he believed the Court should be cautious in challenging the government's assessment of how to balance conflicting claims of such magnitude. This was particularly so when, as here, it was not possible to determine the relative benefits and harms of the policy. He observed that Lord Wilson's 10 questions could not be satisfactorily answered and asked 'is it to be said that the whole matter is all just too difficult and uncertain and that the Secretary of State is therefore disabled from taking the course [of action]?'[82]

In such circumstances, the question was who should make the judgment call, and here he saw the expertise and responsibility of the policymaker as critical.[83]

Lord Brown's disagreement was therefore not confined to the adequacy of justification, as he believed that the Court should not be making this judgment at all; rather, the decision, 'unless demonstrably wrong', should be made by government.[84] That was not a direct challenge to the principle in *Huang* that courts determine proportionality in the individual case, nor did he propose a general principle of deference, also dismissed in *Huang*, but he did consider that deference to the policymaker was appropriate here: 'Of course, the ultimate decision on article 8(2) proportionality must be for the courts but in this particular context the courts should to my mind accord government a very substantial area of discretionary judgment.'[85]

The core of Lord Brown's dissent therefore was the intensity of scrutiny – but 'in this particular context', not as a general proposition. However, his approach would have limited the ability of individuals to challenge refusals under the policy as they would have had to show why their personal circumstances merited special

[78] ibid [90], [91].
[79] ibid [66].
[80] ibid [91].
[81] ibid [66], [78]–[79].
[82] ibid [87].
[83] ibid [91].
[84] ibid [91].
[85] ibid [91].

treatment.[86] His concerns were principled, but there was also a suggestion of political pragmatism: 'In a sensitive context such as that of forced marriages it would seem to me not merely impermissible but positively unwise for the courts yet again to frustrate government policy except in the clearest of cases.'[87]

His criticisms reflected his comments in *EB (Kosovo)* on the government's assessment of the public interest and were a harbinger of future problems for the Court. They were particularly weighty coming from the justice who had led the Court in *Chikwamba*, *Beoku-Betts* and *Mahad*.

The polarisation on this issue was reflected in the content of the speeches. Both Lord Wilson and Lady Hale discussed the evil of forced marriage, but also paid attention to the interference. Lord Wilson spent some time talking about Aguilar and Amber Quila. He mentioned Ms Quila's professional ambitions, her intended university course and degree subject, and even her 'A'-level results.[88] Bibi, while she was discussed sympathetically, received less detailed consideration. It is likely that Lord Wilson seized the presentational advantage of a young, educated, middle class (her parents were teachers) woman who was not from a community associated with forced or even arranged marriage. It may have been a useful tactic to establish that, despite the horrors of forced marriage, the costs of the minimum age requirement were excessive, but it also demonstrated the extent to which arranged marriages between young people had become a stigmatised category, with few calls on public sympathy. This was also noticeable in Lord Brown's dissenting judgment. He opened by saying: 'Forced marriages are an appalling evil.'[89] He was concerned to ensure that the Court did not inadvertently hamper measures to prevent them, but absent from his judgment was sympathy for, let alone an assessment of, the hardship endured by what he called 'innocent couples', the same omission for which the majority criticised the government.[90] It is difficult not to conclude that, like the government, he regarded the claims of very young couples to a family life as relatively minor.

The impact of *Quila* was considerable. It resulted in reversion of the minimum age for entry and sponsorship to 18.[91] It established a common standard for the proportionality assessment across the legal system by adopting in a judicial review the *Huang* standard for appeals. Its approach to proportionality was widely cited in later immigration and non-immigration judicial reviews.[92] In terms of the themes of this book, it demonstrated a commitment to the protection of family life, reflected by a rigorous Article 8 proportionality assessment, which used the framework set out in Article 8(2) appropriate to negative obligation cases.

[86] ibid [93].
[87] ibid [97].
[88] ibid [12]–[16].
[89] ibid [81].
[90] ibid [91].
[91] ibid [92].
[92] eg *R (on the application of Steinfeld) v Secretary of State for International Development* [2018] UKSC 32; *AT* (n 50); *Shahzad (Art 8: legitimate aim) Pakistan* [2014] UKUT 85 (IAC); *B v Independent Safeguarding Authority* [2012] EWCA Civ 977.

As in *ZH (Tanzania)*, the Court anticipated accusations that it was using Article 8 to interfere in immigration policy. In *ZH (Tanzania)*, the Court could lean on the section 55 statutory duty. In *Quila*, the Court suggested that it was really addressing a social policy disguised as an immigration measure. Both Lord Wilson and Lady Hale pointed out that the sole aim of the policy was to deter forced marriage. In Lord Brown's words: 'The Secretary of State's purpose is clear. It was not to control immigration. It was to deter forced marriages.'[93] Lady Hale said: 'The Secretary of State cannot at one and the same time say that she is not doing this for the purpose of controlling immigration and rely upon jurisprudence which is wholly premised on the state's right to control immigration.'[94]

Their immediate point was the disconnect between the government's reliance on immigration-related jurisprudence and the policy's stated aims, and there was no suggestion that the searching proportionality assessment flowed from the non-immigration policy aim; the Court relied on *Huang* to guide the proportionality assessment and pointed out the weak democratic credentials of the Immigration Rules.[95] However, their words served to distance *Quila* from mainstream family reunification Article 8 decisions. Lady Hale also cited the right to marry in international law and, specifically, Article 12, on which she said:

> There is a further reason for holding the interference disproportionate. Although the means used is an interference with article 8 rights, the object is to interfere with article 12 rights. The aim is to prevent, deter or delay marriage to a person from abroad. The right to marry is a fundamental right.[96]

As the discussion on *Baiai* showed earlier, Article 12 is a stronger, less qualified right than Article 8 and the passages quoted here suggested that the Court in *Quila* was keen to suggest that something stronger than normal Article 8 family reunification was in issue.

There was also the Court's finding that the Immigration Rules were not incompatible with human rights, only the individual decision made under them, although the Court was clear that refusals under the Rules would rarely be human rights compliant. This avoided the difficult question already discussed in *Mahad* above of when, if ever, the Immigration Rules would be found invalid for incompatibility with Convention Rights. It seemed probable that the Rules would always be found compliant if there was an option for Article 8 to be applied outside the Rules. Claims for leave outside the Rules would have to be made on a case-by-case basis, increasing the financial and other burdens on applicants. In this way, the Court avoided a direct confrontation with government, but at the cost of ease and certainty in the application of Article 8, a point pursued further in the next chapter.

[93] *Quila* (n 58) [8].
[94] ibid [72].
[95] ibid [54], [61].
[96] ibid [66], [78].

Quila was another vital case in the development of a family reunification jurisprudence. In finding interference disproportionate, the Court held that the government had not adequately justified its policy and it acted to protect a group whose family lives have often been devalued or even trivialised: young couples, particularly those in arranged marriages. At the same time, the Court stressed the non-immigration implications of the decision and showed it was unwilling to find the Immigration Rules unlawful even when they could almost never be lawfully applied, a warning to lawyers about the limits of what the Court was ready to do. Lord Brown's deeply felt dissent was echoed by some critical commentary that believed that the Court had expected too much of the government, suggesting that the decision would leave the Court exposed.[97] This proved to be the case.

VI. A COMPLEX RELATIONSHIP WITH ARTICLE 8

The second phase post-*Huang* decisions discussed in this chapter represent, in many ways, a continuation of those discussed in the first phase. Each of them improved the family reunification rights of binational families. *Baiai* protected the right to marry, *Mahad* made sponsorship easier through recognising a right to rely on third party support, *ZH (Tanzania)* ensured children's interests were a primary consideration and *Quila* protected the family reunification rights of young, married couples. They interrogated the government's justification for interference with family life and recognised the dilemmas faced by sponsors. They show a Court prepared to make rigid administrative rules more flexible, nuanced and cognisant of human diversity and complexity. In so doing, they created a space in which the claims of family life could be heard. Given the consistency of their findings, the Court may be said to have adopted the importance of family life as an underpinning value. The decisions were a major landmark in the history of British immigration law and of British human rights.

However, despite their importance, the impact on lower-level decision-making was not assured. This was exemplified by the High Court judgment in *Mansoor*.[98] Mrs Mansoor, a Yemeni national, was married with seven children. Her husband came to the UK in 1998, and later naturalised. In 2005, Mrs Mansoor and the children joined him. Under the Rules then in force, the children received indefinite leave to enter, but Mrs Mansoor received two years leave as a spouse, and would become eligible for indefinite leave after two years. Before the two years expired, Mr Mansoor was made redundant and made welfare claims for himself and his family. As a result, Mrs Mansoor no longer qualified for indefinite leave and was expected to leave the UK. Her human rights appeals against refusal were repeatedly refused on the grounds that she

[97] The Rt Hon Lady Justice Arden DBE, 'Proportionality: The Way Ahead?' [2013] *PL* 498.
[98] *Mansoor v Secretary of State for the Home Department* [2011] EWHC 832.

could return to Yemen and apply for re-entry when eligible. Alternatively, there was 'no bar whatsoever' to her family returning with her, or family life could continue through electronic contact and visits.[99]

Blake J, in the High Court, found the refusals unlawful and the cases discussed in the past three chapters were central to his decision. *Huang* and *EB (Kosovo)* required a detailed, fact-sensitive assessment of what family life required. The correct test for whether the family could return was reasonableness, not 'insurmountable obstacles' or an equivalent test. After *Chikwamba*, it was disproportionate to expect Mrs Mansoor to return to Yemen to make an application to re-enter. Following *Beoku-Betts*, the Article 8 rights of the entire family, including her children, must be considered. After *ZH (Tanzania)*, the best interests of her children (some of whom were now British citizens) were a primary consideration. Although *Quila* had not yet been heard in the Supreme Court, Blake J drew on the Court of Appeal decision to scrutinise the policy rationale for the two-year limited leave policy, which, he determined, was to impede immigration rights being obtained through sham marriages, and was therefore not applicable to Mrs Mansoor.

Without these decisions, Mrs Mansoor would almost certainly have been without a legal remedy and the case showed how they made a concrete difference. It also demonstrated their limited efficacy. Mrs Mansoor entered legally with a residence permit, although it had now expired and, in this respect, her situation was atypical; most claims involved irregular entry. It is plausible that the Strasbourg Court would also have found a violation even under the margin of appreciation. Yet, her claim was only resolved through an expensive, stressful and time-consuming judicial review, an option not available to many claimants. The Home Office (repeatedly) and several appellate bodies had all dismissed her human rights claims. The refusals and failed appeals took place between 2009 and 2011, so after the *Huang*, *Beoku-Betts*, *EB (Kosovo)* and *Chikwamba* decisions, but their values did not appear to have been absorbed. It seemed that only those with the stamina, resilience and resources to bring further proceedings were able to benefit from them.

These problems may point to why the Court's approach seemed to change between the first and second phases. Chapter five showed that in *Chikwamba* and *EB(Kosovo)*, the Court seemed to be creating a domestic Article 8 jurisprudence based on principles established by the Strasbourg Court but applied domestically and without the margin of appreciation. This was consistent with the Court's powers under the Human Rights Act, but it was politically delicate. The Court was therefore not entirely explicit about what it had done. It engaged principally with domestic rather than Strasbourg cases, used the parties' individual predicament to do much of the persuasive work and was not always clear about what was expected of the lower courts. The consequence was that the

[99] ibid [13].

decisions' effectiveness was somewhat blunted, particularly given the tendency by decision-makers and tribunals to favour conservative interpretations.

In the second post-*Huang* phase, discussed in this chapter, perhaps encouraged by the success of the first phase cases, lawyers used human rights to ask the Court to intervene not only in issues of policy, but also in the Immigration Rules and statute. In response, the Court showed continued support for family reunification but a diminished reliance on the intersection of Article 8 and family reunification. In *Baiai*, this was inevitable; Article 12 was the more relevant and stronger right, but the Court did not suggest that prohibitions on marriage inhibited the exercise of Article 8 rights, although the converse happened in *Quila*. In *Mahad*, the Court relied only on interpretation of the Immigration Rules and made no substantive comment on Article 8, in what seems to have been a considered and pragmatic choice. In *ZH (Tanzania)*, the Court drew on Article 3 of the Convention on the Rights of the Child in applying Article 8 and, critically, on its incorporation into UK law through statute. *Quila* was a pure Article 8 case, but the Court distanced it from mainstream family reunification cases by stressing the non-immigration aim of the policy, and Lady Hale pointed to the relevance of Article 12. The Court also declined to find the Immigration Rules themselves incompatible despite the widespread character of the violation.

While this partial distancing from Article 8 depended partly on happenstance – other avenues had to be available – taken together, the cases suggested a partial reorientation. This impression was reinforced by some other characteristics of this second phase of cases. They were, in general, more directly effective. The statement in *Quila* as to compatibility, while still short of finding the Rules unlawful, was more unequivocal than its equivalent in, for example, *Chikwamba*. This directness was sometimes at a cost to durability or scope. The *Baiai* judgment enabled the government to replace the certificates of marriage scheme with one that avoided the previous errors. By interpreting the Immigration Rules to permit third party support, the Court in *Mahad* provided a rapid and practical solution, but it could easily be overturned by amendments to the Rules, whereupon the entire issue would have to be relitigated. In *ZH (Tanzania)*, the focus on children's nationality and the statutory duty owed to children in the UK provided a solid legal base, but only for a subsection of children impacted by removal and deportation (while still having a wider but more diffuse impact).

In this second phase, the style and structure of judgments were also different. Except for *Mahad*, where human rights were not cited, there was significantly more engagement with Strasbourg cases than during the first phase despite reduced reliance on Article 8. This is demonstrated in Figure 6.1, which is a chart that draws on the content analysis discussed in chapter one.[100] The cases cited in *Baiai* were under Article 12, not Article 8, but the underlying point remains that engagement with the Strasbourg cases was stronger in the second than in the first phase. This suggests that the Court's relationship with the Strasbourg cases

[100] For an explanation of the methodology, see Appendix.

changed through this period, particularly as Figure 6.2 shows that the number of domestic cases cited did not show such a marked pattern.

Figure 6.1 Number of ECtHR cases cited in lead and concurring judgments in the first and second post-*Huang* phases

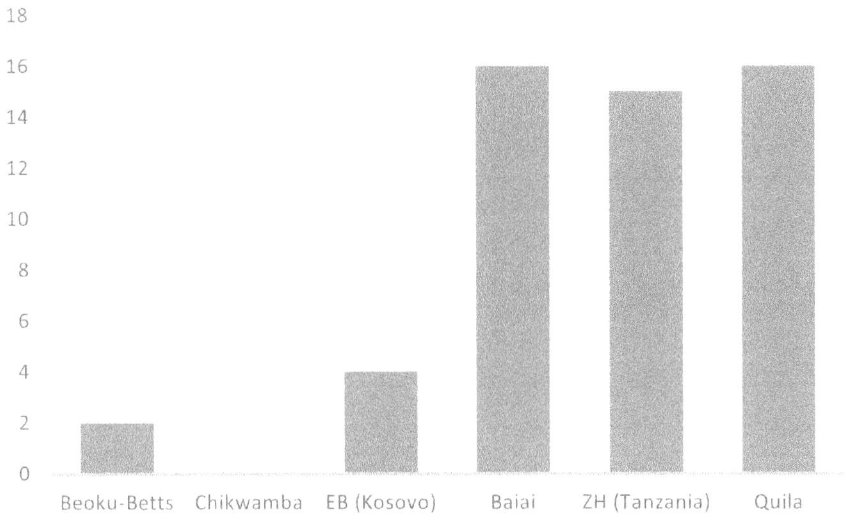

Figure 6.2 Number of domestic cases cited in lead and concurring judgments in the first and second post-*Huang* phases

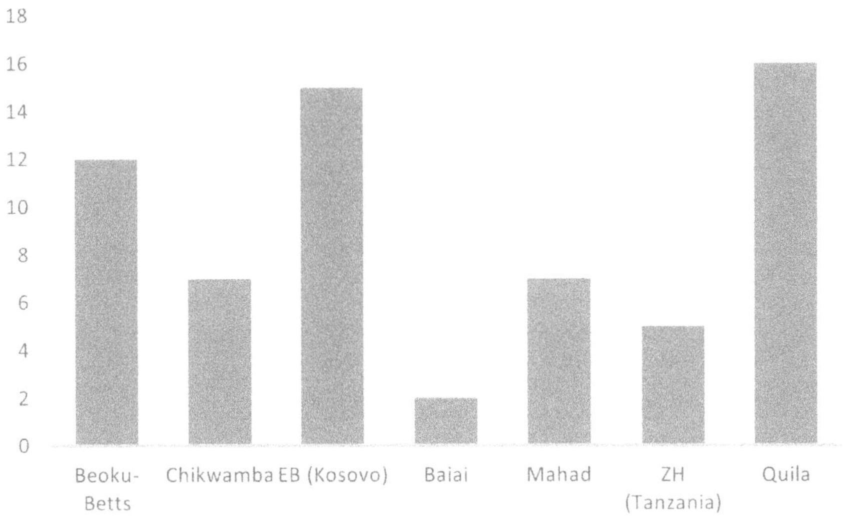

At the same time, Figure 6.3 shows more engagement in the first phase with contextual facts, ie with facts discussed as part of the background rather than to make a legal point, suggesting that these were critical to making the argument.

Figure 6.3 Percentage of paragraphs in lead and concurring judgments that address contextual facts in the first and second post-*Huang* phases

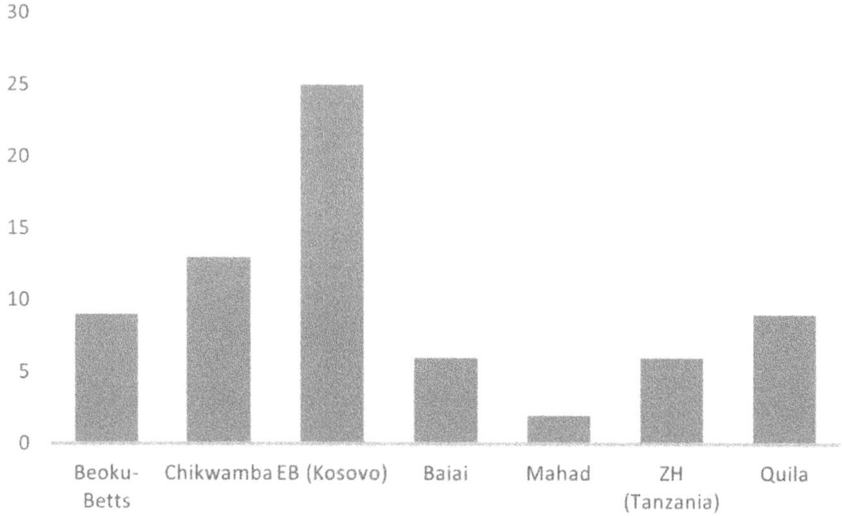

There was also more use of first names in the first phase, as demonstrated in Table 6.1. Using first names is unusual in judgments and could be seen as patronising or overfamiliar. Their use would have been a conscious effort to establish a more personal connection between the reader and the subject. This humanising function seems to have been less critical in the second phase.

Table 6.1 Use of first names about at least one of the parties in the first and second post-*Huang* phases

Case	First names used without surname
Beoku-Betts	Yes
Chikwamba	Yes
EB (Kosovo)	Yes
Baiai	No
Mahad	No
ZH (Tanzania)	No[a]
Quila	Ambiguous[b]

[a] Parties were anonymised.

[b] The second applicant in *Quila* invited the Court to call her Bibi, but it was unclear if this was, in fact, her first name as it was also used in the case name.

All these characteristics suggested a reversion in the second phase cases to the more usual style of Supreme Court judgment writing, but the individuals' situation was still the starting point of the judgments. The cases in both phases mentioned the claimants' problems early in the judgment. This reflected the common thread running through both phases – that family life was the primary concern. Although the second phase cases were framed differently, they were still a challenge to the government because they prioritised the needs of families. In fact, they led to direct changes in policy in ways that the first phase decisions did not: after *Baiai*, the certificates of approval scheme was abandoned, as was the increased minimum age after *Quila*. *Mahad* was instantaneously applicable through the Immigration Rules. *ZH (Tanzania)* did not result in rule changes at that stage, though it brought concrete benefits. The decisions left the Court politically exposed, however, and, perhaps not coincidentally, there were also the first signs of major division. Lord Brown's dissent in *Quila* went much further than his previous partial dissent in *EB (Kosovo)* and suggested awareness of a growing political risk. While his disagreement was formally confined to the circumstances of the case, his language suggested wider frustration: 'Article 8 is a difficult provision which has already led to some highly contentious, not to say debateable, decisions.'[101]

His concern was with deference in the proportionality assessment. He had led the Court in *Chikwamba* and assented in *ZH (Tanzania)*, both proportionality decisions, and it was not clear if he now included them amongst the 'contentious' or 'debateable' decisions. It is significant, however, that he also led the Court in *Mahad*, finding against the government on third party support but through an interpretation of the Immigration Rules without reference to Article 8. His commitment to supporting family life where he found it possible to do so was evident; his enthusiasm for using Article 8 less so.

His reservations can be understood even if they are not shared. The decisions discussed in this chapter and the previous two were made by a judiciary that was committed to protecting family if possible. However, despite some beautifully conceived and constructed judgments, it was not easy to make Article 8 effective in a wider institutional and political climate that prioritised the perceived requirements of immigration control and saw the anti-majoritarian character of human rights as antithetical to democracy. This was even more the case when claims started to question the compatibility of the Immigration Rules, rather than administrative practice. By the time of *ZH (Tanzania)* and *Quila* in 2011, the Court was heading for a confrontation with the government. In 2010, the Labour government was replaced by a Conservative-led coalition government with plans to reform human rights and reduce immigration. Its displeasure was evident; the Minister for Immigration at the time of *ZH (Tanzania)* described himself as 'disappointed' by the decision.[102] The same minister called *Quila* 'another very disappointing judgment'.[103] At this stage, there was no elaboration

[101] *Quila* (n 58) [97].

[102] A Hirsch, 'Landmark Human Rights Ruling Allows Asylum Mother to Remain in UK' *The Guardian* (London, 1 February 2011).

[103] A Travis, 'Government Attacks Judges for Rejecting Marriage Visa Ban' *The Guardian* (London, 12 October 2011).

as to the character of the disappointment, but the next chapter will show that the government was soon more specific.

VII. CONCLUSION

The cases discussed in this chapter and the previous two were unique. It was unprecedented for the Court to find so consistently over a range of cases in favour of migrants and against the government.[104] Yet, this was really a question of perspective. Where the government saw migrants, the Court saw families. Further, these were families that, by definition, included British citizens or residents where refusal would mean either exile or separation. Collectively, they suggest an ethics based on the preservation of the family unit, recognising the claims of citizenship, and the interests of children. These values were not to be cast aside almost as a matter of course in favour of government priorities in immigration control, although they would not always prevail. This led the Court into an unavoidable evaluation of policy. Although this was for the limited purpose of determining proportionality, it concerned an arena where government claimed almost unassailable sovereignty and judges had previously shown great reticence. The Court demonstrated surprising unanimity in this enterprise; Lord Brown offered the only dissent, and this became significant only in *Quila*.

In summary, the Court continued to protect binational families when it could, but Article 8 was a fragile vehicle for achieving this. This was a likely cause of some of the issues identified in the first post-*Huang* phase, including some vagueness about what the Court was doing in those judgments. In the second post-*Huang* phase, discussed in this chapter, the Court was asked to assess not just policy, but the Immigration Rules and statutory provisions, and it looked for ways to avoid relying wholly on Article 8. It also declined to find the Immigration Rules incompatible with Article 8 and reverted to a more conventional style of judgment, engaging more with the Strasbourg jurisprudence and less with the individual circumstances of each claim. However, their findings still protected family life and subjected the government's policy rationale to scrutiny, leaving the Court politically exposed. As the next chapter shows, the Court's role in Article 8 and family reunification became a critical political flashpoint, leading to the final phase in this extraordinary string of decisions.

[104] The government won in *AS (Somalia) v SSHD* [2009] UKHL 32, discussed briefly in ch 1, s VI. While it involved an application for family reunification by two Somali orphans, the question in issue was much broader than the Art 8 claim.

7

*The Supreme Court Rolls Back: The Third Post-*Huang *Phase*

I. INTRODUCTION

THIS CHAPTER ANALYSES three Supreme Court judgments decided between 2015 and 2018 (the third post-*Huang* phase). In these decisions, the Supreme Court retreated on the vexed question of the judicial scrutiny of policy justification and adopted a conservative view of what Article 8 requires of government. In so doing, it undid many of the effects of the decisions discussed in the previous three chapters, although it did not specifically say so. The third phase decisions were made in a new political context: the Conservative-led coalition in government from 2010 was determined to reduce immigration and was antagonistic to judicially determined human rights. The government introduced rule and statute changes that aimed to confine judicial discretion over Article 8 in immigration cases.

There were also changes in the composition of the Court and the revival of a strand of judicial thinking opposed to scrutiny of executive policy.[1] Lord Sumption, appointed in 2012 although he did not sit on the decisions discussed here, was critical of what he called 'litigation which is essentially politics by other means'.[2] Lord Reed, also appointed in 2012, believed in the 'exercise of an appropriate degree of restraint'.[3] Meanwhile, lawyers representing applicants, perhaps emboldened by earlier successes, arguably paid insufficient heed to their limitations, in particular the Court's reluctance to find that the Immigration Rules do not comply with Article 8. The outcome was a series of decisions that were disappointing for those working with migrants and their

[1] *Bank Mellat v Her Majesty's Treasury* [2013] UKSC 39; *R (on the application of Lord Carlile of Berriew QC and others) v SSHD* [2014] UKSC 60.

[2] J Sumption, 'Foreign Affairs in the English Courts since 9/11', Lecture at the Department of Government (London School of Economics, 14 May 2012) 2; see also J Sumption, 'Judicial and Political Decision-Making: The Uncertain Boundary', The FA Mann Lecture, 2011.

[3] The Rt Hon Lord Reed President of the Supreme Court of the United Kingdom, 'Response to a Call for Evidence produced by the Independent Human Rights Act Review', para 31. For a discussion of the different standards of review in proportionality decisions, see M Elliott, 'From Bifurcation to Calibration: Twin-Track Deference and the Culture of Justification' in H Wilberg and M Elliott (eds), *The Scope and Intensity of Substantive Review: Traversing Taggart's Rainbow* (Oxford, Hart Publishing, 2015) 61–90.

families, although they were not entirely negative. It is likely that the Court, after some years of engagement with Article 8, was looking for a way to remove itself from an area where it was exposed to political and legal controversy that threatened to compromise its wider autonomy over human rights.

The next section of this chapter explores the changes in political and legal background that informed the decisions discussed in this chapter. There follows an analysis of three cases: *Ali and Bibi*, *MM (Lebanon)* and *Agyarko*.[4] In these, the Court sought to retreat from a highly exposed position without engaging in an overt reversal. As a result, these decisions were complex, and sometimes confusing. The analysis in this chapter is therefore more technical in character, as I attempt to disentangle the diverse threads of the Court's reasoning to show how an apparently dispassionate doctrinal analysis enabled a strategic reorientation towards the interests of government.

Ali and Bibi in 2015 concerned implementation of a pre-entry language test. The Court found that the test was lawful, and that violations could be avoided through granting leave to enter or remain in the UK outside the Immigration Rules (leave outside the Rules). It was divided on the extent to which the government's public interest justification could be scrutinised. The second decision, *MM (Lebanon)* in 2017, on new financial conditions for sponsorship, showed that the Court had unambiguously withdrawn from scrutiny of the public interest although there were some positive findings on children and sources of financial support. In the final decision, *Agyarko*, the issue was claims by irregular migrants based on family life. The judgment represented a further turn towards prioritising government concerns in human rights adjudication.

There follows a reflection on the third phase decisions, which shows that the Court avoided express repudiation of its previous position through apparently minor adjustments in its legal findings, a closer identification with European Court of Human Rights (ECtHR, Strasbourg Court or Strasbourg) doctrines, including the margin of appreciation, and a language and structure strongly aligned with a government perspective. The chapter ends with a discussion of all three phases of the post-*Huang* jurisprudence, supported by findings from the content analysis first discussed in chapter one and which also appeared in the previous chapter. It demonstrates the adjustments in the way that justices wrote their judgments in order to accommodate this shift.

II. A NEW BACKGROUND

Most of the decisions analysed in previous chapters took place against the background of a Labour government that had passed and implemented the

[4] *R (on the application of Ali and Bibi) v SSHD* [2015] UKSC 68; *R (on the application of MM (Lebanon)) v SSHD* [2017] UKSC 10; *R (on the application of Agyarko) v SSHD* [2017] UKSC 11.

Human Rights Act 1998 and took, at least at first, a positive if highly conditional approach to immigration. When that government was replaced in 2010 by a Conservative/Liberal Democrat coalition, there was not the same parliamentary support for human rights, and attitudes towards immigration hardened. The political climate from 2012 onwards has been extremely bleak for migrants, with Article 8 rights only one explicit target.

Under the coalition government, Conservative ministers occupied the key posts of Home Secretary, Immigration Minister, Justice Secretary and Attorney General. The Conservative Party manifesto had promised to substantially reduce immigration and to replace the Human Rights Act with a UK Bill of Rights.[5] While opposition within government stalled reform of domestic human rights at that stage, the commitment to reduce immigration was taken seriously and dominated immigration policy until 2019.[6] However, achieving this was not straightforward. As the UK was an EU Member State, the government had to focus its efforts on the admission or departure of those from outside the EU, and the entry of non-EU nationals through the student, work and family routes was severely restricted. Family migration was doubly vulnerable as a source of immigration and the conduit for anxiety about integration and social cohesion. The latter had been a concern under Labour, but the distinction between promoting integration after arrival and preventing entry was now blurred. In June 2010, one month after the general election, the government announced a pre-entry language test for spouses and partners that was implemented in the following October. It built on a plan that had been developed but postponed by the previous government and led to the legal challenge that resulted in the *Ali and Bibi* decision discussed below.

The use of Article 8 in immigration cases was increasingly politicised. Hostility to the Human Rights Act was not new, but the main line of attack was now the perceived misuse of Article 8 by foreign criminals to avoid deportation, a question outside the scope of this book.[7] However, family reunification was implicitly included, and the two categories were often discursively conflated. At the Conservative Party conference in 2011, the Home Secretary Theresa May talked of an 'illegal immigrant who cannot be deported because, and I am not

[5] Conservative Party, 'Invitation to Join the Government of Britain: The Conservative Manifesto 2010' (April 2010) 21, 79.

[6] H Fenwick, 'The Human Rights Act or a British Bill of Rights: Creating a Down-Grading Recalibration of Rights against the Counter-Terror Backdrop?' [2012] *PL* 468. The net migration target did not form part of the 2019 Conservative Party manifesto: Conservative Party, 'Get Brexit Done: Unleash Britain's Potential – The Conservative and Unionist Party Manifesto' (2019).

[7] For an overview, see R Hamlin, '"Foreign Criminals," the Human Rights Act, and the New Constitutional Politics of the United Kingdom' (2016) 4 *Journal of Law and Courts* 437. Out of 602 appeals allowed by the immigration tribunals in 2013, 324 involved convicted criminals, who succeeded under Art 8: C Harlow and R Rawlings, 'Striking Back or Clamping Down: An Alternative Perspective on Judicial Review' in J Bell, M Elliott, JNE Varuhas and P Murray (ed), *Public Law Adjudication in Common Law Systems: Process and Substance* (Oxford, Hart Publishing, 2016) 301–26.

making this up, he had a pet cat'.[8] The 'illegal immigrant' had entered legally and outstayed his visa. He was therefore liable only to administrative removal, not criminal deportation. The cat featured only as evidence of family life with his partner and his claim succeeded because the government had failed to follow its own policy. The ensuing media coverage, nicknamed 'Catgate', did little to dispel the impression that the immigration system was excessively lenient towards wrongdoers, despite attempts by lawyers to explain the facts.[9]

A government consultation paper published in July 2011 contained several strands, all of which were directed at making family reunification more difficult.[10] On Article 8, the tone was abrasive; in her foreword, Theresa May said that it was her 'sincere hope [to] bring some common sense back to this, admittedly difficult, area'.[11] The underlying aim was to return to the pre-*Huang* position, where the government determined the public interest and a test of 'insurmountable obstacles' applied.[12] In July 2012, the government made extensive revisions to the Immigration Rules based on the Consultation, including significant changes to the financial criteria for the admission of spouses (discussed later in the chapter under *MM (Lebanon)*) and the creation of a limited set of human rights exceptions in the Immigration Rules (discussed later under *Agyarko*). There was also the removal of almost all rights of admission for elderly or dependent relatives, the extension of the probationary period for spouses and partners from two to five years, and limits on the scope of Article 8 appeals against criminal deportation.

The amendments to the Rules were laid before Parliament in the usual way. In addition, arguing that judges needed parliamentary guidance on Article 8, the government instigated a parliamentary debate, an unusual proceeding for the Immigration Rules. The Home Secretary, Theresa May, explained that:

> Parliament has never before been given the opportunity to set out how it believes it should be possible to interfere with article 8 rights in practice. That meant the courts were left to decide the proportionality of interference with article 8 rights themselves … without the benefit of the views of Parliament.[13]

Thus, the House of Commons was invited to agree that

> this House [recognises] that the right to respect for family or private life in Article 8 of the European Convention on Human Rights is a qualified right and agrees that the

[8] Theresa May, speech at the Conservative Party Conference, London, 4 October 2011, www.politics.co.uk/comment-analysis/2011/10/04/theresa-may-speech-in-full-2/.

[9] See A Wagner, 'Catgate: Another Myth Used to Trash Human Rights' *The Guardian* (London, 4 October 2011); H Wray, 'Greater than the Sum of Their Parts: UK Supreme Court Decisions on Family Migration' [2013] *PL* 838; for an alternative perspective, see D Campbell '"Catgate" and the Challenge to Parliamentary Sovereignty in Law' [2015] *PL* 426.

[10] Home Office/UK Border Agency, *Family Migration: A Consultation* (July 2011).

[11] ibid 3.

[12] ibid 61.

[13] Theresa May MP, HC Deb 19 June 2012, vol 546, col 760.

conditions for migrants to enter or remain in the UK on the basis of their family or private life should be those contained in the Immigration Rules.[14]

The hope was that, if the amended Rules were endorsed by Parliament, courts would accept them as representing the correct balance between the public interest and family life, avoiding the need for leave to be granted on human rights grounds outside the Rules.[15] The debate revealed that opposition as well as government MPs feared being seen as lax on immigration.[16] Only a few understood the implications for those who were not 'murderous, mayhem-causing foreign nationals'.[17]

The amended Rules were only one part of the drive to reduce migration.[18] Also in 2012, legal aid was removed from almost all immigration claims, including Article 8 claims.[19] From 2013, new, 'hostile environment' measures started to take effect, including prohibitions on irregular migrants receiving financial services, driving or renting accommodation, with stronger controls on access to employment and healthcare. The immigration system became increasingly opaque, complex, expensive and unaccountable. The aim was to make life more difficult for unauthorised migrants, but measures also affected regular migrants and even citizens.[20] The hostile environment was a major factor in the *Windrush* scandal, which emerged in 2017 when it was revealed that long-standing residents of Commonwealth origin were made destitute, refused services, detained or expelled from the UK because of uncertainty about their status. There followed warm words about a fairer system, and some minor rule changes, but the bulk of 'hostile environment' laws remain in place.[21]

The focus on Article 8 also continued. The Immigration Act 2014 set out a series of 'public interest considerations' to which a court must have regard when considering Article 8. Those relevant to family reunification comprised statements, for example, that the maintenance of effective immigration controls and the ability of entrants to speak English or be financially independent were in the public interest, and that a relationship formed when residence was unlawful

[14] HC Deb 19 June 2012, vol 546, col 760.

[15] HC Deb 19 June 2012, vol 546, col 762.

[16] Yvette Cooper MP, HC Deb 11 June 2012, vol 546, col 50. Although MPs did not necessarily agree with the proposed changes; see Yvette Cooper MP, HC Deb 19 June 2012, vol 546, cols 775–76; see also the concerns of John McDonnell MP, HC Deb 19 June 2012, vol 546, cols 782–84.

[17] Pete Wishart MP, HC Deb 19 June 2012, vol 546, cols 791–94.

[18] For a discussion of changes during this period, see S York, 'The "Hostile Environment" – How Home Office Immigration Policies and Practices Create and Perpetuate Illegality' (2018) 32 *Journal of Immigration Asylum and Nationality Law* 363.

[19] For a discussion, see S York, 'The End of Legal Aid in Immigration: A Barrier to Access to Justice for Migrants and a Decline in the Rule of Law' (2013) 27 *Journal of Immigration, Asylum and Nationality Law* 106.

[20] M Griffiths and C Yeo, 'The UK's Hostile Environment: Deputising Immigration Control' (2021) 41 *Critical Social Policy* 521.

[21] For a discussion of the Windrush scandal, see A Gentleman, *The Windrush Betrayal: Exposing the Hostile Environment* (London, Faber & Faber, 2019).

would carry little weight. On the other hand, the public interest would not require removal where there was a 'genuine and subsisting parental relationship' with a British citizen child or one who had lived in the UK for seven years. These did not depart significantly from Strasbourg principles and the main intention was to reduce judicial discretion. None of the decisions discussed in this chapter directly involved the provisions of the 2014 Act, but awareness of them and of the government's willingness to legislate would have shaped judicial thinking.

Anti-immigration and anti-human rights sentiment continues to feature in British political life. The Conservative Party manifesto of 2015 again promised to cut immigration and replace the Human Rights Act with a 'British Bill of Rights' that would 'protect' basic rights but reverse human rights 'mission creep'.[22] When the UK left the EU in 2019, even long-standing EU citizens had to apply under the settlement scheme to retain their rights. The current government has legislated to reduce the availability of judicial review for migrants and plans to replace the Human Rights Act with a more restrictive Bill of Rights.[23] The Nationality and Borders Act 2022 continues the trend of highly restrictive legislation.[24]

III. *ALI AND BIBI*: PRE-ENTRY LANGUAGE TESTING

Ali and Bibi v SSHD was a challenge by judicial review to the implementation through the Immigration Rules of a pre-entry language test for spouses and partners, a condition that already applied in several other European countries.[25] At first glance, the test was undemanding, as it required competence only in speaking and listening at the lowest examinable level (A1 Common European Framework of Reference). It therefore could be presented as a reasonable measure that would promote post-entry integration.

The applicants argued that the test was incompatible with Article 8 and was also discriminatory under Article 14. They submitted an expert report written by an interdisciplinary team of researchers led by this author. This showed that it was often impossible to access suitable tuition and tests in a format that did not, in practice, require some ability to read and write in English. Unlike other European states, the government did not ensure that learning materials and

[22] Conservative Party, 'Strong Leadership, a Clear Economic Plan, a Brighter, More Secure Future: The Conservative Manifesto 2015', 29–31 and 73.

[23] Judicial Review and Courts Act 2022, s 2; Ministry of Justice. *Human Rights Act Reform: A Modern Bill of Rights – A Consultation to Reform the Human Rights Act 1998* (CP 588, December 2021); Queen's Speech 2022, www.gov.uk/government/speeches/queens-speech-2022; Bill of Rights Bill (HC 2022–23) [117].

[24] On problems with the Act, see E Lefley, 'Six Especially Ugly Bits of the Revised Borders Bill That Really Should Be Changed' (*Free Movement*, 7 January 2022).

[25] At the time of the hearing, four other European countries had implemented pre-entry language tests; see the expert report available from the author of this book.

testing centres were widely available, and it was especially difficult for applicants from the Global South, particularly those living in rural areas or with little education, to obtain appropriate tuition and pass the test. Implementation had previously been proposed and postponed by the Labour government for these reasons, but was brought forward by the coalition government in November 2010, without addressing these problems and with only very limited exemptions on humanitarian grounds. Some nationalities were exempt from the test because they were 'majority English speaking', but there were inconsistencies in the list. Canada, for example, was exempt although it has a substantial francophone population, but Nigeria, where English is the sole official language and very widely spoken, was not. The report also showed that the benefits of pre-entry learning, as opposed to learning after entry, were minimal, and that government claims as to the costs of providing translation and interpretation facilities to this group were superficial and tendentious.[26]

The applicants claimed that the Rules were incompatible with Article 8, discriminatory and irrational. They had not applied for visas, as they were unwilling to pay for applications that were destined to fail, but it meant that the Court did not have a concrete set of facts on which it could make a specific ruling. It was not surprising, in those circumstances and after *Quila*, that the Court unanimously found that the Immigration Rules, which implemented the test, were compatible with Article 8 as violations could be addressed through granting leave outside the Immigration Rules. While the main challenge to the Rules therefore failed, the Court found that the guidance on when leave should be granted outside the Immigration Rules was drafted too narrowly and was incompatible with Article 8. However, this aspect does not seem to have been fully argued by the applicants and the Court agreed, with some reluctance, to make a declaration on the guidance after further representations. The Court was impliedly critical of the lawyers' overall strategy. Lady Hale, for example, said the applicants had set themselves a 'difficult task' in asking for the Rules to be found unlawful, while Lord Neuberger mentioned the cost of further proceedings as an important reason for agreeing to make a later declaration.[27] While *Ali and Bibi* was a challenging case to bring, it arguably achieved less than it might have.

The Article 14 claim also failed as the Court considered that, while the test was discriminatory, this was justified. However, in a pattern that was repeated in *MM (Lebanon)*, discussed below, the analysis of discrimination was not very searching. Exempting all majority English speaking countries was a defensible step, but treating comparable countries differently was not. However, this was regarded by the Court as the inevitable result of the need for a bright-line rule,

[26] See the expert report available from the author; for scholarly criticism of pre-entry language testing, see A Blackledge, '"As a Country We Do Expect": The Further Extension of Language Testing Regimes in the United Kingdom' (2009) 6 *Language Assessment Quarterly* 6.

[27] *Ali and Bibi* (n 4) [2], [103]; see also [76] (Lord Hodgson).

although administrative convenience is hardly a persuasive justification.[28] Lady Hale also observed that if the exemptions were unlawful, the government could respond by imposing the language test on everyone rather than removing it altogether.[29] This was true; states have reacted to discrimination findings by levelling down rights for everyone.[30] That, however, is precisely the point: a criterion which is considered an excessive burden for one group should not be imposed on another without good reason, and the government must determine its priorities in a non-discriminatory way. Language testing has a history of being used as a tool of racial and colonial domination, and it was disappointing to see so little attention paid to its discriminatory character.[31]

Despite agreement within the Court on compatibility of the Immigration Rules, discrimination and the guidance, there were some significant differences between the judgments. Lady Hale, with whom Lord Wilson agreed, undertook a thorough examination of Article 8 proportionality. She engaged with the expert evidence, citing it or reproducing its content at several points, and followed the Court in *Huang*, *EB (Kosovo)*, *Quila* and *Chikwamba* by declining to show automatic deference to the government's perspective, finding on the quality of the evidence before her. She concluded that language learning had some benefits but that the argument for its necessity was not strong.[32] As there was some public benefit and many applicants could pass it, requiring the test was compatible with Article 8 but the criteria for exemptions were too narrow.

Two separate judgments, by Lord Hodge (with agreement by Lord Hughes) and by Lord Neuberger, were more accommodating to the government and, as they represented the majority, their views prevailed. Firstly, they clearly wanted to discourage further attacks on the Immigration Rules. Lady Hale had found that the Immigration Rules were compatible with Article 8 without saying when they would be incompatible. Lord Hodge said that an Immigration Rule would be incompatible with Article 8 only if it were 'incapable of being operated in a proportionate way'.[33] Lord Neuberger posited only a slightly less demanding standard, saying that the 'evidence does not suggest that implementation of the Rule will achieve its purpose in only a negligible number of cases'.[34] In fact, that was precisely what the evidence did suggest: the language requirement would have only a minimal impact on language proficiency after entry, but this finding enabled him to propose a very demanding test for incompatibility. It is very rare

[28] ibid [58].
[29] ibid [56]–[59].
[30] See ch 3, s IV.
[31] See, eg A Bashford, 'Immigration Restriction: Rethinking Period and Place from Settler Colonies to Postcolonial Nations' (2014) 9 *Journal of Global History* 26.
[32] *Ali and Bibi* (n 4) [45], [34].
[33] ibid [69].
[34] ibid [83].

that a Rule will be 'incapable' of being operated proportionately or will do so only in a tiny number of cases, and this effectively barred a future challenge on these lines.[35]

Secondly, Lord Hodge said that, notwithstanding the appellants' evidence, the Court should not interfere with the government's policy decision: 'the law gives the executive branch a wide margin of appreciation in its assessment of the consequences of its social policy in this sphere'.[36]

He therefore attached more weight than Lady Hale to the government's view on the need for the policy, with consequences for when a violation might arise. Lack of or limited literacy would be insufficient, although 'inordinate' cost or the absence of a suitable test might be.[37] Lord Neuberger considered that courts should be 'very slow indeed' to rely on applicants' expert evidence 'as the sole or main justification for invalidating government policy … on a sensitive social issue'.[38] He suggested that Article 8 applications outside the Rules would prevail in a significant number of cases, but on the basis of compelling individual circumstances, not the weakness of the public interest.[39] In both cases, the consequence was that fewer applications would succeed in a human rights claim outside the Rules than under Lady Hale's approach.

Their view reflected the more executive-oriented strand of jurisprudence which had emerged in the Court, discussed in the introduction to this chapter and which was visible also in Lord Brown's dissent in *Quila*.[40] In Article 8 terms, the question was the extent to which the government must justify its policy choice. Governments do need some flexibility, but the majority was anxious to ensure that it had a free hand. Lord Neuberger, for example, even said that the government should not be asked to predict the precise outcome of policy in case it led to falsified evidence:

> [O]ne must be wary of complaining about the lack of a quantitative or precise assessment of the extent of the likely benefits, *and it is fair to add that no such complaint has been advanced*. Where, as here, such an assessment is not a practical possibility, to insist on one would have two possible consequences, each of which would be unfortunate. First, it could lead to the abandonment of experimental policies, however well thought out they may be and however successfully they may have turned out. *Alternatively, it could encourage artificial or bogus cost–benefit and other quantitative analyses …* (emphasis added)[41]

[35] It was also inconsistent with the Court's approach elsewhere; see C Rowe, 'Falling into Line? The Hostile Environment and the Legend of the "Judges' Revolt"' (2022) 85 *MLR* 105.

[36] *Ali and Bibi* (n 4) [63].

[37] ibid [73].

[38] ibid [96], [94].

[39] ibid [101].

[40] ibid [85]; see also *Lord Carlile* (n 2).

[41] *Ali and Bibi* (n 4) [97].

Despite his qualifying words, this was a straw man argument. The applicants' demands were more modest than Lord Neuberger suggested and their evidence, which was not disapproved by the Court, showed that the government had already presented an 'artificial' analysis that misrepresented the case for the language test. However, by suggesting that the applicants had been too exigent, Lord Neuberger could disguise a shift by the majority in favour of a more deferent approach. In *Huang*, the Court had found that, in evaluating policy justification, 'appropriate weight' should be awarded to the judgment of a person with responsibility for the subject matter and access to special knowledge and advice.[42] This dismissed an a priori theory of deference and courts would evaluate the evidence before them on its overall merits. This was evident in the Court's approach in *Chikwamba*, *Baiai* and *Quila*, all discussed in previous chapters. Lady Hale and Lord Wilson had taken a similar approach here, but the majority now found that the government's view should prevail not because its evidence was more persuasive, but as a matter of principle. The consequence was that government claims as to the need for a policy would not be scrutinised provided a superficially plausible defence of them was given.

The finding that the Immigration Rules were compatible with Article 8 left open the question of when an application should succeed based on an exception granted outside the Rules. When the judgment was finalised in June 2017, it said only that applying the guidance on exceptions outside the Rules 'would breach Article 8 in a "significant number" of instances' without providing more detailed criteria.[43] In response, the government amended the Immigration Rules so that where refusal would breach Article 8 due to its 'unjustifiably harsh' consequences, the language requirement would be waived.[44] 'Unjustifiably harsh' is a problematic standard that featured in all three cases discussed in this chapter. It was not technically incorrect, as Article 8 might lawfully permit outcomes that could be described as 'harsh' in the sense that they authorise a degree of suffering, and therefore an additional and unjustifiable level of harshness would be required for a violation. However, it is a negative term that acts to lower expectations of what Article 8 can achieve. This was a grudging response, therefore, that benefited from the lack of specificity in the judgment and suggested that exceptions would continue to be very rare.

Compared to the second phase decisions, there were differences in how the judgments in *Ali and Bibi* were written and organised. Only Lady Hale acknowledged the human problems behind the claim. Her opening paragraph referred to the applicants' concerns, and she later mentioned their personal circumstances

[42] *Huang v Home Secretary* [2007] UKHL 11 [16].

[43] Order of the Supreme Court in the case of *R (on the application of Ali and Bibi) v SSHD* [2015] UKSC 68, 21 June 2017.

[44] Immigration Rules HC395 Appendix FM, para GEN3.2. Successful applicants would have to wait 10 years instead of five years for a settled status.

and why they did not apply for a visa before starting proceedings.[45] Lord Hodge did not discuss the applicants' position except in a brief, loaded aside that, while it was confusingly worded, suggested concern to prevent the abuse of incoming spouses:

> In each of the appeals a female UK citizen has gone overseas and found a spouse from within a community with which she has a connection. Often it may be a male UK citizen [where] the benefit which flows from language competence is not only improved access to advice in event of mistreatment but, more generally, the ability to lead one's life with a degree of independence and autonomy.[46]

Lady Hale also made the sole reference, apart from a brief mention by Lord Neuberger, to the human right to respect for family life.[47] Otherwise, Article 8 was discussed in terms of its limitations.[48] These differences in style reflected the growing gap in substance between the prevailing approach during the first two post-*Huang* phases, represented here only by Lady Hale and Lord Wilson, and the approach of the majority in *Ali and Bibi*. That the Court was visibly divided would have been a major concern for the Court, and the discussion in the next section on *MM (Lebanon)* shows how it was resolved.

IV. *MM (LEBANON)*: THE MINIMUM INCOME REQUIREMENT

Until 2012, couples applying for family reunification had to meet a relatively straightforward criterion of 'adequate maintenance' that was concerned with the prospective joint income of the couple, set by reference to welfare benefit levels. This was replaced in 2012 by a new minimum income requirement (MIR) under which sponsors, unless in receipt of disability-related benefits, needed to show an income equivalent to an annual income of at least £18,600 pa for at least six months, and often longer, before the application. This was regardless of their partner's actual or potential earnings, unless the partner already worked legally in the UK, or support from third parties. Income shortfall could be met only through very substantial savings held in an approved account for six months prior to application.

When first implemented, 47 per cent of the adult population in the UK could not meet the MIR, with a much higher percentage for some groups (its discriminatory impact is further discussed below), and they were now excluded from sponsoring a partner.[49] British citizens working abroad seeking to return to

[45] *Ali and Bibi* (n 4) [1], [22]–[24].
[46] ibid [64].
[47] ibid [25], [31], [81].
[48] eg ibid [66]–[67] (Lord Hodge), [81] (Lord Neuberger).
[49] H Wray, Grant S, Kofman E and C Peel, 'Family Friendly? The Impact on Children of the Family Migration Rules: A Review of the Financial Requirements' (Children's Commissioner for England, 2015) 59.

the UK had to earn the MIR already irrespective of local wages and to hold a formal UK job offer also at the MIR. These conditions were often impossible to meet, leading to lengthy separations as the sponsor moved ahead of the family to establish the conditions for sponsorship.[50] All applicants had to meet onerous new evidentiary hurdles (for example, as to how wage slips or bank statements were presented), while minor errors in the application could lead to refusal of a very expensive application.[51] The impact of these changes was wide-ranging, and went beyond the UK's ethnic minority population, who were previously the main target of family migration controls.[52] By now, overseas travel was no longer an elite activity but a normal part of life, even for those of relatively modest means, who might therefore meet partners abroad. Greater global mobility meant more migrants coming to the UK, where they formed relationships with citizens and settled residents.[53] All these families were affected by the MIR.

Reports soon emerged of significant numbers of refusals. It was estimated in 2015 that the MIR had caused around 12,500 fewer successful applications each year since implementation in 2012 and at least 15,000 children had been affected.[54] The result was emotional and financial devastation as women had to give birth alone, children were traumatised by repeated separation from a parent and sponsors worked excessive hours, left children with grandparents and moved to find work, or sold houses to acquire the necessary savings. Some families despaired of ever living together, with serious consequences for mental health. The MIR became a source of widespread public and political comment, with critical reports from the All Party Parliamentary Group on Migration and the Children's Commissioner for England, and substantial media and parliamentary interest.[55] Expectations were therefore high when the MIR was challenged through a judicial review that eventually came before the Court in *MM (Lebanon)*. The outcome, however, while not entirely negative, was disappointing overall.

As in *Ali and Bibi*, the applicants proceeded by a judicial review of the MIR, arguing it was incompatible with human rights. This was surprising, given the Court's clear reluctance to find the Immigration Rules incompatible in *Ali and Bibi* and *Quila*. However, the government had initially argued that exemptions through leave outside the Immigration Rules would not be granted, forcing the

[50] ibid 69–70.

[51] ibid 70–74.

[52] See applicants' expert report in *MM (Lebanon)* (n 4), Table 4 available from author; E Kofman, 'Family Migration as a Class Matter' [2018] *International Migration* 33; A Sirriyeh, '"All You Need Is Love and £18,600": Class and the New UK Family Migration Rules' (2015) 35 *Critical Social Policy* 228; on earlier measures, see H Wray, *Regulating Marriage Migration into the UK: A Stranger in the Home* (Abingdon, Routledge, 2011).

[53] Office for National Statistics *Travel Trends 2019* (22 May 2020); Migration Observatory *Net migration to the UK* 29 July 2020.

[54] Wray et al, 'Family Friendly?' 125–27.

[55] All Party Parliamentary Group on Migration *Report of the Inquiry into New Family Migration Rules* (June 2013); Wray et al, 'Family Friendly?' 107.

applicants' lawyers to focus on the Rules themselves.[56] The government dropped this argument before the Supreme Court hearing, presumably because they anticipated losing on it, and this made a challenge to the Rules themselves more difficult, as violations could now be avoided through leave outside the Rules. The case started well, however, with Blake J at first instance finding that, while an income criterion was lawful, the government had failed to establish that the MIR in that form was necessary, and its application would be disproportionate in several defined circumstances.[57] This success was short-lived as the Court of Appeal reversed his judgment because it failed to award 'appropriate weight' to the government's view on necessity.[58]

The Supreme Court found that the Immigration Rules containing the MIR were compatible with Article 8 because its application would not always be disproportionate and because, following the government's concession before the hearing, leave could be granted outside the Immigration Rules if refusal would breach Article 8. It was now clear that the Immigration Rules would always be compatible with human rights provided they could sometimes be met and there was an escape route available via leave outside the Rules. In theory, even an income threshold set absurdly high, for example at £100,000 pa, would be lawful because leave could be granted outside the Rules. The Court's clear aim was to deter further attacks on the Rules as a whole, rather than on individual decisions made under them. Article 8 was not a way to challenge structurally unjust immigration policies but a remedy for occasional egregious unfairness.[59]

This was an unsurprising, if disappointing, outcome. There were, however, some positive findings: the Court emphasised that some cases would succeed outside the Immigration Rules; that, while the MIR itself was compatible with Article 8, the evidential requirements might not be; that alternative sources of funding should be considered; and that the Rules and the Guidance, taken together, did not meet the government's statutory duty to children. However, the judgment contained little detail on these points and, as in *Ali and Bibi*, they could therefore be met through minimal changes.

MM (Lebanon) was a long and complex judgment. Despite its positive aspects, it represented a step back in terms of judicial implementation of human rights. Its full implications in that respect were not easy to discern but had to be inferred from passages scattered through the judgment, possibly because, in this way, the extent of the Court's reorientation was less evident. A close reading, however, reveals the interacting ways by which the Court gave the government

[56] Theresa May MP, HC Deb 19 June 2012, vol 546, cols 762–63.
[57] *MM v SSHD* [2013] EWHC 1900 [123]–[124], [144].
[58] *MM v SSHD* [2014] EWCA Civ 985 [151].
[59] See C Bertram, D Prabhat and H Wray, 'The UK's Spousal and Family Visa Regime: Some Reflections after the Supreme Court Judgment in the MM Case' (*University of Bristol Law School Blog*, 8 March 2017) legalresearch.blogs.bris.ac.uk/2017/03/the-uks-spousal-and-family-visa-regime-some-reflections-after-the-supreme-court-judgment-in-the-mm-case/.

more control over when and how Article 8 would apply in immigration cases. The following subsections address three aspects of the judgment that contributed to this retreat. The first discusses the Court's changed approach to deference. The second considers how the Court limited the potential application of Article 8. The third looks at how the judgment was constructed to reinforce the Court's message.

A. Increased Deference

A revived doctrine of deference, already anticipated by the majority in *Ali and Bibi*, was the single most significant change, but it was not spelled out explicitly. The judgment cited the passage in *Huang* that said that, in deciding proportionality, judges should give 'appropriate' weight to those with responsibility for the subject matter and access to specialist information.[60] This was not disapproved but, elsewhere in the judgment, the Court also said that 'considerable weight' should attach to judgments made by the Secretary of State in the exercise of her constitutional responsibility for immigration policy.[61] This suggested that the 'appropriate' weight was, in fact, 'considerable' and that this was a consequence of the decision-maker's constitutional function, not the quality of the government's arguments in support of the policy, marking a departure from *Huang*. The decision in *Quila* represented an obstacle to this move as the Court had found the government's case for its policy to be inadequate, doing precisely what it now said it should not. The Court circumvented *Quila* by saying that, in *Quila*, there was not an 'immigration dimension' as the aim had been to prevent forced marriages.[62] This was an unconvincing argument. If taken at face value, it suggested a turn towards 'spatial deference', in which some areas of government activity are immune or almost immune from judicial scrutiny: why, otherwise, should an immigration policy automatically be treated differently to a social protection measure? Close examination suggests a further flaw in the logic. The policy in *Quila* was not unique; immigration control is rarely an end in itself, and most immigration policies pursue wider policy objectives: integration, economic benefits, child protection and so on. Elsewhere in *MM (Lebanon)*, the Court noted that the MIR was intended to reduce welfare dependency, and the reduction of immigration was not a 'primary objective'.[63] The distinction from *Quila* therefore was less marked than the judgment suggested.

The Court was helped in its reversion to greater deference by an improved presentation by the government of its case, who had presumably learnt from its problems in *Quila*. It had commissioned a report from the Migration Advisory

[60] *MM (Lebanon)* (n 4) [65].
[61] ibid [75]–[76].
[62] ibid [82].
[63] ibid [16].

Committee (MAC), an independent group of academic economists, on the minimum income needed to ensure the family unit could be supported without being 'a burden on the State'.[64] The £18,600 threshold was, according to the MAC, the point at which a couple was unlikely to receive welfare benefits. The Court described the report as 'a model of economic rationality' that, alongside a public consultation and an impact assessment, established the government's case for its policy.[65] The Court did not mention that the applicants' experts and a report submitted by the Children's Commissioner for England contested not the MAC report itself, but the conclusions drawn from it, as well as the conduct of the consultation and the findings of the impact assessment.[66] A detailed analysis is available elsewhere, but, in summary, the argument was that the government had cherry-picked and manipulated data to overstate the need for and benefits of the MIR.[67] The Court did not disagree with this evidence; it simply ignored it, apart for a reference to 'copious submissions on both sides'.[68] This reflected the new position on deference. If the government's view would prevail provided a prima facie case for it was made out, the applicants' criticism of policy was irrelevant. The lack of an explicit reference to this evidence, however, meant that those reading the judgment would have been unaware of its existence and therefore of the magnitude of the shift in approach.

The change to a position of more deference had a significant impact on applicants' chances of success under Article 8 outside the Immigration Rules. The fact that the policy was regarded as fully justified made it less likely that an individual decision made under the Rules would be found to be disproportionate. As Lady Hale suggested in *Ali and Bibi*, the greater the presumed benefits of a policy, the harder it is to show that they are outweighed by individual hardship.[69] By treating the case for the MIR as fully made out, the Court made violation findings less likely.

B. Limiting the Potential of Article 8

Problems for couples unable to meet the MIR had been increased by the government's guidance to decision-makers on leave outside the Immigration Rules. This said that exemptions under Article 8 should be granted only in 'exceptional

[64] Migration Advisory Committee, *Review of the Minimum Income Requirement for Sponsorship under the Family Migration Route* (November 2011) 6.

[65] *MM (Lebanon)* (n 4) [83] [6], [14].

[66] The author led (different) research teams for both the Children's Commissioner's report and the applicants' evidence: Wray et al, 'Family Friendly'. The expert report is available from the author.

[67] For more on these and other problems with the government's arguments, see H Wray, 'The *MM* Case and the Public Interest: How Did the Government Make Its Case?' (2017) 31 *Journal of Immigration Asylum and Nationality Law* 227.

[68] *MM (Lebanon)* (n 4) [78].

[69] *Ali and Bibi* (n 4) [54].

circumstances' that, in practice, were almost never found.[70] This appeared to contradict *Huang*, which held there was no condition of 'exceptionality'. The Court decided, however, that this revived use of 'exceptional' was lawful as it functioned as a prediction, not a condition, as it did not ask decision-makers to seek out any 'exceptional' factors. This technical difference would mean little to most decision-makers.[71]

The Court further restricted judicial capacity to apply Article 8 by treating the domestic jurisprudence as confined by the margin of appreciation.[72] This international law doctrine assumes that national authorities, including courts if permitted under domestic law, are best placed to apply rights in the local context, so that the supranational court sets only minimum standards. The Human Rights Act could plausibly be interpreted as giving courts power to develop human rights domestically, but the Court now rejected such a view, rebutting the approach implicitly taken in earlier cases. It followed that the boundaries of Article 8 were now a matter only for the government under the limited supervision of the Strasbourg Court, with domestic courts' role confined to ensuring the government did not fall below Strasbourg standards. This, in effect, created a double margin of appreciation, first in the domestic courts, then at Strasbourg, reinforcing a conservative dynamic in the jurisprudence.[73]

A restrained approach was also evident in the Court's approach to discrimination. The discriminatory effects of the MIR had been a source of concern for many.[74] Due to their low wages and exclusion from the labour market, some groups were more affected than others, including women, some ethnic minorities, the young and those living outside Southeast England, with many subject to multiple disadvantages.[75] The government's Policy Equality Statement noted the MIR's indirectly discriminatory impact, but found that this was proportionate to the policy aims and mitigated by minor concessions.[76] The Court rejected the Article 14 discrimination claim with almost no explanation and there was little

[70] *MM (Lebanon)* (n 4) [22]; R Thomas, 'Administrative Justice, Better Decisions, and Organisational Learning' [2015] *PL* 1. The *MM (Lebanon)* judgment [25] said that, between 2012 and 2014, only 26 claims succeeded outside the Immigration Rules, while around 30,000 applications were refused. Evidence disclosed by the Home Office to the author while she was writing the Children's Commissioner's report suggested that almost all 26 claims were allowed only after a successful appeal.

[71] For a discussion of the distinction between these two forms of exceptionality, see ch 4, s V.

[72] *MM (Lebanon)* (n 4) [40], [76].

[73] See the words of Jean-Paul Costa, former President of the ECtHR, cited in M Andenas and E Bjorge, 'National Implementation of ECHR Rights' in A Føllesdal, B Peters and G Ulfstein (eds), *Constituting Europe: The European Court of Human Rights in a National, European, and Global Context* (Cambridge, Cambridge University Press, 2013) 186–262, 186–87.

[74] Wray et al, 'Family Friendly?' 59–64; M Sumption and C Vargas-Silva, 'Love Is Not All You Need: Income Requirement for Visa Sponsorship of Foreign Family Members' (2019) 2 *Journal of Economics, Race, and Policy* 62; MYY Wong, 'The Unequal Price of Love: A Critical Race Feminist Critique of the £18,600 Minimum Income Requirement for Family Reunification under Article 14 ECHR' (2019) 33 *Journal of Immigration, Asylum and Nationality Law* 302.

[75] See the applicants' expert report available from the author.

[76] Home Office, *Policy Equality Statement: Family Migration* (June 2012).

sense that the structural character of the discrimination had been recognised.[77] The MIR fell within the ambit of Article 8 and the government's own materials acknowledged indirect discrimination, so the legal issue was justification.[78] The Strasbourg Court's margin of appreciation in relation to 'general measures of economic or social strategy' was (and remains) narrow when, as here, race, ethnic origin or gender were in issue.[79] Even if a measure was in the public interest, the government should seek to mitigate its discriminatory impact.[80]

Successful discrimination claims at Strasbourg on family reunification have included both indirect and direct discrimination. Indirect discrimination has generally been more direct in its effects than those of the MIR, but the Article 14 argument was nonetheless substantial.[81] However, the Court addressed it only briefly, saying, in effect, that as the government had satisfied the Court under Article 8, it had also fulfilled its Article 14 obligations: 'no separate issue arises in respect of discrimination under article 14'.[82] Even if the Court believed that the discrimination claim could not succeed, it did nothing to reassure affected groups that their concerns were taken seriously.

C. The Judgment

MM (Lebanon) was heard by a panel of seven and was determined through a single judgment led by Lady Hale and Lord Carnwath, with assent by the other justices, including Lord Wilson. This reflected its significance and, it is likely, the Court's wish to publicly reconcile its differences on the deference question. Lady Hale's leadership was particularly significant; she had sat on many of the earlier post-*Huang* decisions, and she and Lord Wilson had supported a more active role for the Court in *Ali and Bibi*. The one-year gap between hearing and judgment suggested that achieving this unified position had been difficult. The judgment was long (104 paragraphs), and it was sometimes difficult to follow. As with the first phase of post-*Huang* decisions, the Court was not entirely

[77] *MM (Lebanon)* (n 4) [78]. This does not seem to have been a unique failing; for a critique of equality assessments carried out in relation to the hostile environment, see Equality and Human Rights Commission, *Public Sector Equality Duty Assessment of Hostile Environment Policies* (November 2020).

[78] For a discussion of the development of this argument before the Strasbourg Court, see S Fredman, 'Emerging from the Shadows: Substantive Equality and Article 14 of the European Convention on Human Rights' (2016) 16 *Human Rights Law Review* 273.

[79] *DH v The Czech Republic* App no 57325/00 (GC, 13 November 2007) [176]. In gender cases, the margin of appreciation has applied principally to measures that aim to remedy women's structural disadvantage; see, eg *Stec and Others v UK* [2006] ECHR 1162.

[80] See, eg *Oršuš and Others v Croatia* App no 15766/03 (GC, 16 March 2010); Fredman, 'Emerging from the Shadows'.

[81] *Biao v Denmark* (2017) 64 EHRR 1; *Vallianatos v Greece* (2014) 59 EHRR12; *Pajić v Croatia* App no 68453/13 (23 February 2016); *Tadeucci and McCall v Italy* App no 51362/09 (30 June 2016); *Abdulaziz v United Kingdom* (1985) 7 EHRR 471.

[82] *MM (Lebanon)* (n 4) [78].

transparent about what it was doing, and its apparently dispassionate language disguised the extent to which the judgment marked a reprioritisation of the concerns of government over those of binational families.

The judgment barely acknowledged the reality facing families separated by the MIR. The second paragraph briefly noted that many individuals found the MIR difficult to meet, but the judgment moved rapidly to a discussion of the government's dissatisfaction with the former rule.[83] The hardships facing applicants were mentioned again later, but as a preliminary to the observation that a rule that caused hardship to many might still be compatible with Convention rights.[84] The impact of the MIR was understated; the Court said that estimates differed as to the proportion of the adult population who could not meet it, failing to mention that reliable sources put it at more than 40 per cent.[85] The judgment emphasised the apparently very low earnings of sponsors under the previous regime without mentioning these figures were contested by the applicants.[86] It also observed that 45 per cent of these previous sponsors would have been unable to meet the MIR, but did not note that this was close to the national figure, so that they were not, in fact, noticeably poorer than the population as a whole.[87] Finally, the Court also did not explore the considerable practical difficulties of meeting the evidential requirements for the MIR.

The government's perspective predominated in other ways too. For example, one sentence began, 'Problems were encountered with [the former] approach', although it was the government, not families, that found it problematic, while the passive voice suggested that the government was the victim of circumstances rather than pursuing its own agenda.[88] The need for change was assumed to be unquestionable: 'Hence the Home Office set about devising an alternative policy.'[89] As mentioned earlier, government claims that the MIR would bring substantial savings in welfare benefits and public services were reported, with no acknowledgement that these were contested.[90]

It is interesting that *MM (Lebanon)* was the first occasion in the decisions discussed in this book that the Court engaged fully with the Strasbourg Article 8 cases. In the first post-*Huang* phase, the Court cited a few cases mainly to demonstrate that Article 8 protected family life. The second phase (see chapter six) saw more discussion, but on specific issues – the interests of children in *ZH (Tanzania)* and Article 8(1) interference in *Quila*. There was also a brief discussion in *Ali and Bibi*. In *MM (Lebanon)*, however, there was a wide-ranging analysis, with

[83] ibid [80].
[84] ibid [81].
[85] ibid [2]; see, eg Sumption and Vargas-Silva, 'Love Is Not All You Need'; Migration Observatory, 'Women, Young People and Non-Londoners Are Most Affected by Changes to Family Migration Policy' (Oxford University, 12 June 2012).
[86] *MM (Lebanon)* (n 4) [4].
[87] ibid [8].
[88] ibid [5].
[89] ibid [27]–[32], [5]–[6].
[90] ibid [16].

a particular emphasis on *Jeunesse*. This, though, was for a particular purpose. While the Court still referred to Article 8's protective function, particularly as regards children, there was also a new stress on its limitations, and the Court was explicit that family reunification engaged a positive, not negative, obligation.[91]

D. Impact of *MM (Lebanon)*

The Court in *MM (Lebanon)* had a clear aim: to end confrontations with the government over Article 8 and immigration that had already led to rule and statute changes. The government's assessment of the public interest in an immigration control measure would not be questioned, Article 8 was a remedy only in exceptional cases, and the interests of families and minorities were barely mentioned. After grappling with Article 8 for some years and faced with a government hostile to both migrants and constitutionalised human rights, the Court removed itself from the fray.

The judgment did have some positive consequences: the Immigration Rules had to be amended to meet the government's duty to children, other financial resources must now be considered, and leave must sometimes be granted outside the Rules. The government, however, again responded minimally. Amendments to the Immigration Rules in July 2017 allowed an application to succeed if, although an applicant could not meet the rules, 'exceptional circumstances' made refusal a breach of Article 8 due to 'unjustifiably harsh consequences'. A wider range of financial resources would occasionally be considered, and decision-makers must consider the best interests of a relevant child.[92] This was something, but not much. 'Unjustifiably harsh', discussed earlier, was a high threshold, the obligation to children was unspecific, alternative financial resources were still not counted routinely and evidential requirements were pitched high. Families accepted under these amendments or in applications granted outside the Rules must wait up to 10 years and make repeated, expensive applications to achieve a permanent status.[93] Presumably, the government hoped to have done enough to comply while minimising the number of additional successful claims.

In summary, *MM (Lebanon)* was the decision in which the Court decisively rolled back on its previous approach and pre-empted attempts to use Article 8 to challenge the overall unfairness of the Immigration Rules, rather than individual decisions made under them. That message was reinforced by the final decision discussed in this chapter, *Agyarko*.

[91] ibid [37]–[44].

[92] Immigration Rules, HC290, 20 July 2017, amending HC395 Appendix FM: Family Members, paras GEN.3.1, GEN.3.2, GEN.3.3.

[93] For a discussion, see G Manning, 'The Minimum Income Requirement for Family Settlement: The Cost of Integration' [2017] *PL* 304; C Desira, 'Home Office Makes Changes to Appendix FM Minimum Income Rule Following MM Case' (*Free Movement*, 10 August 2017); Migration Observatory, 'Migrants on Ten-Year Routes to Settlement in the UK (Oxford University, 27 July 2021).

V. *AGYARKO*: REGULARISATION AND PRECARIOUSNESS

The decision in *Agyarko* was handed down on the same day as *MM (Lebanon)* by the same panel and must be seen as a continuation of the same endeavour.[94] It concerned irregular migrants asking for leave to remain in the UK under Article 8 and whose claims, following *Huang* and *EB (Kosovo)*, could no longer be dismissed through the tests of insurmountable obstacles and exceptionality. The government wanted to revive these tests and decide claims within the Immigration Rules. To this end, it had created limited provision for regularisation within the Rules: paragraphs EX.1(a) and EX.1(b). Its argument was that these paragraphs covered almost all instances when Article 8 would be violated, making grants of leave outside the Immigration Rules very rare indeed.

Paragraph EX.1(a) allowed a parent to remain in the UK if there was a 'genuine and subsisting parental relationship' with a child who was a British citizen child or had lived in the UK for at least seven years and, in either case, could not reasonably be expected to leave the UK. Paragraph EX.1(b) applied to an applicant with 'a genuine and subsisting relationship' with a British citizen, refugee or settled partner where there were insurmountable obstacles (defined as 'very significant difficulties') to family life continuing outside the UK.[95] It was intended that almost all cases would now be determined under these exceptions, with leave outside the Rules, according to guidance, only where 'exceptional circumstances' would lead to 'unjustifiably harsh consequences', bearing in mind that precarious family life attracted little weight.[96]

Agyarko concerned paragraph EX.1(b), the exception for partners. The unrelated applicants, Ms Agyarko and Ms Ikuga, entered as visitors in 2003 and 2008 respectively and overstayed. They were in long-term relationships with British citizens but had no children in the UK. Neither had criminal records and Ms Ikuga had fertility problems and other serious health issues for which her partner provided care. If removed from the UK, it was unclear that either could return, but their applications for leave to remain were refused. The question was whether paragraph EX.1(b) and the guidance for leave outside the Rules, taken together, complied with Article 8. The Court found unanimously in favour of the government but, as in *MM (Lebanon)*, the extent of the retreat was not made explicit. The Court's reference point was the Strasbourg decisions, particularly *Jeunesse*, which was mentioned 11 times in the judgment, usually by reference to its limitations (despite the violation finding in *Jeunesse*).[97] In this way, it did not have to address the extent to which the decision in *Agyarko* represented a step backwards from its own previous decisions.

The first issue was the resurrection of 'insurmountable obstacles' in the Immigration Rules. The Court found this was lawful as leave outside the Rules

[94] *Agyarko* (n 4).
[95] HC395 Appendix FM, paras EX1, EX2.
[96] *Agyarko* (n 4) [45].
[97] See, eg ibid [33], [43], [49], [53], [54].

was available 'in exceptional circumstances' if a refusal on this basis violated Article 8.[98] The finding that the Rules were lawful was unsurprising; after *Ali and Bibi* and *Mahad*, the Immigration Rules were effectively invulnerable to incompatibility findings provided leave could be granted on human rights grounds outside the Rules. The key question therefore was whether the guidance on leave outside the Rules was compatible with Article 8. The new version of exceptionality and the test of 'unjustifiably harsh' had already been approved in *MM (Lebanon)* and were accepted here also.[99] That left 'precariousness', a concept that derived from the Strasbourg cases. The government's definition arguably went further than Strasbourg by including relationships entered into when residence was lawful, whereas, at Strasbourg, it was almost always confined to irregular migrants.[100] This was, however, accepted by the Court.[101] As a consequence, an Article 8 claim involving an irregular or non-settled migrant, unless they were the parent of a resident child, could succeed only if there were insurmountable obstacles to relocation or exceptional circumstances that made removal unjustifiably harsh, bearing in mind that family life was precarious. This was a long way from the reasonableness test in *EB (Kosovo)* and the rejection of 'exceptionality' in *Huang*.

Article 8 claims that do not involve children are very difficult to win and the claimants in *Agyarko* claims might never have succeeded, but there was now almost no space for them, as later lower court decisions confirmed.[102] More significant, perhaps, was the indirect impact of *Agyarko*, when combined with *Ali and Bibi* and *MM (Lebanon)*, on the relationship between the Immigration Rules and Article 8. Under *Huang*, Article 8 compliance was an objective, judicially determined standard and the Immigration Rules had only a limited bearing on it; refusal under the Rules was 'the point at which to begin, not end, consideration of the claim under article 8', although appropriate weight would be given to the government's view on proportionality, including as expressed through the Immigration Rules.[103] Over time, it became clear that the Immigration Rules would never be declared incompatible with Article 8 provided leave could be granted outside the Rules. While this presented some practical problems (what would happen if the Rules were impossible to meet?), it had some logic and, as the government preferred applications to be decided within the Rules, there was an incentive for it to keep the Rules compliant with Article 8.

[98] ibid [48].

[99] ibid [55]–[56].

[100] See ch 3, s VB.

[101] *Agyarko* (n 4) [50]–[53]; C Yeo, 'Supreme Court Upholds Minimum Income Rule of £18,600 to Sponsor Foreign Spouses in *MM* Case' (*Free Movement*, 22 February 2017); see also R Warren, 'Private Life in the Balance: Constructing the Precarious Migrant' (2016) 30 *Journal of Immigration, Asylum and Nationality Law* 124. This position was later explicitly endorsed in a different context in *Rhuppiah v SSHD* [2018] UKSC 58 [43].

[102] See, eg *TZ (Pakistan) v SSHD* [2018] EWCA Civ 1109; *Mudibo v SSHD* [2017] EWCA Civ 1949; *EQ (AP) v SSHD* [2017] CSOH 111; see also B Shabbir, 'A Familiar Nemesis: The Court of Appeal on "Insurmountable Obstacles"' (*Free Movement*, 6 December 2017).

[103] *Huang* (n 42) [6].

After *Agyarko* and *MM (Lebanon)*, however, Article 8 claims had to be 'exceptional' and consequences must be 'unjustifiably harsh' to succeed outside the Immigration Rules. This met the government's desire to have almost all decisions made within the Immigration Rules, which would also make life more straightforward for applicants but it turned Article 8 into a more relative standard. The reference point was what the Rules required, and a successful claim must stand out from the ordinary run of refusals however harsh the Rules. There must be limits to this; an egregiously non-compliant provision in the Rules might still result in successful claims outside the Rules. However, the version of Article 8 that emerged was still a narrow one. The government's language in the Rules and the Guidance could be defended as technically compatible with Article 8, but they were negative in tone. Although claims such as those in *Agyarko* would rarely succeed at Strasbourg, the overall message was that the government's priorities were now even more critical.

The turn towards government interests was reflected in how the *Agyarko* judgment was structured and expressed. The seven-judge panel delivered a single judgment led by Lord Reed. The opening sentence set the tone: 'These appeals are concerned with applications made by foreign nationals, residing unlawfully in the UK, for leave to remain here as the partners of British citizens with whom they have formed relationships during the period of their unlawful residence.'[104]

The contrast with the language of earlier decisions was stark. The applicants' unlawful presence was mentioned twice in the first sentence. They were not named until midway through the judgment, consistent with their distancing from the centre of concern, and the judgment was written in ways that reduced the likelihood of an empathic response from the reader. For example, it was mentioned twice that Ms Agyarko had three children in Ghana, and that she had not visited them since 2003.[105] Failure to visit was an inevitable consequence of her insecure position in the UK, but the impression that she was an indifferent mother was left to hang. This can be contrasted with the more sympathetic treatment of Ms Chikwamba, who was in a similar position.[106] Ms Ikuga's personal and medical difficulties were often described through reported speech ('it was said that …'), suggesting scepticism.[107] The distancing language was reinforced by the dismissive tone of the conclusions, with repeated use of the word 'nothing': 'nothing' to suggest exceptional circumstances, 'nothing' to displace the earlier finding that the application must fail, 'nothing' to undermine previous conclusions.[108] It seemed that, for the Court, the family life of these applicants was indeed 'nothing', while the interests of their partners were dismissed briefly and legalistically. The right of a citizen to live 'unhindered' in the UK 'does not

[104] *Agyarko* (n 4) [1].
[105] ibid [20], [21].
[106] See ch 5, s C.
[107] *Agyarko* (n 4) [26]–[30].
[108] ibid [70], [73].

entitle a British citizen to insist that his or her non-national partner should also be entitled to live in the UK, when that partner may lawfully be refused'.[109] The term 'insist' suggested that this was an unreasonable expectation, not an understandable desire to live with loved ones.

VI. REFLECTIONS ON THE THIRD PHASE DECISIONS

Agyarko is the final family reunification decision discussed in this book, although the Court continued to rule on Article 8 and deportation or private life.[110] It concluded a remarkable period in the history of immigration and human rights. *Huang* (chapter four) and the first and second post-*Huang* phases (chapters five and six) showed a Court ready to use Article 8 to protect families in unprecedented ways. The third phase, discussed in this chapter, saw the Court retrace its steps. The result is that the government has little work to do to justify its policies, and Article 8 is interpreted narrowly.

The scale of rollback should not be overstated. The impact of Article 8 is still visible in the immigration system, although more often in the form of exceptions within the Immigration Rules or under the statutory provisions that have not come before the Court than as a free-standing obligation.[111] The parents of children resident in the UK, particularly if the children are citizens, are in a stronger position than before and some couples can make use of the limited provision in the Rules for third party financial support. Insurmountable obstacles to relocation are occasionally found to exist. In all these cases, achieving a settled status is a long and expensive process for families, but it is possible. In addition, it is impossible to know the counterfactual: what might the government have done if it had not been bound by Article 8? Both the minimum income requirement and the pre-entry language test could have been set at a more demanding level, for example. The current government's desire to repeal the Human Rights Act may be influenced by its populist and divisive character, but the Conservatives have wanted to reform the Act since they entered government in 2010 precisely because it limits their freedom of action.

The third phase decisions did, however, change the human rights climate in family reunification at the structural level. They achieved four things. Firstly, the Immigration Rules will never be found incompatible with human rights provided there is an opportunity for leave to be granted outside the Rules. Secondly, the courts will not assess the government's reasons for policy even when it interferes with family life. It is interested only in whether a particular case causes egregious hardship. This makes violation findings less likely as the proportionality assessment will assume that the policy serves the public interest. Thirdly, the

[109] ibid [68].
[110] *KO (Nigeria) & Ors v SSHD* [2018] UKSC 53; *Rhuppiah* (n 101).
[111] Nationality, Immigration and Asylum Act 2002, s 117b (inserted by Immigration Act 2014, s 19).

constraints imposed by Article 8 on the government will only be those established by the Strasbourg Court. The Human Rights Act cannot be used to develop a domestic Article 8 jurisprudence that was shaped by Strasbourg but took account of national conditions. The margin of appreciation means that the Strasbourg jurisprudence develops only cautiously, and the result is likely to be more conservative domestic interpretations. Finally, the Court endorsed the government's use of terms such as 'exceptional circumstances', 'unjustifiably harsh' or 'insurmountable obstacles', because they could be applied in ways that comply with Article 8 even though these are not the most obvious interpretations. The consistent application of Article 8 therefore depends on decision-makers and the Tribunal understanding and applying the correct interpretation. While the Tribunal can be expected to apply the law correctly in most cases, and success rates in Tribunal appeals are quite high despite the problems noted in earlier chapters, appeals require financial and personal resources that are not available to everyone and take months to be heard and decided.[112] While immigration decision-makers are often competent and conscientious, they are not legally trained and are subject to institutional pressures. The government can continue to apply exemptions narrowly, knowing that it will often not be successfully challenged.

All these factors collectively made Article 8 a less effective check on government conduct. This was not surprising. There was no longer a majority on the Court in favour of the former approach and the political context had changed. As a purely legal matter, the Court could have maintained its previous stance, at least for a while. Although the 2012 changes to the Immigration Rules were debated in Parliament, they were still only rules of practice, whereas the Court's obligations under the Human Rights Act derived from statute. A searching approach to policy and domestic interpretation of the Strasbourg jurisprudence were both compatible with the Human Rights Act and could still have been applied to applications for leave outside the Immigration Rules. However, the Immigration Act 2014, while not strictly relevant to these decisions, showed the government's determination to act, and there was a growing wider risk to the entire human rights jurisdiction.[113]

VII. REFLECTIONS ON *HUANG* AND THE THREE PHASES

This section considers how the third phase decisions shape understanding of the Supreme Court's family reunification jurisprudence in its entirety. It draws on

[112] In 2017, 56% of appeals against immigration decisions were successful: D Stevenson, 'Immigration Tribunals Lose Their Way in Overcomplicated Human Rights Rules' (*Free Movement*, 9 October 2018).

[113] Ministry of Justice, *Human Rights Act Reform: A Modern Bill of Rights – A Consultation to Reform the Human Rights Act 1998* (CP 588, December 2021); Queen's Speech 2022, www.gov.uk/government/speeches/queens-speech-2022.

the content analysis that has already been briefly used in chapter six to reflect on how the jurisprudence emerged, evolved and subsided. In so doing, it maintains the categorisation adopted in this and previous chapters. After *Huang* (discussed in chapter four), there was the first post-*Huang* phase (chapter five), in which the Court used Article 8 to ensure executive policy fully considered family life. In the second phase (chapter six), the Court was asked to engage with the Immigration Rules and statute. It still prioritised family life, but did not rely only or at all on Article 8. In the third phase (this chapter), the Court reverted to a position that limited the actual and potential impact of Article 8.

The first observation is that the case law seems to have become increasingly problematic. *Huang* was a crisp 22-paragraph judgment handed down two months after the hearing. *MM (Lebanon)* contained 110 paragraphs and took one year to be decided (followed by 74 paragraphs and 10 months in *Agarko*). A length of 110 paragraphs is not unusual in a Supreme Court judgment, and this book has argued that judges in all phases were sometimes elliptical in their reasoning.[114] It is the increasing length and the increasing delay, both demonstrated in Figure 7.1, that suggest problems, particularly when, as Table 7.1 shows, the average length and wait for judgment did not change in the same period. This impression is reinforced by the panels of seven justices instead of the usual five for *MM (Lebanon)* and *Agyarko*.

Figure 7.1 Length of entire judgment in paragraphs and time in months between hearing and judgment

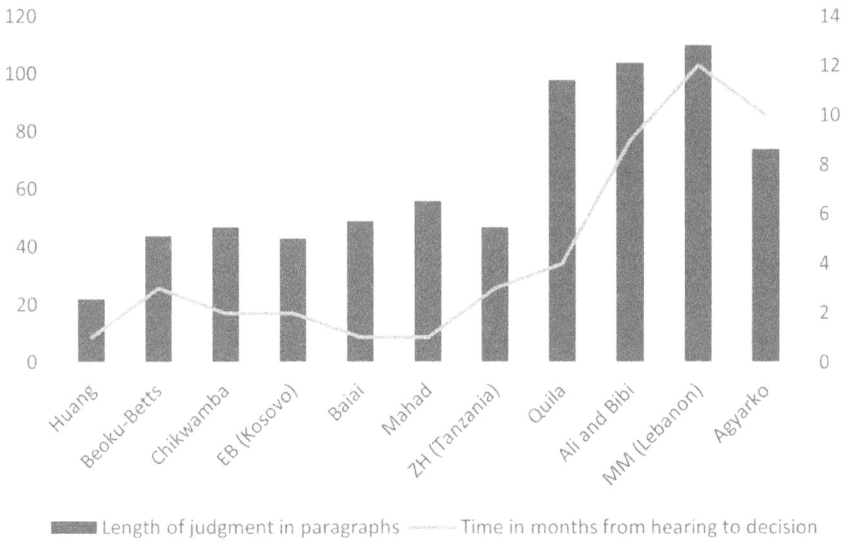

[114] For example, *Miller v Secretary of State for Exiting the European Union* [2017] UKSC 5, heard in the same year as *MM (Lebanon)* and *Agyarko*, had 283 paragraphs.

Table 7.1 Average length and wait for House of Lords/Supreme Court judgments in 2007 and 2017

	Average length of House of Lords/Supreme Court judgments	**Average time between hearing and judgment (rounded to nearest month)**
2007	77	2
2017	74	4

There was also a change to the language and organisation of the judgments through the period. Examples have already been cited, but an overview shows the pattern. *Huang* and the first phase judgments made little reference to the Strasbourg cases, reflecting their focus on domestic human rights. In both the second and third phases, the Court engaged more deeply, although still not consistently, with the Strasbourg cases, as Figure 7.2 shows.

Figure 7.2 Number of ECtHR cases cited in lead and concurring judgments

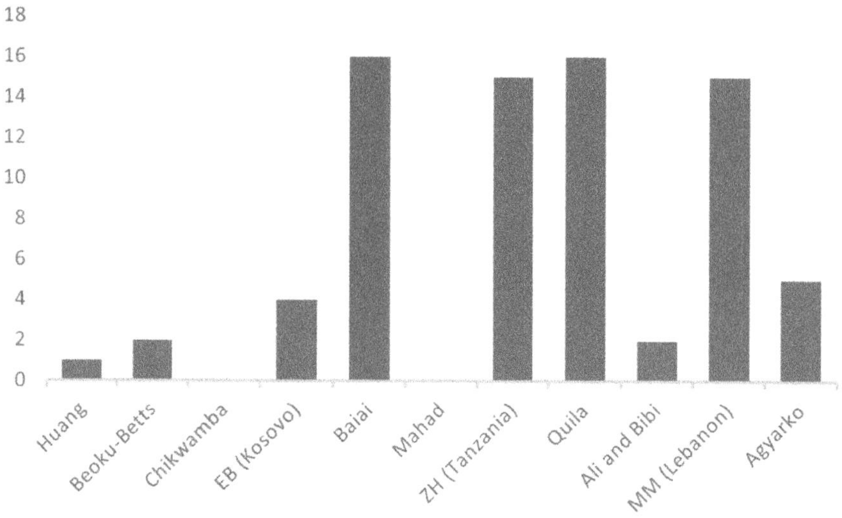

Raw numbers do not tell us the depth of the Court's engagement with the decisions they did cite. As Figure 7.3 shows, when the frequency of references to Strasbourg cases is counted, the picture looks roughly similar in that prolonged engagement with the Strasbourg cases did not begin until the second post-*Huang* phase. The impression that the third phase was somewhat less engaged must be understood in the context of multiple references in *MM (Lebanon)* and *Agyarko* to *Hesham Ali*, a decision of the Court on deportation that extensively reviewed the Strasbourg cases.[115]

[115] *Hesham Ali (Iraq) v SSHD* [2016] UKSC 60.

Figure 7.3 Total number of references to ECtHR cases within leading and concurring judgments

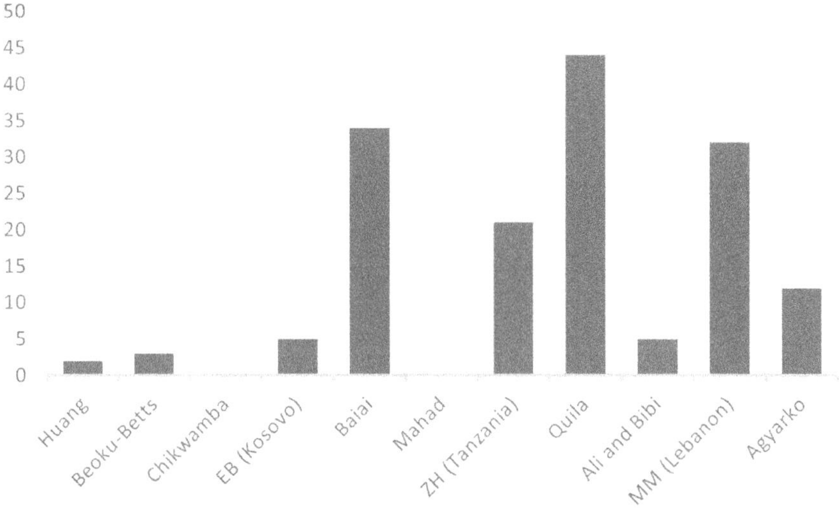

Figure 7.4 shows that no such pattern was visible in the number of domestic cases cited, suggesting that the change was in the approach to the Strasbourg cases.

Figure 7.4 Total number of domestic cases cited in lead and concurring judgments

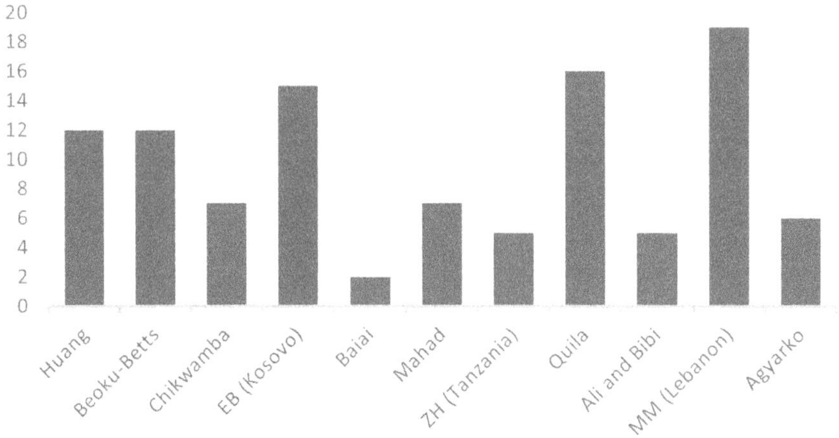

If engagement with Strasbourg did not begin until the second post-*Huang* phase, the purposes for which they were cited changed between the second and third phase. I have suggested that the second phase saw the Strasbourg cases as a source of rights, whereas the emphasis in the third phase was on ensuring that the public interest in removing or refusing migrants was fully considered. This is demonstrated in Figure 7.5, which shows increased references to the public interest during the third phase.

Figure 7.5 Use of 'public interest' or related terms in lead and concurring judgments (*Baiai* and *Mahad* excluded)

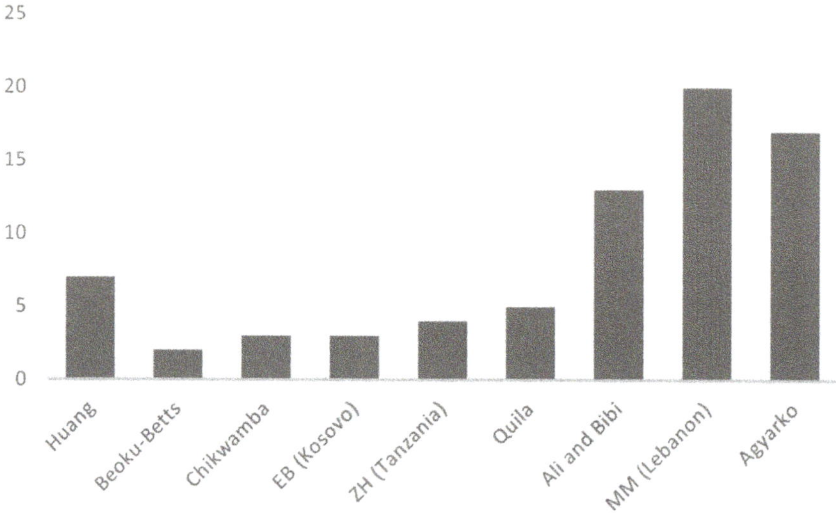

There were also increased references over time within the decisions to the margin of appreciation (see Figure 7.6), beginning with *Quila*, and arguably reflecting growing interest in the relationship between domestic and supranational courts, and with how the limits of Article 8 protection should be determined.

Figure 7.6 References to margin of appreciation in lead and concurring judgments (*Mahad* excluded)

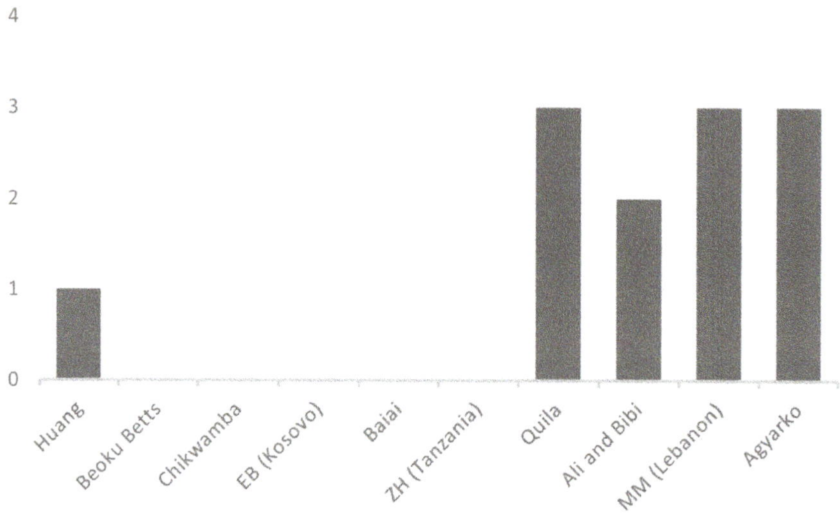

Also of note is the increase in references to positive obligations, seen in Figure 7.7. The spike in such references in *Quila* reflected its focus on whether family life existed under Article 8(1), where positive obligations were pertinent.[116] The fall relative to *Quila* in the third phase cases is again a likely consequence of the references in those cases to *Hesham Ali*, which had addressed the question of positive obligations in some depth.

Figure 7.7 References to positive obligations in lead and concurring judgments (*Baiai* and *Mahad* excluded)

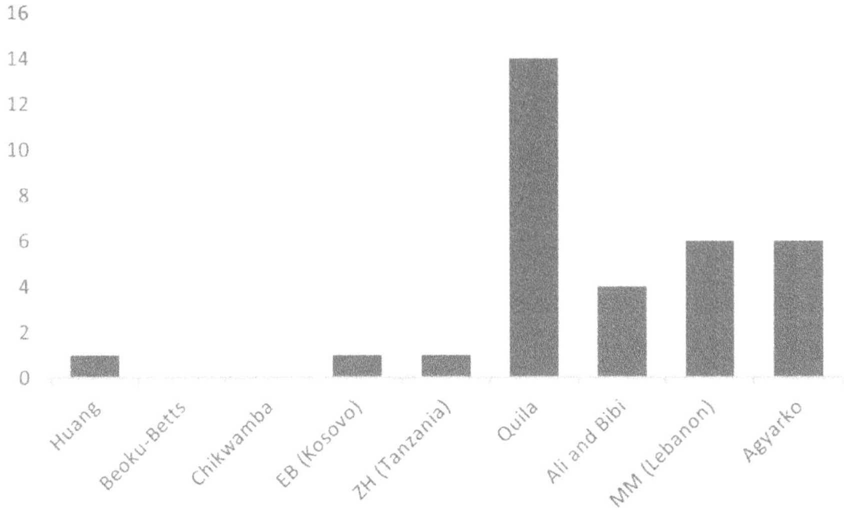

As the cases progressed, therefore, the Strasbourg jurisprudence became steadily more important but this was primarily in terms of its limits, as the Court became more preoccupied with meeting government concerns. As it did so, there was correspondingly less interest in the personal difficulties and circumstances of the applicants. As Figure 7.8 shows, there was not a steep decline through the period, but there was a marked drop between the first and second phases, for the reasons discussed in chapter six. There was, however, a difference in where applicants' circumstances first appeared in judgments, as demonstrated in Figure 7.9. It suggests that, in the third phase, the problems for families were no longer the first consideration.

[116] See ch 6, s V.

Figure 7.8 Percentage of paragraphs devoted to facts in lead and concurring judgments

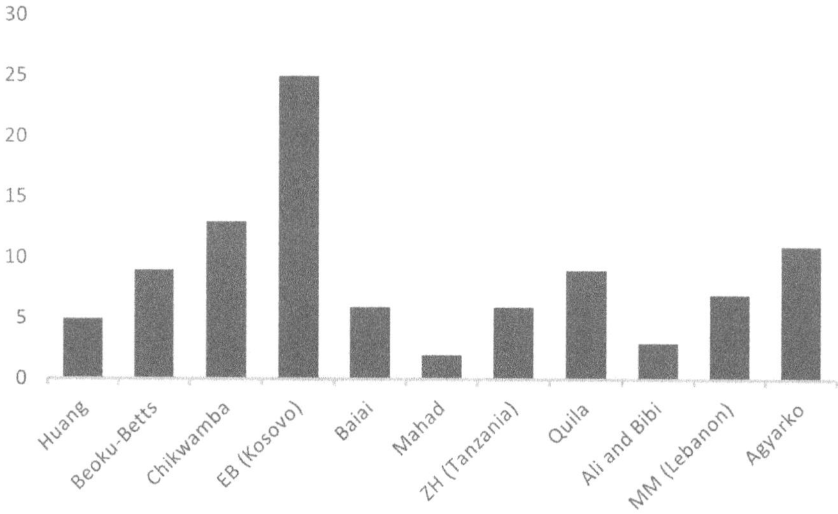

Figure 7.9 Decile of the judgment in which applicants' circumstances were first discussed

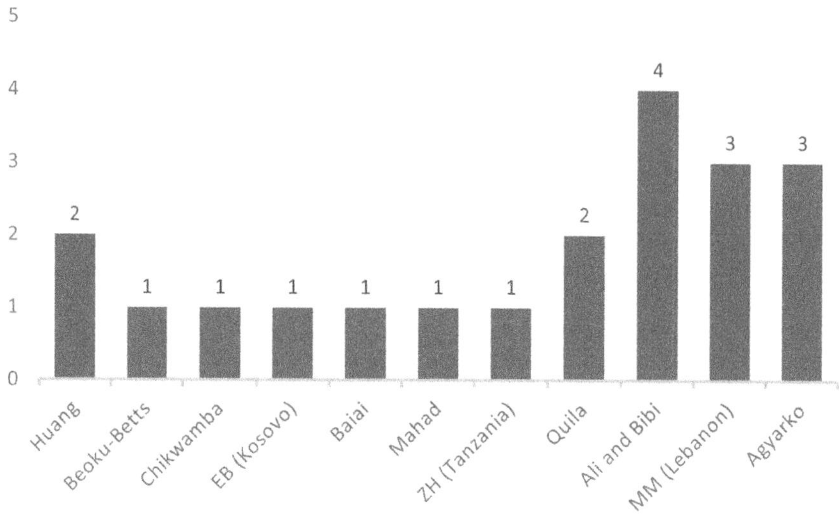

There was also more interest in questions of regular or lawful entry and residence. Seven of the decisions featured applicants who were in the UK without leave, but the regularity of their residence barely featured until the final case of *Agyarko*, where it was the central issue (see Figure 7.10).

Figure 7.10 References to unlawful, irregular or unauthorised entry or residence in relevant decisions

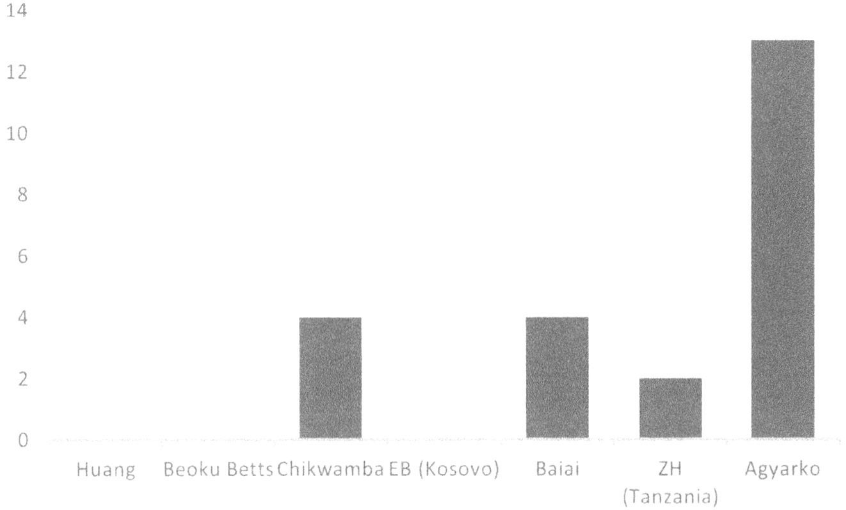

The preceding discussion has suggested that the Court's view of its function changed during the cases. Over time, it became less engaged with Article 8 as a means of protecting families and more with ensuring that government interests were given sufficient consideration. The consequence was that Article 8 was no longer a means of addressing the structural exclusion of individuals and minority groups but was a legal obligation like any other, with the Court reverting to an umpire role between two parties. A possible indication of this is the marked increase in language associated with the attribution of legal responsibility, as seen in Figures 7.11 and 7.12. Figure 7.11 shows the raw use of this language and Figure 7.12 shows it in relation to the length of the judgments, revealing a less marked but still noticeable distinction between the first and second phase cases and the third phase ones.

Figure 7.11 Use of the terms 'impose', 'oblige' and 'duty', variants and synonyms (set out in the Appendix) in lead and concurring judgments

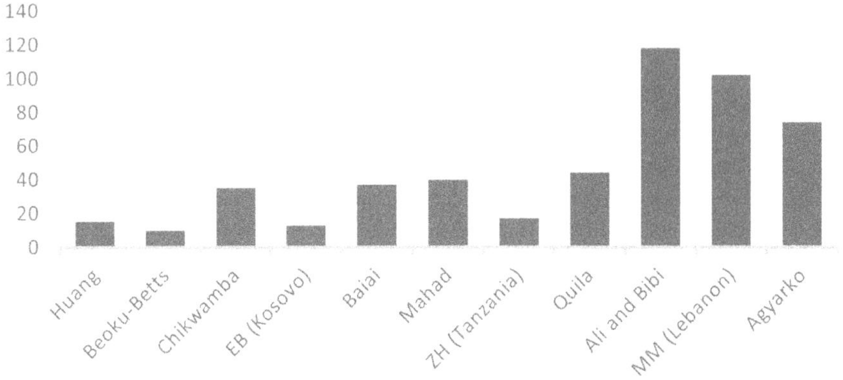

Figure 7.12 Use of the terms 'impose', 'oblige' and 'duty', variants and synonyms in lead and concurring judgments as a percentage of the number of paragraphs in these judgments

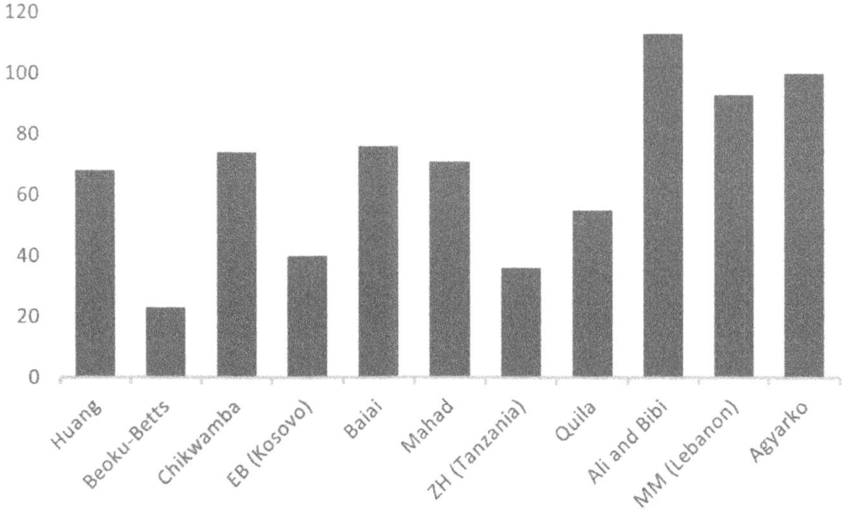

The content analysis reported here supports five key arguments made through the interpretation of the decisions analysed in this book. Firstly, judgments did more than make statements of law; they were constructed to promote or prioritise certain perspectives and to persuade the reader of a moral as well as a legal case. This was often done in indirect ways, through the structure, ordering and language of the judgments. Secondly, constructing a case for the protection of family life under Article 8 was not straightforward. The first phase decisions barely engaged with the Strasbourg cases. The second phase did so in relation to specific and limited arguments, which did not rely only on the intersection between Article 8 and family reunification. As the Court came under pressure, it continued to engage with Strasbourg Article 8 cases, but with an increasing emphasis on their limits and on the positive character of the obligation, as well as on government interests and priorities, which started to take centre stage. This was not a straightforward process, and judgments both became longer and took longer to decide. Thirdly and relatedly, the individuals and families behind each claim became less central to the analysis, first in terms of the attention they received and then their priority in the argument. The fourth argument is that, as the Court retreated from a close scrutiny of government policy, human rights became a set of legal rules rather than principles that could address structural imbalances within the law, and the Court became correspondingly more concerned with the attribution of precisely defined legal responsibilities. Finally, the Supreme Court is shown to have been acutely conscious of how its judgments would impact on its relationship with other constitutional actors. There was arguably a degree of overcorrection in this respect as the Court moved from barely considering the public interest, the limits of Article 8 and concerns over irregular migration to an intense focus on it.

Taken in its entirety, the analysis in this and the previous three chapters suggests that the Court was a strategic actor throughout, in the sense that it did not 'make decisions in a vacuum' but attended to 'the preferences and likely actions of other key players, including their colleagues, judicial superiors, politicians, and the public'.[117] This was not openly acknowledged, however. On the surface, the Court '[sustained] the myth that adjudication involves nothing but principled deliberation'.[118]

VIII. CONCLUSION

This chapter has analysed three Article 8 family reunification decisions that were heard against an increasingly antagonistic background. On the one hand, the government was determined to limit the impact of Article 8 as much as possible and to avoid decisions made by judges outside the Immigration Rules. On the other, lawyers had seen, during the first and second post-*Huang* phases, that the Court was alert to the need to protect family life and perhaps paid insufficient attention to the limits of what it was willing to do. The outcome was that the Court emphatically withdrew from the battle and rolled back to a position that largely resembled that which prevailed before *Huang*, although there remained some elements of additional protection. In *Ali and Bibi*, on the pre-entry language test, the panel agreed that the test was compatible with Article 8 as leave outside the Immigration Rules could be used to address violations. While there was disagreement as to scrutiny of the public interest, a more deferent approach prevailed. In *MM (Lebanon)*, the Court declined to question the government's assessment of the public interest and found that, subject to some modest changes, the minimum income requirement was lawful. *Agyarko* reinforced that position in its analysis of exceptions within the Immigration Rules that purported to ensure Article 8 compliance. Overall, the Court reverted to an executive-oriented position not just in terms of deference, but also in its interpretation of the Strasbourg cases, as well as in its language and in the weight and priority awarded to various interests. It also declined to engage in any depth with discrimination claims. The retreat to this position was always a probability, given the hostile wider climate, including the government's

[117] L Epstein and K Weinshall, *The Strategic Analysis of Judicial Behavior: A Comparative Perspective* (Cambridge, Cambridge University Press, 2021) 1–2.

[118] R Mann and MC Hübner, 'What Judges Don't Say – Judicial Strategy and Constitutional Theory' (*Law Log – WZB Rule of Law Center*, 2015) 21.

'strike back' measures and changes to the Court's composition.[119] While earlier chapters showed the potential of Article 8, the lack of durability demonstrated in this chapter shows the difficulty of using Article 8 in family reunification claims and invokes a deeper question: what can be expected of Article 8? This is a question of law and politics that is addressed in the next chapter.

[119] Harlow and Rawlings, 'Striking Back or Clamping Down', 301–26.

8

A Better Article 8 is Possible

I. INTRODUCTION

THE PREVIOUS CHAPTER ended by asking what can be expected of Article 8 in family reunification claims. This chapter attempts to address that question. It is underpinned by the belief that Article 8 has accorded insufficient weight to family life in family reunification claims and it imagines how these claims would proceed if family were as important as immigration control. It draws on the domestic and European Court of Human Rights (ECtHR, Strasbourg Court or Strasbourg) judgments (including dissenting judgments) discussed in this book, and its aim is to extend existing principles to make family more important. The chapter is therefore a 'moral reconstruction' that is 'sensitive' to practice, and that recognises the pressures on judges.[1] It is also focused on what the Strasbourg Court might do as it is clear from the decisions discussed in the previous chapter that the Supreme Court will not now exceed the Strasbourg jurisprudence and may even be prohibited from doing so in future.[2] Even so, it is still an idealistic exercise, given resistance in many European states to the application of human rights to immigration cases; the Strasbourg Court is unlikely to move ahead substantially if it cannot bring most states with it. Some judges may have personal sympathy for binational families, but they cannot make immigration less important for governments and there is no realistic route to a judicially endorsed right to family reunification without wider public consensus.

While caution is justified, undue pessimism is not. Political climates do not last for ever. Change at Strasbourg has been slow, but chapter three showed that it is real, and it may, in time, go further. Advances have been in those areas where states have already made international law commitments, such as children's rights, discrimination or forced migration.[3] These are therefore likely to be at the forefront of change, but the analysis of the domestic cases in chapters four to six showed that a more vigorous application of Article 8 can have an impact

[1] K Möller, *The Global Model of Constitutional Rights* (Oxford, Oxford University Press, 2012) 20–22.

[2] Bill of Rights Bill (HC 2022–23) [117].

[3] *Rodrigues Da Silva and Hoogkamer v The Netherlands* [2006] ECHR 86; *Jeunesse v Netherlands* [2014] ECHR 1309; *Biao v Denmark* [2016] ECHR 455; *AM v Denmark* App no 6697/18 (GC, 9 July 2021).

in many aspects of family reunification. They also showed that using Article 8 as a vehicle for change is not straightforward. They raise the question of whether using human rights law is the most appropriate way to improve the position of binational families. This preliminary issue is addressed in the next section of this chapter, which considers the limitations of human rights but concludes that there are benefits to pursuing remedies through the law, provided legal arguments form part of a wider social movement for reform. The chapter then turns to how those arguments should be made. This requires a return to the technical issue that has arisen repeatedly through the book: whether family reunification is a positive or negative obligation. I explain why, with reservations, I continue treating family reunification as engaging a positive obligation.

That decision shapes the following sections, which consider how Article 8 can be made legally more effective. The first issue is family life. I argue that the current approach, which recognises family life between spouses and between parents and children, needs to be supplemented by a flexible and fact-sensitive method of recognising wider family relationships. The discussion then turns to the public interest, and the argument here is in two parts. The first notes that, in positive obligation cases, the issue is not the public interest as understood in negative obligation cases, whose boundaries are determined by the state within the limits of Article 8(2), but the 'general interest', a potentially wider concept that can incorporate the benefits for society of keeping families together. The second part of this discussion looks at the specific general interest in immigration control. The argument is that states should explain the reasons for their policy choices so that an assessment of their actual, as against their presumed, benefits can take place. There follows an analysis of the doctrine of precarious residence, which has functioned to exclude almost all claims to family reunification. I propose adjustments to make it more reflective of the reality of binational family life. The chapter finally addresses the position of sponsors, whose interests have often been absent from the jurisprudence, and suggests ways to give them more explicit consideration. The chapter closes with two short case studies, which demonstrate how the changes proposed in this chapter would create a more even balance between the needs of immigration control and those of families.

II. WHY HUMAN RIGHTS?

The analysis in this book has suggested that judicially implemented human rights have limited capacity to effect concrete change, at least where family reunification is concerned. Gains have been modest and provisional, and one possible interpretation of the book is that it provides ammunition for human rights sceptics. While I recognise why that argument could be made, I am more optimistic. I see the claims of binational families as a struggle for justice and recognition that is never definitively won, and which cannot take place in a single domain. Judicial human rights do not replace other forms of contestation but have a distinct role to play in articulating, realising and embedding standards that have achieved some degree of wider social acceptance. It is more than merely preaching to the converted.[4]

Critiques of judicial human rights tend towards the same conclusion, that law is an inadequate tool. There are two principal objections. One, which I call the 'sceptical argument', says that human rights provide only individual answers to structural problems, diverting energy and attention from the need to effect wider social change. The other, which I call the 'democratic argument', objects to the involvement of judges in decisions that should be arrived at through political contestation and debate. As the next two subsections show, I accept that both arguments have a point, but they indicate the need for realism and caution, rather than abandonment of the project.

A. The Sceptical Argument

A substantial literature critiques the incoherence, indeterminacy and inefficacy of human rights as a concept: 'There is nothing at the core of the onion, no centre or kernel that gives human rights their overall shape.'[5] This has made them liable to co-option for a range of purposes, including by governments and international organisations. They become an elite project that supports a vast bureaucratic apparatus, that fails to prevent widespread abuse and that legitimises authoritarian acts and neocolonial interventions.[6] Some scholars see a link between the growth in human rights discourse and the rise of neoliberalism, arguing that human rights function to individualise and depoliticise claims caused by the structural injustices and inequalities that neoliberal policies have created, providing a relatively harmless outlet for pressures that might otherwise be destabilising.[7] There is not a clear causal relationship between the rise of human rights and the pursuit of neoliberal economic policies, but human rights have certainly failed to remedy the devastating inequalities associated with these policies, while their hegemonic grip on the 'political imagination' has made the creation of alternative understandings of emancipation and resistance more

[4] V Guiraudon, 'European Courts and Foreigners' Rights: A Comparative Study of Norms Diffusion' (2000) 34 *International Migration Review* 1107.

[5] C Douzinas, *Human Rights and Empire: The Political Philosophy of Cosmopolitanism* (Abingdon, Routledge-Cavendish, 2007) 14.

[6] D Kennedy, 'International Human Rights Movement: Part of the Problem?' (2002) 15 *Harvard Human Rights Journal* 101; S Hopgood, *The Endtimes of Human Rights* (Ithaca, NY, Cornell University Press, 2013); Douzinas, *Human Rights and Empire: The Political Philosophy of Cosmopolitanism*.

[7] eg S Marks, 'Four Human Rights Myths' in D Kinley, W Sadurski and K Walton (eds), *Human Rights: Old Problems, New Possibilities* (Cheltenham, Edward Elgar Publishing, 2013) 217–35.

difficult.[8] Meanwhile, human rights are, in practice, far from 'universal', with multiple exclusions, including often of non-citizens.[9]

These tensions are more pronounced when human rights become legal rights. Legal rights are predominantly 'first generation' rights relating to individual freedom, such as those in the European Convention on Human Rights (ECHR), rather than collective social rights. Legal remedies require personal resources and resilience, which are often unavailable to those who most need protection. The scope of protection is limited by the qualified character of rights, doctrines such as the margin of appreciation, and the transformation of broad aspirations into positivistic standards that can address only a limited range of concrete problems. The outcome is that a few individuals achieve a solution, but the underlying structural injustice remains intact; as Douzinas points out, 'liberal jurisprudence often appears as an ex post facto rationalisation of the workings of power'.[10] The current position of the Supreme Court described at the end of the previous chapter might seem to justify such scepticism. The right to respect for family life is mainly confined to some British citizen children and their parents, and it often depends on families making repeated expensive applications and appeals. While this assists a few individuals, the outcome is the legitimisation by the courts of highly restrictive rules that exclude significantly higher numbers than those they replaced.

The picture is, however, more complex. Firstly, while the government draws legitimacy from judicial endorsement, there is no obvious causal connection between the domestic human rights regime in 2000 and the introduction of a more restrictive family migration regime in 2012, which reflected changed political priorities more than an opportunistic attempt to use human rights as legal cover. On the contrary, it is possible that, without the constraints of the Human Rights Act, the government would have gone further. The Migration Advisory Committee's report could have justified a significantly higher minimum income requirement than the one that was adopted.[11] The language test was set at the lowest assessable level, and below that in other European states.[12]

Whether to rely on human rights is a pragmatic question of identifying the best way to establish concrete gains on a particular issue. Chapters four to six show that, at least so far as Article 8 and family reunification is concerned, they

[8] S Moyn, 'A Powerless Companion: Human Rights in the Age of Neoliberalism' (2014) 77 *Law & Contemporary Problems* 147.

[9] B Ibhawoh, 'Human Rights for Some: Universal Human Rights, Sexual Minorities, and the Exclusionary Impulse' (2014) 69 *International Journal* 612; A Gündogdu, *Rightlessness in an Age of Rights: Hannah Arendt and the Contemporary Struggles of Migrants* (Oxford, Oxford University Press, 2014).

[10] Douzinas, *Human Rights and Empire: The Political Philosophy of Cosmopolitanism*, 11.

[11] See ch 7, s III.

[12] See ch 7, s IV.

can make a difference to some extent and in the right context.[13] If that were not the case, the government would not have made such strenuous efforts to control their application by the courts. The problems with Article 8 lie not with its inherent incapacity, but with the environment in which it operates. Relying on the courts to protect human rights on their own without wider social and political consensus is always likely to disappoint; the protection of human rights is a broad enterprise, requiring interaction between a range of actors, a strategic approach, and varied forms of advocacy and activism.[14]

B. The Democratic Argument

Chapter two showed that the British constitution has one dominant characteristic: the principle of parliamentary sovereignty. The association of democracy with parliamentary supremacy has led to a strongly majoritarian conception of democracy and this has affected the perception of judicially determined human rights within the UK. There is deep resistance towards any perceived encroachment by judges on questions considered to be the preserve of the legislature.

Resistance to early proposals for a human rights statute often came from the political left, although criticism of the Human Rights Act has come mainly from the libertarian right.[15] The basic objections are remarkably similar, however. In 1979, Griffith said that 'law is not and cannot be a substitute for politics'.[16] In 2016, Lord Sumption said that 'politics is quite simply a better way of resolving questions of social policy than judge-made law'.[17] In both cases, the better way forward was said to be through strengthening the institutions and mechanisms of representative democracy, although the perceived danger was different in each case. For Griffith, the risk was that establishment-minded judges would undermine a programme of progressive social change. For Sumption, the objections concern democracy, personal autonomy and responsibility.[18]

[13] For a discussion of the impact of human rights litigation in the Dutch context, see S Van Walsum (2009) 'Against All Odds: How Single and Divorced Migrant Mothers Were Eventually Able to Claim Their Right to Respect for Family Life' (2009) 11 *European Journal of Migration and Law* 295.

[14] G De Burca, *Reframing Human Rights in a Turbulent Era* (Oxford, Oxford University Press, 2021); Moyn, 'A Powerless Companion: Human Rights in the Age of Neoliberalism', 160; Douzinas, *Human Rights and Empire: The Political Philosophy of Cosmopolitanism.*

[15] JAG Griffith, 'The Political Constitution' (1979) 42 *MLR* 1; J Sumption, 'The Limits of Law' in N Barber, R Ekins and P Yowell (eds), *Lord Sumption and the Limits of the Law* (Oxford, Hart Publishing, 2016) 15–26.

[16] Griffith, 'The Political Constitution'.

[17] Sumption, 'The Limits of Law, 24.

[18] Sumption's views have been criticised by many distinguished scholars, eg Barber et al, *Lord Sumption and the Limits of the Law*; M Loughlin, 'What Would John Griffith Have Made of Jonathan Sumption's Reith Lectures?' (2019) 90 *The Political Quarterly* 785; B Hale, 'Dame Frances Patterson Memorial Lecture 2019: Law and Politics – a Reply to Reith' (2019) 24 *Judicial Review* 205;

Despite its initial early resistance, the liberal left has largely converted to judicial involvement in human rights, due to expansion in centralised executive power, growth in international human rights and changed perceptions of the judiciary, leading a new understanding of what law might do.[19] There is a further key point. Critics such as the left-wing legal scholar JAG Griffith and his contemporaries hoped that political mobilisation would forge a majority for profound social change.[20] There is now less confidence in this possibility and greater awareness of the danger that the rights of minorities can be marginalised or overridden by majoritarian political systems, particularly in times of crisis or hardship. Modern democratic systems routinely include anti-majoritarian elements that limit this risk, including judicial involvement in rights protection, and this is generally considered part of a progressive constitution.[21] Resistance to judicial involvement in human rights is thus less about defending democracy and more about defending a particular version of it.

That does not make judicial involvement in human rights adjudication unproblematic. It puts the judiciary under a new spotlight and sometimes in an uncomfortable position. Governments may seek to distance themselves from difficult decisions by leaving judges to take the blame. Questions about the social, ethnic and gender composition of the judiciary and the appointments process rightly become more prominent. Judges may need support from independent structures that can examine a wider range of issues more intensively, perhaps collaborating with the courts in suitable cases.[22] Problems of access to courts, whether individually or via pressure groups, should be resolved. There is no silver bullet, however. In a liberal state, an independent judiciary is the final arbiter of what is lawful, including under the Human Rights Act or any successor statute. Questions of legality include questions about the lawfulness of policy, which only the judiciary can answer; the issue is how best to equip judges to make decisions that adequately reflect the balance of interests. At a time when both human rights and the judiciary have been under prolonged

R Spano, 'The Democratic Virtues of Human Rights Law – A Response to Lord Sumption's Reith Lectures', Inaugural Bonavero Institute Annual Human Rights Lecture (The Old Hall, Lincoln's Inn, London, 20 February 2020).

[19] See KD Ewing, 'The Human Rights Act and Parliamentary Democracy' (1999) 62 *MLR* 79; C Bickerton, 'The Left's Journey from Politics to Law' in R Ekins and G Gee (ed), *Judicial Power and the Left* (London, Policy Exchange, 2017) 56–61; Loughlin, 'What Would John Griffith Have Made of Jonathan Sumption's Reith Lectures?', 785–93.

[20] Loughlin, 'What Would John Griffith Have Made of Jonathan Sumption's Reith Lectures?', 785–93.

[21] SE Lemieux and DJ Watkins, 'Beyond the "Countermajoritarian Difficulty": Lessons from Contemporary Democratic Theory' (2009) 41 *Polity* 30; CF Zurn, *Deliberative Democracy and the Institutions of Judicial Review* (Cambridge, Cambridge University Press, 2007).

[22] The Equality and Human Rights Commission has had a troubled history, with regular changes in strategic direction, and is seriously underfunded in terms of such a task; D Barrett, 'The Regulatory Space of Equality and Human Rights in Britain: The Role of the Equality and Human Rights Commission' (2019) 39 *Legal Studies* 247.

attack for resisting executive illegality, it is this question, rather than a binary opposition between rights and democracy, that needs to be addressed.[23]

The issue, however, is not what lawyers and scholars think about human rights, but how to win wider acceptance for what they think within government and wider civil society. Making this case, particularly when it involves immigration, cannot be undertaken only by lawyers. Both the sceptical and the democratic critiques therefore revolve around the same point: human rights, particularly the civil and political rights represented by the ECHR and the Human Rights Act, cannot be the main means of achieving a just society. That does not mean that they are irrelevant. Within a context of wider campaigning and advocacy, success in a human rights claim can serve to concretise and embed protection. Admittedly, this is an uneven process, but strategic litigation, provided it is carefully conceived, can help to remedy wider injustice:

> European human rights case law does matter … under particular preconditions: repeat litigation and legal mobilisation by interested civil society and minority actors, support by political and other influential elites, as well as advocacy by human rights organisations capable of exerting pressure and linking Court rulings to policy issues and reforms.[24]

This cautious but positive perspective has informed the approach taken in this chapter. It particularly influenced the decision to continue to treat family reunification as a question of positive obligations, discussed briefly in the next section.

III. STICK OR TWIST? THE CASE FOR TREATING FAMILY REUNIFICATION AS A POSITIVE OBLIGATION

Chapter one showed that family reunification may be seen as engaging negative or positive obligations. The Strasbourg Court usually treats it as involving a positive obligation and therefore adopts a 'fair balance' proportionality assessment. In so doing, it signifies its acceptance that the human right to family life does not take priority over state sovereignty in immigration, the 'Strasbourg reversal'.

For several reasons, I decided not to argue here for family reunification to be treated as a negative obligation. That means accepting the logic of state sovereignty over immigration as a political and legal fact despite its contestation by scholars and persuasive arguments for open, or more open, borders.[25]

[23] *R (on the application of Miller and Dos Santos) v Secretary of State* [2017] UKSC 5; *R (on the application of Miller) v The Prime Minister* [2019] UKSC 41.

[24] D Anagnostou, 'Does European Human Rights Law Matter? Implementation and Domestic Impact of Strasbourg Court Judgments on Minority-Related Policies' (2010) 15 *International Journal of Human Rights* 721, 738.

[25] See ch 3, s IV. Several authors have criticised the presumed necessity of borders, eg T Hayter, *Open Borders: The Case against Immigration Controls* (London, Pluto Press, 2004); R Jones (ed),

To argue otherwise, however, would be to argue for the reversal of decades of the Strasbourg jurisprudence, would alienate state parties and would discard the evolutionary development of the jurisprudence. It is also not clear that it would have the desired effect. Although the Strasbourg Court has usually treated family reunification as a positive obligation, the problem has not been that designation but the lack of a sufficiently rigorous proportionality assessment, and that is not confined to positive obligation cases. Where family reunification has been treated as a negative obligation, scrutiny of the public interest has also been perfunctory.[26] Treating Article 8 as a negative obligation does not therefore guarantee that the right to family life is given more weight, and arguing for it is not worth the additional obstacles to acceptance. At a pragmatic level, it is more productive to argue not that immigration control is too important, but that family life is also important.

My proposal is that family life should carry the same weight as immigration control, and this is compatible with a positive obligation fair balance assessment. Indeed, it is impossible to see how the assessment of a positive obligation can start from the position that one general interest factor is a priori more important than the right itself, so this is the minimum legally coherent interpretation. At the end of the assessment, either family life or immigration control will prevail, but a positive obligation proportionality assessment allows that decision to be made on a close evaluation of relevant factors in the individual case.

IV. FAMILY LIFE BEYOND THE 'CORE' FAMILY

This book has shown a disjuncture between the reality of family life and its meaning in the Strasbourg cases. Chapter one showed family to be a dynamic web of relationships that extends beyond the immediate household and whose needs fluctuate through the life cycle. Chapter three, however, explained that the Strasbourg Court usually confines family life, at least in family reunification cases, to married couples, or minor children and their parents ('core' family relationships), for whom admission may be needed as 'the most adequate means … to develop family life'.[27] For family life to exist with other family members, or for there to be interference in that family life, there must be 'further elements of dependency, involving more than the normal emotional ties'.[28] The result is that

Open Borders: In Defense of Free Movement (Atlanta, University of Georgia Press, 2019); L de Noronha and GM Bradley, *Against Borders: The Case for Abolition* (London, Verso Books, 2022); for a legal argument, see B Schotel, *On the Right of Exclusion: Law, Ethics and Immigration Policy* (Abingdon, Routledge, 2013).

[26] *Omoregie and Others v Norway* [2008] ECHR 761; *Berrehab v The Netherlands* [1988] ECHR 14.

[27] *Sen v Netherlands* (2003) 36 EHRR 7.

[28] *Uner v Netherlands* App no 46410/99 (18 October 2006) [44].

most relationships between adults are excluded from the scope of Article 8.[29] This approach may have its roots in historical uncertainty as to whether a proportionality assessment is possible in positive obligation cases. If not, engagement of Article 8(1) would lead straight to a violation finding. Now that it is well established that positive obligations do involve a proportionality assessment, there is no reason to be cautious in extending the meaning of family life, but the advantages of a continuing narrow approach for states are obvious; excluding relationships from the scope of Article 8(1) means the claim fails without ever moving to a proportionality assessment under Article 8(2), where governments must defend their policies.

The result of the Court's approach is that an artificial and static concept of family life prevails as soon as analysis moves beyond the core family. The changes in relationships, residence and care arrangements for adult relatives that are a normal part of family life and the significance of wider family support are not recognised. Dependency is difficult to establish as it is interpreted predominantly as financial dependency (which can continue without family reunification), and physical care by paid carers is seen as an adequate substitute for family care. The requirement for 'more than normal family ties' means that common family relationships cannot qualify even if circumstances change. On the rare occasions family life is found to exist, there is usually no interference as it can continue as before and there is no obligation to allow it to develop. It is, however, artificial to see the desire to provide support to an ageing parent, a troubled adult child or a traumatised sibling as 'developing' family life.[30] What is family life if not the underlying obligations of care, interdependence and support performed in different ways over the lifecycle between different individuals? Chapter one showed family to be a dynamic and fluctuating web of relationships that extends beyond the immediate household. The ties and responsibilities are always present even if they have not yet crystallised in a form that requires the parties to live together.

Rejecting the claims of adult relatives places a heavy burden on the (often female) citizens of migrant descent who must undertake caring responsibilities across international borders.[31] It also means that the migration history defines the character of family life forever. The relationship that exists between a daughter in her 20s who leaves behind a fit, active mother in her middle years becomes the only family life that can legally exist between the pair, even if the daughter is herself now a naturalised citizen of the new state and the mother is widowed, ill and vulnerable. An aunt whose nephews and nieces have been orphaned is equally unable to show that family life now requires her to care for them. This approach treats the recognition that family life exists as contingent on the choice

[29] For a more extended discussion, see ch 3, s IIIC.

[30] For a discussion, see C Draghici, 'Adult Children and Elderly Parents in Strasbourg Proceedings: A Misconstrued Approach to "Family Life"' (2018) 32 *International Journal of Law, Policy and the Family* 42.

[31] See H Askola, '(No) Migrating for Family Care in Later Life: *Senchishak v Finland*, Older Parents and Family Reunification' (2016) 18 *European Journal of Migration and Law* 351.

to emigrate for which the consequences must be accepted. It reflects the individualised character of the civil and political rights of which Article 8 forms part, and it discriminates against sponsors of migrant origin who are the most likely to have dependent relatives living abroad. As Judge Spielmann observed in the first instance decision in *Shevanova*:

> Giving precedence to the criterion of dependency to the detriment of that of normal affective ties strikes me as a very artificial approach to determining the existence of 'family life'. It seems inconceivable to me that so little importance can be attached to the affective ties between a mother and her son that they can fall outside the scope of 'family life'.[32]

A more nuanced and realistic way to assess family life outside the core family is therefore needed. My suggestion is that incorporating at least some elements of an ethics of care into the meaning of family life under Article 8(1) would better reflect the reality of family life. This is not because family life only involves 'care' in the traditional sense of looking after the vulnerable, but because an 'ethics of care' better encapsulates what makes family life so important, offering a richer account than dependency and focusing on the overall character of family life. States may respond that this would open the door to a vastly increased number of claims, but if this is the case, then it is an Article 8(2) argument. The claim would still be subject to a proportionality assessment, which would require states to explain the reasons for refusal, rather than the claim being pre-emptively excluded.

The starting point for care theory is that we are relational and have a deep interconnectedness with our family.[33] Family members are those with whom we have the strongest and thickest ties, but they are not limited to those with whom we have a close blood or legal relationship. Caring is also not confined to situations of special vulnerability requiring an unusual level of dependency, but refers to the relationships that are necessary for human well-being and flourishing: 'In the human realm, it refers to an activity of support that seeks to maintain, continue, or restore one's capacity to be, speak or act.'[34]

An ethics of care brings to light the gendered and racialised dimensions of a conception of family life that ignores both the invisible labour that care requires and assumptions about who needs or deserves care.[35] It also embraces partiality, in the sense that we are not, in the immediate sense, responsible for all human

[32] *Shevanova v Latvia* App no 58822/00 (GC, 15 June 2006), Partially Concurring Opinion of Judge Spielmann [4].

[33] For a discussion, see V Held, *The Ethics of Care as Moral Theory* (Oxford, Oxford University Press, 2005); D Engster and M Hamington, 'Introduction' in D Engster and M Hamington (eds), *Care Ethics and Political Theory* (Oxford, Oxford University Press, 2015) 1–16.

[34] F Brugère, *Care Ethics: The Introduction of Care as Political Category* (Leuven, Peeters Publishers, 2019) 68.

[35] F Brugère, 'Caring Democracy as a Solution against Neoliberalism and Populism' in P Urban and L Ward (eds), *Care Ethics, Democratic Citizenship and the State* (London, Palgrave Macmillan, 2016) 137–59.

beings equally, and particularism, in that we have a relationship with specific individuals. It thus enables relationships to be assessed on their merits, but in a less rigid way than under the criteria currently used by the Court. An ethics of care can be usefully applied in a legal context, and was reflected in the passage in *Huang*, discussed in chapter four, that spoke of the 'core value' that Article 8 exists to protect:

> Human beings are social animals. They depend on others. Their family, or extended family, is the group on which many people most heavily depend, socially, emotionally and often financially. There comes a point at which, for some, prolonged and unavoidable separation from this group seriously inhibits their ability to live full and fulfilling lives.[36]

If an ethics of care were applied to the wider family relationships that are currently almost always excluded, finding whether family life exists and has been respected under Article 8(1) would be assessed by the strength of the connection between the individuals concerned and their need to be together, without requiring dependency in any particular form or 'more than normal emotional ties'. It would be context and time contingent; the aunt with orphaned nephews and nieces may always have had a strong connection to them but only needs to care for them when they are orphaned. The same applies to a son whose elderly parent has been widowed or a mother whose adult child develops a serious illness. Care theory therefore can help to articulate a version of family life that more closely corresponds to how family life evolves through time. It avoids an artificial distinction between family life that can be 'developed' under Article 8 and family life that cannot, and ensures that the threshold for Article 8(1) interference is not artificially raised by adopting a static, unchanging view of family life. This would not, on its own, mean that Article 8 applications succeed, but it would mean that more applications meet the Article 8(1) threshold and therefore can be considered under Article 8(2), where the claim will be set against the public interest. Assuming this assessment is sufficiently rigorous, a point pursued in the next two sections of this chapter, it would inhibit government complacency and narrow policies that exclude certain family relationships from consideration.

V. THE PUBLIC INTEREST 1: THE 'GENERAL INTEREST' AND FAMILY LIFE

The impact of treating family reunification as a positive obligation is most visible when discussing proportionality. In a negative obligation claim, the government commits or proposes to commit an act which interferes with an ECHR right and

[36] *Huang v SSHD* [2007] UKHL 11 [18]; R Manning, 'Care, Normativity, and the Law' in Engster and Hamington, *Care Ethics and Political Theory*, 127–45.

the applicant argues that the government should refrain. In qualified rights such as Article 8, the government identifies the public interest served by the policy, which must correspond to one of the legitimate aims set out in the text of the Convention right. The public interest is thus confined to these specific matters and the government decides which apply in this instance. The question is therefore whether the personal interests of the applicant outweigh the public interest raised by the government.

In a positive obligation case, the government is accused of failing to act and the proportionality assessment cannot be carried out as prescribed in Article 8(2).[37] The Strasbourg Court therefore asks whether a fair balance has been struck 'between the competing interests of the individual and of the community as a whole'.[38] This is a more generalised and subjective assessment, to which the Article 8(2) legitimate aims have only a 'certain relevance'; instead, the question is whether failure to act is sufficiently in the 'general interest' to justify interfering with the right.[39] The meaning of the 'general interest' is unclear, and the assessment and burden of proof are less structured than in a negative obligation case.[40]

In almost all family reunification cases, the only 'general interests' considered are immigration control and the best interests of children; other concerns do not feature.[41] However, there is no reason why the 'general interest' cannot be more widely assessed and include 'the multidimensional consequences and the multitude of interests that might be affected'.[42] There is a 'general interest', for example, in enabling families to enjoy a stable life together or in citizen children growing up fully integrated in their country of nationality even if the family unit would not be destroyed by expulsion. Sponsors are part of the community, and their welfare is also a public good. Family separation can increase their unhappiness and marginalisation as their lives are forcibly divided and disrupted. It is in the general interest that they do not have to sell homes, work excessive hours to meet minimum income requirements or divide their lives between different countries. Family reunification policies are felt more by some social and ethnic groups, and reducing the impact on them would increase social cohesion. Importing these considerations would not just be another way of asserting the original family life right in question, but would recognise that family-oriented

[37] See ch 1, s IVC.

[38] *Jeunesse* (n 2) [106].

[39] *Rees v United Kingdom* [1986] ECHR 11 [37]. The Court sometimes also uses the term 'fair balance' as the final stage in a negative obligation Art 8(2) assessment.

[40] D Xenos, *The Positive Obligations of the State under the European Convention of Human Rights* (Abingdon, Routledge, 2012) 61–71.

[41] But see the words in *MA v Denmark* App no 6697/18 (9 July 2021) [165], cited later in this section.

[42] V Stoyanava, 'The Disjunctive Structure of Positive Rights' (2018) *Nordic Journal of International Law* 344, 376.

policies promote the wider good. As the Grand Chamber acknowledged in *MA v Denmark*, 'family reunification may … favour preserving social cohesion and facilitate integration'.[43]

VI. THE PUBLIC INTEREST 2: IMMIGRATION CONTROL

The previous section argued that the 'general interest' in a fair balance assessment can be broader than the public interest in immigration control. However, immigration control considerations are included in the list of relevant factors developed by the Strasbourg Court and are likely always to be a key component in the assessment.[44] Chapter three demonstrated that these considerations are not treated as a factor of variable or contestable weight but as an objective and unchangeable necessity. The aims and effectiveness of the policy and the degree to which it responds to an established need are not considered. The outcome is that the case for that policy, as against one that is less restrictive, does not have to be made and the fair balance test favours the state by reducing opportunities for judicial scrutiny.

This is not a necessity but a choice. Chapter one explained that, while the Strasbourg Court is often more accommodating to states in positive obligation cases, the usual reasons for caution in positive cases do not apply in family reunification. There is also no reason why governments should not explain why they chose these restrictions; immigration controls are rarely an end in themselves but are designed to achieve other aims, such as labour market stability or social cohesion, and courts can assess the policy's coherence and weight according to those aims. To do so would increase openness and accountability and discourage policies that are superficially plausible but poorly conceived or politically eye catching. It is also a realisable expectation; immigration policies do not usually involve sensitive information relating to state security and the request is not for 'a quantitative or precise assessment of the extent of the likely benefits' but for an explanation of how the government decided that the policy is necessary despite its impact on families.[45] Some policies will be easy to defend; a requirement, for example, that the couple must have an income that is equivalent to the minimum wage would be uncontroversial, but one that needed more or required that the income must come only from certain sources would need more explanation.

The benefits of such an approach are apparent from those instances where judges have adopted a more interrogative approach. For example, in *Quila*,

[43] *MA v Denmark* (n 41) [165]; see also T Strik, B de Hart and E Nissen, *Family Reunification: A Barrier or Facilitator of Integration? A Comparative Study* (Oisterwijk, Wolf Publishers, 2013).

[44] *Jeunesse* (n 2) [107].

[45] *Ali and Bibi v SSHD* [2015] UKSC 68 [97].

the government was unable to show any benefit arising from the minimum age requirement. Lady Hale in *Ali and Bibi* found that implementing a pre-entry language test was lawful but that the government could show only a very limited benefit to the public. The House of Lords in *Chikwamba* found that the aim of a policy prohibiting in-country applications was to deter unlawful entry so was not relevant to those entering in good faith to make an asylum claim. The Strasbourg Court has been more reticent, and chapter three showed that it has been more stringent with states only in unusual cases, but the discussion of *Biao* in chapter three showed the potential.[46]

With the possible exception of *Quila*, none of the instances cited in this discussion prevented the government from having an immigration policy on the issue in question, but the policy had to be adjusted to avoid being too broad. Judges did not decide policy but required governments to explain why the policy was more important than family life. Political constitutionalists would argue that such scrutiny is the job of the legislature, but, without robust judicial supervision, it can be difficult for minority voices to be heard in that forum. As Judge Martens observed,

> the European Court of Human Rights has to ensure, in particular, that State interests do not crush those of an individual, especially in situations where political pressure – such as the growing dislike of immigrants in most member States – may inspire State authorities to harsh decisions.[47]

Immigration laws reinforce existing ethnic, gender and other inequalities, and it may be argued that discrimination claims under Article 14 provide a sufficient remedy for unfair policies. However, Article 14 is of limited efficacy in this context. States can respond to Article 14 violations not by enhancing protection for the disadvantaged group, but by levelling down rights; there is no longer any discrimination, but there is also no protection for family life. That happened after the sex discrimination finding in *Abdulaziz* and, following *Biao*, the Danish government replaced the combined attachment requirement with other, more restrictive criteria.[48] Governments, if they are careful, can often achieve their aims by crafting policies that do not fail under Article 14. One reason is that, so far, Article 14 has been applied only where discrimination is direct or, if indirect,

[46] See ch 3, s IV.

[47] *Gül v Switzerland* (1996) 22 EHRR 93, Dissenting Opinion of Judge Martens [15].

[48] On implementation of the judgment in *Abdulaziz v UK* (1985) 7 EHRR 471, see H Wray, *Regulating Marriage Migration into the UK: A Stranger in the Home* (first published Farnham, Ashgate, 2011, Abingdon, Routledge, 2016) 65–67; on *Biao v Denmark*, see New to Denmark, 'New Rules for Family Reunification for Spouses' (8 June 2018); see also K De Vries, 'Rewriting *Abdulaziz*: The ECtHR Grand Chamber's Ruling in *Biao v. Denmark*' (2016) 18 *European Journal of Migration and Law* 467. See further the Dissenting Opinion of Judge Yudkivska in *Biao v Denmark* and the UK Supreme Court's dismissal of the discriminatory effects of an exemption to language testing in *Ali and Bibi* (n 45) [56]–[59].

has a clear and immediate discriminatory impact.[49] However, the causes of inequality in family migration controls are often more remote: the increased impact, for example, on marginal groups of universal criteria such as income requirements or language tests, and the greater involvement of ethnic minorities in family reunification. This impact may be too indirect for an Article 14 claim (although perhaps it should not be), but it is a good reason for the Article 8 assessment to be relatively exacting in this context.

In brief, there are valid arguments for subjecting government claims to more active scrutiny under Article 8 than has occurred so far. Practicalities, however, still need to be resolved. As the House of Lords pointed out in *Huang*, certainty is necessary to ensure that the immigration system is 'workable, predictable, consistent and fair as between one applicant and another'.[50] Not all courts can therefore be expected to undertake this role. It would be difficult, for example, to expect first instance tribunals, who decide thousands of claims and where consistency is critical, to assess the strength of the government's claims on each occasion. Meanwhile, the Strasbourg Court sees itself as having primarily a supervisory function, ensuring that domestic courts have properly addressed relevant considerations. Such supervision, however, can extend to ensuring that the domestic courts undertake, at some stage during domestic appellate proceedings, a sufficiently rigorous assessment of government justification. This would be consistent with its supervisory function, would avoid the problem of a double margin of appreciation, applied first at the domestic and then at the supranational level, and would lead to a more effective and dynamic supervisory regime.[51]

There is a risk that such scrutiny would be ineffective if governments engage in 'artificial or bogus cost–benefit … analyses'.[52] Chapter seven observed that, in *MM (Lebanon)*, the applicants argued that the apparently sophisticated government case for the UK's minimum income requirement was based on faulty logic and selective analysis.[53] Applicants' lawyers must be vigilant in challenging exaggeration or manipulation, and courts must be ready to consider their arguments. The problem in *MM (Lebanon)* was not that evidence was unavailable, but that the Supreme Court chose to disregard it. That this was a choice is clear

[49] Examples of direct discrimination include *Abdulaziz* (n 48); *Pajic v Croatia* App no 68453 (23 February 2016); *Hode and Abdi v United Kingdom* App no 22341/09 (6 November 2012); examples of indirect discrimination include *Tadeucci and McCall v Italy* App no 51362/09 (20 May 2004); *Biao* (n 3). For a discussion, see Council of Europe, *Guide on Article 14 of the European Convention on Human Rights and on Article 1 of Protocol 1 to the Convention* (updated 31 August 2021) 73–74.

[50] *Huang* (n 36) [16].

[51] See the words of Jean-Paul Costa, former President of the ECtHR, cited in M Andenas and E Bjorge, 'National Implementation of ECHR Rights' in A Føllesdal, B Peters and G Ulfstein (eds), *Constituting Europe: The European Court of Human Rights in a National, European, and Global Context* (Cambridge, Cambridge University Press, 2013) 186–262, 186–87.

[52] *Ali and Bibi* (n 45) [97].

[53] See ch 7, s IVA.

from Lord Neuberger's earlier words in *Ali and Bibi* about similar evidence that analysed the government's case for a pre-entry language test: 'any court should be very slow indeed before relying on such evidence as the sole or main justification for invalidating government policy'.[54] In other words, there was a presumption in favour of the government's view independent of its quality, a form of institutional or even formalist deference.

Failure by national courts to consider these points could form part of the arguments made to the Strasbourg Court as to the sufficiency of examination by the national authorities. The Strasbourg Court could then find a violation or carry out its own enquiry. This would not necessarily mean an all-or-nothing finding. In *Ali and Bibi*, for example, Lady Hale accepted that the language test criterion was lawful and 'benign', but found that its benefits were minor and obstacles to passing were considerable. This had a bearing on when its application was proportionate:

> Given the comparatively modest benefits of the pre-entry requirement, when set against the very substantial practical problems which some will face in meeting it, the only conclusion is that there are likely to be a significant number of cases in which the present practice does not strike a fair balance as required by article 8.[55]

The ability of such a critical approach to make better informed and more nuanced decisions becomes clear if one returns for the final time to the questions that were outlined in the introductory chapter and have been referred to several times since then. As chapter one explained, the court's understanding of the public interest could be relevant to all of the following questions:

1. What public (or general) interest does the measure serve?
2. How effective is it?
3. Is it necessary in this case?
4. Is its application disproportionate?

A negative answer to either question 1 or 2 is possible. More likely is that they will be answered positively but in a qualified way, and this will inform the answers to questions 3 and 4. For example, if a minimum income policy aims to prevent welfare dependency under questions 1 and 2, the parties' access to other resources would be material to question 3. Such an approach would engage actively with state concerns and offer a pragmatic resolution of the tension between respect for the democratic process and the claims of family life. It would also represent a significant shift from the dominant position at Strasbourg, where only question 4 is addressed, and even then is subject to a condition of exceptionality, discussed in the next section.[56]

[54] *MM (Lebanon) v SSHD* [2017] UKSC 10 [94].
[55] *Ali and Bibi* (n 45) [54]; see also [41]–[45].
[56] See ch 3, s VB.

VII. PRECARIOUS RESIDENCE AND EXCEPTIONALITY

The overwhelming weight currently awarded to the public interest in immigration control results in the precariousness doctrine, which, in turn, leads to the exceptionality condition. If immigration policy is not contestable, a claim cannot be based on the unfairness of the policy. It follows that family life created when residence rights are 'precarious' is at the risk of the individuals involved, and admission will be required only in 'exceptional' circumstances.

The precariousness doctrine originated in resistance to irregular migrants who presented states with a 'fait accompli' in terms of their family life, but it has been extended so that it treats all failures to meet immigration laws in the same way, effectively making those laws immune to human rights scrutiny.[57] There is a presumed equivalence between, for example, a person who has repeatedly deceived the authorities and starts a relationship after a deportation order and a couple who have married after meeting outside the state but find that harsh entry requirements do not allow them to live together. Precariousness therefore renders binational families indefinitely subject to state-generated laws, however harsh, and raises the question of the function of Article 8 if it accepts the legitimacy of all state measures.

Many might sympathise with applicants unable to challenge entry criteria, but not with irregular migrants. Yet, the distinction should not be overstated. Irregularity is not an absolute condition, but a category in and out of which many migrants fall due to the complexity and expense of immigration processes.[58] It is also a structural feature of an unequal world where there are few opportunities for legal migration, particularly from poor and unstable regions. The culpability attaching to and the consequences of the infringement of immigration laws need to be addressed in context and alongside other factors such as the reasons for entry and the state's toleration of presence.

As chapter three observed, the Strasbourg Court has recently adopted a more nuanced position in this regard, notably in *Rodrigues da Silva and Hoogkamer*, *Nunez* and *Jeunesse*, but it is not clear whether this represents an evolving principle or is a response to the increased emphasis on children's rights. There are strong arguments for a more flexible approach. Human connection is a universal need that cannot conveniently be suspended for lengthy periods while status is resolved. It is ironic in this context that academic literature has shown that a couple's credibility in the immigration system depends on showing that their relationship is 'pure', ie it is untainted by instrumental considerations.[59]

[57] *Omoregie* (n 26) [64]; *Roslina Chandra and Others v the Netherlands* App no 53102/99 (13 May 2003).

[58] A Kubal, 'Conceptualizing Semi-legality in Migration Research' (2013) 47 *Law and Society Review* 555.

[59] H Wray, 'The "Pure" Relationship, Sham Marriages and Immigration Control' in J Miles, R Probert and P Mody (eds), *Marriage Rites and Rights* (Oxford, Hart Publishing, 2015) 141–65; A Andrikopoulos, 'Love, Money and Papers in the Affective Circuits of Cross-Border Marriages: Beyond the "Sham"/"Genuine" Dichotomy' (2021) 47 *Journal of Ethnic and Migration Studies* 343;

However, the precariousness doctrine expects a couple to anticipate the likely problems and not allow their relationship to develop if they know they may be separated by immigration controls. Intimate relationships should therefore apparently be governed by instrumental factors, but only those that benefit the state. In this way, the Court reflects the fear that underpins much family migration policy: that family and state are in competition for an individual's loyalties, and the state may lose.[60]

In summary, the precariousness doctrine leans excessively towards the state, and draws on idealised and unrealistic expectations of human behaviour. A better position would be to build on the approach in *Nunez* and *Jeunesse* and treat the absence of immigration status as a variable factor, not the dominant one. A court might therefore give weight to a history of deception but should not exclude a couple just because they cannot meet onerous conditions. There should also be a degree of realism and humanity in recognising that human beings will always form significant relationships. When immigration enforcement has not taken place over many years, the prospect of separation will recede and attachments will deepen. This is, as Lord Bingham observed in *EB (Kosovo)*, how 'minds work'.[61]

If precariousness becomes one variable factor, then the test for success is no longer that only 'exceptional' cases can succeed. Instead, a fair balance assessment would ask whether, in all the circumstances, it is reasonable either for family life to be enjoyed elsewhere or for the family to be separated. That is the test adopted by the House of Lords in *EB (Kosovo)* and which was implicitly abandoned in *MM (Lebanon)* and *Agyarko*. While it may currently be unpopular with governments, it would provide a more equal balance between the interests of immigration control and the personal and community interests in protecting family life. It would make the precariousness test more flexible, giving more discretion to judges but also enabling realistic and humane assessments that, over time, would set new guidelines, ensuring a reasonable degree of consistency and predictability.

VIII. SPONSORS AND CITIZENSHIP

States generally recognise an obligation to permit family reunification.[62] However, governments also heavily regulate who may be admitted, with

AM D'Aoust, 'A Moral Economy of Suspicion: Love and Marriage Migration Management Practices in the United Kingdom' (2018) 36 *Environment and Planning D: Society and Space* 40.

[60] A Macklin, 'Epilogue – Love Triangle: Nation, Spouse, Citizen' in AM D'Aoust (ed), *Transnational Marriage and Partner Migration: Constellations of Security, Citizenship, and Rights* (New Brunswick, Rutgers University Press, 2022) 259–73.

[61] *EB (Kosovo) v SSHD* [2008] UKHL 41 [15].

[62] JH Carens, 'Who Should Get In? The Ethics of Immigration Admissions' (2003) 17 *Ethics & International Affairs* 95.

racialised, gendered and increasingly classed dimensions.[63] Meanwhile, citizenship is a dynamic, multidimensional concept that is imagined in many ways across multiple domains so that individuals and the government may understand the term in different ways.[64] The result is a frequent disconnect between what citizens expect from their government and government assertions of power over the admission of their family members, leading to anger and a deep sense of personal betrayal. In the words of one outraged sponsor:

> It's just so wrong on every level. To say that you can have your family somewhere else, I mean that's just ridiculous. Why should I have to go and live somewhere else? I'm entitled to live here, why should I have to go and move my family half way round the world in order to have a family together?[65]

Yet a proper assessment of the sponsor's situation barely features in most proportionality assessments. The Strasbourg Court invariably observes that states are not under an obligation to permit binational families to live together on the territory and it does not treat states' immigration policies as contestable under Article 8. The emphasis is therefore on the migrant's situation, family life is treated as an abstract entity that can exist anywhere and the implicit expectation is that sponsors should be ready to leave their home to enjoy family life.[66] In practice, it can be difficult for sponsors to show why their interests should prevail. If they are mentioned at all, it is generally to show that family life can continue either elsewhere or through other means, such as visits or electronic communication.[67]

Citizenship rights have not been totally disregarded in Article 8 claims. As observed in chapter three, children's nationality has been treated as a pertinent factor.[68] This point was explored by the Supreme Court in *ZH (Tanzania)*, and it is worth recalling what was said of the children in that case:

> [T]hey have an unqualified right of abode here; they have lived here all their lives; they are being educated here; they have other social links with the community here; they have a good relationship with their father here … Nor should the intrinsic importance of citizenship be played down. As citizens these children have rights which they will not be able to exercise if they move to another country. They will lose the advantages of growing up and being educated in their own country, their own culture and their own language.[69]

[63] B De Hart, 'Love Thy Neighbour: Family Reunification and the Rights of Insiders' (2009) 11 *European Journal of Migration and Law* 235; S Bonjour and L Block, 'Ethnicizing Citizenship, Questioning Membership: Explaining the Decreasing Family Migration Rights of Citizens in Europe' (2011) 20 *Citizenship Studies* 778.

[64] R Lister, 'Inclusive Citizenship: Realizing the Potential' (2007) 11 *Citizenship Studies* 49.

[65] M Griffiths, '"My Passport Is Just My Way Out of Here": Mixed-Immigration Status Families, Immigration Enforcement and the Citizenship Implications' (2021) 28 *Identities* 18, 25.

[66] For a close analysis of the racialised and gendered aspects of the Court's position, see De Hart, 'Love Thy Neighbour' 235–31.

[67] See ch 3, s VA.

[68] *Jeunesse* (n 2) [115]–[119]; *TuquaboTekle and Others v The Netherlands* App no 60665/00 (1 December 2005), [2005] ECHR 803 [47]; *Sen* (n 27) [40].

[69] *ZH (Tanzania) v Secretary of State for the Home Department* [2011] UKSC 4 [31]–[32].

Lady Hale's words acknowledge that, in the context of Article 8 and children, citizenship is not just a bare right of residence but involves cultural, social and emotional ties, although the purpose in that context was to emphasise the specific injustice to children, who cannot choose where to live. However, similar considerations arise in Article 8 private life claims by adults, where social, not legal, citizenship is in issue. In *Slivenko*, the Grand Chamber said of the applicants who had been expelled from Latvia as a family: 'They were thus removed from the country where they had developed, uninterruptedly since birth, the network of personal, social and economic relations that make up the private life of every human being.'[70]

While the Article 8 deportation cases have not been encouraging in recent years, a relevant factor in decisions remains the deportee's 'solidity of social, cultural and family ties with the host country and with the country of destination'.[71] In brief, therefore, courts have sometimes acknowledged that ties to a state merit legal recognition.

However, this largely disappears when it comes to family reunification, unless children are present. In effect, sponsors must accept the consequences of their choice, whether that was to form a relationship with a non-national or to migrate, leaving family members behind. The sponsor's interests are not specifically mentioned in the Strasbourg Court's list of relevant factors in family reunification, although they are implicitly included in references to 'the extent of the ties in the Contracting State' and 'insurmountable obstacles' in the country of origin.[72] Chapter three shows that the former is usually considered perfunctorily while the latter is a minimal standard that is rarely, if ever, determinative, and which focuses on problems with the destination country, not on what the sponsor must give up. There have been some attempts in the domestic courts to recognise sponsors' concerns. The UK Supreme Court, in its first and second phase decisions (chapters five and six), showed awareness of and sympathy for their predicament without articulating a concrete principle. Lower courts have occasionally asserted that citizenship means more than a bare right to enter and remain. The Court of Appeal, when it heard *Quila*, distinguished the position of the applicants in *Abdulaziz* from those in *Quila*. In *Abdulaziz*, the Strasbourg Court noted that the applicants were 'settled' migrants who contracted marriages after coming to the UK and could therefore live elsewhere. This was not the case for the British citizens in *Quila*, who had a constitutional right to live in the UK and to marry: 'For the state to make exile for one of the spouses the price of exercising the right to marry and embark on family life requires powerful justification – considerably more powerful … than existed in *Abdulaziz*.'[73]

[70] *Slivenko v Latvia* App no 48321/99 (9 October 2003) [96].
[71] *Maslov v Austria* App no 1638/03 (23 June 2008) [71].
[72] *Jeunesse* (n 2) [107].
[73] *Quila v SSHD* [2010] EWCA Civ 1482 [48] (Sedley LJ).

This passage was not approved by the Supreme Court when it heard *Quila*. It did not need it to find a violation and, correctly in my view, emphasised the *Abdulaziz* sponsors' close connections to the UK.[74] The Supreme Court later endorsed the government's view that legal citizenship confers no obligation on the British state to permit family reunification with citizens, who only have a personal right to enter and live in the UK 'without let or hindrance'.[75] Yet, despite the problems with it, the passage by the Court of Appeal in *Quila* points the way to the appropriate question on sponsors' interests: when should involuntary exile be considered the price of family life?

In binational families, one family member will always live outside their country of nationality, but the decision as to which is a personal one that will be dictated by many considerations: family, work, health, cultural, political, religious and social factors. The state should only interfere in the decision when there are strong reasons to do so. However, the absence of detailed consideration of sponsors' interests in the fair balance assessment renders their concerns invisible. If these interests were treated as a separate component in the assessment, the assessment would recognise that refusal compels the sponsor (and other family members) either to accept separation or to renounce 'the network of personal, social and economic relations that make up the private life of every human being' and that it is wrong to force citizens or long-term residents to choose between family and home without compelling reasons. The price of love and family should not, as the Court of Appeal pointed out, be exile unless there is a powerful justification, and sponsors' interests must be explicitly and sympathetically centred.

IX. FAMILY LIFE AND IMMIGRATION: THE NEW APPROACH IN PRACTICE

This chapter's premise is that the current approach to Article 8 family reunification, as demonstrated in the Strasbourg cases and in the chapter seven Supreme Court decisions, awards insufficient weight to family life. The chapter has discussed various ways in which an Article 8 assessment would unfold differently if family life were more significant. These include a different approach to family life, a broader sense of the general interest, more scrutiny of government claims, adjustment to the doctrines of 'precariousness' and 'exceptionality', and proper consideration of sponsors' interests. The outcome would be a more evenly weighted fair balance assessment.

[74] *Quila v SSHD* [2011] UKSC 45 [33] (Lord Wilson).

[75] Immigration Act 1971, s 1(1). Even this right is qualified as citizens may be subject to a 'temporary exclusion order' of up to two years at a time (with the possibility of renewal) under Counter-Terrorism and Security Act 2015, ss 2–4.

This can be demonstrated by considering two hypothetical examples that draw on the factual scenarios in the failed Strasbourg claims in *Omoregie* (a claim for regularisation by a failed asylum seeker) and *Senchishak* (a claim for admission of an elderly, infirm parent), although not all details have been included and some assumptions have been made.[76] Each case study is analysed first under existing Strasbourg principles and then under the adjusted approach. It is not possible to say with certainty that the adjusted approach would result in a violation finding, but the fair balance assessment would give more weight to family life.

A. Case Study 1: The Failed Asylum Seeker

Facts: A is a young man and a national of an African country, Upsilon. He entered a European state, Zeta, without authorisation and claimed asylum. While waiting for his claim to be decided, he began a relationship with B, a citizen of Zeta. Six months later, A and B began living together. Two months after that, his asylum claim was refused. Over the next few years, A appealed the asylum refusal, A and B married and they had a daughter C, who is also a citizen of Zeta. B's application to sponsor A as a spouse was refused because A was not lawfully resident and B's earnings were insufficient. Eventually all asylum and spouse application appeals failed, and A was expelled. A is subject to a re-entry ban, B still cannot meet the income threshold for sponsorship and A cannot return to Zeta for the foreseeable future.

Current framework: A, B and C have lived together, and expulsion interferes with family life. The issue is proportionality and whether the expulsion decision represents a fair balance between competing interests. As A did not have an immigration status when the relationship began, family life is treated as 'precarious' and exceptional circumstances are needed to find a violation. C's best interests are a primary consideration, but it is not clear how much weight they would carry for a father. Since *Omoregie*, the Court has shown more flexibility (for example, in *Jeunesse*), but chapter three observed its gendered character. Other factors, such as B's wish to remain in her home and the justification for an income threshold in that form, are of little significance, but whether the state has consistently applied its immigration policy to A's case could be relevant. If it is impossible for B and C to join A in Upsilon (because, for example, there is a civil war), that would be material, but differences in the standard of living or the interruption to B's career prospects or other interests are not.

Proposed framework: Under the framework discussed in this chapter, A's lack of immigration status is still a factor, but so is the fact that the relationship began while he had a right to remain in international law. Also relevant is whether he

[76] *Omoregie* (n 26); *Senchishak v Finland* [2014] ECHR 1295.

later sought regularisation or deceived the authorities. Both B and C's situations are relevant; what would they give up if they leave Zeta to follow A? What would be the impact on C of growing up outside her country of birth and nationality? What would be the consequences for B in relation to her career, social and family life, and other responsibilities? If B and C remain in Zeta without A, how will the separation affect them? What is the wider impact of creating a fractured family unit, where family life can only be enjoyed occasionally and via extensive travel, and a child has only an intermittent and distant relationship with her father? The government also needs to explain why the income threshold is necessary, and the Court would consider the risks of allowing B to return even if it is not met. Overall, and after considering these factors, the question is whether refusing to allow A to live with B and C is reasonable.

B. Case Study 2: The Elderly Parent

Facts: D moved 20 years ago to a European state, Kappa, from her country of birth, Sigma, which shares a border with Kappa. Since then, she has lived lawfully in Kappa, working and bringing up a family. Her parents and sister remained in Sigma. Her sister and then her father died, by which time D's mother E was in poor health. She moved in with her granddaughter in Sigma, but this did not work out well. D shuttled between Kappa and Sigma to care for E, putting considerable strain on her own and her family's well-being. She tried to find a care home in Sigma, but nothing was suitable as family members are expected to care for aged relatives. Eventually, D brought E to Kappa on a visit visa and then asked permission for her to stay permanently. The application took four years to be finally determined, during which time E lived with D in Kappa. The claim was eventually refused and E faces expulsion to Sigma.

Current framework: The first question is whether Article 8(1) is engaged, ie is there interference with family life? In *Senchishak*, the Court said that until the mother came to Kappa, there was no family life as the parties had lived apart, while co-residence after she came to Kappa did not constitute family life as it was created knowing that it might not continue. There was therefore no need to consider proportionality. This was a harsh finding, and another panel might find that family life exists, but expulsion is still not interference given the background situation and precarious residence, or that there was interference, but it was proportionate. Likely factors in the 'fair balance' proportionality assessment are that E has few ties to Kappa, that care in Sigma is possible, if not ideal, that the granddaughter can assist, and that D can provide financial support and travel to Sigma to see her mother. It is unlikely therefore that a violation would be found.

Proposed framework: Family life is treated in a different way. Instead of dividing it into two segments – before and after E's arrival in Kappa – the overall character of the relationship is considered. D and E have always been close and

D's wish to have E live with her is a normal stage in the parent–child relationship. As family life exists, the issue is 'fair balance'. While the factors mentioned above still apply, some new elements are considered. Firstly, the government's justification of the rule that prohibits E's entry is relevant. If the concern is access by elderly relatives to expensive health and social care, the magnitude of the risk and whether it can be mitigated (in ways that do not reinforce other social inequalities, such as through excessively expensive insurance) are relevant. Another factor is D's personal situation: what will be the impact on her and her family if she must support E from afar? The fact that D moved E to live with her before asking for permission is of limited relevance if, as in *Senchishak*, this was lawful. Although a court might not want to penalise a state's relative generosity in this regard, the fact that cohabitation has now lasted for several years shows that it is a viable solution. Overall, the test is whether refusal is reasonable.

C. Case Studies: Discussion

This chapter has proposed adjusting the fair balance assessment to give family life more holistic consideration and greater weight. This would not guarantee admission in any specific case, but would shift the balance some degrees towards the protection of families. While there is currently little support among states and consequently the Strasbourg Court for a new approach, the proposals are not outlandish. Chapter three has shown a slowly increasing degree of flexibility by Strasbourg. The applicants in the case studies above would have stood a good chance of success under the UK's immigration regime of the early 2000s even without the intervention of Article 8. The political pendulum may have swung in an anti-migrant direction at present, but it can swing back. In that scenario, the Strasbourg Court could recognise a new consensus, and raise standards across Europe.[77]

It could be argued that the proposals are too modest. By working within the positive obligation framework, they continue to accept the logic of immigration controls, disregarding the primacy of the family life right and accepting that people need permission to cross borders. The analysis has therefore disregarded arguments for open borders. This is not because they are unconvincing in principle but because they are far removed from the current realm of the possible, and the aim here is to imagine a world that is within grasp even if it is not right now. The argument made here is less ambitious but also less improbable; it asks courts to treat the protection of family life as a serious obligation that carries weight against immigration control.

[77] Scholars have argued that consensus does not require unanimity but a clear trend: K Dzehtsiarou, *European Consensus and the Legitimacy of the European Court of Human Rights* (Cambridge, Cambridge University Press, 2015); L Wildhaber, A Hjartarson and S Donnelly, 'No Consensus on Consensus? The Practice of the European Court of Human Rights' (2013) 33 *Human Rights Law Journal* 248, 241.

X. CONCLUSION

In the Strasbourg family reunification cases, immigration control is presented as a force of nature, a monolithic entity that cannot be avoided or negotiated. That position was reflected in the later UK Supreme Court decisions discussed in chapter seven. The consequence is that there is little obligation on states to recognise, let alone justify, the painful personal dilemmas of binational families to whom all the 'risks' of migration are passed. The state is thereby assumed to be more secure: the refusal is in the 'public interest'. Yet, the question that is rarely asked is what precisely is the public interest and for whom does it operate? Instead, immigration controls are normalised and naturalised to the point that it is considered unreasonable to ask that they should bend to the needs of citizens and residents. The passing of risk to the individual is the counterpart of the individualisation of rights for which human rights have been criticised. In both cases, the wider context of how risk is created and allocated, and how control is exercised over narratives of immigration control and justice, is ignored.[78] It reproduces an artificial divide between private and public interests, and subordinates the former to the latter in ways that entrench gender and racial inequalities.

This chapter has proposed ways to dismantle this monolithic presence through changes in how family life and the public interest are understood, a more critical approach to government claims, a new approach to 'precarious' residence, the removal of the exceptionality test and greater consideration to the needs and concerns of sponsors. The outcome would be a right to family reunification that continues to recognise that the general interest, at least as currently understood, requires immigration controls but also requires strong and secure family units. Primarily, it would recognise that human rights exist to protect humans from, in the words cited earlier of Judge Martens, being 'crushed' by the state. The tension between immigration control and the protection of family life cannot easily be resolved in a world where immigration control carries such weight and where states resist supranational regulation. It is important, however, to be clear eyed about the hardships and unpalatable choices involved, to challenge legal doctrines that conceal state-oriented judicial choices and to make the case for the wider values that are at stake.

[78] On risk and justice, see B Hudson, *Justice in the Risk Society: Challenging and Re-affirming 'Justice' in Late Modernity* (London, Sage, 2003); on risk as cultural, governmental, individualised and constructed, see J Arnoldi, *Risk* (Cambridge, Polity, 2009) 38–66.

9

Concluding Remarks

I. INTRODUCTION

THIS BOOK HAS made four main arguments, which have been substantiated through a close and contextual analysis of cases decided by the European Court of Human Rights (the Strasbourg Court, Strasbourg) and, more extensively, 11 family reunification judgments decided by the UK's Supreme Court, formerly the House of Lords (the Court). The first argument is that the cases show that Article 8 has had only a limited impact on the ability of states to regulate family reunification. There have been some gains, but they are not extensive, reflecting the difficulties facing judges in advancing the protection of human rights without wider social and political consensus. The second is that there is an irreconcilable tension between the duty to protect family life and state claims to sovereignty over immigration, so that adjudicating on Article 8 family reunification claims is complex, difficult and value laden. Judges must strategise and act tactically, whether the aim is to give more effect to Article 8 or to limit its impact. The third is that, despite the problems, legal coherence requires that family life must, at a minimum, be given the same weight as the demands of immigration control. Achieving this would be a major advance that is not realisable in the immediate future, but it is possible within the dominant positive obligation framework, through several incremental steps. The final argument is that, in family reunification Article 8 claims, the claims of family life and the suffering caused by restrictive immigration controls have been insufficiently acknowledged when set against state claims to sovereignty over immigration, so that aiming for a more expansive version of Article 8 family reunification rights is a worthwhile objective.

The ways in which these arguments have been addressed in the book are discussed in this chapter. It starts by considering the limited impact that both the Strasbourg Court and the Supreme Court cases have had on family reunification policy, suggesting limits on what judges can achieve on their own. It goes on to point out how the Supreme Court has acted strategically as a moral and political agent throughout, advancing, retreating and crafting judgments to disguise problems and promote specific aims. It then considers the legal character of Article 8 and why, legally speaking, the needs of families should be treated as being at least as important as immigration control. It ends by returning to the interests at stake in Article 8 family reunification cases and why the argument for a more family-friendly version is morally as well as legally compelling.

II. THE IMPACT OF ARTICLE 8 ON IMMIGRATION POLICY

The analysis in chapter three of the large number of Strasbourg Article 8 family reunification cases described the gains there as 'modest', and this is equally true of the domestic jurisprudence. The Supreme Court hears about 50–60 cases a year, all of them on questions of law 'of the greatest public or constitutional importance affecting the whole population'.[1] That it heard 11 family reunification cases in a 10-year period, alongside others on Article 8 and deportation or extradition, suggests that family reunification presented problems for many, and that families, lawyers and judges saw the Human Rights Act as having the potential to assist them. However, this book has shown that it is, in fact, difficult to use Article 8 to support binational family life despite the promise of the early cases.

The starting point in the Supreme Court domestic cases was *Huang* in 2007, discussed in chapter four, which reversed lower court decisions that had made Article 8 claims almost impossible to win. It found that appellate courts should reach their own decision on human rights compatibility, giving them an autonomous role in developing Article 8 protection. Courts must give 'appropriate weight' to the government's view on proportionality, but there was no separate doctrine of judicial deference, and the government's view on the necessity of its policy would not automatically prevail. The Immigration Rules were not assumed to embody the correct Article 8 balance and there was no precondition of exceptionality for an Article 8 violation finding. While the Court still anticipated only a few claims succeeding, it opened the way to a more flexible, judicially shaped Article 8 jurisprudence.

There followed three cases discussed in chapter five (the first post-*Huang* phase) that showed what this could mean. *Beoku-Betts* concerned the appeals legislation, and it made claims easier to bring by finding that the Article 8 rights of all family members, not just those of the applicant, should be considered in an appeal. *Chikwamba* determined that it would often be disproportionate to require an applicant for in-country regularisation to return to their country of origin to make their application, again enabling claims to be brought more easily. *EB (Kosovo)* decided that delay due to a dysfunctional immigration system could reduce the weight awarded to the public interest in immigration control. More significantly, it confirmed that there was no test of 'insurmountable obstacles' in Article 8 cases; instead, the question was whether it was reasonable for the family to move abroad. The decisions were a cause for celebration for migrants and those working with them, and suggested that the Court was willing to use

[1] www.supremecourt.uk/.

its human right jurisdiction to establish a domestic Article 8 family reunification jurisprudence, a step that was consistent with both the doctrine of the margin of appreciation and the Human Rights Act.

Chapter six analysed four decisions (the second post-*Huang* phase) that were also good news for migrants and their families. Each protected binational family life, but none did so only or at all through using Article 8. *Baiai* concerned the right to marry and was therefore decided under Article 12 of the European Convention on Human Rights (ECHR), a strong right, and the Court explicitly compared it to the more qualified right in Article 8. *Mahad*, on whether funds from third parties could be used to meet the financial criteria for admission, was brought as an Article 8 claim but was decided in the applicants' favour through interpretation of the Immigration Rules without reference to Article 8. *ZH (Tanzania)* ensured that children's interests, particularly British citizen children's interests, were a primary consideration in decisions concerning their parents, including those concerning the parents' expulsion. It has been a hugely influential case, which discussed children's rights under Article 8 in depth, but its authority derived, in significant part, from additional obligations on the government through a statutory duty towards children. Finally, *Quila* found that an increase in the minimum age to 21 for entry or sponsorship for spouses and partners, designed to reduce the incidence of forced marriage, would normally breach Article 8 if the marriage was not forced, although the Immigration Rules were not found unlawful. It was decided on Article 8 alone, but the Court emphasised the non-immigration character of the restriction in question. In all these decisions, therefore, family life received additional protection, but Article 8 was not the driving force or, if it was, the immigration context was minimised.

The third post-*Huang* phase, examined in chapter seven, took place against increasing government resistance to the Court's role in determining the scope of Article 8 protection, amended Immigration Rules and legislation, and a political drive to reduce immigration. It consisted of three decisions, including two where lawyers argued that the Immigration Rules were incompatible with Article 8 – an ambitious, arguably overambitious, claim. Over the course of these decisions, the Court maintained some gains, particularly on the rights of children (which were protected by statute), but unambiguously withdrew from any critique of government policy and accepted the government's conservative position on the character of the obligations created by Article 8. The first decision, *Ali and Bibi*, on the implementation of a pre-entry language test for spouses and partners, accepted that the test would breach Article 8 in a significant number of cases, but these could be managed through grants of leave outside the Immigration Rules. The Court was openly divided on the issue of deference, with the majority taking the view that the Secretary of State's view on the need for a policy should receive 'considerable weight', a more deferent approach than the 'appropriate weight' formulation used in *Huang*. The second decision, *MM (Lebanon)*, on the minimum financial requirements for spouses, was clear that governments would easily persuade courts that their policy was necessary, making Article 8 a question only of the personal circumstances of the claimant, not the strength of the public interest, which was assumed. Article 8 violations, which the Court acknowledged would happen with some regularity, could again be addressed through leave granted outside the Immigration Rules. The final decision, *Agyarko*, addressed provisions within the Immigration Rules designed to cater for possible Article 8 violations. Despite their rather narrow formulation, the Court accepted the government's position that they would cover almost all cases, with only a very few succeeding outside the Rules. Both *MM (Lebanon)* and *Agyarko* emphasised that the Court considered itself bound by the margin of appreciation in the same way as the Strasbourg Court and would not consider whether Article 8 required more in the domestic context, handing authority back to the government.

The outcome of all these decisions is that Article 8 is now an occasional remedy, particularly for families in the UK with British citizen children, and only a limited constraint on policy. The Immigration Rules will never be found incompatible with Article 8 if violations can be addressed through leave outside the Rules, the government must do little to justify its policy and courts will not go beyond the state-centric approach of the Strasbourg Court. The government could, if it wished, implement Immigration Rules that clearly violate Article 8 and force individuals to bring individual appeals outside the Rules in each case, a time-consuming and expensive process that many will be unable to undertake. Article 8 has also had no impact on less visible obstacles to family reunification: very high visa fees and other costs, prolonged routes to settlement and demanding evidential requirements.

However, it would be wrong to say that Article 8 has not acted at all as a structural constraint. At present, the government prefers to keep the Immigration Rules in line with an admittedly conservative interpretation of Article 8. In this way, while it must recognise the impact of Article 8 in a few cases, there is less likelihood of unpredictable developments through judicial interpretations. To the extent that this creates a degree of consistency and predictability, it is of value to applicants too, although much depends on the quality of the initial decision-making. It is also possible that fear of adverse Article 8 findings has held the government back from going further through, for example, increasing the minimum income or the pre-entry English language requirement. Human rights obligations have therefore shaped government policy to some degree, although the full extent is unknowable. However, the Court's restrained approach means that this can be done in a minimal way within the Rules, in the knowledge that few cases will succeed outside them.

This outcome suggests a limited role for human rights in ensuring the needs of families are sufficiently considered and reinforces the function of human rights as an individual remedy for those in a position to enforce them. They have also been used to legitimise harsh policies, such as the minimum income requirement. This is a decidedly more negative picture than that hoped for after the early decisions. However, what happened in the earlier decisions must not be overstated. In the first phase, the Court addressed the interpretation of statutory appeal provisions and executive policy outside the Immigration Rules. Even then, it was not very specific about what it was doing in terms of Article 8 and the Human Rights Act. In the second phase, it did address problems with the Immigration Rules as well as policy, but did not rely entirely or at all on Article 8 and did not find the Immigration Rules unlawful even when their application would breach Article 8 in a substantial number of cases. Once the government's antagonism was clear, the Court retreated on the question of deference to executive policy and the government's view on what Article 8 required, although it is not clear how much this was a tactical question or reflected a new outlook following changes in the composition of the Court; it is likely that both played a part.

In either event, it is clearly very difficult for courts to use Article 8 to protect binational families even if there is the will and irrespective of what might be legally justifiable. As well as the likely confrontations with government, there are practical difficulties. Article 8 requires fact-sensitive decisions and does not adapt easily to a mass decision-making system. As the discussions in chapters four and five showed, courts cannot easily change attitudes within the Tribunal and elsewhere in the immigration system, which draw, in turn, on institutional culture as well as wider social attitudes. Respect for family life in the immigration context requires more than good judicial decisions; it also requires wider social, cultural and political change.

III. THE SUPREME COURT AS A MORAL AND POLITICAL ACTOR

The book has shown that the Court acted strategically, expanding its authority where it could and retreating when the political controversy became damaging. At the time of *Huang*, judicial autonomy and the protection of family life were mutually reinforcing. By the time of *MM (Lebanon)* and *Agyarko*, protecting family life threatened the Court's position and it retreated from a conflict that it could only lose.[2] It is likely that the direction of the Court was driven by some justices more than others, and there was some dissent, but it is significant that the first decision, *Huang*, and the last two, *MM (Lebanon)* and *Agyarko*, were single judgments; the unity of the Court and the coherence of the law

[2] The Court acted courageously on later occasions; see, eg *Miller and Dos Santos v Secretary of State* [2017] UKSC 5; *Miller v The Prime Minister* [2019] UKSC 41. However, after Lord Reed, who gave the lead judgment in *Agyarko* (discussed in ch 7), became President of the Court in 2020, the Court became 'less confident and more deferential': see NR Langen, 'Under Lord Reed, the Court Has Retreated into Itself' (*The Justice Gap*, 27 July 2021); see also A Horne, 'Has the UK Supreme Court Reformed Itself?' (*Prospect Magazine*, 5 August 2021), www.prospectmagazine.co.uk/politics/supreme-court-lord-reed-reforming-itself-child-benefit-cap-law; L Graham, 'The Reed Court by Numbers: How Shallow is the 'Shallow End'?' (*UK Constitutional Law Blog*, 4 April 2022); C Gearty, 'In the Shallow End' (2022) 44 *London Review of Books*.

were shared institutional priorities. There was a considerable distance between the first and last judgments, yet the Court succeeded in moving between them without expressly contradicting itself. Judgments involved sophisticated legal arguments, as could only be expected, but the analysis showed that they also depended on choices as to language, structure, emphasis and selection of legal materials. Judgments were written to persuade readers that the legal approach adopted in them was inevitable, correct and represented a seamless progression, even though they were not always consistent with each other. It was only through a close analysis of the structure, emphases, vocabulary, ellipses and simplifications that their constructed character became apparent.

Huang talked in a new way about the importance of family life and the protective function of Article 8. The first phase post-*Huang* decisions went further in humanising the applicants, describing their personal circumstances and dilemmas in some detail. There was, however, relatively little engagement with the Strasbourg cases or with the specific character of obligations and powers under the Human Rights Act. The Court was doing something new with human rights, but there seemed to be a reluctance to say so explicitly even though such a step was consistent with its constitutional function and the Human Rights Act. In the second post-*Huang* phase, the Court avoided an over-reliance on Article 8. There was also less interest in the individual circumstances and more engagement with relevant Strasbourg cases, although the predicament of the applicants, not the government's immigration-related concerns, was still the starting point. The third post-*Huang* phase also engaged with the Strasbourg cases, particularly in *MM (Lebanon)*, but with a greater emphasis on the limits of protection. There were increasing references to the public interest in controlling immigration, the margin of appreciation and the positive character of the Article 8 obligation, all concepts that function to delimit the impact of Article 8. The Court reverted to a more distanced, impersonal style, with little consideration of or empathy with the individuals affected, and their interests were not prioritised within the judgments. There was also a close identification with the concerns of government.

The judgments were imbued with values. This was obvious when Lord Bingham devoted a fifth of his judgment to a young man's traumatic history in *EB (Kosovo)*, but it was also true when the Court in *Agyarko* mentioned the applicants' unlawful residence twice in the first sentence. These values were likely to have been both personal and institutional, and the two may sometimes have been in tension. Some judges would have regarded any policy scrutiny as inappropriate or would have had limited sympathy for applicants. Others may have seen no alternative but to accept a constrained position. It is improbable that Lady Hale and Lord Wilson lost their pro-family inclinations or stopped seeing policy scrutiny as central to proportionality between *Quila* and *MM (Lebanon)*; it is more likely that they accepted the need for a cautious and united approach in the face of growing government hostility. While this was a disappointment for binational families, it is unsurprising. The Court showed itself to be a strategic political actor, in the sense that it was driven by more than pure legal analysis and aimed to achieve certain ends, which would themselves adapt over time to changes in the personal and institutional values of justices and in response to other constitutional actors, particularly the government. The Court would always respect the express will of Parliament in legislation, but it also sought to avoid open conflict with the executive, at least on this issue. Its strategisation was not always obvious, however. Particularly in its later cases, the Court sustained the myth of objective adjudication motivated only by legal principle.

IV. A COHERENT LEGAL INTERPRETATION OF ARTICLE 8

This book has argued that, in family reunification claims, Article 8 can and should start from the position that family life is of equal importance to immigration control. This is a normative but also legal argument because even a conservative interpretation of Article 8 requires that family life is not a priori given less weight than immigration control. The problem has been that this position is rarely acceptable to states who wish to retain tight control over admissions, and their support is necessary for the maintenance of the international human rights regime. The book has shown that judges who want to make family life more important find it difficult to do so because it is likely to lead to confrontations with the government, even if their conclusions are defensible legally. In consequence, as chapter three demonstrated, the Strasbourg Court has developed its Article 8 family reunification jurisprudence in a cautious manner, adopting doctrines and principles that usually, but not always, favour state sovereignty over migration above the protection of family life. Where it has found violations, the underpinning principles can be hard to pin down. The UK's Supreme Court has also not always been explicit about how it is applying principles domestically, and it has now accepted a government-oriented version of Article 8.

This observation led to chapter eight of the book. While it observed that criticisms of judicialised human rights reveal their limits and the need for them to be part of a wider social and political process, it argued that legal avenues should not be abandoned. Human rights litigation can contribute to and concretise wider political and social movements. The Strasbourg cases have, slowly and cautiously, expanded the scope of Article 8 in family reunification, with momentum in cases involving children, forced migrants or discrimination where states are subject to wider obligations in international law. Political, legal and social climates change; until 1985 and the *Abdulaziz* case, it was not even clear that family reunification claims engaged Article 8. There is no legal reason why the Article 8 family reunification cannot develop further.

Chapter eight therefore looked at areas of the Article 8 jurisprudence that might evolve in a more propitious climate, notably on the inclusion of family members beyond the nuclear family, a wider understanding of the general interest, judicial scrutiny of government claims as to the necessity of immigration controls in that form, precarious residence and the interests of sponsors. Taken together, these changes would create the contours of a right to family reunification that would treat family life as having equal importance with immigration control. In any decision, either family life or immigration control would eventually prevail, but it would be a more evenly balanced contest based on a detailed assessment of all relevant factors.

In that analysis, I continued to treat Article 8 as a positive obligation. In so doing, I accepted states have a pre-existing right to control the admission and stay of non-nationals, so that the admission of a family member required a positive act of the state. While scholars have cogently argued that there is no such pre-existing legal right, it is a political fact that is recognised by courts, including the Strasbourg Court and the Supreme Court. I therefore decided to adopt the pragmatic approach of working within the same confines because I want to make an argument that is intelligible to those who must work within existing systems and because treating family reunification as a positive obligation still permits a more generous and flexible treatment of family reunification claims. Most of the reasons for treating positive obligations cautiously – the uncertain character of the obligation, the problems of assessing public interest considerations and the cost to states – do not apply to family reunification. The limits on what is considered possible jurisprudentially, even within a positive obligation framework, are not primarily legal in character.

Further, while a positive obligation does not give lexical priority to the right in the manner of a negative obligation, even a cautious interpretation of Article 8 as a positive obligation cannot logically start from the position that respect for family life carries *less* weight than immigration control. In a positive obligation case, the right is balanced with the 'general interest'. As chapter eight showed, the general interest will include immigration control factors and can also include other considerations, such as the wider benefits of family unity. There is no reason why one of those considerations should a priori be awarded more weight than the right itself even if, after a careful assessment, the right does not prevail. Treating family life as having at least the same importance as immigration control is the minimum requirement of a coherent legal interpretation of Article 8.

V. FINAL WORDS: MAKING FAMILY MATTER

My argument that family should be regarded as having at least the same importance as immigration control when considering Article 8 and family reunification is also normative. I will therefore end by restating why states should be encouraged through human rights norms towards a more family-oriented immigration regime. Chapter one noted that, absent immigration control factors, family is the fundamental and primary unit through which human beings find nurture, care, emotional and material support, and companionship. Its significance can hardly be overstated. Later chapters have shown that, in family reunification jurisprudence (with limited exceptions relating to children, forced migrants and where there is clear discrimination), the significance of family largely disappears, and immigration concerns predominate. As chapter one also noted, family reunification cannot be treated in the same way as labour migration, where governments make instrumental calculations as to the value of admitting an individual migrant. Rather, they have a responsibility to their citizens and other long-term residents, which means that states rarely prevent family reunification altogether even if otherwise committed to low levels of immigration. Quota systems are also rare in family reunification, and they feel instinctively wrong; the claim is for something too fundamental to be a matter of pure chance.[3] In other words, there is something special about family migration; the claim is stronger because of what is at stake and who is affected.

People want to live with their family members and find separation difficult to endure. That became clear when the coronavirus pandemic led to border closures and some families found themselves abruptly and unexpectedly separated, leading to campaigns organised around slogans such as '#Love is not tourism'.[4] If restrictions resulting from a pandemic that killed millions of people led to an outcry because of the misery they caused, reasons for keeping families apart indefinitely under immigration controls need to be just as weighty. However, the suffering caused by controls that go further than necessary is often not visible because of who endures it: predominantly citizens of migrant heritage, the poor, the less well educated. They are forced into a transnational lifestyle, not as members of an elite who choose to exercise their privileged mobility, but because they have no other option, and their suffering attracts little attention despite the loneliness, guilt, mental ill-health, stress and financial consequences. In that light, vague justifications for sweeping restrictions seem inadequate, arbitrary and discriminatory. Cogent and pressing reasons should be present if a citizen or long-term resident must choose between their home and their child, partner, parent, sibling or indeed any person where the ties are such that there is an obligation or need to live in proximity.

That is not how the world is currently organised, and this principle is easily displaced by the dominant and apparently urgent requirements of immigration control and the overbearing weight of state sovereignty. One of the hardest parts of writing this book was to keep engaging with the subject matter on my own terms and not to become overwhelmed by a state-dominated perspective. The sense that it is not legitimate to question state policy was sometimes evident in the decisions discussed in this book. A British citizen, for example, had no right

[3] The USA operates a quota system for wider family members and Austria has a scheme for the family members of sponsors who are not citizens.

[4] B de Hart and C Carella, '#LoveIsNotTourism: Cross-Border Couples, Citizenship and Belonging during the Covid-19 Crisis' *Family Migration in Times of Crisis* Workshop convened by Radboud University Network on Migrant Inclusion (RUNOMI) 15 June 2021.

to 'insist' on being joined by a partner when there was no existing right in British immigration law.[5]

Even though my vision of a rebalanced immigration system is an ideal, I believe that it is a worthy one that should shape our actions wherever possible. Policymakers, decision-makers and judges must work within the confines of their authority and power. But where they have choices, these can and should be exercised in that direction so far as possible. This would be congruent with the spirit of human rights, as more than an occasional legal remedy but as a structural force that shapes interactions between state and individual. It would recognise that an interpretation of Article 8 that routinely puts state concerns above implementation of the right is incoherent. It would enable more families to flourish and would build momentum for an immigration system that puts the welfare of families at its centre.

[5] *R (on the application of Agyarko) v SSHD* [2017] UKSC 11 [68].

Appendix: Content Analysis Methodology

THE CONTENT ANALYSIS discussed in chapters six and seven examined the 11 Supreme Court decisions analysed in this book. The aim was to identify differences in the way that the Court wrote and structured its judgments in the *Huang* judgment and in the three post-*Huang* phases discussed in chapters four to seven, each of which represented a different response to the judgment in *Huang*. All the decisions substantively analysed in this book are included in each part of the content analysis except where expressly stated.

The content analysis method was chosen because it provides an additional degree of objectivity to the interpretation of the cases. The exercise bears some resemblance to discourse analysis in that it concerns the construction of a social reality through legal texts. However, in this instance, the constructions were not primarily discovered through the analysis but had already been identified, and were then confirmed, refined, nuanced or amended by the content analysis. The analysis has not adopted the methods specific to discourse analysis but does adopt a critical approach to the text, looking at linguistic choices, structure, citation practice and other matters. It does therefore share some of the insights and overall approach of discourse analysis.

The analysis subjected the 11 cases to a focused examination that engaged with selected elements of the text: sometimes single words or case names and, on other occasions, a couple of sentences or a paragraph. The decision as to which elements to examine emerged from a reading of the cases, although the results of the content analysis sometimes led to consideration of new elements or to the reinterpretation and recategorisation of the cases. It was therefore an iterative process. The analysis was quantitative, in that it noted the frequency with which certain words, phrases or passages occurred, as well as other simple numerical measures such as the number of paragraphs or of European Court of Human Rights judgments cited. However, it also had qualitative elements as it was sometimes necessary to determine the meaning of passages before they were counted or categorised. The qualitative aspects required some judgment calls. It was sometimes difficult, for example, to decide if a passage discussing facts represented context or was part of the legal analysis. All facts may be legally relevant, and it is not always easy to decide the function of a particular passage. Similarly, it also had to be decided how to categorise passages quoted from other judgments. There was therefore a degree of subjectivity, but the methodology discussed below was designed to ensure a reasonable degree of reliability. Subjectivity was not the only risk, however. An attempt was made to identify the number of passages that addressed the public interest in immigration control, but this proved impossible, given the intricate character of the reasoning and the interweaving of facts and law. The same issue arose in relation to positive obligations and legitimate aim. It was therefore decided simply to count the occurrence of relevant terms regardless of context. This still gave some interesting results, but limited weight should be put on them. This is reflected by their function in the book, where they support rather than lead the main analysis.

The categories of analysis were data driven in that they emerged from a prior reading of the text but had, of necessity, to be confined to those that can be made subject to, and which could usefully be addressed through, a content analysis. They were primarily of use in reinforcing or challenging previous interpretations, and several parts of the analysis in this book are more nuanced as a result. The categories and, where appropriate, sub-categories are set out below.

The units of analysis were the 11 House of Lords/Supreme Court cases. Concurring judgments, even if very brief, were included, except for Category 9 (see below), which considered the position within each judgment of discussion of the applicants' personal circumstances. Because brief assenting judgments can go before or after the lead judgment, position within the whole judgment can be misleading, so, in that one instance, position within the lead judgment was considered. Dissenting judgments were excluded, however, except when the overall length of each case was measured. They could not be treated as part of the main judgment due to their opposing perspective, but they could not easily be analysed separately due to problems of consistency. They were usually shorter, said little about the facts and cited fewer cases. Deciding whether a judgment was dissenting was not always straightforward, however. It was decided to treat Lord Brown's judgment in *EB (Kosovo)* as dissenting because, while it did not disagree on every point, the underlying point of disagreement was fundamental, as it clearly was in *Quila*. The position was more complex in *Ali and Bibi*. Here, Lady Hale gave the lead judgment, followed by two concurring judgments. There was unanimity on one key point, but Lady Hale was in a minority on a second. It was decided to treat all the judgments as in concurrence due to agreement on the main issue.

A further problem arose in the treatment of the two decisions that do not address Article 8: *Baiai* and *Mahad*. The reasons for their inclusion were discussed in chapter six and, because they were seen as part of the cohort of cases, they were included in the content analysis wherever possible. The only exceptions, identified in the table below, were when the analysis concerned Strasbourg cases (*Mahad*) or Article 8 specifically (*Mahad* and *Baiai*). In addition, when analysing the language used to discuss irregular migrants, I only included decisions that involved such migrants.

In each judgment, relevant segments were identified and categorised. Some segments were relevant to more than one category, but each segment would be allocated to only one sub-category within each category. Depending on the category, the segment might be a case name, a word, a few lines, a single paragraph or several paragraphs. Some parts of the judgments were not relevant to this exercise and were therefore disregarded. Several steps were taken to minimise the risk of error and subjectivity. Two cases were analysed as a pilot before the categories and sub-categories were finalised and the main analysis (including the two pilot cases again) was undertaken. In the main analysis, ambiguities were decided against my existing hypothesis. To check reliability, the entire exercise was carried out again two years later without having first reviewed the original data, which was compared only after the second analysis. Only minor discrepancies were identified, and these were resolved by carrying out those aspects of the analysis for a third time.

Category number	Category	Definition and notes	Subcategories	Identification of data tables
1	Number of ECtHR cases cited in lead and concurring judgments	Includes cases mentioned in quotations; each case is counted only once. *Mahad* excluded	None – value	Figures 6.1 and 7.2
2	Percentage of paragraphs that address contextual facts in lead and concurring judgments	This includes paragraphs that address facts as background rather than to arrive at a legal conclusion; Percentages rounded to nearest percentage point	None – value	Figures 6.3 and 7.8
3	Use of first names	First names are used for at least one party or family member. First names used with surname are excluded	3.1 Yes; used first names 3.2 No; did not use first names	Table 6.1
4	Length of judgment in paragraphs	Quantity of numbered paragraphs	None – value	Figure 7.1
5	Time between hearing and judgment in months	Taken from information at head of judgments; rounded to nearest month	None – value	Figure 7.1

(continued)

(Continued)

Category number	Category	Definition and notes	Subcategories	Identification of data tables
6	References to the public interest	Occurrence of the term 'public interest' or the cognate terms 'general interest, 'competing interests', 'interests of the community', 'interests of society', 'public order', 'interests of immigration control', interests of national security, public safety or the economic well-being of the country'. *Baiai* and *Mahad* excluded.	None – value	Figure 7.5
7	References to 'positive obligations'	References to 'positive obligation', 'positive duty', 'obligation to admit', 'general obligation to respect', 'duty to allow' or 'to facilitate' family to live together. *Baiai* and *Mahad* excluded	None – value	Figure 7.7
8	References to 'the margin of appreciation'	*Mahad* excluded	None – value	Figure 7.6
9	Position within judgment of discussion of applicants' circumstances	Decile of lead judgment in which applicants' circumstances first discussed	9.1 First decile 9.2 Second decile etc	Figure 7.9

(continued)

(Continued)

Category number	Category	Definition and notes	Subcategories	Identification of data tables
10	Use of term 'impose', 'oblige', 'obligation' 'duty' or synonyms	Use of 'impose', 'oblige', 'require' (in any tense or mood), or 'duty', 'obligation' or 'requirement' (in singular or plural), and 'imposition'. First column =raw number; second column =ratio to paragraphs in judgments as %	None – value	Figures 7.11 and 7.12
11	Number of domestic cases cited	Number of UK cases cited from any UK court or tribunal	None – value	Figures 6.2 and 7.4
12	Total number of times ECtHR cases are cited	Frequency with which ECtHR case names appear in leading and concurring judgments. *Mahad* excluded	None – value	Figure 7.3
13	References to 'lawful', 'unlawful', 'irregular', 'regular', 'legal' or 'illegal' residence	Frequency with which those terms appear in *Huang*, *Beoku-Betts*, *Chikwamba*, *EB (Kosovo)*, *Baiai*, *ZH (Tanzania)*, *Agyarko*	None – value	Figure 7.10

Bibliography

Abrams, K, 'What Makes the Family Special?' (2013) 80 *Chicago Law Review* 7.

Adler, M, *Administrative Justice in Context* (Oxford, Hart Publishing, 2010).

Ahmed, F and Perry, A, 'The Quasi-entrenchment of Constitutional Statutes' (2014) 73 *CLJ* 514.

Ahmed, F and Perry, A, 'Constitutional Statutes' (2016) 37 *OJLS* 461.

Allan, TRS, 'Human Rights and Judicial Review: A Critique of "Due Deference"' (2006) 65 *CLJ* 671.

Amos, M, 'Separating Human Rights Adjudication from Judicial Review – *Huang v Secretary of State for the Home Department and Kashmiri v Secretary of State for the Home Department*' (2007) 6 *European Human Rights Law Review* 679.

Anagnostou, D, 'Does European Human Rights Law Matter? Implementation and Domestic Impact of Strasbourg Court Judgments on Minority-Related Policies' (2010) 15 *International Journal of Human Rights* 721.

Andenas, M and Bjorge, E, 'National Implementation of ECHR Rights' in A Føllesdal, B Peters and G Ulfstein (eds), *Constituting Europe: The European Court of Human Rights in a National, European, and Global Context* (Cambridge, Cambridge University Press, 2013) 186–262.

Anderson, B, *Us and Them? The Dangerous Politics of Immigration Control* (Oxford, Oxford University Press, 2013).

Anderson, E, 'Democracy: Instrumental vs. Non instrumental Value' in T Christiano and J Christman (eds), *Contemporary Debates in Political Philosophy* (Oxford, Blackwell, 2009) 213–27.

Andrikopoulos, A, 'Love, Money and Papers in the Affective Circuits of Cross-Border Marriages: Beyond the "Sham"/"Genuine" Dichotomy' (2021) 47 *Journal of Ethnic and Migration Studies* 343.

Arden, M, 'Proportionality: The Way Ahead?' [2013] *PL* 498.

Arnoldi, J, *Risk* (Cambridge, Polity, 2009).

Arvind, TT and Stirton, L, 'Legal Ideology, Legal Doctrine and the UK's Top Judges' [2016] *PL* 418.

Askola, H, '(No) Migrating for Family Care in Later Life: *Senchishak v Finland*, Older Parents and Family Reunification' (2016) 18 *European Journal of Migration and Law* 351.

Barber, N and Young, A, 'The Rise of Prospective Henry VIII Clauses and Their Implications for Sovereignty' [2016] *PL* 112.

Barrett, D, 'The Regulatory Space of Equality and Human Rights in Britain: The Role of the Equality and Human Rights Commission' (2019) 39 *Legal Studies* 247.

Barry, B, *How Judges Judge: Empirical Insights into Judicial Decision-Making* (Abingdon, Routledge, 2020).

Bashford, A, 'Immigration Restriction: Rethinking Period and Place from Settler Colonies to Postcolonial Nations' (2014) 9 *Journal of Global History* 26.

Bates, E, 'The Birth of the European Convention on Human Rights and the European Court of Human Rights' in J Christoffersen and M Madsen (eds), *The European Court of Human Rights between Law and Politics* (Oxford, Oxford University Press, 2013) 17–42.

Beck-Gernsheim, E, 'The Marriage Route to Migration: Of Border Artistes, Transnational Matchmaking and Imported Spouses' (2011) *Nordic Journal of Migration Research* 60.

Bellamy, R, 'Political Constitutionalism and the Human Rights Act' (2011) 9 *International Journal of Constitutional Law* 86.

Benhabib, S, *The Rights of Others: Aliens, Residents and Citizens* (Cambridge, Cambridge University Press, 2004).

Bevan, C, 'Self-Represented Litigants: The Overlooked and Unintended Consequence of Legal Aid Reform' (2013) 35 *Journal of Social Welfare and Family Law* 43.

Bhabha, J, *Child Migration and Human Rights in a Global Age* (Princeton, Princeton University Press, 2011).
Bickerton, C, 'The Left's Journey from Politics to Law' in R Ekins and G Gee (eds), *Judicial Power and the Left* (London, Policy Exchange, 2017).
Bingham, T, 'The European Convention on Human Rights: Time to Incorporate' in T Bingham (ed), *The Business of Judging: Selected Essays and Speeches: 1985–1999* (Oxford, Oxford University Press, 2000) 131–40.
Bingham, T, 'Maccabaean Lecture in Jurisprudence – The Judges: Active or Passive' (2006) 139 *Proceedings of the British Academy* 55.
Bingham, T, 'The Rule of Law' (2007) 66 *CLJ* 67.
Bingham, T, 'The Human Rights Act' (2010) 6 *European Human Rights Law Review* 568.
Bingham, T, *The Rule of Law* (London, Penguin Books, 2010).
Bingham, T, *Lives of the Law: Selected Essays and Speeches* (Oxford, Oxford University Press, 2011).
Bjorge, E, 'National Supreme Courts and the Development of ECHR Rights' (2011) 91 *International Journal of Constitutional Law* 5.
Blackledge, A, '"As a Country We Do Expect": The Further Extension of Language Testing Regimes in the United Kingdom' (2009) 6 *Language Assessment Quarterly* 6.
Block, L, 'Regulating Membership: Explaining Restriction and Stratification of Family Migration in Europe' (2015) 36 *Journal of Family Issues* 1433.
Bonjour, S and Block, L, 'Ethnicizing Citizenship, Questioning Membership: Explaining the Decreasing Family Migration Rights of Citizens in Europe' (2011) 20 *Citizenship Studies* 778.
Bonjour, S and Cleton, L, 'Co-constructions of Family and Belonging in the Politics of Family Migration' in E Carmel, K Lenner and R Paul (eds), *Handbook on the Governance and Politics of Migration* (Cheltenham, Edward Elgar Publishing, 2021) 161–72.
Bonjour, S and de Hart, B, 'A Proper Wife, a Proper Marriage: Constructions of "Us" and "Them" in Dutch Family Migration Policy' (2013) 20 *European Journal of Women's Studies* 61.
Bonjour, S and Duyvendak, JW, 'The "Migrant with Poor Prospects": Racialized Intersections of Class and Culture in Dutch Civic Integration Debates' (2017) *Ethnic and Racial Studies* 882.
Bonjour, S and Kraler, A, 'Family Migration as an Integration Issue? Policy Perspectives and Academic Insights' (2015) 36 *Family Issues* 1407.
Bosch March, C, 'Backsliding on the Protection of Migrants' Rights? The Evolutive Interpretation of the Prohibition of Collective Expulsion by the European Court of Human Rights' (2021) 35 *Journal of Immigration Asylum and Nationality Law* 315.
Brady, A, *Proportionality and Deference Under the UK Human Rights Act: An Institutionally Sensitive Approach* (Cambridge, Cambridge University Press, 2012).
Breeze, R, '"Enemies of the People": Populist Performances in the Daily Mail Reporting of the Article 50 Case' (2018) 25 *Discourse, Context & Media* October 60.
Brettell, C, 'Marriage and Migration' [2017] *Annual Review of Anthropology* 81.
Brooks P, 'The Law as Narrative and Rhetoric' in P Brooks and P Gewirtz (eds), *Law's Stories: Narrative and Rhetoric in the Law* (New Haven, Yale University Press, 1998) 14–21.
Brugère, F, 'Caring Democracy as a Solution against Neoliberalism and Populism' in P Urban and L Ward (eds), *Care Ethics, Democratic Citizenship and the State* (London, Palgrave Macmillan, 2016) 137–59.
Brugère, F, *Care Ethics: The Introduction of Care as Political Category* (Leuven, Peeters Publishers, 2019).
Bryceson, D and Vuorela, U, 'Transnational Families in the Twenty-first Century' in D Bryceson and U Vuorela (eds), *The Transnational Family: New Frontiers and Global Networks* (Oxford, Berg Publishers, 2020) 3–30.
Cahill-O'Callaghan, R, 'The Influence of Personal Values on Legal Judgments' (2013) 40 *Journal of Law and Society* 596.
Cahill-O'Callaghan, R, 'Reframing the Judicial Diversity Debate: Personal Values and Tacit Diversity' (2015) 35 *Legal Studies* 1.

Cahill-O'Callaghan, R, *Values in the Supreme Court: Decisions, Division and Diversity* (Oxford, Hart Publishing, 2020).
Campbell, D, '"Catgate" and the Challenge to Parliamentary Sovereignty in Law' [2015] *PL* 426.
Campbell, J, 'The Role of Lawyers, Judges, Country Experts and Officials in British Asylum and Immigration Law' (2020) 16 *International Journal of Law in Context* 1.
Carens, JH, 'Who Should Get In? The Ethics of Immigration Admissions' (2003) 17 *Ethics & International Affairs* 95.
Carens, JH, *The Ethics of Immigration* (Oxford, Oxford University Press, 2013).
Carling, J, Menjívar, C and Schmalzbauer, L, 'Central Themes in the Study of Transnational Parenthood' (2012) 38 *Journal of Ethnic and Migration Studies* 191.
Carver, N, 'Displaying Genuineness: Cultural Translation in the Drafting of Marriage Narratives for Immigration Applications and Appeals' (2014) 3 *Families, Relationships and Societies* 271.
Chakrabarti, S, 'Rights and Rhetoric: The Politics of Asylum and Human Rights Culture in the United Kingdom' (2005) 32 *Journal of Law and Society* 131.
Charsley, K, Bolognani, M and Spencer, S, 'Marriage Migration and Integration: Interrogating Assumptions in Academic and Policy Debates' (2017) 17 *Ethnicities* 469.
Charsley, K, Storer-Church, B, Benson, M and Hear, N, 'Marriage-Related Migration to the UK' (2012) 46 *International Migration Review* 861.
Charsley, K, Agusita, E, Wray, H, Mohabir, R, Coombs, C and Ballmi, P, 'Kept Apart: Couples and Families Separated by the UK Immigration System' (Bristol, University of Bristol, 2020).
Cholewinski, R, 'Family Reunification and Conditions Placed on Family Members: Dismantling a Fundamental Human Right' (2002) 4 *European Journal of Migration and Law* 271.
Christie A, 'The Best Interests of the Child in UK Immigration Law' (2013) 16 *Nottingham Law Journal* 16.
Christoffersen, J and Madsen, MR, 'Introduction' in J Christoffersen and MR Madsen (eds), *The European Court of Human Rights between Law and Politics* (Oxford, Oxford University Press, 2013) 1–13.
Clayton, G, 'Prediction or Precondition? The House of Lords Judgment in *Huang and Kashmiri*' (2007) 21 *Journal of Immigration Asylum and Nationality Law* 311.
Consterdine, E, 'Managed Migration under Labour: Organised Public, Party Ideology and Policy Change' (2015) 41 *Journal of Ethnic and Migration Studies* 1433.
Craig, P, 'Judicial Review and Anxious Scrutiny: Foundations, Evolution and Application' [2015] *PL* 60.
Crawford, C, 'Dialogue and Declarations of Incompatibility under Section 4 of the Human Rights Act 1998) (2013) *Denning Law Journal* 43.
D'Aoust, AM, 'In the Name of Love: Marriage Migration, Governmentality, and Technologies of Love' (2013) *International Political Sociology* 258.
D'Aoust, AM, 'A Moral Economy of Suspicion: Love and Marriage Migration Management Practices in the United Kingdom' (2018) 36 *Environment and Planning D: Society and Space* 40.
Darbyshire, P, *Sitting in Judgment* (Oxford, Hart Publishing, 2011).
De Burca, G, *Reframing Human Rights in a Turbulent Era* (Oxford, Oxford University Press, 2021).
De Hart, B, 'Love Thy Neighbour: Family Reunification and the Rights of Insiders' (2009) 11 *European Journal of Migration and Law* 235.
De Hart, B, 'Superdads: Migrant Fathers' Right to Family Life before the European Court of Human Rights' (2015) 18 *Men and Masculinities* 448.
De Hart, B, 'The Odd Couple: Gender, Securitization, Europeanization and Marriages of Convenience in Dutch Family Migration Policies (1930–2020)' in AM D'Aoust (ed), *Transnational Marriage and Partner Migration: Constellations of Security, Citizenship and Rights* (New Brunswick, Rutgers University Press, 2021) 31–48.
De Hart, B and Bessels, E, 'Everything Went According to the Rules: Female Citizen Sponsors' Legal Consciousness, Intimate Citizenship and Family Migration Law' (2021) 28 *Identities* 37.
De Hart, B and Carella, C, '#LoveIsNotTourism: Cross-Border Couples, Citizenship and Belonging during the Covid-19 Crisis' *Family Migration in Times of Crisis* Workshop convened by Radboud University Network on Migrant Inclusion (RUNOMI) 15 June 2021.

De Hart, B, van Rossum, WM and Sportel, I, 'Law in the Everyday Lives of Transnational Families: An Introduction' (2006) 3 *Oñati Socio-Legal Series* 991.

De Noronha, L, *Deporting Black Britons: Portraits of Deportation to Jamaica* (Manchester, Manchester University Press, 2020).

De Noronha, L and Bradley, GM, *Against Borders: The Case for Abolition* (London, Verso Books, 2022).

De Vries, K, 'Rewriting *Abdulaziz*: The ECtHR Grand Chamber's Ruling in *Biao v. Denmark*' (2016) 18 *European Journal of Migration and Law* 467.

Dembour, M, *When Humans Become Migrants: Study of the European Court of Human Rights with an Inter-American Counterpoint* (Oxford, Oxford University Press, 2015).

Dickson, B, *Human Rights and the United Kingdom Supreme Court* (Oxford, Oxford University Press, 2013).

Dixon, D, *Democracy and the Human Rights Act: Republican Analysis of Citizen Power*. (Abingdon, Routledge, 2017).

Douzinas, C, *Human rights and empire: the political philosophy of cosmopolitanism*. (Abingdon, Routledge-Cavendish, 2007).

Draghici, C, 'Adult Children and Elderly Parents in Strasbourg Proceedings: A Misconstrued Approach to "Family Life"' (2018) 32 *International Journal of Law, Policy and the Family* 42.

Draghici, C, *The Legitimacy of Family Rights in Strasbourg Case Law: Living Instrument or Extinguished Sovereignty* (Oxford, Hart Publishing, 2017).

Dustin, M and Phillips, A, 'Whose Agenda Is It? Abuses of Women and Abuses of "Culture" in Britain' (2008) 8 *Ethnicities* 405.

Dzehtsiarou, K, *European Consensus and the Legitimacy of the European Court of Human Rights* (Cambridge, Cambridge University Press, 2015).

Edwards, R, 'Judicial Deference under the Human Rights Act' (2002) 65 *MLR* 859.

Eekelaar, J, 'Beyond the Welfare Principle' (2002) 14 *Child and Family Law Quarterly* 237.

Eekelaar, J, 'The Role of the Best Interests Principle in Decisions Affecting Children and Decisions about Children' (2015) 23 *International Journal of Children's Rights* 3.

Elliott, M, 'Constitutional Legislation, European Union Law and the Nature of the United Kingdom's Contemporary Constitution' (2014) *European Constitutional Law Review* 379.

Elliott, M, 'Beyond the European Convention: Human Rights and the Common Law' (2015) 65 *Current Legal Problems* 85.

Elliott, M, 'From Bifurcation to Calibration: Twin-Track Deference and the Culture of Justification' in H Wilberg and M Elliott (eds), *The Scope and Intensity of Substantive Review: Traversing Taggart's Rainbow* (Oxford, Hart Publishing, 2015) 61–90.

Engster, D and Hamington, M, 'Introduction' in Engster D and Hamington M (eds), *Care Ethics and Political Theory* (Oxford, Oxford University Press, 2015) 1–16.

Epstein, L and Weinshall, K, *The Strategic Analysis of Judicial Behavior: A Comparative Perspective* (Cambridge, Cambridge University Press, 2021).

Ewing, KD, 'The Human Rights Act and Parliamentary Democracy' (1999) 62 *MLR* 79.

Farahat, A, 'The Exclusiveness of Inclusion: On the Boundaries of Human Rights in Protecting Transnational and Second Generation Migrants' (2009) 11 *European Journal of Migration and Law* 253.

Farahat, A, 'Enhancing Constitutional Justice by Using External References: The European Court of Human Rights' Reasoning on the Protection against Expulsion' (2015) 28 *Leiden Journal of International Law* 303.

Fenwick, H, 'The Human Rights Act or a British Bill of Rights: Creating a Down-Grading Recalibration of Rights against the Counter-Terror Backdrop?' [2012] *PL* 468.

Fielding, NG, 'Judges and Their Work' (2011) 20 *Social & Legal Studies* 97.

Fischman, JB and Law, DS, 'What Is Judicial Ideology, and How Should We Measure It?' (2009) 29 *Washington University Journal of Law* 133.

Flynn, D, 'New Borders, New Management: The Dilemmas of Modern Immigration Policy' (2005) 28 *Ethnic and Racial Studies* 463.

Ford, R, Jennings, W and Somerville W, 'Public Opinion, Responsiveness and Constraint: Britain's Three Immigration Policy Regimes' (2015) 41 *Journal of Ethnic and Migration Studies* 1391.

Fortin, J, 'Are Children's Best Interests Really Best? *ZH Tanzania) (FC) v Secretary of State for the Home Department*' (2011) 74 *MLR* 932.

Fortin, J, 'Children's Rights – Flattering to Deceive' (2014) 26 *Child and Family Law Quarterly* 51.

Fredman, S, 'Emerging from the Shadows: Substantive Equality and Article 14 of the European Convention on Human Rights' (2016) 16 *Human Rights Law Review* 273.

Freeman, G, 'Can Liberal States Control Unwanted Migration?' (1994) 534 *The Annals of the American Academy of Political and Social Science* 17.

Furusho, CY, 'The "Ideal Migrant Victim" in Human Rights Courts: Between Vulnerability and Otherness' in M Duggan (ed), *Revisiting the 'Ideal Victim': Developments in Critical Victimology* (Bristol, Bristol University Press 2009) 123–40.

Gearty, C, *Can Human Rights Survive?* (Cambridge, Cambridge University Press, 2006).

Gearty, C, 'In the Shallow End' (2022) 44 *London Review of Books*.

Gebrial, D, 'Decolonising Desire: The Politics of Love' (*Versobooks.com*, 2017) 13.

Gedalof, I, 'Unhomely Homes: Women, Family and Belonging in UK Discourses of Migration and Asylum' (2007) 33 *Journal of Ethnic and Migration Studies* 77.

Gee, G, Hazell, R, Malleson, K and O'Brien, P, *The Politics of Judicial Independence in the UK's Changing Constitution* (Cambridge, Cambridge University Press, 2015).

Gentleman, A, *The Windrush Betrayal: Exposing the Hostile Environment* (London, Faber & Faber, 2019).

Glen, P, 'The Removability of Non-citizen Parents and the Best Interests of Citizen Children: How to Balance Competing Imperatives in the Context of Removal Proceedings' (2012) 30 *Berkeley Journal of International Law* 1.

Goderis, B and Versteeg, M, 'Human Rights Violations after 9/11 and the Role of Constitutional Constraints' (2012) 41 *Journal of Legal Studies* 131.

Goodman, SW, 'Controlling Immigration through Language and Country Knowledge Requirements' (2011) 34 *West European Politics* 235.

Gordon, IR, Scanlon, K, Travers, T and Whitehead, CME, *Economic Impact on the London and UK Economy of an Earned Regularisation of Irregular Migrants to the UK* (London, Greater London Authority, 2009).

Gordon, M, *Parliamentary Sovereignty in the UK Constitution: Process, Politics and Democracy* (Oxford, Hart Publishing, 2015).

Grande, E, Schwarzbözl, T and Fatke, M, 'Politicizing Immigration in Western Europe' 26 (2009) *Journal of European Public Policy* 1444.

Greer, S and Wildhaber, L, 'Revisiting the Debate about "Constitutionalizing" the European Court of Human Rights' (2012) 12 *Human Rights Law Review* 655.

Griffith, JAG, 'The Political Constitution' (1979) 42 *MLR* 1.

Griffiths, M, '"My Passport Is Just My Way Out of Here": Mixed-Immigration Status Families, Immigration Enforcement and the Citizenship Implications' (2021) 28 *Identities* 18.

Griffiths, M and Yeo, C, 'The UK's Hostile Environment: Deputising Immigration Control' (2021) 41 *Critical Social Policy* 521.

Guiraudon, V, 'European Courts and Foreigners' Rights: A Comparative Study of Norms Diffusion' (2000) 34 *International Migration Review* 1107.

Gunaratnam, HJ, Bhattacharyya, Y, Davies, G, Dhaliwal, W, Jackson, E and Saltus, R, 'Un/deserving Migrants and Resisting Dehumanisation' in HJ Gunaratnam, Y Bhattacharyya, G Davies, W Dhaliwal, E Jackson and R Saltus (eds), *Go Home?: The Politics of Immigration Controversies* (Manchester, Manchester University Press, 2017) 120–40.

Gündogdu, A, *Rightlessness in an Age of Rights: Hannah Arendt and the Contemporary Struggles of Migrants* (Oxford, Oxford University Press, 2014).

Guthrie, C, Rachlinski, JJ and Wistrich, AJ, 'Blinking on the Bench: How Judges Decide Cases' (2007) 93 *Cornell Law Review* 1.

Hacker, D, *Legalized Families in the Era of Bordered Globalizations* (Cambridge, Cambridge University Press, 2017).
Hale, B, 'Maccabaean Lecture in Jurisprudence: A Minority Opinion?' (2008) 154 *Proceedings of the British Academy* 319.
Hale, B, 'Families and the Law: The Forgotten International Dimension' (2009) 21 *Child and Family Law Quarterly* 413.
Hale, B, 'Dame Frances Patterson Memorial Lecture 2019: Law and Politics – A Reply to Reith' (2019) 24 *Judicial Review* 205.
Hamlin, R, '"Foreign Criminals," the Human Rights Act, and the New Constitutional Politics of the United Kingdom' (2016) 24 *Journal of Law and Courts* 437.
Hampshire, J, 'Disembedding Liberalism? Immigration Politics and Security since 9/11' in TE Givens, GP Freeman and D Leal (eds), *Immigration Policy and Security: US, European and Commonwealth Perspectives* (Abingdon, Routledge, 2009) 109–29.
Hanne, M and Weisberg, R, 'Introduction' in M Hanne and MR Weisberg (eds), *Narrative and Metaphor in the Law* (Cambridge, Cambridge University Press, 2018) 1–12.
Hanretty, CA, *Court of Specialists – Judicial Behavior on the UK Supreme Court* (Oxford, Oxford University Press, 2020).
Hansen, R, *Citizenship and Immigration in Post-War Britain: The Institutional Origins of a Multicultural Nation* (Oxford, Oxford University Press, 2000).
Harlow, C and Rawlings, R, 'Striking Back or Clamping Down: An Alternative Perspective on Judicial Review' in J Bell, M Elliott, JNE Varuhas and P Murray (eds), *Public Law Adjudication in Common Law Systems: Process and Substance* (Oxford, Hart Publishing, 2016) 301–26.
Hayter, T, *Open Borders: The Case against Immigration Controls* (London, Pluto Press, 2004).
Held, V, *The Ethics of Care as Moral Theory* (Oxford, Oxford University Press, 2005).
Hester, M, Chantler, K, Gangoli, G, Devgon, J, Sharma, S and Singleton, A, *Forced Marriage: The Risk Factors and the Effect of Raising the Minimum Age for a Sponsor, and of Leave to Enter the UK as a Spouse or Fiancé(e)* (Bristol, University of Bristol, 2007).
Hickman, T, *Public Law after the Human Rights Act* (Oxford, Hart Publishing, 2010).
Hiebert, J, 'The Human Rights Act: Ambiguity about Parliamentary Sovereignty' [2013] *German Law Journal* 2253.
Hilbrink, E, 'Adjudicating the Public Interest in Immigration Law: A Systematic Content Analysis of Strasbourg and Luxembourg Case Law on Legal Restrictions to Immigration and Free Movement' (PhD Thesis, Vrije Universiteit Amsterdam, 2017).
Hoffmann, L, 'The COMBAR Lecture 2001: Separation of Powers' (2002) *Judicial Review* 137.
Honohan, I, 'Reconsidering the Claim to Family Reunification in Migration' (2009) 57 *Political Studies* 768.
Hopgood, S, *The Endtimes of Human Rights* (Ithaca, NY, Cornell University Press, 2013).
Hudson, B, *Justice in the Risk Society: Challenging and Re-affirming, 'Justice' in Late Modernity* (London, Sage, 2003).
Hunt, M, 'Sovereignty's Blight: Why Contemporary Public Law Needs the Concept of, "Due Deference"' in N Bamforth and P Leyland (eds), *Public Law in a Multi-Layered Constitution* (Oxford, Hart Publishing, 2003) 339–48.
Hunt, M, Hooper, H and Yowell, P (eds), *Parliament and Human Rights: Redressing the Democratic Deficit* (Oxford, Hart Publishing, 2015).
Hunter, R and Rackley, E, 'Lady Hale: A Feminist Towering Judge' in R Abeyratne and I Porat (eds), *Towering Judges: A Comparative Study of Constitutional Judges* (Cambridge, Cambridge University Press, 2021).
Hunter, R, McGlynn, C and Rackley, E, 'Feminist Judgments: An Introduction' in R Hunter, C McGlynn and E Rackley (eds), *Feminist Judgments: From Theory to Practice* (Oxford, Hart Publishing, 2010).
Ibhawoh, B, 'Human Rights for Some: Universal Human Rights, Sexual Minorities, and the Exclusionary Impulse' (2014) 69 *International Journal* 612.
Jones, R (ed), *Open Borders: In Defense of Free Movement* (Atlanta, University of Georgia Press, 2019).

Joppke, C, 'Why Liberal States Accept Unwanted Immigration' (1988) 50 *World Politics*, (January) 266–93.
Jowell, J, 'Judicial Deference: Servility, Civility or Institutional Capacity' [2000] *PL* 592.
Juss, SS, 'Free Movement and the World Order' (2004) 16 *International Journal of Refugee Law* 289.
Kavanagh, A, *Constitutional Review under the Human Rights Act* (Cambridge, Cambridge University Press, 2009).
Kavanagh, A, 'Defending Deference in Public Law and Constitutional Theory' (2010) 126 *LQR* 222.
Kennedy, D, 'International Human Rights Movement: Part of the Problem?' (2002) 15 *Harvard Human Rights Journal* 101.
Kesby, A, 'Internal Borders and Immigration Control: New Prospects and Challenges' (2010) 2 *European Human Rights Law Review* 176.
King, JA, 'Institutional Approaches to Judicial Restraint (2008) 28 *OJLS* 409.
Klaassen, M, 'Between Facts and Norms: Testing Compliance with Article 8 ECHR in Immigration Cases' (2019) 37 *Netherlands Quarterly of Human Rights* 157.
Klatt, M and Meister, M, *The Constitutional Structure of Proportionality* (Oxford, Oxford University Press, 2012).
Klinck, DR, 'Criticising the Judges: Some Preliminary Reflections on Style' (1986) 31 *McGill Law Journal* 655.
Klug, F and Wildbore, H, 'Follow or Lead? The Human Rights Act and the European Court of Human Rights' (2010) 6 *European Human Rights Law Review* 621.
Knight, C and Cross, T, 'Public Law in the Supreme Court 2011–2012' (2012) 17 *Judicial Review* 330.
Kofmann, E, 'Family Migration as a Class Matter' (2018) *International Migration* 33.
Kouroutakis, A, 'The Henry VIII Powers in the Brexit Process: Justification Subject to Political and Legal Safeguards' (2021) 9 *The Theory and Practice of Legislation* 1 97.
Kratochvíl, J, 'The Inflation of the Margin of Appreciation by the European Court of Human Rights' (2011) 29 *Netherlands Quarterly of Human Rights* 324.
Kubal, A, 'Conceptualizing Semi-legality in Migration Research' (2013) 47 *Law and Society Review* 555.
Lagoutte, S, 'Surrounding and Extending Family Life: The Notion of Family Life in the Case-Law of the European Court of Human Rights' (2003) 21 *Mennesker og Rettigheter* 292.
Lambert, H, 'The European Court of Human Rights and the Right of Refugees and Other Persons in Need of Protection to Family Reunion' (1999) 11 *International Journal of Refugee Law* 427.
Lavrysen, L, *Human Rights in a Positive State: Rethinking the Relationship between Positive and Negative Obligations under the European Convention on Human Rights* (Cambridge, Cambridge University Press, 2016).
Leinonen, J and Pellander, S, 'Court Decisions over Marriage Migration in Finland: A Problem with Transnational Family Ties' (2014) *Journal of Ethnic and Migration Studies* 1488–1506.
Lemieux, SE and Watkins, DJ, 'Beyond the "Countermajoritarian Difficulty": Lessons from Contemporary Democratic Theory' (2009) 41 *Polity* 30.
Letsas, G, *Theory of Interpretation of the European Convention on Human Rights* (Oxford, Oxford University Press, 2007).
Lister, R, 'Inclusive Citizenship: Realizing the Potential' (2007) 11 *Citizenship Studies* 49.
Liversage, A and Rytter, M, 'A Cousin Marriage Equals a Forced Marriage: Transnational Marriages between Closely Related Spouses in Denmark' in A Shaw and A Raz (eds), *Cousin Marriages: Between Tradition, Genetic Risk and Cultural Change* (Oxford, Berghahn, 2015) 130–53.
Loughlin, M, 'What Would John Griffith Have Made of Jonathan Sumption's Reith Lectures?' (2019) 90 *The Political Quarterly* 785.
Macdonald, I, 'ECHR Article 8: Bringing the UK Courts Back in Step with Strasbourg' (2008) 22 *Journal of Immigration Asylum and Nationality Law* 293.
Macklin, A, 'Epilogue – Love Triangle: Nation, Spouse, Citizen' in D'Aoust, AM (ed), *Transnational Marriage and Partner Migration: Constellations of Security, Citizenship, and Rights.* (New Brunswick, Rutgers University Press, 2022) 259–73.
Malleson, K, 'The Evolving Role of the Supreme Court' (2011) 4 *PL* 754.

Mann, R and Hübner, MC, 'What Judges Don't Say – Judicial Strategy and Constitutional Theory' (2015) *Law Log – WZB Rule of Law Center* 21.

Manning, G, 'The Minimum Income Requirement for Family Settlement: The Cost of Integration' [2017] *PL* 304.

Manning, R, 'Care, Normativity, and the Law' in D Engster and M. Hamington (eds), *Care Ethics and Political Theory* (Oxford, Oxford University Press, 2015) 127–45.

Marks, S, 'Four Human Rights Myths' in D Kinley, W Sadurski and K Walton (eds), *Human Rights: Old Problems, New Possibilities* (Cheltenham, Edward Elgar Publishing, 2013) 217–35.

Masterman, R, 'Aspiration or Foundation? The Status of the Strasbourg Jurisprudence and the "Convention Rights" in Domestic Law' in H Fenwick, G Philipson, R Masterman (eds), *Judicial Reasoning under Human Rights* (Cambridge, Cambridge University Press, 2017) 57–86.

McLaren, L, *Immigration and Perceptions of National Political Systems in Europe* (Oxford, Oxford University Press, 2015).

Metcalfe, E, 'The Strange Jurisprudence of Lord Hoffmann: Human Rights and the International Judge' (2009) 2 *UCL Human Rights Review* 35.

Möller, K, *The Global Model of Constitutional Rights* (Oxford, Oxford University Press, 2012)

Mowbray, A, *The Development of Positive Obligations under the European Convention on Human Rights by the European Court of Human Rights* (Oxford, Hart Publishing, 2004).

Moyn, S, 'A Powerless Companion: Human Rights in the Age of Neoliberalism' (2014) 77 *Law & Contemporary Problems* 147.

Mullen, T, 'Reflections on *Jackson v Attorney General*: Questioning sovereignty' (2007) 27 *Legal Studies* 1.

Murkens, J, 'Judicious Review: The Constitutional Practice of the UK Supreme Court' (2018) 77 *CLJ* 349.

Mustasaari, S, 'The "Nuclear Family Paradigm" as a Marker of Rights and Belonging in Transnational Families' (2015) *Social Identities* 359.

Neudorf, L, 'The Supreme Court and the New Judicial Independence' (2012) 1 *Cambridge Journal of International and Comparative Law* 25.

Niemi-Kiesiläinen, J, Honkatukia, P and Ruuskanen, M, 'Legal Texts as Discourses' in G Svensson and M Davies (eds), *Exploiting the Limits of Law* (Farnham, Ashgate, 2007) 69–88.

Ockelton, M, 'Article 8 ECHR, the UK and Strasbourg: Compliance, Cooperation or Clash? A Judicial Perspective' in KS Ziegler, E Wicks and L Hodson (eds), *The UK and European Human Rights: A Strained Relationship?* (London, Hart Publishing, 2015) 215–24.

Onazi, O, 'Towards a Subaltern Theory of Human Rights' (2009) 9 *Global Jurist* No 8.

Oomen, B, *Rights for Others: The Slow Home-Coming of Human Rights in the Netherlands* (Cambridge, Cambridge University Press, 2014)

Paterson, A, *Final Judgment: The Last Law Lords and the Supreme Court* (Oxford, Hart Publishing, 2013).

Paul, R, 'Strategic Contextualisation: Free Movement, Labour Migration Policies and the Governance of Foreign Workers in Europe' (2013) 34 *Policy Studies* 122.

Pellander, S, 'Traces of Dependency: Manifestations of Elderly Family Migration across Policy Arenas' ('The Problematisation of Family Migration' workshop, University of Amsterdam, 4–5 June 2015).

Pobjoy J, 'The Best Interests of the Child Principle as an Independent Source of International Protection' (2015) 64 *ICLQ* 327.

Posner, R, 'Judges' Writing Styles (And Do They Matter?)' (1995) 62 *Chicago Law Review* 1421.

Posner, R, *How Judges Think* (Cambridge, MA, Harvard University Press, 2008).

Prabhat, D and Hambly, J, 'Bettering the Best Interests of the Child Determination: Of Checklists and Balancing Exercises' (2017) 25 *International Journal of Children's Rights* 754.

Qureshi, A, Morris, M and Mort, L, 'Beyond the Hostile Environment' (London, Institute for Public Policy Research, 2021).

Rackley, E, 'The Art and Craft of Writing Judgments: Notes on the Feminist Judgments Project' in R Hunter, C McGlynn and E Rackley (eds), *Feminist Judgments: From Theory to Practice* (Oxford, Hart Publishing, 2010) 44–56.

Rawlings, R, 'Review, Revenge and Retreat' (2005) 68 *MLR* 3 378.

Regine, R, 'Strategic Contextualisation: Free Movement, Labour Migration Policies and the Governance of Foreign Workers in Europe' (2013) 34 *Policy Studies* 122.

Robinson, D, *Judicial Discretion in the House of Lords* (Oxford, Oxford University Press, 1998).

Rowe, C, 'Falling into Line? The Hostile Environment and the Legend of the "Judges' Revolt"' (2022) 85 *MLR* 105.

Sachdeva, S, *The Primary Purpose Rule in British Immigration Law* (Stoke on Trent, Trentham Books, 1993).

Salazar Parreñas, R, 'Transnational Fathering: Gendered Conflicts, Distant Disciplining and Emotional Gaps' (2008) 34 *Journal of Ethnic and Migration Studies* 1057.

Salt, J, 'International Migration and the UK. Annual Report of the UK SOPEMI Correspondent to the OECD' (London, UCL Migration Research Unit, 2009).

Samuels, H, 'Feminizing Human Rights Adjudication: Feminist Method and the Proportionality Principle' (2013) 21 *Feminist Legal Studies* 39.

Sawyer, C, 'Not Every Child Matters: the UK's Expulsion of British Citizens' (2006) 14 *International Journal of Children's Rights* 157.

Schinkel, W, *Imagined Societies. A Critique of Immigrant Integration in Western Europe* (Cambridge, Cambridge University Press, 2017).

Schotel, B, *On the Right of Exclusion: Law, Ethics and Immigration Policy* (Abingdon, Routledge, 2013).

Seddon, D, 'Case Comment: *Beoku-Betts v Secretary of State for the Home Department*' (2008) 22 *Journal of Immigration Asylum and Nationality Law* 358.

Seddon, D, 'Case Comment: *EB (Kosovo) v Secretary of State for the Home Department*' (2008) 22 *Journal of Immigration Asylum and Nationality Law* 360.

Simmons, T, 'Sexuality and Immigration: UK Family Reunion Policy and the Regulation of Sexual Citizens in the European Union' (2008) 27 *Political Geography* 213.

Sirriyeh, A, '"All You Need Is Love and £18,600": Class and the New UK Family Migration Rules' (2015) 35 *Critical Social Policy* 228.

Sirriyeh, A, *The Politics of Compassion – Immigration and Asylum Policy* (Bristol, Policy Press, 2018).

Smyth, C, 'The Best Interests of the Child in the Expulsion and First-Entry Jurisprudence of the European Court of Human Rights: How Principled Is the Court's Use of the Principle?' (2015) 17 *European Journal of Migration and Law* 70.

Somerville, W, *Immigration under New Labour* (Bristol, Policy Press, 2010).

Spielmann, D, 'Allowing the Right Margin: The European Court of Human Rights and the National Margin of Appreciation Doctrine: Waiver or Subsidiarity of European Review?' (2012) 14 *Cambridge Yearbook of European Legal Studies* 381.

Spijkerboer, T, 'Structural Instability: Strasbourg Case Law on Children's Family Reunion' (2009) 11 *European Journal of Migration and Law* 271.

Staiano, F, 'Good Mothers, Bad Mothers: Transnational Mothering in the European Court of Human Rights' Case Law' (2013) 15 *European Journal of Migration and Law* 155.

Steyn, L, 'Deference: A Tangled Story' [2005] *PL* 346.

Stoyanava, V, 'The Disjunctive Structure of Positive Rights' (2018) 87 *Nordic Journal of International Law* 344.

Strik, T, de Hart, B and Nissen, E, *Family Reunification: A Barrier or Facilitator of Integration? A Comparative Study* (Oisterwijk, Wolf Publishers, 2013).

Sumption, J, 'The Limits of Law' in N Barber, R Ekins and P Yowell (eds), *Lord Sumption and the Limits of the Law* (Oxford, Hart Publishing, 2016) 15–26.

Sumption, M and Vargas-Silva, C, 'Love Is Not All You Need: Income Requirement for Visa Sponsorship of Foreign Family Members' (2019) 2 *Journal of Economics, Race, and Policy* 62.

Taylor, R, 'Putting Children First: Children's Interests as a Primary Consideration in Public Law' (2016) 28 *Child & Family Law Quarterly* 46.

Tew, Y, 'And They Call It Puppy Love: Young Love, Forced Marriage and Immigration Rules' (2012) 71 *CLJ* 18.

Thomas, R, *Administrative Justice and Asylum Appeals* (Oxford, Hart Publishing, 2011).

Thomas, R, 'Administrative Justice, Better Decisions, and Organisational Learning' [2015] *PL* 1.

Thym, D, 'Respect for Private and Family Life under Article 8 ECHR in Immigration Cases: A Human Right to Regularize Illegal Stay?' (2008) 57 *ICLQ* 87.

Thym, D, 'Residence as Defacto Citizenship? Protection of Long Term Residence under Article 8 ECHR' in R Rubio-Marin (ed), *Human Rights and Immigration* (Oxford, Oxford University Press, 2014) 106–44.

Trotter, S, 'The Child in European Human Rights Law' (2018) 81 *MLR* 452.

Tsakyrakis, S, 'Proportionality: An Assault on Human Rights' (2009) 7 *International Journal of Constitutional Law* 468.

Turner, J, 'The Family Migration Visa in the History of Marriage Restrictions: Postcolonial Relations and the UK Border' (2015) 17 *British Journal of Politics & International Relations* 623.

Turner, J, *Bordering Intimacy: Postcolonial Governance and the Policing of Family* (Manchester, Manchester University Press, 2020).

Turner, J and Espinoza, MV, 'The Affective and Intimate Life of the Family Migration Visa: Knowing, Feeling and Encountering the Heteronormative State' (2021) 26 *Geopolitics* 357.

Van Walsum, S, 'Against All Odds: How Single and Divorced Migrant Mothers Were Eventually Able to Claim Their Right to Respect for Family Life' (2009) 11 *European Journal of Migration and Law* 295.

Van Walsum, S, Jones, G and Legene, S, 'Belonging and Membership. Postcolonial Legacies of Colonial Family Law in Dutch Immigration Policies' in M Schrover and DM Molony (eds), *Gender, Migration and Categorisation. Making Distinctions between Migrants in Western Countries, 1945–2010* (Amsterdam, Amsterdam University Press, 2013) 149–73.

Vaughan, A, 'The Tribunal's New Role in Article 8 Statutory Appeals' (2007) 21 *Journal of Immigration Asylum and Nationality Law* 129.

Viljoen, F and Louw, L, 'State Compliance with the Recommendations of the African Commission on Human and Peoples' Rights, 1994–2004' (2004) 101 *The American Journal of International Law* 1.

Wallace Goodman, S, 'Controlling Immigration through Language and Country Knowledge Requirements' (2011) 34 *Western European Politics* 235.

Walsh, C, 'Unhappy Families and Use of Article 8 for Failed Asylum Seekers' (2009) *Denning Law Journal* 153.

Warren, R, 'Private Life in the Balance: Constructing the Precarious Migrant' (2016) 30 *Journal of Immigration, Asylum and Nationality Law* 124.

White, S, 'Brexit and the Future of the UK Constitution' (2022) 43 *International Political Science Review* 359.

Wildhaber, L, 'The European Court of Human Rights in Action' (2004) 21 *Ritsumeikan Law Review* 83.

Wildhaber, L, Hjartarson, A and Donnelly, S, 'No Consensus on Consensus? The Practice of the European Court of Human Rights' (2013) 33 *Human Rights Law Journal* 241.

Wilding, J, 'Droughts and Deserts. A Report on the Immigration Legal Aid Market' (Brightion, University of Brighton and Joseph Rowntree Charitable Trust, 2019).

Williams, R, 'Structuring Substantive Review' [2017] *PL* 99.

Wong, MYY, 'The Unequal Price of Love: A Critical Race Feminist Critique of the £18,600 Minimum Income Requirement for Family Reunification under Article 14 ECHR' (2019) 33 *Journal of Immigration, Asylum and Nationality Law* 302.

Wray, H, 'An Ideal Husband? Marriages of Convenience, Moral Gate-Keeping and Immigration to the UK' (2006) 8 *European Journal of Migration and Law* 303.
Wray, H, 'Moulding the Migrant Family' (2009) 29 *Legal Studies* 592.
Wray, H, *Regulating Marriage Migration into the UK: A Stranger in the Home* (first published Farnham, Ashgate, 2011, Abingdon, Routledge, 2016).
Wray, H, 'Greater than the Sum of Their Parts: UK Supreme Court Decisions on Family Migration' [2013] *PL* 838.
Wray, H, 'Family Migration and New Labour' in S Juss (ed), *Research Companion to Migration Theory and Practice* (Farnham, Ashgate, 2013) 639–60.
Wray, H, '"A Thing Apart": Controlling Male Family Migration to the United Kingdom' (2015) 18 *Men and Masculinities* 424.
Wray, H, 'The "Pure" Relationship, Sham Marriages and Immigration Control' in J Miles, R Probert and P Mody (eds), *Marriage Rites and Rights* (Oxford, Hart Publishing, 2015) 141–65.
Wray, H, 'The MM Case and the Public Interest: How Did the Government Make Its Case?' (2017) 31 *Journal of Immigration Asylum and Nationality Law* 227.
Wray, H, 'What Do States Regulate When They Regulate Spousal Migration?' in AM D'Aoust (ed), *Transnational Marriage and Partner Migration: Constellations of Security, Citizenship and Rights* (New Brunswick, Rutgers University Press, 2022) 88–105.
Wray, H, Agoston, A and Hutton, J, 'A Family Resemblance? The Regulation of Marriage Migration in Europe' (2014) 16 *European Journal of Migration and Law* 209.
Wray, H, Grant, S, Kofman, E and Peel, C, 'Family Friendly? The Impact on Children of the Family Migration Rules: A Review of the Financial Requirements' (Children's Commissioner for England, 2015).
Wright, J, 'Interpreting Section 2 of the Human Rights Act 1998: Towards an Indigenous Jurisprudence of Human Rights' [2009] *PL* 595.
Xenos, D, *The Positive Obligations of the State under the European Convention of Human Rights* (Abingdon, Routledge, 2012).
Yap, PJ, 'Defending Dialogue' [2012] *PL* 527.
York, S, 'The End of Legal Aid in Immigration: A Barrier to Access to Justice for Migrants and a Decline in the Rule of Law' (2013) 27 *Journal of Immigration, Asylum and Nationality Law* 106.
York, S, 'The "Hostile Environment" – How Home Office Immigration Policies and Practices Create and Perpetuate Illegality' (2018) 32 *Journal of Immigration Asylum and Nationality Law* 363.
Young, A, 'Will You, Won't You, Will You Join the Deference Dance?' (2014) 34 *OJLS* 392.
Yuval-Davis, N, Anthias, F and Kofman, E, 'Secure Borders, Safe Haven and the Gendered Politics of Belonging: Beyond Social Cohesion' (2005) 28 *Ethnic and Racial Studies* 513.
Zurn, DF, *Deliberative Democracy and the Institutions of Judicial Review* (Cambridge, Cambridge University Press, 2007).

Index

Z

www.ingramcontent.com/pod-product-compliance
Ingram Content Group UK Ltd.
Pitfield, Milton Keynes, MK11 3LW, UK
UKHW021543041026
15470UKWH00019B/868

9 781509 902576